Around Scotland

A Touring Guide

by

Ken & Julie Slavin

Cadogan Books
London

To the late
Annabel Macdonald of Bornish, South Uist
and all her family

ISBN 0 946313 10 5

Published by Cadogan Books Ltd 1983
15 Pont Street, London SW1
First published in USA by Hippocrene Books, Inc.
171 Madison Avenue, New York, N.Y., 10016

Typeset in Great Britain by
M.C. Typeset, Chatham, Kent
Printed and bound by
Biddles of Guildford

By the same authors:
The Tuareg
Land-Rover, the Unbeatable 4 × 4

Acknowledgements

We would like to thank the Scottish Tourist Board (in particular Libby Anderson and Anne Macsween) for their help, and also the Highlands and Islands Development Board. We are grateful to Land-Rover Limited (in particular Roger Ball) for the loan of the Land-Rover while we were researching the book.

Sources of reference used in compiling this book:
Blue Guide– Scotland, Ernest Benn Ltd.
The Story of Scotland by Janet Glover, Faber.
Mary, Queen of Scots by Antonia Fraser, Granada.
The Highland Clearances by John Prebble, Penguin.

Bibliography

Boswell, J., *Journal of a Tour to the Hebrides with Samuel Johnson.*
Fraser, A., *Mary, Queen of Scots*, Weidenfeld & Nicholson.
    King James VI of Scotland, I of England, Weidenfeld & Nicholson.
Glover, J.R., *The Story of Scotland*, Faber.
Johnson, Dr S., *Journey to the Western Islands*
Prebble, J., *Culloden*, Penguin.
    Glen Coe, Penguin.
    Mutiny, Penguin.
    The Highland Clearances, Penguin.
Royal Scottish Geographical Society, *Shetland and Oil.*
Trantner, N., *Portrait of the Border Country.*

(Light Reading)
Beckwith, L., *The Hills is Lonely*, Arrow Books.
    The Sea for Breakfast, Arrow Books
    and other books.
Mackenzie, C., *Whisky Galore*, Penguin.
Munro, N., *Para Handy Tales*, Pan.

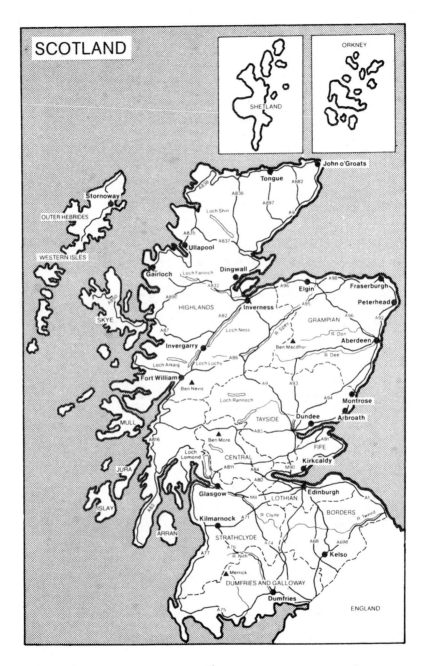

SCOTLAND

SHETLAND

ORKNEY

John o'Groats

Tongue

A836 A882

A838 A897

Loch Shin A9

A835

A837

Stornoway

OUTER HEBRIDES

Ullapool

WESTERN ISLES

Gairloch   Loch Fannich   Dingwall

A832   A96   Elgin   A98   Fraserburgh

A890   HIGHLANDS   A95   Peterhead

SKYE   A82   Inverness   GRAMPIAN   A96   A92

A87   Loch Ness   R Spey   R Don   Aberdeen

Invergarry   Ben Macdhui   R Dee

Loch Arkaig   A86   Loch Lochy

Fort William   A9   A93

Ben Nevis   Loch Rannoch   A94   Montrose

MULL   TAYSIDE   Dundee   Arbroath

A816   Ben More   A85   FIFE   A91

Loch Lomond   CENTRAL   Kirkcaldy

JURA   A811   A84   M90

A80

ISLAY   Glasgow   M8   LOTHIAN   Edinburgh   A1

A83   Kilmarnock   A71   R Clyde   BORDERS   R Tweed

ARRAN   STRATHCLYDE   A74   A68   A698   Kelso

A76

A77   R Nith

Merrick   DUMFRIES AND GALLOWAY

Dumfries

A75   ENGLAND

4

Contents

Introduction

Scotland is a country for which we both have very strong feelings and the only difficulty in writing a guide book is in deciding what must be left out, because with attractions for so many people it is virtually impossible to cater for all throughout the country. The Directory sections are designed to help you plan your holiday as easily and successfully as possible, while the tours of the regions aim to show you all the most important places.

We have not quoted admission charges because they inevitably change periodically and can therefore be misleading. Times of opening and closing are also subject to change, so we recommend that you regard the times listed as an indication. The Scottish Tourist Board is one of the most efficient, active and comprehensive in the world, and we cannot stress too often that application should be made to their offices for any queries of a specific nature at whatever level.

Throughout the text you will come across the following abbreviations: NTS – National Trust for Scotland; STB – Scottish Tourist Board; NNR – National Nature Reserve. The text has been written on the assumption that the reader will have a good map to hand at the same time. *Scotland Touring Map*, scale 5 miles:1 in. (8 km) is recommended, published by the STB.

When touring historical monuments or places of historical interest reference has been made to the characters involved, but space has not been allowed for background history to be included. References to incidents and sites concerning the best-known figures in Scotland's history, such as St Margaret, David I, Robert the Bruce, William Wallace, Mary Queen of Scots and Bonnie Prince Charlie (the Young Pretender), as well as the best-known literary figures, such as Scott, Stevenson and Burns, occur throughout the book, and it is advisable to refresh your memory on these periods in Scottish history, the better to enjoy the time spent at sites.

Dumfries & Galloway

This part of Scotland, occupying its southernmost coast and bordering with England, tends to be overlooked by visitors to Scotland because it is neither remarkably scenic in its own right, nor directly on the way to the more impressive scenery. It is significant in Scottish history both for the establishment of Christianity and for subsequent military and royal incidents. The area around Dumfries is best known for its associations with Robert ('Rabbie') Burns, 1759–96, the poet whose most famous works are of south-west Scotland (the other major 'Burns' town being Ayr in Strathclyde). This southern coastline from the Solway Firth west is not startlingly beautiful but nor is it spoilt by excessive development, or main arterial roads (as is the West Coast somewhat, up towards Glasgow) so it shouldn't just be omitted from your itinerary. The whole region offers nice surprises and hidden-away corners, but quite different from the Highlands, except for the extensive Galloway Forest Park, 200 square miles (322 sq km) of magnificent mountainous forest straddling the boundary with Strathclyde.

The first route through Dumfries and Galloway that we describe is the A74 leading directly to Glasgow from England, entering the region at Gretna and leaving it north of Beattock and Moffat.

I: Gretna – Lockerbie – Moffat

Gretna Green instantly conjures up images of hasty, illicit or secret marriages and eloping couples; since Scottish law continued to recognise the legality of a marriage by witnessed declaration long after the laws in England were tightened up on this, the English were obliged to cross the border, usually to have a local blacksmith do the deed. At the eastern end of the Scottish border at Lamberton Bar (on the A1 where it crosses into Scotland), similarly used at that time, it was the tollkeeper who was most called upon. In Gretna you can see sundry related curios at the Smithy.

At **Kirkpatrick Fleming**, about three miles (5 km) north, is the cave where Robert the Bruce was hidden by Irving for three months, and possibly had his experience with the spider (though this is also held to have happened when he was on Rathlin). Next to the house inhabited by Irving, the cave is now accessible by pathway, but in Bruce's day only by rope from the small tower above which was connected by secret passage to the house (passage now closed). It is not a natural formation, having been hewn out of the rock by stone-age troglodytes whose primitive tools were discovered in the river below.

Just a few miles (4 km) further, note the Merkland Cross, fifteenth century, at **Kirtlebridge**. The next village is Ecclefechan where the

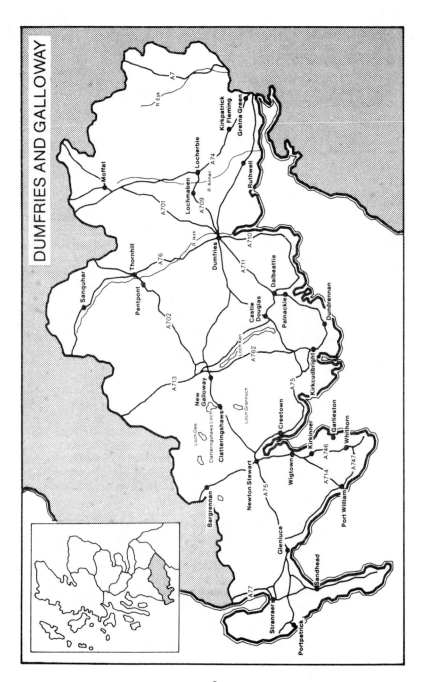

DUMFRIES AND GALLOWAY

essayist Thomas Carlyle was born, in 1795, in the Arched House which is now a NTS museum with, among other items of great interest, some of Carlyle's correspondence with Goethe. The house was built by his father and uncle who were both master masons; you can see Carlyle's tomb in the churchyard.

There is a fifteenth century ruined stronghold 2½ miles (3 km) away on the B725, which is Hoddam Castle, and a mile (2 km) north-east of Ecclefechan is Birrens, a very well excavated ruined Roman fort. Nearby (about 2½ miles (3 km) north) is Burnswark (or Birrenswark) a Roman artillery range on a prominent hill with earthworks, and probably the site of a tenth century battle, the English defeating the opposing forces of mainly Scots and Norsemen.

At **Lockerbie**, a pleasant little market town, take the left turning to **Lochmaben** about four miles (6 km) along the A709 to see the remains of the immense fourteenth century Lochmaben Castle where the Bruce family lived. Robert the Bruce was born here (or at Turnberry, up the west coast towards Ayr). Note his statue in the town. The great castle at the southern end of Castle Loch was enjoyed by James IV and also by Mary Queen of Scots who brought Darnley here in 1565. According to tradition it was she who introduced from France the tasty little fishes into the surrounding lochs, apparently a rare delicacy, but they require netting as they won't take bait. (It is actually more likely that monks brought them into Scotland.) When the massive castle fell into neglect a great many of its stones were used for buildings in the town.

The manor house of Rammerscales, about a mile (2 km) off the A709 between Lockerbie and Lochmaben, was built in the eighteenth century.

Rejoining the A74, the road continues northwards through barren, unmemorable scenery to **Moffat** (Beattock), about 14 miles (23 km) further on. Moffat is an airy, sedate spa town (its sulphur springs were popular in the last century) with a very broad main street lined with shops, cafes, dignified buildings, and trees in the middle. Of the various cafes, we can recommend one called 'Coffee 'n Cream' which is just along the pavement from the mouth-watering Moffat Toffee Shop, where a dazzling array of toffees are sold (the 'specials' are made to secret family recipes in their local toffee factory). Note the fountain in this street with its fine curly-horned ram figure on the top (symbolising the importance of sheep farming locally) known as Colvin Fountain. The inventor of tarmacadam, John McAdam, who died in 1836, is buried in the churchyard here.

Taking the A701 north from Moffat in six miles (10 km) you reach the 'Devil's Beef Tub', an enormous crater-like hollow in the hills, so-called because it was used for concealing stolen cattle in raiding days. Another natural local feature is the magnificent 200-foot (61 km) waterfall by the A708 heading north-east into Borders, known as Grey Mare's Tail as it is where Tail stream falls from Loch Skene towards the Moffat Water. Be very careful to stick to the low path here, as nasty accidents have happened to more adventurous scramblers.

II: Ruthwell – Dumfries – Sanquhar

Taking the A75 from Gretna, out along the north shore of the Solway Firth you pass Annan after about nine miles (14 km), the road leading through agricultural countryside, here and there commanding pleasant views of the water. At **Ruthwell** (which is locally pronounced 'Rivvel'), some five miles (8 km) beyond Annan on the B724 the church contains a Cross of exceptional significance as a Christian monument, 18 feet (5.5m) tall, dating from the early eighth century with fascinating elaborate carvings. There is a museum in Ruthwell, in a cottage built on the site of the very first Savings Bank, founded in 1810, giving a lot of information about the Savings Bank Movement. (About 2½ miles (4 km) east of here between the B724 and the A75, are the lovely Kinmount Gardens with very pleasant woodland walks. Late spring is best for rhododendrons.)

Turn left at Ruthwell to reach first Brow Well, where Robert Burns was instructed by his physician friend to bathe, to help his illness (an unsuccessful treatment as he died three days later, back in Dumfries), and further round the coast, to Caerlaverock Castle, one of the most unusual castles in south-west Scotland, noted particularly for its extraordinary triangular shape. It is late thirteenth century, with repairs carried out 300 years later, then extended in the seventeenth century. Apart from its striking symmetrical fortified exterior, what makes these red ruins remarkable is the elegant Renaissance style of the seventeenth century rooms around the triangular courtyard. The castle stands majestically in the waters of the old moat. The Caerlaverock National Nature Reserve along the Nith estuary is an area noted for barnacle geese and other wildfowl, and is also the natterjack toad's most northerly breeding place.

From here follow the B725 along the Nith firth right up to **Dumfries**, and its quaint, attractive waterfront. This is the prettiest part of the town, with a six-arched footbridge (partly fifteenth century), at one end of which is the seventeenth century Old Bridge House with period rooms, part of the Observatory, an interesting museum incorporating an eighteenth century windmill, and a camera obscura. The first bridge over the Nith here was wooden, and built by Devorguilla Balliol. Dumfries has long been a prosperous and busy town, though its population has now grown to 28,000 as it includes Maxwelltown on the west bank of the Nith (connected now by four bridges). It has many associations with Robert Burns as he spent the last few years of his life here, but it has been a royal burgh since the late twelfth century. In 1306 Robert the Bruce murdered Comyn here, effectively opening the protracted war of independence, as Comyn was with John Balliol (Edward I's choice as king of Scotland (1292–96) instead of Robert the Bruce). Devorguilla Balliol, who founded various religious houses (as well as Balliol College in Oxford), was John's mother; it was either she or her father who founded the thirteenth century Franciscan Greyfriars Friary where

Comyn was slain, which stood opposite Greyfriars Church (1866) in Castle Street. In 1746 the Young Pretender passed through Dumfries on his retreat.

In many towns and villages of the south-west you would be hard pressed not to notice that Robert Burns spent most of his 37 years here; (the Scottish Tourist Board have organised a 'Burns Heritage Trail', details from 'Land o' Burns Centre', Alloway, or Kyle and Carrick District Council, TIC, 30 Miller Road, Ayr, or the STB in Edinburgh (*see* Introduction p. 00). At Dumfries you can see where he lived, where he drank, where he worshipped and where he was buried. His first apartment, not open to the public, is that which he called 'Stinking Vennel' because an open drain ran through it conveying rotting offal from the butchers' market down to the Nith, but his next home here was luckily more salubrious and now serves as a museum, Burns' House in Burns Street. The Globe Inn (established 1610) off the High Street was his favourite tavern, and is a pleasant pub to this day. If you take a drink or inexpensive lunch here, you will see the chair he used to sit in, amongst other related items, and his bedroom is preserved. In St Michael's Church (1750) you can see the Burns family pew and outside is the ornate and elaborate Grecian tomb wherein the bodies of Robert, his wife and some of their children now lie. On his death he was simply buried in the churchyard, transferred to this mausoleum in 1815; his wife Jean lived on at their home until her death in 1834. On the former Tolbooth, Midsteeple (1707) in the town centre is a relief map of Dumfries in Burns' day.

Leaving Dumfries on the A76 one mile (2 km) north is the ruined Lincluden Abbey, constructed in the twelfth century for Benedictine nuns, and made collegiate in 1339. The abbey buildings have largely disappeared, leaving just the choir and south transept of the little church (note the stone carvings depicting the life of Christ on the screen at the entrance to the choir, and the extravagant fifteenth century tomb of Princess Margaret, daughter of Robert II and Countess of Douglas).

A further five miles (8 km) up the A76 takes you to Ellisland, where Robert Burns tried (and failed) to make a success of farming by introducing new methods. He rented the 100-acre (40 ha) plot, and was granted £300 to build the farmhouse. Among the poems he produced here are 'Auld Lang Syne' and 'Tam o' Shanter'. The newly-restored Granary gives an impression of Burns the farmer.

About 10 miles (16 km) west, through Dunscore, Craigenputtock farm was where Thomas Carlyle lived from 1828–33, and where he wrote most of *Sartor Resartus*.

The A76 here follows Nithsdale, from Dumfries as far as Kirkconnel, with the A702 branching off west at **Thornhill**. Between Penpont (where the explorer James Thompson was born, in 1858 – memorial at Thornhill, the place of his schooling) and Moniaive is Tynron, a hill with a fort where Robert the Bruce is said to have laid low after murdering Comyn. Tynron Juniper Wood is a 12-acre (5 ha) nature reserve. The

Renwick Monument is just above Moniaive, and commemorates James Renwick, 1662–88, who was executed in Edinburgh (aged 26) as the last of the Covenanter martyrs.

If you wander around **Moniaive** there are various craft workshops to visit: at Woodhead Cottage, Craigdarroch, see how cowhide may he fashioned by competent leather-workers; at Dalya Craft, Kirkland, makers of hardwood furniture welcome visitors between 9 am and 5 pm. Finish up at the Glencairn Workshops where pine furniture is made, and you can sit down over a cup of coffee for a while in the coffee shop.

Maxwelton House, east of Moniaive on the A702, is where Annie Laurie was born in 1682 (about whom the famous ballad poem was written, originally by William Douglas of Fingland), and the house, seventeenth century, includes part of a fourteenth to fifteenth century castle. There is a museum here of agricultural, dairy and early kitchen implements.

Back in Nithsdale, at Carronbridge the road forks, the A702 leading up over barren moorland to Dalveen Pass, following the line of a Roman road, and passing the well-preserved ruin of Morton Castle (built around 1480) by Morton Loch, a mile or so (2 km) after the fork. Further on, the seventeenth century church at Durisdeer has a striking monument in black and white marble by Van Nost, to the Duke and Duchess of Queensberry, who died in 1711 and 1709 respectively.

The left fork is the A76 leading now to Drumlarig Castle commanding fine views of Nithsdale, 18 miles (29 km) north of Dumfries. Built of pale pink sandstone in the latter part of the seventeenth century by the Douglas family (on the site of an earlier Douglas stronghold), this is now the home of the dukes of Buccleuch and Queensberry. With four towers, and 17 lead turrets, around a central court, the castle houses a treasure trove of furniture, famous paintings, and superb antiques. (Note the silver chandelier, weighing 126 pounds (57 kg), of 1680.) Retreating northwards, the Young Pretender spent a night here in 1746 and you can see a variety of his posessions in the bedroom he used. The paintings include Rembrandt's 'Old Woman Reading' and works by Holbein, Murillo, Rowlandson and Couet as well as many family portraits. The old kitchen is a delightful setting for a snack and cup of tea to keep you going while exploring the beautiful grounds. Dogs aren't encouraged to visit except on a lead as there are peacocks strutting freely in the gardens. Extensive nature trails, and a woodland children's play area are very enjoyable in good weather.

After this, **Sanquhar** is the next port of call on the A76 and is a royal burgh town famous for the 1680 Covenanters' Declaration of Sanquhar, by Richard Cameron and his supporters, who later formed the Cameronian regiment though Cameron had been killed soon after the first declaration, at a skirmish near Cumnock, 17 miles (27 km) further on. James Renwick (monument, Moniaive) made a second declaration in 1685 but the Cross to which these were affixed no longer exists, the place is marked by a monument. William Adam built the town's Tolbooth, in 1735, now containing a museum of local interest, featuring a clock tower, and Sanquhar also has Britain's first Post Office dating from 1783, a year prior to the Mail Coach Service starting.

About eight miles (13 km) after Sanquhar you cross the boundary into Strathclyde.

III: New Galloway – Newton Stewart – Stranraer

Leaving Dumfries on the A75, an unclassified road to the north at Henderland leads up to the Glenkiln reservoir, lying amidst lonely country, but worth visiting for its Sculpture Park. Placed around the reservoir you can see works by Henry Moore ('King and Queen'), Epstein, Rodin and others.

The A75 divides at Crocketford, the A712 taking the north-west direction towards New Galloway, passing Corsock House Gardens in five miles (8 km) with attractive water garden and superb rhododendrons (especially in late spring).

New Galloway is a very small royal burgh (300 inhabitants), with an important hydro-electric scheme, and a fifteenth to seventeenth century ruin, Kenmure Castle, the seat of the Gordons of Lochinvar for a long time, the Viscounts Kenmure, who received Mary Queen of Scots during her tour of this area in 1563, and after her defeat at Langside in 1568 it was Lochinvar who gave her the clothes in which to disguise herself for her flight. Kenmure Castle overlooks Loch Ken, nearly 10 miles (16 km) long, on either side of which roads lead through pleasant scenery to Kirkcudbright, and to Castle Douglas.

The A713 northwards from New Galloway crosses lonely moorland and pasture known as 'The Glenkens', flanking Galloway Forest Park, a splendid 150,000 acres (60,750 ha) of forest, moor, mountain and loch, including lochs Trool and Doon (Castle Doon, early fourteenth century, used to be on an island in the loch but was moved to avoid being submerged when the loch level was raised to become a reservoir, the castle originally known as Castle Balliol, held by King John Baliol). The forest is rich in wildlife, and has at least 10 peaks above 2,000 feet (610m), Merrick being the highest at 2,766 feet (844m), making outstanding walking country. (Get hold of a copy of *Galloway Forest Park Guide* in Newton Stewart if you plan to spend time in the area.)

The A712 heads west out of New Galloway, then south-west after Clatteringshaws, where the best stretch of scenery begins as the road skirts the southern edge of the Forest Park. The Deer Museum at Clatteringshaws Loch is in converted farm buildings and has imaginatively displayed material on deer, wild goats, live trout and the botany and mineralogy of the district. A short walk from here takes you to Bruce's Stone (NTS) on Moss Rapploch, which records Robert the Bruce's victory over the English at a battle here in 1307 during the war of independence. Also near here is the western approach to Raider's Road, a 10-mile (16 km) forest drive through woods where you can see many

13

species of birds, coming out on the A762. Murray's Monument is an obelisk beside the A712 in memory of Alexander Murray, 1775–1813, who was born and brought up as a shepherd boy in these hills but became a professor of oriental languages at Edinburgh.

Newton Stewart is a pleasant little town on the River Cree, given a charter in 1677 by Charles II, and developed after that by William Stewart, son of the Earl of Galloway. The two churches, of Minigaff and Penninghame are both by William Burn, the nineteenth century architect. It forms a good base for touring, especially for exploration of the forest park, and the Machars district due south.

The A714 northwards from Newton Stewart takes you along the course of the Cree and the right turn at Bargrennan leads into the heart of Galloway Forest Park, Glen Trool. This part was once a refuge for Robert the Bruce, and the Bruce Stone, standing amidst peaceful green scenery overlooking Loch Trool, marks the place where he overwhelmed the English by rolling boulders down on top of them.

The A712 joins up with the A75 at Newton Stewart, and leads out to the south-west towards **Glenluce** (15 miles/24 km on), traditionally the home of the Wizard, Michael Scot, about whom legends abound. Glenluce Abbey, founded in 1192 and visited by Mary Queen of Scots in 1563, is now but a meagre ruin. Little of the church's fine Early English structure remains standing, bar the gable ends, but the fifteenth century vaulted chapter house is still a noble feature, with a superb arched entrance and central stone pillar. Note the red clay interlocking water pipes which are probably unique. Glenluce is at the head of Luce Bay, and the Sands of Luce were for many years a threat to the good soil beyond as their dunes were constantly shifting but they are now held firm by Corsican pine trees.

Off the A75 three miles (5 km) east of Stranraer are the Castle Kennedy Gardens, of the stately nineteenth century Lochinch Castle which is not open to the public. The old ruin of Castle Kennedy, late fifteenth century, is on an isthmus in the grounds between two lochs, now thoroughly overgrown, but it is the gardens that are the attraction, especially the avenue of huge monkey-puzzle trees planted about 100 years ago, and the large round lily pond. The gardens were transformed, in 1847, from a tangle to their original seventeenth century plan, and the pinetum was the first in Scotland.

Stranraer, with its attractive harbour and quayside houses, is a busy market town as well as car ferry port for Larne in Northern Ireland, as is Cairnryan on the east side of the loch. It is often used as a touring base for the Rhinns of Galloway, the double peninsula forming Scotland's south-west corner. The town has a local history museum in London Road, the Wigtown District Museum, with material on Sir John Ross, the Arctic explorer (1777–1856) who lived at North West Castle here (now a hotel). There is also a Curling Rink with a viewing gallery.

The Rhinns' main centre is **Portpatrick** on the west coast, a pleasant and popular holiday resort, and important in the past as the best harbour for regular sailings to Northern Ireland, but with the advent of steam-powered boats, mid-nineteenth century, Stranraer took on the trade and Portpatrick's little harbour was abandoned. You can see the ruins of the early sixteenth century Dunskey Castle just south of the town on a small headland, but take great care on the cliffs here.

In the centre of the north arm of the peninsula is the ruined Lochnaw Castle beside a loch, a seventeenth century building with an older tower. The former castle was on an island in the loch. The lighthouse (Corsewall) on the north coast was built by the engineer Robert Stevenson, 1772–1850, (grandfather of Robert Louis Stevenson), famed for his lighthouses, notably Bell Rock.

The south arm of the Rhinns merits a longer investigation, firstly at Kirkmadrine off the A716 near **Sandhead**, where inscribed stones were discovered, believed to be the earliest Christian monuments in Britain (fifth to twelfth century), signifying the successful penetration of Christianity in this part of Scotland within a few years of St Ninian's arrival at Whithorn. The stones are displayed and explained in a show case outside the church in whose ancient churchyard they were found.

A couple of miles (3 km) south, visit Ardwell House Gardens and south again, the Logan Botanic Garden to see unusual trees, shrubs and plants flourishing in the mild Gulf Stream climate. (Logan has a walled garden, featuring a formal pond and trees include cabbage palms and the Brazilian Gunnera manicata, the largest-leafed outdoor plant to grow in Britain.) The Logan fish pond is a tidal rock pool originally built in 1800 as a fish larder for Logan House, but now stocked with 'tame' sea fish, mainly cod.

The southerly tip of the peninsula is Mull of Galloway, a rugged escarpment of 200 feet (61m).

IV: Dalbeattie – Kirkcudbright – Whithorn

Leaving Dumfries on the A710, down the west side of the Nith estuary, the ruins of Sweetheart Abbey, (or New Abbey) are six miles (10 km) along the route. The Abbey takes its unexpected name from the fact that Devorguilla Balliol, who founded the abbey in memory of her husband, was buried in front of the high altar with her husband's heart. (John Balliol predeceased her by 21 years.) She founded the abbey for Cistercians in 1273, but the existing red sandstone ruins show mainly the church, scarcely any of the monastic buildings having survived. The church has beautiful features (the great west window, the main arches and central tower), not least of which is the containing wall, made up of massive boulders, enclosing some 30 acres (12 ha) in all. Devorguilla Balliol (*see* p. 00) also founded Balliol College in Oxford, and a memorial slab in the abbey is from Balliol College (1966) marking the original site of her tomb.

From Sweetheart Abbey the A710 approximately follows the coast round to Dalbeattie, skirting Criffel (a hill of 1,686 feet/570m at its highest point, and not difficult to climb from Glen Burn). Arbigland, east of the road, with formal and water gardens set in woods around a small bay with sandy beaches, is where John Paul (father of the sailor John Paul who changed his name to Paul Jones, and became founder of the US Navy) worked as a gardener. His son was born in 1747, dying in France in 1792 after an eventful and colourful life. At the church in Kirkbean on the A710 he is commemorated by a font presented by the US Navy. Rounding the headland at the mouth of the firth, Mote of Mark is a 20-acre (8 ha) site of an ancient hill fort.

Dalbeattie on the Urr Water is a little grey granite town known in the nineteenth century for exporting the local stone. It is worth stopping at the Woodside Studio Gallery in William Street for its exhibitions of paintings, usually of local subjects. Out in the estuary of the Urr, Rough Island is a bird sanctuary, overlooked from the west by Orchardton Tower, off the A711 several miles (4 km) south of Dalbeattie, near Palnackie. Orchardton Tower is a rare and very good example of a ruined round tower house of the fifteenth century (built by John Cairns), in a green and rural setting. In Palnackie, see the North Glen Gallery where glass blowing is demonstrated, and welding.

The A711 curves its way round the coast but not running beside the sea until it reaches Kirkcudbright Bay. Smaller roads lead down to the shore, with shallow sandy bays. You get long views over the Solway Firth from the road.

Some seven miles (11 km) from Kirkcudbright you reach Dundrennan with the ruins of a Cistercian abbey founded in 1142 probably by David I. Falling into neglect in the early seventeenth century, its stones were quarried for building houses in the village. Dundrennan Abbey is noted as the last place on Scottish soil where Mary Queen of Scots rested on 15 May, 1568, composing her last letter to Elizabeth I pleading sanctuary in England, before embarking from Port Mary (then called Burnfoot) to Workington across the Solway Firth, in the greatest secrecy, with her red hair shorn for disguise, and sailing in a humble fishing boat. The transepts are the finest remnant of the church, and the entrance to what was the chapter house, with a beautiful example of a thirteenth century pointed doorway.

Kirkcudbright (pronounced Kir-coo-bri) is a picturesque burgh town on the Dee which takes its name from Kirk of Cuthbert, the saint whose bones were once sheltered in an ancient church here. Near the wide waterfront off the High Street is the dominant ruin of a castellated mansion with turrets, McLellan's Castle, built in 1582 from the stones of the old friary, by Sir Thomas McLellan, whose imposing tomb and effigy are now in the nineteenth century Greyfriars Church. In the church you can also see a fragment of the thirteenth century Franciscan friary, where it is believed that Mary Queen of Scots stayed in 1563 on her tour of the region. Little else survives of the old town. (John) Paul Jones was imprisoned in the sixteenth to seventeenth century Tolbooth (accused of manslaughter when his ship's carpenter died after a flogging), which stands beside the Mercat Cross (1610). The town is very popular with artists, and the painter E.A. Hornel bequeathed his eighteenth century Broughton House in the High Street to the town when he died in 1933. It houses a collection of his work, a library and antique furniture, set in a pleasant garden. In St Mary's Street the Stewartry Museum is worth a visit for the varied historical displays including an exhibition focussing on (John) Paul Jones, who changed his name to Jones after he killed the ring leader of a mutinous crew, an incident he profoundly regretted for the rest of his life. Perhaps he was a man of many regrets, because in 1778 he looted the plate from a house on St Mary's Isle (the peninsula south of Kirkcudbright) later returning all of it to its owner, the Countess of Selkirk.

Before continuing along the main coastal route, **Castle Douglas** is 10 miles (16 km) to the north, (6 miles/12 km direct from Dalbeattie). It has no castle of its own, taking its name from a merchant by the name of William Douglas who developed the town in 1789 with his new fortune. It has three parallel streets and is a busy centre with good shopping facilities. Try and get to the market auction, usually on a Monday, at the top of the town. The town had been subject to the ruthless 'Black' Douglases of Threave long before this, and their gaunt stronghold, Threave Castle (now ruined) stands on an island in the Dee two miles (3 km) away, its forbidding countenance surely reflecting the nature of its creator, Archibald the Grim, Lord of Galloway who died here in 1400. The castle was built between 1369 and 1390 with five storeys of a single room, each one connected by a corner tower spiral stair, comprising in all a great tower, 70 feet (21 m) high.

Off the A75 two miles (3 km) south of Castle Douglas are Threave Gardens with a NTS Visitor Centre. The Victorian house, not open to the public, is a School of Practical Gardening, and the estate consists of a series of gardens with shrubberies and shrub roses, rockeries, water gardens, heath banks, a walled garden, vegetable gardens, woodlands and glasshouses, where everything seems to grow effortlessly and profusely. Nearby is the Threave Wildfowl Refuge, a roosting and feeding place for the many geese and ducks of the Dee.

Returning to the coastal route and the A75, you come to **Gatehouse of Fleet**. The Angel Hotel in the High Street is a convenient stop for coffee or a meal, and there are interesting forest walks to take from the Murray Forest Centre, half a mile (1 km) east. There is an exhibition in a log cabin here depicting the broad-leafed tree species in Fleet Forest. Just outside Gatehouse note the eighth century Christian Cross in the churchyard of Anwoth Church, itself built in 1627.

Cardoness Castle is a stark four-storeyed tower house ruin of the fifteenth century, worth visiting to see its original stairway, fireplaces and vaulted basement ceiling. Initially it belonged to the de Cardines, hence the name. Where the road bends up towards Creetown it overlooks Ravenshall Point just east of Kirkdale Burn. Some 250 yards (228 m) east of the burn on the shore is the narrow entrance to Dirk

Hatteraick's Cave, the largest of several caves along here. Half a mile (1 km) north of the road, up a side road, is Cairn Holy with two neolithic tombs, (stone age and bronze age).

Carsluith Castle on the A75 is a ruined sixteenth century fortified manor house of the L-plan. Creetown is across the estuary from Wigtown, where there was a ferry link at one time, referred to as 'Port-an-Ferry' in Scott's novel *Guy Mannering*. The Kirkmabreck Quarries nearby produced the granite from which much as been built, including the local houses, and Liverpool Docks! Before reaching Newton Stewart, there are very attractive forest walks up around Larg Hill and Bruntis Lochs, in Kirroughtree Forest.

Skirting round the south of Newton Stewart, pick up the A714 to **Wigtown**, focal point of the area often referred to as the 'Quiet Country', and itself an unhurried royal burgh town of 1457, whose pleasantly spacious main street has a bowling green in the centre and a narrow pend, or arch, at each end. In the thirteenth century Devorguilla Balliol founded yet another priory here, but no trace remains. At the river mouth there used to be a harbour, and a castle on the mound, but Wigtown is probably best known for the sorry tale of the Wigtown Martyrs, two women aged 62 and 18 who in 1685 were tied to a stake in the estuary and left to drown in the incoming tide, for refusing to betray their covenanting beliefs. The Martyrs' Stake standing in solitude on the mud flats of the estuary indicates where the two Margarets (Lachlan and Willson) met their death, but they are now buried in the churchyard, along with three men hanged for the same reason. Note the descriptive headstones. The Martyrs' Monument was erected in 1858. West of Wigtown along the B733 about three miles (5 km) are the Standing Stones of Torhouse, a 60-foot (18 m) diameter circle comprising 19 stones, probably bronze age.

After Kirkinner, on the A746, (note its Celtic Cross in the churchyard) take the B7004 to the left, towards Garlieston to follow the line of the coast. Garlieston is typical of a fishing village whose harbour trace has declined to nothing, attractively situated on a tiny bay. Beyond Cruggleton Bay on the B7063 is a badly ruined castle (a Comyn fortress) and Norman church, Cruggleton Church, which is a rare example of such architecture in this part of Scotland. Cruggleton Castle is now merely a single arch beside the shore.

This minor road continues almost to the tip of the headland, ending at Isle of Whithorn, not actually an island though the low neck of land joining the promontory to the mainland could easily have been submerged at one time. This has a very active harbour, being the headquarters of Wigtown Bay Sailing Club, and shark or tope fishing expeditions are organised out into the deeps now and then. The ruined St Ninian's Chapel, built around 1300, was probably used by overseas pilgrims to Whithorn, and the tower house overlooking the village is late seventeenth century.

St Ninian's Cave, on the rocky foreshore about three miles (5 km) west of here off the A747, can only be reached on foot and is where St Ninian is supposed to have spent many hours in prayer and meditation. The little votive crosses on the rocks have been there since the eighth century.

Whithorn deserves special attention, as the place where Ninian, a local man who went to Rome on a pilgrimage and to study, first introduced Christianity to Scotland, 397 years after the birth of Christ, building a little church of stone here on his return, by this time aged about 37. The church was clad in white plaster, earning the name of White House, or 'huit aern', from which Whithorn is obviously derived. The remains of this building have been excavated but in order to preserve them they have had to be covered. A priory was founded here in 1160 to serve the shrine which was, for hundreds of years, a place of pilgrimage for people of many nations and many walks of life. From Scotland the pilgrims included Robert the Bruce (in 1329), James III, James IV (who came nearly every year) and James V. It is approached today from the wide main street of Whithorn through a seventeenth century archway, the 'pend', flanked by sculptured pillars of the fifteenth century, also the way to the museum, which gives an exceptionally well explained history, and includes important Early Christian artefacts. Relatively little remains of the priory.

This part of the region is known as 'The Machars', and the A747 travels up the western coast, hugging the shore from Barsalloch Point to Auchenmalg Bridge before looping slightly inland to reach Glenluce. At Barsalloch Point, on the right of the road, is an iron age fort on a 60-foot (18 m) rise above the sea called Barsalloch Fort, encircled by a clearly defined ditch. At the southerly end of Monrieth Bay with its fine stretch of sandy beach, you can see the remains of a double concentric standing stone circle, known as Wren's Egg Stone Circle.

There is an Otter Memorial in bronze commemorating Gavin Maxwell, author, above St Medan's Chapel of Monrieth. His grandfather, Sir Herbert E. Maxwell, a literary figure of this district, is buried here. Gavin Maxwell grew up at House of Elrig, north of Port William. Port William is an attractive village with a neat harbour and generous main square, increasingly popular as a seaside resort. You can take a boat trip from here to the Scar Rocks bird sanctuary.

Drumtrodden Stones, a couple of miles (4 km) north-east on the A714, are two groups of clear bronze age cup and ring markings on natural rock, with three standing stones a short distance away.

Chapel Finian, back on the coast road, was a tenth century (or eleventh century) chapel to St Findbarr, of which only foundations, traces of an old well, and part of a wall remain. Inland from here is Old Place of Mochrum, a fifteenth to sixteenth century castle with two towers, not open to the public.

Access to Sites and Places of Interest

Arbigland
May–Sep. 1400–1800 Tue., Thur., Sun.
Fee.

Ardwell House Gardens
Mar.–Oct. 1000–1800 Mon.–Sat.
Donation.

Caerlaverock Castle
Standard.

Caerlaverock NNR
Permission necessary for sanctuary area
(NCC, SW Region)

Cardoness Castle
Standard.

Carsluith Castle
Standard.

Castle Kennedy Gardens
Easter–late Sep. 1000–1700 daily except Sat.
Fee.

Clatteringshaws Loch
Deer Museum
Easter–Sep. 1000–1700 daily.

Corsock House Gardens
May 1430–1800 Sun.
Fee.

Cruggleton Church
Any reasonable time, key from farm (Mr
Fisher).

Dalbeattie
Woodside Studio
0930–2100 daily.
Fee.

Drumcoltran Tower
Standard.

Drumlanrig Castle
May–late Aug. castle: 1400–1800 (last
entry 1715); grounds: 1200–1800.
Fee.

Dumfries
Burns House
Apr.–Sep. 1000–1300, 1400–1900 Mon.–
Sat., 1400–1900 Sun.; Oct.–Mar. 1000–
1200, 1400–1700 Mon.–Sat.
Fee.

Museum (including Old Bridge House)
Apr.–Sep. 0930–1900 Mon.–Sat., 1400–
1900 Sun.; Oct.–Mar. 0930–1600 Mon.–
Sat., 1400–1600 Sun.

Dundrennan Abbey
Standard.

Ellisland
All reasonable times.

Glenluce Abbey
Standard.

Kinmount Gardens
Apr.–Oct. 1000–1700 daily.
Fee.

Kirkcudbright
Broughton House
Apr.–Oct. 1100–1300, 1400–1600 Mon.–
Fri.; Nov.–Mar. 1400–1600; Tue. & Thur.
Fee.

McLellan's Castle
Standard.

Stewartry Museum
Easter–Oct. 1000–1200, 1300–1700 Mon.–
Sat.
Fee.

Lincluden Abbey
Standard.

Logan
Botanic Gardens
Apr.–Sep. 1000–1700
Fee.

Sea Fish Pond
Easter–Sep. 1000–1200, 1400–1730 Sun.,
Mon., Wed.–Fri.
Fee.

Maxwelton House
May–Sep. 1430–1700 Wed. & Thur.
Fee.

Murray Forest Centre
0900–1800 daily.

Orchardton Tower
0930–1900 Mon.–Sat., 1400–1900 Sun.

Palnackie
North Glen Gallery
1000–1800 daily.

Raiders' Road Forest Drive
End May–Sep. 0900–dusk daily.
Fee (50p coins required for machine).

Sanquhar Museum
Apply: Mr. T.A. Johnstone,
35 High Street.

Sweetheart Abbey
Standard.

Threave
Castle
Standard.

Gardens
0900–sunset daily.
Walled garden and glasshouses: 0900–
1700.
Visitor Centre open Apr.–Oct.
Fee.

Wildfowl Refuge
Conducted parties daily except Mon. by previous arrangement with the Warden (Bridge of Dee 242).

Whithorn Priory
Standard.

Wigtown District Museum
0930–1330, 1400–1700 Mon.–Fri., 0930–1300 Sat.

Hotels and Guest Houses

Annan
Corner House Hotel.
(Annan 2754)

Auchencairn
Balcary Bay Hotel.
(Auchencairn 217)

Solwayside Guest House.
(Auchencairn 280)

Canonbie
Cross Keys Hotel.
(Canonbie 205)

Castle Douglas
Douglas Arms Hotel.
(Castle Douglas 2231)

Castle Kennedy
Eynhallow Hotel.
(Dunragit 256)

Creetown
Creetown Arms Hotel.
(Creetown 284)

Crocketford
Galloway Arms Hotel.
(Crocketford 240)

Dumfries
Aberdour Hotel,
Newall Terrace.
(Dumfries 4825)

Fulwood Private Hotel,
Lovers Walk.
(Dumfries 2262)

Station Hotel,
49 Lovers Walk DG1 1LT.
(Dumfries 4316)

Eskdalemuir
Hart Manor Hotel.
(Eskdalemuir 217)

Glencaple
Nith Hotel.
(Glencaple 213)

Gretna Green
Gretna Chase Hotel.
(Gretna 257)

Gretna Hall Hotel.
(Gretna 257)

Hightae
Royal Four Towns Hotel.
(Lochmaber 402)

Kirkbean
Cavens Guest House.
(Kirkbean 234)

Lochmaben
Beaufort Guest House.
(Lochmaben 295)

Lockerbie
Lockerbie House Hotel.
(Lockerbie 2610)

Moffat
Allanton House Hotel,
21–22 High Street.
(Moffat 20343)

Craigieburn Hotel,
Selkirk Road.
(Moffat 20229)

The Arden House Guest House,
DG10 9HG.
(Moffat 20220)

Moniaive
Craigdarroch Arms Hotel.
(Moniaive 205)
(New Abbey 244)

Newton Stewart
Bruce Hotel.
(Newton Stewart 2294)

Kirroughtree Hotel,
Minnigaff.
(Newton Stewart 2141)

Port William
Commercial Hotel.
(Port William 243)

Portpatrick
Fernhill Hotel.
(Portpatrick 220)

Roslin Hotel,
Heugh Road.
(Portpatrick 241)

Sanquhar
Blackaddie House Hotel,
Blackaddie Road.
(Sanquhar 270)

Stranraer
Bucks Head Hotel,
Hanover Street DG9 7RP
(Stranraer 2064)

21

Torrs-Warren Hotel,
Stoneykirk.
(Sandhead 204)

Thornhill
Buccleuch and Queensberry Hotel.
(Thornhill 30215)

Wigtown
Fordbank Country House Hotel.
(Wigtown 2346)

Accommodation for the Young

Dumfries
Ae Valley Outdoor Centre,
Gubhill.
(Parkgate 289)
Contact: Director of Education,
30 Edinburgh Road,
Dumfries DG1 1JQ.
(Dumfries 63822 ext. 45)

Moffat
Hartfell House,
Hartfell Crescent DG10 9AL.
(Moffat 20153)

Camping & Caravanning

Amisfield
Glen Clova Caravan Site,
Amisfield by Dumfries.
(Amisfield 710447)

Castle Douglas
Loch Ken Holiday Centre,
Parton.
(Parton 282)

Crocketford
Brandedleys by Dumfries.
(Crocketford 250)

Dalbeattie
Islecroft Caravan Site,
Mill Street.
(Dalbeattie 610012)
Bookings: Stewartry Dist. Council Sub Office,
Town Hall Buildings,
Dalbeattie.
(Dalbeattie 610286)

Dumfries
Craigsview Caravan Site,
296 Annan Road.
(Dumfries 3812)

Eastriggs
Central Road Caravan Site.
(Eastriggs 304)

Ecclefechan
Cressfield Country Hotel Caravan Site.
(Ecclefechan 281/345)

Gatehouse of Fleet
Auchenlarie Holiday Farm.
(Mossyard 251)

Glenluce
Whitecairn Caravan Park,
Whitecairn.
(Glenluce 267)

Gretna
The Braids Caravan Park,
Annan Road.
(Gretna 409; Kirkpatrick Fleming 630)

Kirkcudbright
Kippford Caravan Park,
Kippford.
(Kippford 636)

Lochmaben
Lochmaben Caravan Site,
Castlehillgate.
Booking: Annan & Eskdale Dist. Council,
Silverlaw,
Annan.
(Annan 3311)

Lockerbie
Halleaths Caravan Park.
(Lochmaben 321)

Moffat
Camping Club Site,
Ladyknowe.
(Moffat 20436)
Booking: Sites, Camping Club of GB & Ireland,
11 Lower Grosvenor Place,
London.
(out of season only)

Moniaive
Woodlea Hotel.
(Moniaive 209)

Port Logan, Stranraer
New England Bay Caravan Club Site.
(Ardwell 275)

Sanquhar
Castleview Caravan Site.
(Sanquhar 291)

Stranraer
Aird Donald Caravan Park.
(Stranraer 2025)

Self Catering Accommodation

Annan
Mrs Jamieson,
Woodhead,
Annan.
(Eastriggs 383)

Borgue
Mr Gray,
Inglestone Farm,
Borgue.
(Borgue 208)

Castle Douglas
R.H. Ball,
Barncrosh Farm,
Castle Douglas.
(Bridge of Dee 216)

G.M. Thomson & Co.,
27 King Street,
Castle Douglas DG7 1AB.
(Castle Douglas 2701)

Colvend
G.M. Thomson & Co.,
27 King Street,
Castle Douglas DG7 1AB.
(Castle Douglas 2701)

Corsock
Mr & Mrs N. Gray,
Caldow Lodge,
Corsock DG7 3EB.
(Corsock 286)

Creetown
Mrs B. McMillan,
Creetown Caravan Park,
Creetown.
(Creetown 377)

Dalbeattie
Mrs Campbell,
24 Maxwelltown Drive,
Dumfries DG2 9JH.
(Dumfries 3754)

Dumfries
Mrs E.J. Harkness,
Netherhall,
Kirkmahoe DG1 1RE.
(Amisfield 710244)

Mrs C.M. Schooling,
Locharthur House,
Beeswing,
Dumfries.

G.M. Thomson & Co.,
27 King Street,
Castle Douglas DG7 1AB.
(Castle Douglas 2701)

Ecclefechan
Mrs J.D. Clark,
Whins Farm,
Ecclefechan,
Lockerbie DG11 3LW.
(Ecclefechan 257)

Gatehouse of Fleet
Auchenlarie Holiday Farm,
Gatehouse of Fleet DG7 2EX.
(Mossyard 251)

Miss E. McMurray,
Culraven,
Kirkcudbright DG6 4SG.
(Borgue 247)

Glenluce
Mr & Mrs Rankin,
Whitecairn Farm Caravan Park,
Glenluce,
Newton Stewart,
Wigtownshire DG8 0NZ.
(Glenluce 267)

Gretna
Mrs Irving,
Stubby Knowe,
Gretna.
(Chapel Knowe 207)

Kippford
P.R. Aston,
Kippford Caravan Park,
By Dalbeattie.
(Kippford 636)

J. & G. McLellan Ltd,
River View Park,
Kippford DG5 4LG.
(Kippford 204)

J. & E. Thomson,
Doonpark Caravan Park,
Kippford by Dalbeattie.
(Kippford 259)

Kirkcudbright
Mrs I.M. Blacklock,
Little Sypland,
Kirkcudbright.
(Kirkcudbright 30592)

Mrs Jean W. Clark,
Valleyfield Farm,
Kirkcudbright DG6 4NH.
(Twynholm 213)

Mrs J. Picken,
Torrs,
Kirkcudbright.
(Townhead 256)

G.M. Thomson & Co.,
27 King Street,
Castle Douglas DG7 1AB.
(Castle Douglas 2701)

Moniaive
Smiths Gore, Chartered Surveyors,
28 Castle Street,
Dumfries.
(Dumfries 63066)

New Galloway
I.G. McLaren,
Meadowbank,
New Galloway DG7 3RL.
(New Galloway 282)

Newton Stewart
Ian S. Lowth,
Conifers Leisure Parks,
Kirroughtree,
Newton Stewart DG8 6AN.
(Newton Stewart 2107 & Lowestoft 62292)

Scottish Country Cottages,
2d Churchill Way,
Bishopbriggs,
Glasgow G64 2RH.
(041 772 5920)

Portpatrick
Mrs N. McCaig,
Port o'Spittal Farm,
Portpatrick DG9 9AD.
(Portpatrick 232/213)

Port William
J.H.G. Korner,
House of Elrig,
Port William DG8 9RF.
(Port William 242)

Robinson-Wyllie Ltd,
Culbae,
Whauphill.
(Kirkinner 249)

Sandyhills
Barend Properties Ltd,
Sandyhills,
Dalbeattie.
(Southwick 663 & Lowestoft 62292)

Stranraer
P.R. Manning,
Drumlochart Caravan Park,
Lochnaw,
Stranraer DG9 0RN.
(Leswalt 232)

Mrs. M. Whaite,
Meikle Mark Farm,
Stranraer DG9 8HX.
(Stranraer 2366)

Whithorn
Mrs W. Brown,
Boyach,
Whithorn DG8 8LA.
(Whitehorn 324)

Mrs McMiken,
Prestrie,
Whithorn DG8 8JZ.
(Whithorn 417)

Wigtown
Mrs J.S. Rhind,
Clauchrie,
Wigtown DG8 9DH.
(Wigtown 2251)

Golf

Annan
Powfoot Golf Course.
(Cummertrees 227)

Castle Douglas
Castle Douglas Golf Course,
Abercromby Road.
(Castle Douglas 2801)
Secretary: R.W. Blackett,
'Ardale', Abercromby Road,
Castle Douglas.
(Castle Douglas 2665)

Dalbeattie
Colvend Golf Course,
Sandyhills.
(Dalbeattie 610712)

Dalbeattie Golf Club.
(Dalbeattie 610259)

Gatehouse of Fleet
Gatehouse Golf Club,
c/o The Secretary,
5 Markethill.

Kirkcudbright
Kirkcudbright Golf Course,
Stirling Crescent.
(Kirkcudbright 30752)

Moffat
Moffat Golf Course,
Coateshill.
(Moffat 20020)

Newton Stewart
Newton Stewart Golf Club.
(Newton Stewart 2981)

Port William
St Medan Golf Club.
(Port William 358)

Stranraer
Stranraer Golf Club,
Creachmore by Stranraer.
(Leswalt 245)

Wigtown
Wigtown & Bladnoch Golf Club.
(Wigtown 3354)

Sea Angling

Auchenmalg
Pollack, wrasse from rocky shores, flatfish,
bass, mullet and rays from sandy beaches.
Pollack, coalfish, cod, whiting, wrasse,

lesser spotted dogfish, bullhuss, spurdog, tope, rays, conger from boats.
Boats: A. Carter, Castle Daly, Auchenmalg. (Auchenmalg 250)

Drummore
Pollack, wrasse from rocky shores, flatfish, bass, mullet and rays from sandy beaches. Pollack, coalfish, cod, whiting, wrasse, lesser spotted dogfish, bullhuss, spurdog, tope, rays, conger from boats.
Boats: Steven Woods, Craigmillar Guest House, Main Street. (Dummore 372)

Garlieston
Mackerel, cod, pollack and coalfish from the shore. Mackerel, cod, pollack, ray, plaice, dab, flounder and coalfish from boats.
Boats: Mrs James McGinn, North Crescent. (Garlieston 664)
T. Bradshaw, 10 North Crescent. (Garlieston 643)

Isle of Whithorn
Cod, coalfish, dogfish, conger, pollack, mackerel, wrasse from the shore. Cod, rays, flatfish, spurdog, dogfish, mackerel, conger and tope from boats.
Boats: 'Osprey': J. Scoular, Tonderghie. 'Evening Star': Sam Archer, c/o Harbour Master.
'Snow Goose': K. Lonsdale, Main Street. 'Manulea': E.C. McGuire, Burnside. (Whithorn 468)
J. McGinn, Randolph Crescent, Garlieston. (Garlieston 239)
Mr Hannah, Boathirer, Port William. (Port William 434)

Game Fishing

Ae Water
Trout.
Permits: J.P.M. Johnstone, Glenae, Amisfield, Dumfries.
(Amisfield 236)

Annan River
Halleaths Water.
Salmon, sea trout, brown trout.
Permits: weekly tickets (only three issued per week) and season tickets (limited numbers) from Messrs McJerrow, & Stevenson, Solicitors, Lockerbie.
(Lockerbie 2123)

Newbie Estates.
Salmon, sea trout, brown trout.
Permits: Mrs Clark, Newbie Mill, Annan.
(Annan 2608)

Salmon, sea trout, brown trout.
Permits: Red House Hotel, Wamphray, Moffat.
(Johnstone Bridge 214)

Annan River and Moffat Water
Salmon, sea trout, brown trout.
Permits: Upper Annandale Angling Association: J. Black, 1 Rosehill, Grange Road, Moffat.
(Moffat 20104)

Annan River, Kinnel, Dryfewater
Applegirth Estate.
Salmon, sea trout, grilse.
Permits: Smiths Gore, 64 Warwick Road, Carlisle.
(Carlisle 27586)

Black Loch
Brown trout, American brook trout.
Permits: B. Stevens, Three Lochs Caravan Park, Kirkcowan, Newton Stewart.
(Kirkcowan 304)

Brown trout (stocked).
Permits: Galloway Deer Museum, Clatteringshaws; New Galloway & Talnotry Caravan Park, Newton Stewart.

Bladnoch River
Salmon, grilse.
Permits: Newton Stewart Angling Association: R.W. McDowall, 4 Arthur Street, Newton Stewart.
(Newton Stewart 2163)

Cairn River, Nith River
Salmon, sea trout, brown trout.
Permits: D. McMillan, 6 Friars Vennel, Dumfries.
(Dumfries 2075)

Canonbie Liddle
Lower Liddle Ticket.
Salmon, sea trout, herling, brown trout.
Permits: Esk & Liddle Fisheries Association:
Secretary: R.J.B. Hill, Solicitor, Langholm, Dumfriesshire.
(Langholm 80428)

Esk River and Liddle
All waters ticket.
Salmon, sea trout, herling, brown trout.
Permits: Esk & Liddle Fisheries Association:
Secretary: R.J.B. Hill, Solicitor, Langholm, Dumfriesshire.
(Langholm 80428)

J. Irving Wylie, River Watcher,
Byreburnfoot, Canonbie.
(Canonbie 279)

Nith River
Tidal stretch at Dumfries and short stretch
above weir.
Salmon, grilse, sea trout, brown trout.
Permits: Director of Finance,
Municipal Chambers,
Dumfries.
(Dumfries 3166)

And tributaries, Kello, Crawick, Euchan
and Mennock Waters.
Salmon, sea trout, brown trout.
Permits: Upper Nithsdale Angling Club:
William Forsyth, Secretary, Solicitor,
Sanquhar, Dumfriesshire.
(Sanquhar 241)

Salmon, sea trout, brown trout, grayling.
Permits: Mennockfoot Lodge Hotel,
Sanquhar, Dumfriesshire.
(Sanquhar 382)

Tarf River
Brown trout, sea trout.
Permits: B. Stevens,
Three Lochs Caravan Park,
Kirkcowan,
Newton Stewart.
(Kirkcowan 304)

Urr River
Salmon, sea trout, brown trout.
Permits: Tommy's Sports Shop,
20 King Street,
Castle Douglas.

Salmon, trout.
Permits: Caldow Lodge self-catering
cottages,
Corsock, Castle Duglas.
(Corsock 286)

Hotels with Shooting and Stalking

Beattock
Auchen Castle Hotel.
(Beattock 407)
Game and rough shooting.

Dalry
Milton Park Hotel.
(Dalry 286)
Rough shooting.

Dumfries
The Ben Guest House,
29 Newall Terrace.
(Dumfries 62950)
Rough shooting.

Glencaple
Nith Hotel.
(Glencaple 213)
Game, wildfowl, rough shooting.

Kirkcolm
Knocknassie House Hotel.
(Ervie 217)
Wildfowl, rough shooting.

Newton Stewart
Corsbie Villa Guest House,
Corsbie Villa, Corsbie Road.
(Newton Stewart 2958)
Game, wildfowl, rough shooting.

Creebridge House Hotel.
(Newton Stewart 2372)
Game, wildfowl, rough shooting.

Duncree Guest House.
(Newton Stewart 2001)
Game, wildfowl, rough shooting, stalking.

Palnackie
Barlochan House Hotel.
(Palnackie 287)
Game shooting.

Cycling

Dumfries
Dumfries Cycles,
25 Glasgow Street.
(Dumfries 65152)

Newton Stewart
Ken Gunn,
Longcastle Schoolhouse,
Whauphill.
(Kirkinner 276)

Stranraer
John Reilly Cycle Market,
32 Bridge Street.
(Stranraer 4517)

Where to Eat

Castle Kennedy
Eynhallow Hotel.
(Dunragit 256/643)

Dumfries
Station Hotel,
Lovers Walk.
(Dumfries 4316)

The Globe Inn,
56 High Street.
(Dumfries 2335)

Moffat
Beechwood Country House Hotel.
(Moffat 20210)

Newton Stewart
The Creebridge House Hotel.
(Newton Stewart 2121)

Stranraer
Bay House Restaurant,
Cairnryan Road.
(Stranraer 3786)

Torrs Warren Hotel,
Stoneykirk.
(Sandhead 204)

Car Hire

Castle Douglas
Harvey Moore,
Vehicle Engineers,
53 Academy Street.
(Castle Douglas 3448)

Dumfries
Gordon Bisset,
Laurieknowe Service Station.
(Dumfries 5059)

SMT Self Drive Hire,
York Place.
(Dumfries 5291/2)

Steeple Taxis Ltd,
Dumfries Station.
(Dumfries 5643/5050)

Kirkcudbright
St Mary's Service Station.
(Kirkcudbright 30696)

Stranraer
Lithgow Car Sales Ltd.,
Hanover Square.
(Stranraer 2833/3939/3364)

Rosefield Motors (Ayr) Ltd,
West End Garage,
Leswalt Road.
(Stranraer 3636/7)

John Wilson, (Hanover Square) Ltd,
Hanover Square.
(Stranraer 3939)

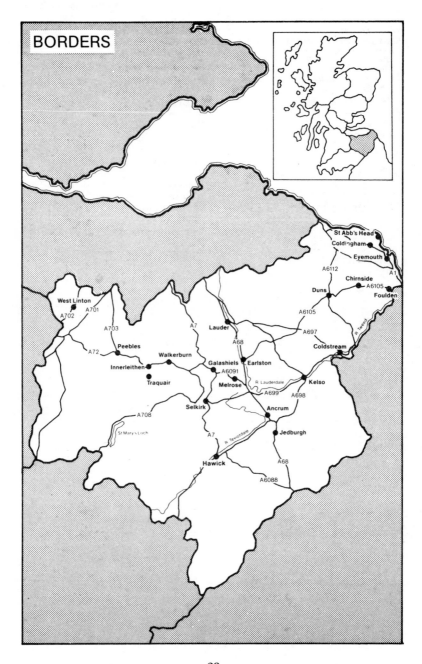

BORDERS

St Abb's Head
Coldingham
Eyemouth
A6112
Chirnside
Duns   A6105
A6105   Foulden
West Linton
A702   A701
A703   A7   Lauder   A697   R Tweed
A72   Peebles   A68   Coldstream
Walkerburn
Innerleithen   Galashiels   Earlston
Traquair   A6091
Melrose   R Lauderdale
A699   Kelso
A698
A708   Selkirk   Ancrum
St Mary's Loch   A7   R Teviotdale   Jedburgh
Hawick   A68
A6088

28

Borders

I: Jedburgh – Melrose – Peebles – Hawick

A good road for scenery from England to Scotland is the A68, from Carter Bar in the Cheviot Hills to Jedburgh, and Edinburgh, switch-backing over the foothills with repeated 'blind summit' warnings, the hills that in centuries past formed a natural defence against invasion. A mile south of Jedburgh grows a 'one thousand year old' oak tree, the Capon Tree, believed to be the hanging tree for Jedburgh.

The immediate view of **Jedburgh** is dominated by the magnificent Abbey ruin, one of David I's four great Border Abbeys. The Monastery is mostly gone, but the Abbey, though roofless, remarkably still has three-storey window ranges, a Norman doorway and west front, and the wheel window (St Catherine's wheel). The Castle, contemporary with the Abbey and popular with Scottish royalty, was a handy target for the marauding English, as were so many border monuments, and was ultimately destroyed. It was here in 1285 that Alexander III was warned of disaster on the occasion of his wedding feast, (for a description of his death *see* chapter 6, p. 000 Kinghorn). On the site a prison was built in 1823, now the Jail Museum with interesting exhibits. The chill stone room beside the Abbey was an old prison cell. Opposite the Abbey, the Tourist Information Centre has details of the Town Trail, a historical tour which includes Queen Mary's House, now a museum. Mary Queen of Scots became dangerously ill, and stayed here to recover in 1566. Museum exhibits include a portrait of Bothwell, and his restored death mask. The Jed Water is spanned by a medieval triple-arched bridge, Canongate, crossed over by Queen Mary, and two centuries later by Bonnie Prince Charlie. Finding himself welcome, the Prince stayed a while at 9 Castlegate. The Tourist Information Centre also has details of Jedburgh's one-week Festival held every July.

Ancrum, on the A68 several miles north, is famous for the Battle of Ancrum Moor in 1544, when the Scots gained an advantage over the English. Lilliardsedge is named after Maid Lilliard who fought in battle undeterred by losing both legs. Her epitaph reads 'Fair Maid Lilliard lies under this stane. Little was her stature but great was her fame. Upon the English loons she laid many thumps. And when her legs were cuttit off she fought upon her stumps.' Lilliardsedge Park is now a caravan and camping park with play areas, garden centre, shop, tavern and kitchen, in pleasant setting with trees.

St Boswells, named after Boisel, a prior at the seventh century Old Melrose Monastery, is on the crossing of the A68 by the A699 and offers golfing and riding (stables at Glenside House, The Green) within easy reach of Lilliardsedge.

'The Scott Country' covers the area of Galashiels, Selkirk, Melrose and Dryburgh as it is the area most closely associated with Sir Walter Scott, in which he spent the last 20 years of his life. **Galashiels** is known for textiles (also the Scottish College of Textiles) and is a busy industrial town. **Selkirk** is built on a hillside with its mills at the foot, by the river. In front of the Court House (now Town Hall) is a statue of Scott who was County Sheriff of Selkirk for over 30 years. Off the market place is a very unusual museum with exhibits of Edwardian and Victorian ironmongery, and the local (1910) ambulance. There is a striking statue of Mungo Park, eighteenth century explorer, and a memorial for the 79-out-of-80 Selkirk men killed at Flodden in 1513 (the returning hero was bearing an English banner). The 'Flodden Flag' is displayed in the Public Library and Museum.

The Tweed Valley is known for its scenery. The wide meandering river, fishermen standing midstream, lies between wooded hills flanked by poplars. Scott's View (signposted) is a superb position from which to appreciate the landscape, and is approached through unspoilt countryside, with old beech trees. The Eildon hills are legandary: King Arthur had his Knights lie 'in enchanted sleep' beneath the volcanic peaks.

There are varied and beautiful walks, best reached by footpath alongside the **Melrose** golf course. Notes on recommended walking routes may be obtained from the Tourist Information Centre, Priorwood. Priorwood Gardens specialise in the cultivation of flowers for drying, and have a NTS Visitor Centre as well as a picnic area. These are beside the Abbey, best-known feature of Melrose, though rugby fans know it as the place where 'seven-a-side' rugby was first played. The Abbey was built by David I to replace the seventh century Monastery of Old Melrose, 2½ miles (4 km) east, but was frequently destroyed by English invaders. Robert the Bruce rebuilt it and it was rebuilt again in the fifteenth century, but since 1545 it has been a ruin, many of the original stones gradually pillaged for other buildings. Some of the remaining stonework shows elaborate carving. The Abbey Museum, on the other side of Cloisters Road, has a collection of Roman finds from the Trimontium of the 'triple peaks' of the Eildon hills.

Scott named his house Abbotsford as it is near the place where the abbots used to ford the river. Scott fans must visit the mock-baronial memorial, partly designed and furnished by Scott, where he did a great deal of his writing.

Shaded by grand old trees, Dryburgh Abbey stands as a majestic ruin in well-tended grounds. Once an important monastery, (see postcard on sale at gate with sketch of how it must have looked in its heyday), it was built on a horseshoe loop in the Tweed, convenient for channelling off fresh water. Founded in 1150 it was sacked three times by the English, twice in the fourteenth century, then once and for all by Hertford and his men in the troubled mid-sixteenth century. From the higher points of the ruin there are rewarding views both of layout and setting. In the north transept chapel of the abbey church lies Sir Walter Scott's tomb. As his

Queen Mary's House, Jedburgh, Borders.

great-grandfather had owned the abbey lands, his family upheld the privilege of 'stretching their bones' there.

Earlston, northwards on the A68, is a peaceful village with wide main street. Note the smoothly-weathered stone of the houses and the traditional tiled walls of the butcher's shop (Donaldson's). There's a characterful old pub on the main street, 'The Black Bull'. Thomas Learmont ('Thomas the Rhymer', thirteenth century poet-prophet) lived here, hence the inscription 'Auld Rhymer's race lies in this place' on the church wall.

Lauderdale follows the course of the Leader, banked by sloping sheep pastures with dry-stone wall enclosures. The valley is dotted with attractive residences, and a fine single-arch bridge spans the river. **Lauder**, a sleepy little 'royal burgh' town, has an uncommon seventeenth century church with octagonal spire.

Following the Tweed upstream from Galashiels, the A72 runs along the north bank with a quieter road on the south bank. At **Walkerburn**, eight miles (13 km) west, the Museum of Wool Textiles throws light on the local wool industry. One mile (2 km) south of Innerleithen, crossing the bridge to Traquair, is the historic Traquair House, supposedly the only home in Scotland to have been lived in continuously since the tenth century, and visited by a total of 27 Scottish and English monarchs. Despite its size (four storeys, dozens of windows, long slate roofs) and forest backdrop, the impression is more domestic than stately, and there's plenty to see inside and out, including a priest's room with secret stairs, 200-year old brewhouse, still operational and licensed to sell its own Traquair House Ale. There are craft workshops in the summer.

Peebles, amidst lovely wooded hills, overlooks a wide stretch of the river and is a great area for walking, especially the Glentress Forest, three miles (5 km) west, which is 2,000 acres (810 ha) of the oldest state forest in southern Scotland. The Cross Kirk at Peebles is a thirteenth century ruin of interest, and the Tweed Bridge, although considerably widened, still displays its fifteenth century origins. The Library and Local History Museum are contained in the Chambers Institution on the main street. At 15 Violet Bank there is an Angling School, ideal for anyone looking for instuction in trout and salmon fishing.

Neidpath Castle, a mile (2 km) to the west, stands on a grassy hill beside the river. Once a robust stronghold it was eventually taken by Cromwell after damage was sustained during a long siege. Further along the A72 is Drochil Castle, half manor house, half fortress. The regent Morton started the building in 1570 but was executed in 1582 before completing it. The style of building of the hall next to the towers is a fine example of the period.

North of here, **West Linton** on the A702 was once an important meeting place for drovers coming across the Pentland Hills with their herds, but is now a quiet village, well placed for the Scottish National Camps Association to have an Outdoor Centre, the Broomlee Centre. The Pentlands are a range of hills running about 16 miles (26 km) south-west of Edinburgh and about five miles (8 km) in width, offering good upland walks with long views.

From Neidpath, the course of the Tweed and the B712 on its west bank continue southwards through pretty wooded scenery, past Dawyck House and Gardens and then Tinnis Castle, before the road joins the A701. Dawyck House Gardens, with chapel designed by William Burn, provide yet more woodland walks, as well as specimen trees and shrubs, narcissi and rhododendrons. Tinnis Castle is an early sixteenth century building abounding in legend (for example, it is one of the many sites of Wizard Merlin's grave).

West and south-west from Selkirk run the Ettrick and Yarrow valleys. Once densely afforested and a renowned hiding place for wanted men, the forest was the inspiration of ballads and poems (even by such as Wordsworth and Scott), but it is now transformed to peaceful moorland by the introduction of large flocks of sheep.

The Yarrow valley leads to Bowhill, two miles (3 km) west of Selkirk, an eighteenth century house with outstanding art collection (including paintings by Leonardo, Gainsborough, Reynolds, Canaletto and Raeburn) and period French furniture. The grounds are very attractive for children, with nature trails and adventure play area in the woods. Newark Castle, still beside the Yarrow, is a ruined fifteenth century keep, and the setting for Scott's *Lay of the Last Minstrel*.

Nearing St Mary's Loch, at the head of the valley, Dryhope Tower, built around 1600, can be seen from the road. Wat of Harden, famous freebooter, married 'the flower of Yarrow', or Mary of Dryhope, who lived in the four-storey tower. Tibbie Shiels Inn, on the spit of land separating St Mary's Loch and Loch of the Lowes, was a favourite rendezvous for such as Walter Scott, Thomas Carlyle, R.L. Stevenson and James Hogg. A seated statue of the poet Hogg, known as 'the Ettrick shepherd' (1770–1835) can be seen near the west end of the spit, but there is a monument to him at Ettrick, where he was born and is buried.

Hawick, the Scottish textile centre, is 18 miles (29 km) south of Selkirk on the A7. It is a busy town with an interesting museum (especially relating to knitwear), and art gallery with monthly exhibitions. There are also riverside walks, hot houses and gardens.

South again, the lonely B6399 road leads down to Hermitage Castle, a remote and forbidding ruin by Hermitage Water. Mainly fourteenth century, the ruin is outwardly in excellent condition, with keep, four corner towers and arches at east and west ends. Inside are the remains of the thirteenth century tower; also see the bakehouse, and the lavatory shafting above it.

II: Kelso – Coldstream – Eyemouth – St Abb's Head

Kelso, east of the A68 on the A699 where the Tweed and Teviot rivers meet, is a historic market town with the ruin of David I's greatest Border Abbey, founded in 1128. In 1545 it was almost razed to the ground by

Hertford, who slaughtered the 100 men defending it and left only the west façade, transepts and tower, and two bays of the nave. The elaborate north-west transept, still intact, is an impressive sight from the road. Kelso's other feature is the elegant, well-preserved Georgian square, but note also the horseshoe set in the road, marking where the Young Pretender's horse is said to have cast a shoe, beside 29 Roxburgh Street. Never a fortified town, Kelso partly depended on **Roxburgh** Castle for its defence, but Roxburgh (a substantial 'royal burgh') was finally seized in the fifteenth century from the English by the Scots, who utterly destroyed it and the castle.

Floors Castle, a mile (2 km) north-west of Kelso, and the seat of the Duke of Roxburghe, was built by William Adam in the 1720s, and added to 125 years later (creating its present appearance) by William Playfair. There is a tree in the grounds that marks the spot where James II was killed by the bursting of a cannon in 1460.

In the immediate vicinity there are several interesting sites to visit: Smailholm Tower to the west, Mellerstain House off the A6089, Greenknowe Tower at Gordon, and Hume Castle directly north of Floors Castle. Smailholm Tower is a very good and comprehensible example of a Border tower, in a lovely situation on a grassy knoll with rocky outcrops. Note the homely touch to the sixteenth century construction of a small privy, with seat, window and even lantern niche.

Mellerstain House pays tribute to both William Adam who built both wings, and his son Robert who completed it in 1778, some 40 years later, and whose superb ceilings and decoration help to make it one of Scotland's most exquisite eighteenth century mansions, set in a splendid park with formal terraced gardens at the rear. The collection of antique furniture (with Chippendale, Sheraton and Hepplewhite pieces), and paintings by such as Constable, Veronese, Van Goyen, Gainsborough, Allan Ramsay, Nicholas Maes, Oswald Birley and Bassano, are shown to best advantage in such elegant surroundings (note the famous Adam library).

On the A6015 just west of Gordon, Greenknowe Tower, built in 1581, is a fortified house in very good condition, still with its iron gate.

The original thirteenth century Hume Castle was ruined after falling into Cromwell's hands in 1651, and rebuilt in late eighteenth century with sham medieval battlements. It now sits squatly on the crest of a hill 600 feet (183 m) above sea level commanding excellent views of the district.

South-east of Kelso the B6352 leads to the English border beside the Bowmont Water. A couple of miles before the border the river separates the twin villages of Town Yetholm, and Kirk Yetholm (once known for being the home of the Scottish gypsies), where the famous 250-mile (402-km) Pennine Way walk begins. South-west of here, between Morebattle and Oxnam (off the B6401) is a fourteenth century ruined tower, at Cessford.

To the north-east of Kelso on the A698 following the Tweed

downstream lies **Coldstream** above a loop in the river. From a few miles to the west almost to the east coast, the Tweed forms the border with England, and Coldstream was, in the past, convenient for couples eloping from England for quick marriages, as at Gretna in the west (Scottish law being more lenient). The Tweed Bridge, 300 feet (91 m) long, was built in 1766 by Smeaton, but the site had long been used as a fording place for the military. The town is known mostly as the headquarters of the Coldstream Guards, raised by General Monk in 1659. The museum is on their original premises. There is an obelisk at the east end of the town commemorating Charles Majoribanks, first member of Parliament for Berwickshire after the Reform Bill of 1832. (Further along the border at **Lady Kirk** just across the river, and the border, from Norham is a church built by James IV in 1500 as a token of his gratitude at having escaped drowning. Of the tower, only the lower part is original, the rest was added in 1743 from a William Adam design.)

Turn off the A6112 from Coldstream towards Duns, and onto the B6360 to visit the attractive church at Fogo, with unusual outside seventeenth century stairway leading up to a laird's loft. **Duns** is another quiet market town, rebuilt on its present site after being totally destroyed in 1545 by the English when it stood on the slopes of Duns Law nearby. The medieval philosopher, John Duns Scotus, is said to originate from here (his statue stands in the park), but it is also the birthplace of the late Jim Clark, motor racing champion, whose trophies are on display in the Jim Clark Room in the Burgh Chambers.

North of Duns, off the A6112, on the summit of a ridge overlooking the wooded valley beneath, an energetic walk of about 1½ miles (2½ km) takes you up to the remains of Edin's Hall Broch (defensive tower), within an earthwork enclosure older still, with lesser enclosures close by. This is one of very few such brochs in southern Scotland and dates to about the end of the first century. Just north-west of here, at Abbey St Bathan's on a fine stretch of the Whiteadder Water, is a village church with a prioress' tomb from a thirteenth century church dedicated to St Bathan who succeeded St Columba. The countryside here, known as Lammermuir, is exceptionally pretty and ideal for walkers, with moors over 1,700 feet (518 m) above sea level, woods, downs and small roads wending their way through them. Eastwards from Duns, on the A6105 are a number of places of interest to visit briefly.

Two miles (3 km) from Duns, Manderston is an imposing Edwardian country house with beautiful gardens, especially when the rhododendrons are in bloom. Edrom is just north of here off the A6105, and has an original Norman arched doorway reconstructed in the churchyard of the parish church. The A6105 skirts Chirnside, where there is another Norman doorway, this time incorporated in the tower of the parish church, and then continues to Foulden. There is an old tithe barn here with outside stairs leading to the second storey. South of Foulden, at Paxton just north of the B6461, the Union Suspension Bridge spanning the Tweed was built in 1820 by Samuel Brown, as the first such bridge in Britain for road traffic.

From the A1 on the east coast it is worth diverting to see **Eyemouth**, a lively yet unpretentious seaside resort where commercial fishing creates employment, especially the export of shellfish. Visitors may examine the lobster tanks here, and the attractive little harbour stretching upriver from the sea.

Coldingham, inland from Coldingham Bay (noted for the colours of its pebbles), has the remains of a thirteenth century Priory, built to replace a seventh century Nunnery which was burnt by the Danes around 870 on St Abb's Head. The Priory was damaged in 1545 by Hertford, then destroyed by Cromwell in 1648, leaving only north and east choir walls, now embodied in the parish church, with Gothic Early English arcade.

St Abb's Head is constantly alive with sea birds making full use of its craggy cliffs. Along the rocky coast to the west, the ruined Fast Castle also perches on the cliffs in a dramatic, if precarious, position. You have to walk to reach these remains, and care must be taken to avoid any accidents on foot. The coastline of the Borders has very little sand to offer, but the pebbly beaches and steep cliff paths around St Abb's, West Loch and Coldingham Bay don't deter holidaymakers who always throng to this corner in summertime.

Access to Sites and Places of Interest

Abbotsford House
Late Mar.–Oct. 1000–1700 Mon.–Sat., 1400–1700 Sun.
Fee.

Coldstream Museum
Easter–Sep. daily, afternoons.
Fee.

Dawyck House Gardens
Easter–Sep. 1200–1700 daily.
Fee.

Drochil Castle
By arrangement.
(Aberlady 201)

Dryburgh Abbey
Standard.

Duns
Jim Clark Room
1000–1300, 1400–1800 Mon.–Sat. 1400–1800 Sun.
Fee.

Floors Castle
Early May–late Sep. 1230–1730 grounds & gardens; 1330–1730 house. Daily except Fri. & Sat.
Fee.

Greenknowe Tower
Standard.

Hawick Museum and Art Gallery
Apr.–Oct. 1000–1700 Mon.–Sat., 1400–1700 Sun.; Nov.–Mar. 1000–1600 Mon.–Sat.
Fee.

Hermitage Castle
Standard.

Hume Castle
Any reasonable time. Key from Breadalbane Guncraft, below Castle.

Jedburgh
Abbey
Standard.

Queen Mary's House
Mar.–Oct. 1000–1200, 1300–1730 daily.
Fee.

Jail Museum
1000–1200, 1300–1700 Mon.–Sat., 1300–1700 Sun.
Fee.

Kelso Abbey
Standard.

Manderston House
Mid May–Sep. 1400–1730 Thur. & Sun.
Fee.

Mellerstain House
May–Sep. 1330–1730 (last adm. 1700)
daily except Sat.
Fee.

Melrose

Abbey
Standard.

Priorwood Gardens
Easter–mid Oct. 1000–1800 Mon.–Sat.,
1330–1730 Sun.; mid Oct.–24 Dec. 1400–
1730 Mon., 1000–1730 Tue.–Sat.
Donation.

Neidpath Castle
Easter–mid Oct. 1000–1300, 1400–1800
Mon.–Sat., 1300–1800 Sun.
Fee.

Peebles
Chambers Institution
0900–1200, 1330–1900 Mon., Tue., Thur.,
Fri., 0900–1200, 1330–1730 Wed.
Cross Kirk
Standard.

Selkirk
Museum of Old Ironmongery
1000–1700 Mon.–Wed., Fri., Sat., 1000–
1300 Thur.
Donation.

Smailholm Tower
Standard.
Key and descriptive notes from nearby
farm.

Traquair House
Easter–early Oct. 1330–1730 daily, but
open from 1030 in July and Aug. Last house
adm. 1700.
Fee.

Walkerburn
Museum of Wool Textiles
0900–1700 Mon.–Fri. Also between Easter
and Sep. 1100–1600 Sat., 1400–1600 Sun.
Fee.

Hotels and Guest Houses

Coldingham
Shieling Hotel,
Coldingham Bay TD14 5PA.
(Coldingham 216)

Duns
Black Bull Hotel.
(Duns 3200)

Galashiels
Kingsknowes Hotel,
Selkirk Road TD1 3HY.
(Galashiels 3478)

Hawick
The Buccleuch Hotel.
(Hawick 2368)

Kirklands Hotel,
West Stewart Place.
(Hawick 2263)

Innerleithen
Tighnuilt House Hotel.
(Innerleithen 830491)

Kelso
House o'Hill Hotel.
(Kelso 2594)

Melrose
Burts Hotel,
Market Square.
(Melrose 2285)

Peebles
Cringletie House Hotel,
Eddleston.
(Eddleston 233)

Green Tree Hotel.
(Peebles 20582)

Riverside Hotel,
Glasgow Road.
(Peebles 20776)

Selkirk
Heatherliehill Hotel.
(Selkirk 21200)

St Boswells
Buccleuch Arms Hotel.
(St Boswells 22243)

Walkerburn
Tweed Valley Hotel,
Galashiels Road.
(Walkerburn 220)

Accommodation for the Young

Coldingham
Coldingham Youth Hostel,
The Mount.

Galashiels
Scottish College of Textiles,
Hall of Residence,
Netherknowe,
Tweed Road TD1 3HQ.
(Galashiels 3474)
Contact: Hall Secretary.
Easter, July and Sep.

Hawick
Snoot Youth Hostel,
Roberton TD9 7LY.

Jedburgh
Ferniehurst Youth Hostel TD8 6NX.

Kelso
Kelso Racecourse Hostel,
Kelso Racecourse.
(Kelso 2822)
Contact: M.P. Nisbet, Secretary, Kelso
Races Ltd, Kelso. (Kelso 2311)
All year (excl. race days).

Melrose
Melrose Youth Hostel,
Priorwood TD6 9EF.
Apr.–Sep.

Camping and Caravanning

Coldingham
Drone Hill Caravan Park.
(Coldingham 425/426)
Apr.–Oct., overnight holding area.

Coldstream
Coldstream Camping Site,
Leet Green.
Booking Enquiries:
Environmental Health Dept,
Berwickshire District Council,
8 Newton Street, Duns.
(Duns 2331)
Easter–Oct.
No touring caravans, no motor caravans.

Eyemouth
J. Wood & Sons,
Northburn Caravan Park.
(Eyemouth 50372/50622)
Mar.–Oct., latest time of arrival 1800 hrs.

Galashiels
Kinknowe Caravan Park,
Off Wood Street.
(Galashiels 2124)

Hawick
Hawick Riverside Caravan Park,
Hornshole Bridge.
(Hawick 73785)
Apr.–Oct., prior booking required, latest
time of arrival 2200 hrs.

Innerleithen
Tweedside Caravan Site,
Montgomery Street.
Booking Enquiries:
Mr H. Collins,
Craig Dhu, Peebles Road,
Innerleithen.
(Innerleithen 830260)
Apr.–Oct., latest time of arival 1930 hrs.

Lauder
Thirlestane Castle Caravan Site,
Thirlestane Castle.
(Lauder 542)
Easter–Oct.

Melrose
Melrose Gibson Park Caravan Site.
Booking Enquiries: Parks Dept,
Ettrick & Lauderdale District Council,
Galashiels.
(Galashiels 4751 ext. 47)
Apr.–Oct., prior booking required, latest
time of arrival 2100 hrs, overnight holding
area.

Peebles
Crossburn Caravan Park,
Edinburgh Road.
(Peebles 20501)
Apr.–15 Oct., prior booking required,
latest time of arrival 2300 hrs.

Selkirk
Victoria Park Caravan & Camping Site,
Victoria Park,
Buccleuch Road.
(Selkirk 20897)
Booking Enquiries: Parks Dept,
Ettrick & Lauderdale District Council,
Galashiels.
(Galashiels 4751 ext. 47)
Apr.–Oct., prior booking required, latest
time of arrival 2200 hrs, overnight holding
area.

Golf

Coldstream
Hirsel Golf Course,
Kelso Road.
(Coldstream 2678)

Duns
Duns Golf Course,
Hardens Road.

Kelso
Kelso Golf Club,
Berrymoss.
(Kelso 2482)

Melrose
Melrose Golf Club,
Dingleton.
(Melrose 2855)

Selkirk
Selkirk Golf Club,
Selkirk Hills.
(Selkirk 20621)

Riding Schools

Bowhill Riding Centre
Bowhill,
Selkirk.
(Selkirk 20400)
Accommodation: not available at Centre,
but hotel or B & B can be arranged locally.
Excellent caravan site in Selkirk.

Bowmont Trekking Centre
Belford on Bowmont,
Yetholm,
Kelso.
(Yetholm 362)
Accommodation: farmhouse
accommodation (full board or B & B) is
available on the premises. Hotel
accommodation can be arranged in Kelso
or B & B in Yetholm.

Burnhouse Mains Riding Centre
Burnhouse Mains,
Stow,
Galashiels.
(Fountainhall 217)
Accommodation: hotels and B & B
arranged locally.
Season: all year.

The Cheviot Connemara Stud
Primside Mill,
Yetholm,
Kelso.
(Yetholm 364)
Accommodation can be arranged in local
hotels, holiday cottage and B & B in the
village.

Cossars Hill Farm Riding Centre
(BHS recognised)
Ettrick Valley,
Selkirk.
(Ettrick Valley 259)
Accommodation: own and local self-
catering accommodation.
Season: May–Sep. inclusive.

Ellwyn Glen Riding Centre
Dingleton Mains,
Eildon Estate,
Melrose.
(Melrose 2908)
Accommodation: own farmhouse at riding
school – full board, B & B. Hotels arranged
locally.
Season: all year.

Ferniehirst Mill Lodge
Jedburgh.
(Jedburgh 3279)
Accommodation: own new licensed private
hotel.

Gamescleuch Riding Centre
Gamescleuch,
Ettrick,
Selkirk.
(Ettrick Valley 257)
Accommodation own B & B at Riding
Centre; self-catering cottages and caravans
can be arranged.
Season: all year.

Priorwood Pony Trekking Centre
Priorwood Youth Hostel,
Melrose.
(Melrose 2521)
Location: centre of Melrose – 300 yards
(274 m) from Melrose Square on the St
Boswells road.
Accommodation: full board or self-catering
in youth hostel. Hotel and B & B can be
arranged locally.

Game Fishing

Acreknowe Reservoir
Brown trout.
Permits: Stotharts,
6 High Street,
Hawick.
or
The Pet Shop,
1 Union Street,
Hawick.
(Hawick 2231)

Ale Water, Teviot River, Slitrig Water,
Borthwick Water, Rule Water
Brown trout, salmon.
Permits: Stotharts,
6 High Street,
Hawick.
(Hawick 2231)

Alemoor Loch
Brown trout.
Permits: Hawick Angling Club,
6 Sandhead,
Hawick.
(Hawick 3771)
or
Stotharts,
6 High Street,
Hawick.

Blackadder Water
(About 13 miles/21 km)
Brown trout.
Permits: Greenlaw Angling Club,
A. Lamb,
'Waterford',
Wester Row,
Greenlaw.

Coldingham Loch
Brown and rainbow trout.
Permits: Dr E.J. Wise,
West Loch House,
Coldingham.
(Coldingham 270)

Hellmoor Loch
Brown trout.
Permits: Hawick Angling Club,
6 Sandhead,
Hawick.
(Hawick 3771)

Peebles
Angling School,
15 Violet Bank.
(Peebles 20782)

Coarse Fishing

Esk and Liddle Water and tributaries
Permits: R.J.B. Hill,
Bank of Scotland Buildings,
Langholm,
Dumfriesshire.

Crooked Loch
Pike, perch.
Permits: The Pet Shop,
1 Union Street,
Hawick.

St Mary's Loch
Pike, perch, eel.
Permits: St Mary's Angling Club,
St Mary's Loch.

Cycling

Kelso
J. Byers Cycle Agent,
24 Horsemarket,
Kelso.
(Kelso 3692)
Bicycles for adults and children. Bicycle
repair carried out.

Peebles
George Pennel Cycles,
3 High Street,
Peebles.
(Peebles 20844)
Bicycles for adults. Bicycle repair service.

Walkerburn
Tweed Valley Hotel.
(Walkerburn 220)
Bicycles for adults and children.

Where to eat

Innerleithen
Cadden View Bed & Breakfast,
14 Pirn Road.
(Innerleithen 830208)

Kelso
Cross Keys Hotel,
36–37 The Square.
(Kelso 23303)

House O'Hill Hotel,
Sprouston Road.
(Kelso 24594)

Melrose
George & Abbotsford Hotel,
High Street.
(Melrose 2308)

Peebles
Hydro Hotel,
Innerleithen Road.
(Peebles 20602)

Walkerburn
Tweed Valley Hotel.
(Walkerburn 220)

Car Hire

Coldstream
J. & M. Stuart,
30 Market Square.

A. & J. Waite,
19 Priory Bank.
(Coldstream 2394)

Duns
T.F. Buckle & Son,
3A Trinity Park.
(Duns 2221)

G. Waddell,
10 Tannage Brae.
(Duns 2340)

Eyemouth
George Anderson,
St Andrews Garage.
(Coldingham 251)

Galashiels
Chalmers McQueen Ltd,
Albert Place.
(Galashiels 3304/2729)

P. Chisholm & Sons,
Bridge Street.
(Galashiels 2363)

D.S. Dalgleish & Son,
Melrose Road & Arcade Garage.
(Galashiels 4767)

Strathclyde

The Strathclyde region covers a large area of south-western Scotland, fringed by Dumfries and Galloway in the south, and by the Highlands in the north. Glasgow is more or less centrally positioned in the region, so we take first the area south of Glasgow, then the City of Glasgow itself, and finally the area to the north.

Part One
I: Douglas – Lanark – Hamilton – Bothwell

First we follow routes already started in the Dumfries and Galloway section, namely from Moffat (I), New Cumnock (II), and Ballantrae, on the west coast (III).

The A74 crosses the Dumfries and Galloway/Strathclyde boundary some eight miles (13 km) north of Beattock through fairly featureless moorland country. At Elvanfoot the A702 doubles back south-westwards, up through the Dalveen Pass to link up with the A76 in Nithsdale (*see* Dumfries and Galloway, p. 7). About a mile (2 km) along this road, the B7040 branches west along the Elvan Water to Leadhills and Wanlockhead (1,370 feet/418 m), the highest two villages in Scotland, and very exposed in bleak windswept surroundings. Formerly there were gold, silver and lead mines here, and in the sixteenth century James V and Mary of Guise both had crowns made partly of gold mined here. At **Leadhills**, the Alan Ramsay Library, founded in 1741, has rare editions, and detailed mining documents of that period. (In the Leadhills churchyard is the gravestone of a man called John Taylor, who lived to the age of 137!) At Wanlockhead the Scottish Lead Mining Industry Museum, is in a converted miner's cottage, with many mining exhibits. Outdoors you can see a beam engine on display.

Back on the A74, just north of Abington the road forks. The A702 heads north-east towards Edinburgh, passing through Lamington, where there is a Norman doorway to see in the church (1721), as well as a sixteenth century tower. To the north-west from here you can see the great mass of Tinto (2,325 feet/709 m) which people used to climb carrying a stone as a form of penance. There must have been far harsher penances, considering the superb view once you get to the top (as far as Antrim in Ireland on a clear day). Perhaps the best walk up is from Thankerton on the A72, though it is not difficult from other directions. Beyond Lamington at Coulter there is an early medieval castle mound beside the railway station, originally with a moat round it. **Biggar** is 2½ miles (4 km) on, and is well worth stopping at for the most unusual Gladstone Court Museum, a convincing reconstruction of nineteenth

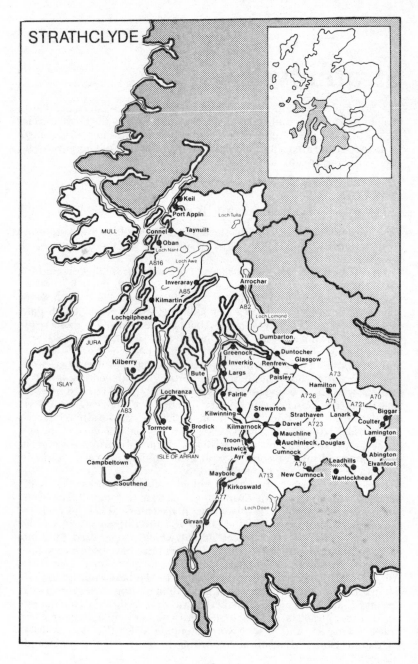

STRATHCLYDE

Keil
Port Appin
Loch Tulla
Connel Taynuilt
Oban
MULL
Loch Nant
A816 Loch Awe
Inveraray Arrochar
A85
Kilmartin A82
Loch Lomond
Lochgilphead
Dumbarton
JURA Greenock Duntocher
Kilberry Inverkip Renfrew Glasgow
Bute Largs Paisley A73
ISLAY Hamilton A70
Fairlie A726 A71 A721
Lochranza Kilwinning Stewarton Strathaven Lanark Biggar
Tormore Brodick Kilmarnock Darvel A723 Coulter
Mauchline Lamington
Troon Auchinleck Douglas
Campbeltown Prestwick Cumnock Abington
ISLE OF ARRAN Ayr A76 Leadhills Elvanfoot
Southend Maybole New Cumnock Wanlockhead
Kirkoswald A713
A77
Loch Doon
Girvan

42

century living in a small Scottish township, including a schoolroom, a bank and various shops, as well as a restored seventeenth century farmhouse.

The alternative fork near Abington is the continuing A74, leading to the crossroads with the A70 where you turn left for a couple of miles (3 km) to **Douglas**. Here you will find St Bride's, a partly ruined fourteenth century church whose choir is a mausoleum. The tombs include that of 'good' Sir James (killed in Spain fighting the Moors in 1330 during his attempt to carry the heart of Robert the Bruce to the Holy Land). One of the 'Black' Douglases, he was renowned for barbaric border raids, and his staunch support of Robert the Bruce. His heart is in one of the caskets below glass on the floor, together with that of Archibald 'Bell-the-Cat', Earl of Angus, a 'Red' Douglas whose nick-name derives from his part in the hanging from a bridge in 1482, of a group of innocent men, fiercely resented for being favoured by the king. Note also the unusual frieze here of the 10 children of James and Beatrice Douglas. The Douglas motto is 'Never Behind', in accordance with which the clock on the tower, possibly given by Mary Queen of Scots in 1565, chimes three minutes early, even to this day, (Scotland's oldest working public clock). You can see a stone monument on the way to St Bride's Church, carved with an ear and a pair of scissors, testimony to the outrage committed in 1684 on a Covenanter called James Gavin, a tailor whose own scissors were used to cut off his ears before being exiled to the West Indies. (He engraved the memorial himself on his eventual return to Scotland.)

Turning right onto the A70 from the A74 you reach **Lanark** by taking a left turn after about seven miles (11 km), onto the A73. Lanark has one of the most important livestock markets in Scotland and is a busy, ancient royal burgh town, above the River Clyde. Its charter was granted by David I in 1140, and a celebration of the event takes place every June for one week. Another festival here is 'Whuppitty Scourie' on 1 March, probably pagan, when children run three times round the church waving balls of paper to banish winter and herald spring. William Wallace's warring career began at Lanark when he slayed an English soldier in an argument, fled to some cliffs known as Cartland Crags nearby, and while in hiding here heard of his wife's murder, whereupon he gathered a band of sympathisers to return to Lanark seeking vengeance. They overthrew the English garrison, killed its commander, and so began a lifetime of rebellion. Wallace was perhaps Scotland's greatest ever patriot, and a hero of Robert Burns. You can walk to Cartland Crags from the imposing Cartland Bridge built by Telford, just west of the town, over the Mouse Water. There are other pleasant walks in the lush green countryside around, and from Blackhill (NTS) there are good views across the Clyde valley. In Lanark you can see the remains of the church where Wallace was (probably) married, the pointed arches of the Church of St Kentigern, twelfth century, whose original bell still tolls in its position in front of the Church of St Nicholas,

1774. Above the door to the tower is a statue of Wallace, made by a Lanark man in 1822. Wallace is believed to have lived in Castlegate. The racecourse is still used, and has one of the oldest racing trophies in existence, the sixteenth century Silver Bell.

A mile (2 km) south of the town on a small by-road is New Lanark, an experimental eighteenth to nineteenth century model industrial village with an explanatory exhibition and 'heritage trail'.

Taking the A72 towards Glasgow, you come to **Crossford** about five miles (8 km) on, and Craignethan Castle, a masterpiece of medieval defensive design which is easy to comprehend, well-preserved and strikingly complete. Once a stronghold of the Hamilton family who were solidly behind Mary Queen of Scots, the castle was partly dismantled after her desperate flight to England, but 100 years later a new mansion was built in the spacious court. It is in a delightful setting of parkland and wooded crags. One of the features of Craignethan is the defensive caponier, possibly the oldest in Britain.

After Craignethan the A72 leads through an increasingly built-up landscape, roughly following the course of the Clyde, crossing the path of the M74, to **Hamilton**, a royal burgh town (about 47,000) since the mid-fifteenth century, previously called Cadzow but renamed when James II granted the charter to the first Lord Hamilton. Hamilton Palace was in the area now designated as Strathclyde Country Park, but had to be demolished in the 1920s when coal workings there caused serious land subsidence. Hamilton owed its prosperity and development to coal until just after the Second World War. When that resource was used up, it turned to industries such as metal casting, and the manufacture of bricks, carpets, electrical goods etc. Strathclyde Country Park is an exemplary achievement in an urban area, with 1,600 acres (648 ha) of parkland offering diverse recreational activities, especially at the extensive loch (a diverted section of the Clyde) which is a national watersports centre. The park, by the M74, was opened in 1976, having been a depressing area of coal workings before that, and now has a camping and caravan site, as well as a nature reserve and golf course.

In Hamilton the Burgh Museum is worth visiting, at 129 Muir Street. There is material on the town's industrial development (with a section on Sir Harry Lauder, 1870–1950, writer and famous interpreter of Scottish songs) and the museum also includes the Regimental Museum of the Cameronians (Scottish Rifles). The building was originally an inn (1696), with a hall extension added 100 years later. Beyond the museum, Mote Hill is the site of the earlier town where the sixth century Netherton Cross used to stand (now in the churchyard of the parish church). The nineteenth century Mausoleum is also near here and is exceptional for its powerful echo. The interior of the square building is octagonal, and the original bronze doors are copies of door panels in the Baptistry, Florence. Because of the echo, formal use of the chapel was out of the question. The Old Church in Hamilton is by William Adam (1732), and stands beside the ancient Cross. The Hamilton District Museum just south of the

M74, has local history, agricultural and transport exhibits.

South of Hamilton on the A723 is **Strathaven**, (pronounced Strayven) which also has a local history museum, the John Hastie Museum, as well as a ruined fifteenth century castle, sometimes called Avondale Castle, and a restored Town Mill with theatre, craft workshop and exhibitions.

West of Hamilton is **East Kilbride**, the first modern satellite town in Scotland, completed in 1947. Note the two recent churches – St Mark's Episcopal Church (1956) which is triangular in elevation, and the Church of Scotland Church (1964) which is seven-sided. There is a monument to the eighteenth century anatomist brothers, John and William Hunter, who were born in this parish. North-east of Hamilton there is a shrine, Carfin Grotto, dedicated to Our Lady of Lourdes, much visited by pilgrims.

Proceeding towards Glasgow, visit the impressive **Bothwell** Castle situated dramatically on green slopes above the Clyde, one of the finest thirteenth century castles in Scotland. From the car park there is a five to ten minute walk through the rhododendron woods to reach the substantial red military ruin, first built by Walter de Moravia around 1270 (his grave slab is in St Bride's Church, Bothwell town, which also has a Burne-Jones east window), but subsequently rebuilt in the 1330s by John de Kilburn (master mason), having been partly dismantled after Bannockburn. It was dismantled again almost at once (under the 'scorched earth' policy of the day) before passing into 'Black' Douglas hands in 1361. It was taken from them after the 1455 defeat by James II, only to be exchanged for a 'Red' Douglas property (Hermitage Castle) in 1492. A mansion which was built beside it in the seventeenth century (pulled down in 1926) caused further ruination by using its stones, so the existing ruin is a very interesting mixture of military and domestic architectural styles. Note particularly the original keep, separated from its court by a moat, cut partly from the rock, and the lack of fireplace in the great hall, indicating a central hearth.

Not far from here is Blantyre which has the extremely worthwhile David Livingstone National Memorial. Livingstone was born here in 1813 and grew up working as a mill 'piecer' in one of the tenements of Shuttle Row which is now restored to house a fascinating and varied collection of exhibits, both local and relating to his African missionary work and explorations.

II: New Cumnock – Mauchline – Kilmarnock

On the A76 after **New Cumnock** it is about six miles (9 km) to **Cumnock**, where the road is crossed by the A70. Outside the Town Hall you will see a bust of James Keir Hardie, the early socialist leader and founder of the Independent Labour Party in 1893. He was born in 1856, lived most of his life in Cumnock, and died in 1915. Alexander Peden, leading Covenanter divine, is also buried here (in unconsecrated ground, having been buried initially at Auchinleck, a couple of miles

(4 km) up the A76, but re-interred by English troops).

Auchinleck has associations with James Boswell (1740–95), who was Dr Johnson's famous biographer, and travelling companion. The ancient parish church was extended in the twelfth century, and again in the seventeenth century, by David Boswell, the later extension forming the Boswell Museum. The Boswell Mausoleum (1754) is also here, containing at least five generations of Boswells, including James, whose Georgian house is on the Auchinleck Estate nearby. The house was built in 1757–79 by James' father, Alexander, Lord Auchinleck the judge, who also built the Mausoleum.

Some six miles (9 km) beyond Auchinleck is **Mauchline**, well-known for its connections with Robert Burns; in 1788 he married Jean Armour at Gavin Hamilton's house near Mauchline Tower (fifteenth century). At the north end of the village is the Burns Memorial Tower, a museum not far from Mossgiel Farm where he worked as a young man. The newly married couple lived in a cottage which is now the Burns House Museum, with Jean's room furnished in the style of the period. In the churchyard nearby (scene of *The Holy Fair*) four of their daughters are buried. Poosie Nansie's Hostelry was a well-loved haunt of Burns and provided the setting for part of *The Jolly Beggars*. It is still a pub, and a very nice place to stop for a drink.

Turning left onto the A758 at Mauchline you pass Highland Mary's Monument, supposedly marking the spot where Robert Burns and Mary Campbell, his great love, parted. A right turn in a couple of miles (3 km) takes you to **Tarbolton** which is associated with the earlier parts of Burns' life, where his family lived at Lochlea. It was here that Burns and some friends founded their literary and debating society, The Bachelors' Club (NTS) in 1780 in a seventeenth century house, and where he became initiated as a Freemason the following year.

Travelling up from Mauchline, **Kilmarnock**, home of Johnnie Walker whisky, is a busy, noisy, sprawling town where several roads meet. It too, has Burns' connections, as his first edition of poems was printed here in 1786 – see the Kay Park Monument (1879), which has an 80-foot (24 m) tower, and houses a museum with a Burns Library, including the first edition of his poetry, and exhibits concerning his life and work. The Dick Institute is the town's other museum, off London Road, with archaeological, natural history and geological material from the vicinity, as well as an art gallery. Off the Glasgow Road you will see Dean Castle, fourteenth to fifteenth century, which has displays including weapons, armour and musical instruments, with an interesting nature trail in the grounds. The last Earl of Kilmarnock was executed in London at Tower Hill for having participated in the 1745 Rebellion.

Taking the A735 out of Kilmarnock towards **Stewarton**, Rowallan Castle stands abut a mile (2 km) to the east of the road and is a sixteenth and seventeenth century mansion. The road proceeds northwards to Glasgow from Stewarton. East of Kilmarnock on the A71, **Darvel** is the birthplace of the man who discovered penicillin, Sir Alexander Fleming

(1881–1955), and there is an attractive garden as a memorial. Further along, north of the road is a rocky promontory, Loudenhill, where Robert the Bruce defeated the Earl of Pembroke in 1306 with his 600 men against 6,000. After this the road joins Strathaven in about eight miles (16 km).

III: Ballantrae – Ayr – Arran – Largs – Paisley

The A77 is the coast road from Stranraer to Ayr, keeping close to the rocky shore most of the way. Stranraer is at the head of Loch Ryan which was used as an anchorage by the Romans. Starting out along the A77 you reach Craigcaffie Castle within four miles (7 km) beside the road. It is a square keep built in the late sixteenth century. (The foundations are thirteenth century, and are said to have been laid on sacks of wool to compensate for the boggy land.)

Following Glen App towards Ballantrae at its northerly end is Glenapp Castle, 1870, whose gardens offer pleasant woodland walks, an aviary and a walled garden. **Ballantrae** isn't the setting for *The Master of Ballantrae* by R.L. Stevenson, as is often assumed, but Stevenson did visit here once, reporting afterwards that he was stoned by the locals for his unconventional clothes. The ruined Ardstinchar Castle, visited by Mary Queen of Scots in 1563, stands above the village.

The B7044 branches inland here to join the A765, a road usually taken by visitors to Galloway Forest Park (*see* p. 13). The coast road hugs the shore, which is often seaweed festooned, with a few sandy bays, presenting fine views across the firth to Arran. At **Girvan** there is a lively harbour and a wide waterfront, with good beaches, making it a crowded resort in the summer. A popular excursion is the ferry trip to Ailsa Craig, the island mountain 10 miles (15 km) offshore, 1,114 feet (340 m) high and easily climbed from the east (sheer cliffs face the shores of Ireland on its west side). Only at low tide can you walk around it. It once belonged to Crossraguel Abbey, further up the A77, when it is said to have been used as a place of exile for uncooperative monks. Later it was a refuge for Catholics, during the Reformation, and now it is a haven for many sea birds. It has its own export, a special kind of granite ideal for curling stones, called ailsite.

The A77 leaves the coast some five miles (8 km) north of Girvan and at **Kirkoswald** you can visit Souter Johnnie's House, ('souter' meaning cobbler), the thatched cottage where John Davidson lived, the original of Robert Burns' *Tam o' Shanter*. Now an NTS museum, it has a number of cobbler's tools as well as Burns items, and there are actual-size stone figures outside of Douglas Graham, of Shanter Farm ('Tam o' Shanter'), Souter Johnnie, the innkeeper and his wife, carved by James Thom, a local sculptor.

Crossraguel Abbey, founded in 1244 by the Earl of Carrick, is some two miles (4 km) beyond, and is still sufficiently intact to show how it must have been in its heyday, particularly the gatehouse, probably the best in Scotland (a sixteenth century addition when it was necessary to build stronger defences), each floor of which has the original window seats and lavatories. The Abbey was founded for Cluniac monks from Paisley who enjoyed the special privilege of being able to mint their own coins, and who occupied it for 350 years. The lands were much coveted, especially by a certain Earl of Cassillis, who, in 1570, in an endeavour to wrest the abbey lands from him, is supposed to have had one poor lay abbot, Allan Stewart, roasted in soap at Dunure Castle, due north of Crossraguel on the edge of the sea (now a ruin but once visited by Mary Queen of Scots early in her 'western progress' of 1563). The chapter house of the abbey is still impressive, with superb vaulting spreading from an elegant central column.

Two miles (4 km) further you come into **Maybole**, regarded as the centre of the Carrick district, a busy town scattered over a hill, whose castle was a seat of the earls of Cassillis, and whose Tolbooth preserves the tower of a Kennedy mansion (seventeenth century). The earls of Carrick owned this coastal territory before the Kennedys, and the earls of Cassillis after them. There is a ruined fifteenth century Collegiate Church just south of the main road, whose sacristy was enlarged to accommodate a burial place for the Kennedys.

Returning to the coast road, Turnberry Castle is the other place (with Lochmaben) claiming to be Robert the Bruce's birthplace (1274). It is now a ruin, probably since 1307 (when Bruce came over from Arran), as a result of the intrigue which revolved around getting Bruce crowned, of which Turnberry was certainly a centre. A lighthouse is just beside the castle remains, perhaps even built on the site of its old courtyard. The golf courses here are internationally renowned, and presided over by an enormous hotel.

Just north of Turnberry is one of the highlights of this stretch, Culzean (pronounced Cullain) Country Park and Castle. The castle was built between 1777–92 by Robert Adam, and is one of his most exceptional achievements, constructed around an ancient Kennedy tower, sprawled above the sea, and incorporating beautiful interior features. Note particularly the round drawing room, with carpet specially woven at Maybole, and finely restored plaster ceilings (repainted to Adam's original colour scheme), and the lovely oval staircase, as well as the Eisenhower room commemorating President Eisenhower's connection with the castle. (The National Guest Flat was given to him for his lifetime when he was still a General.) The castle was given to the NTS in 1945. Out of doors, the grounds consist of 565 acres (229 ha) of delightful park and woodland with a long-established mellow walled garden, a swan pond, varied sea shore, a camellia house and much else besides. You are well advised to go first to the converted farm buildings, also by Robert Adam, (Adam Home Farm) where there is an excellent Park Centre, starting point for planned walks and an Interpretation Centre in the widest sense. There is also a pleasant restaurant and a shop. This Country Park, opened in 1969, was the first such in Scotland.

Approaching Ayr, just south of the town is Alloway, a small village well-known as Robert Burns' birthplace. He was born in a cottage (Burns Cottage with adjoining museum, containing an important collection which includes the Family Bible) that was just a clay hut until his father rebuilt it, where he lived till he was 7, (the cottage then became an ale house for a number of years). His father is buried at Alloway Kirk, the ruined church through whose window 'Tam o' Shanter' witnessed a witches' orgy in the poem. Opposite is the Land o' Burns Visitor Centre, with audiovisual theatre and agricultural museum. The rather grand Grecian Monument (1820) nearby is another museum with Burns relics, just above the River Doon where it is spanned by a thirteenth century single-arched bridge (Brig o' Doon, renowned as 'Tam o' Shanter's' means of escape from the witches, who couldn't cross running water). At Rozelle House, off the road to Ayr, Alloway has the MacLaurin Art Gallery which has paintings as well as exhibitions of photography, local history and craft (see the Ayrshire embroidery work), and a nature trail in its extensive grounds.

Ayr is the principal town and resort of this coastline, with good beaches here and there along Ayr Bay, up to Troon. For holiday makers there are ample facilities including three golf courses, three heated swimming pools, two museums, (the Tam o' Shanter Inn in High Street is preserved in the eighteenth century style of Burns' time, and the Carnegie Library in Main Street, over the New Bridge, includes a local history section), a racecourse, fishing amenities and a number of buildings and monuments of interest. The early sixteenth century Loudoun Hall in Boat Vennel, near the river, is the town's oldest building and is a beautifully preserved example of domestic architecture from that era.

Ayr has been a royal burgh since about 1200, but there was a settlement here for some 400 years before that. William Wallace is remembered here mainly for the Burning of the Barns of Ayr in 1297, when he set fire to Edward I's temporary barracks, housing 500 people; he watched the blaze from a spot north of Tarbolton, now a landmark with a tower built in 1860, the Barnweil Monument. In 1298 Bruce destroyed the castle to prevent its occupation by the English. Its location is not certain as many of its stones were removed by Cromwell in 1652 for building his great fort. This spread over 12 acres (5 ha), now disappeared apart from some bits of wall, and St John's Tower restored in 1914, from the top of which you can see across open countryside and the Firth of Clyde. The old church of St John was swallowed up by Cromwell's fort, so he financed a replacement church, Auld Kirk (or new church of St John), which is reached under an arch through an alley off the High Street, Kirk Port. It was built in 1654–56 and restored in 1952 as a war memorial, preserving three lofts and the original pulpit's timber panelling. Burns was baptised at this church. From the churchyard, notice the view of the Auld Brig, constructed in the thirteenth century and Ayr's only bridge for the next 500 years, featured by Burns in his poem *Twa Brigs*. There is a statue of Burns (1891, by Lawson) outside the station, and one of Wallace (1832, by James Thom) in a niche at the Wallace Tower down the High Street. From Ayr you can take the *Waverley* steamer (the world's last sea-going paddle steamer) for a cruise on the Clyde.

From Ayr to Glasgow along the coast and the banks of the Clyde the landscape is, for Scotland, dull and mainly industrial, the better part being the less built-up stretch between Ardrossan and Gourock, which has views over open moorland country inland, and over the Clyde estuary to the west. The route is punctuated with busy resorts, golf courses and some sandy beaches.

You are in **Prestwick** before you realise that you have left Ayr, but despite its proximity it retains its own identity, mostly for its golf courses and its international airport, developed here because of its remarkable record for being fog-free, becoming the RAF Ferry Command Headquarters, and the USAF Air Transport Command during the Second World War, and gaining international civil airport status afterwards.

A signpost west off the Ayr road approaching Prestwick directs you to Bruce's Well, now surrounded by a bungalow housing scheme. It was here that Robert the Bruce, sick with leprosy, is said to have collapsed with fatigue, water spurting out of the ground where his spear struck. He drank and felt restored, later founding a leper hospital here, and a chapel whose remains can still be seen, before his death in 1329 (of leprosy).

Troon is on the neck of land jutting into the Firth of Clyde that separates the Bays of Ayr and Irvine. Much more peaceful than Ayr and Prestwick, it is a popular golfing centre (with five golf courses within easy reach) and has fine beaches. The port, slightly apart from the tourist centre, is always busy and has shipbuilding and breaking yards. Three miles (5 km) off-shore to the south-west is the bird sanctuary of Lady Island.

Dundonald is a village to the north-east of Troon with a historic ruined castle on the hill. Dundonald Castle is now a poor remnant of the thirteenth century stronghold inhabited by Robert II, first of the line of Stuart kings. He died here, as did his son, Robert III, after which the castle fell into neglect. Stones from it were used by the first Earl of Dundonald to build his mansion, Auchans, in 1644, a mile (2 km) to the south, which is also now in ruins. At Dreghorn, north of Dundonald you can see a plaque commemorating J.B. Dunlop, the veterinary surgeon who invented the pneumatic tyre and was born here in 1840 (died 1921).

Two miles (4 km) west is **Irvine**, an industrial town with a coal port and chemical factories. Though mainly modern in appearance, Irvine is a royal burgh town with distant roots. In 1297 Wallace's supporters signed the Treaty of Irvine here with England, abandoning their loyalty to him and causing him to seek new support further north. Mary Queen of Scots came here, to the thirteenth century Seagate Castle, in 1563 (an occasion honoured to this day by Marymass every year, festivities for a week during August, culminating in the crowning of the queen and a procession past the old church, now ruined but still showing its tower, and a huge hearth and chimney. Robert Burns worked as a flax-dresser in Irvine from 1781–83, until the shop in which he worked burnt down one New Year during the celebrations. His lodging house was in Glasgow Vennel, indicated by a plaque. The Irvine Burns Club Museum is in Eglinton Street, and two miles (3 km) north is Eglinton Castle (1796) with its 100-foot (30 m) tower and public gardens. At the Harbourside in Irvine is the Magnum Leisure Centre with a variety of sport facilities including ice-skating, squash, and swimming, set in 150 acres (61 ha) beside the beach. There is also a theatre and a cinema.

The journey to Paisley can be short-cut north of Irvine, from **Kilwinning** (named after St Wynin who built a church there in the sixth century, on the site of the ruined twelfth century abbey) along the A737 through **Beith**, or through **Kilbirnie** (with an interesting fifteenth and sixteenth century church) and Lochwinnoch. You can reach the Muirshiel Country Park from Lochwinnoch and the Castle Semple Water Park just beyond, both centres of the Clyde-Muirshiel Regional Park, the latter created for boating and coarse fishing (no motor boats). Semple Collegiate Church is an early sixteenth century ruin. The area north-west of Lochwinnoch is lonely upland without roads, Hill of Stake, 1,713 feet (522 m), standing in its midst.

The A78 from Irvine soon runs into **Saltcoats** (named from the saltworks that James V established) and the adjoining **Ardrossan**, formally planned in 1806 by Peter Nicholson. Both are popular as holiday resorts despite an uninspiring setting. Saltcoats has a harbour with an unusually housed Maritime Museum in the Old Customs House, with material on the coal trade and the saltworks of the town. North Ayrshire Museum is in the old parish church (eighteenth century) past the railway station, and has exhibits showing local industrial development. You can see the Horse Island bird sanctuary from the shore. Ardrossan Castle, a hillside ruin overlooking Ardrossan Bay (lovely views) was built in the twelfth century, taken from the English by Wallace, and eventually destroyed by Cromwell.

Ardrossan is a port for sailings to **Arran**. The only other approach to the Isle of Arran is across the Kilbrannan Sound from Kintyre (Claonaig port) to Lochranza in the north of the island. The Ardrossan ferry goes to Brodick, taking almost an hour, and is extremely busy in summer (book your car ticket in advance) for Arran has been a popular holiday destination since the early 1700s (at one stage people came here just to take the milk from the wild goats, believing it to have vital medicinal properties), and is still much enjoyed for its unspoilt scenery and tourist facilities (golf, fishing, boating, pony trekking, etc). It belongs to the Hamilton family (to whom it was awarded royal charter in 1503) and the NTS, who have managed to ensure that its picturesque mountains, moorland and coastline remain unspoilt. It is roughly 20 miles by 10 (32 × 16 km), with mountainous country to the north, moorland to the south. Goatfell is the highest peak, at 2,866 feet (874 m). If you are energetic you can walk up it starting from near Brodick Castle, or go rock-climbing on Cir Mhor (2,618 feet/798 m), to the north-west. Brodick Castle, on the north shore of Brodick Bay, is in good condition, dating from the thirteenth, seventeenth and nineteenth centuries, and houses Hamilton family treasures, some ornate plasterwork, and fine paintings by, among others, Turner and Watteau. It also has two delightful gardens, an eighteenth century walled garden and a 60-acre (24 ha) rhododendron garden. Brodick is Arran's main village, and the Arran Nature Reserve is just on its northern outskirts. Lochranza has an ancient ruined castle (thirteenth and fourteenth century, enlarged in the sixteenth century), its two towers still standing, handsomely situated over the sea. On his return from Rathlin in Ireland in 1306 Robert the Bruce landed here before reaching the mainland, fired with determination for his cause after studying the spider's tactics, now legendary.

The road runs down the western shores of Arran, reaching an area with abundant prehistoric remains, which can only be visited on foot (there is a signed path just over the Machrie stream near Tormore). You can also walk down to King's Cave on the shore (about a mile/2 km), said to have been inhabited by Fingal (Finn MacCoul) and by Robert the Bruce (though in neither case is it the cave with which the man is connected). The road that cuts across the middle of the island is called the String and was first constructed in 1817. Along the south coast of Kilmory is a stone-age or bronze-age compartmented cairn, Torrylin Cairn, in which the skeletons of six bodies were found, two children and four adults. Now just a mound, you get to it by the footpath beside the village post office; there is a larger burial cairn east of the village, Cairn Ban. Holy Island, off the east coast, is a conspicuous craggy peak (1,000 feet/305 m) standing in Lamlash Bay. It was named after a saint, buried at Shiskine near the west coast, who lived to be 120 years old, St Molaise. Saint's Cave on Holy Island has some runic markings, said to refer to the Norsemen who died at Largs in 1263. (After the Battle of Largs, the Norse King Hakon reassembled his battered and defeated fleet here in Lamlash Bay.)

Back on the mainland, some seven miles (11 km) north of Ardrossan you will see the fifteenth century Hunterston Castle off the road, with its eighteenth century house and large walled garden. Opposite the island of Great Cumbrae (usually just called Cumbrae) is **Fairlie**, an attractive little resort with a sixteenth century keep standing above it, covered in ivy, in a glen with a rushing waterfall. The Kelburn Country Centre offers nature trails, pony treks, pleasant gardens and various exhibitions from a complex of eighteenth century farm buildings.

Largs is two miles (3 km) north of here and is the most attractive and stylish of the resorts along this coast, set below a screen of hills with lovely views west. The Battle of Largs which took place in 1263 is a famous landmark in Scottish history as it ended the era of Norse control in mainland Scotland, and ceded to Scotland the Hebrides and the Isle of Man, islands they had held for 400 years. The battle, fought partly at sea and partly on land because strong winds blew the Viking galleys ashore, was between Alexander III and Hakon, King of Norway, and lasted two days resulting in a Scots' victory. The battlefield is marked by the Pencil Monument at Bowen Craig down a path by the sea, to the south of Largs. Every year in September the town holds a nine-day Viking Festival to commemorate the incident, demonstrating the strong historical link between Scotland and Norway. Another interesting aspect of the Battle of Largs is that it may have led to the thistle becoming Scotland's emblem. Supposedly, a Norseman was creeping up on Alexander's men at night, barefoot for a surprise attack, when he trod on a thistle and let out a cry of such pain as to raise the alarm among the Scots, and save the situation for Scotland. (A similar incident is acredited to the Battle of Luncarty against the Danes in 990.) In Largs you can't mistake the parish church on the Esplanade, Church of St Columba, built by Alexander Ross in 1877, but the finest feature of the town is Skelmorlie Aisle in Bellman's Close. This was originally the north transept of the old church but converted by Sir Robert Montgomerie of Skelmorlie in 1636, to a mausoleum with some of the best Renaissance work to be seen in Scotland. Beneath an elaborately painted wooden barrel vault stands a superb monument to Sir Robert and his wife. Next door the Largs Historical Society has a small museum with interesting photographs, bygones and books.

Brisbane Glen is called after General Sir Thomas Brisbane who was born here, and became Governor of New South Wales in Australia. (The city of Brisbane in Queensland is also named after him, it then being all a part of New South Wales.) Through his early interest in astronomy he erected three stone columns on The Mound which still stand there today.

Largs is the port for the **Cumbrae** ferries, a popular service which takes only 10 minutes to cross to Cumbrae Slip, and 30 minutes to Millport. The island (12 mile/19 km circumference) has a single road encircling it, much enjoyed by cyclists in summer. Millport is the only town and a pleasant family resort in peaceful surroundings. Its Museum of the Cumbraes deals with local history, special emphasis on Victorian and Edwardian times, and Butterfield Church, 1849, was consecrated Cathedral of Argyll and The Isles in 1876.

As you continue north up the mainland coast you will catch a glimpse of sixteenth century Knock Castle shaded by trees, then Skelmorlie Castle a couple of miles (4 km) on, well-situated on an incline just south of Wemyss Bay (pronounced Weems) which is a ferry port for the island of **Bute**, a service that takes 30 minutes, to **Rothesay**.

Rothesay is an ancient royal burgh and the most popular of the Clyde Island coastal resorts, with an unusual round-shaped historic ruined castle. The earliest record of it is in 1230 when it was stormed by Norsemen (the damage they inflicted can still be seen, and then again in 1263 at the time of the attempted Norse invasion of Scotland and the Battle of Largs, when the castle again fell to Norsemen. Of the Stuarts, Robert II, Robert III, James IV and James V all enjoyed it as a royal residence. The two latter built the great tower, as they used it for an operational base against the Lords of the Isles. The castle was burned in 1685 and remained derelict until the nineteenth century when the 2nd and 3rd Marquesses of Bute restored it. The ruins are still imposing with a circular wall which is unique in Scotland, four round towers, and the great tower, which has the great hall on its first floor. The great hall contains some interesting pieces including a lively tapestry and a bronze bust. Behind the castle you will find the Bute Museum where you can learn about the local prehistoric sites and the nature trails on the island. Exhibits include material on archaeology and natural history. The road up to the north of the island skirts the Kyles of Bute, the narrow straits separating Bute from the Cowal peninsula (from which side the Kyles can best be viewed).

North of Wemyss Bay, at Inverkip (where there is a nuclear power station) you can head inland up to Cornalees Bridge, another Clyde-Muirshiel Regional Park Centre. Get a leaflet from the Visitor Centre on the two-mile (3 km) Cornalees Trail which includes two interesting aqueducts.

The coast road passes Cloch Lighthouse (1797) opposite Dunoon where the Clyde sweeps round past **Gourock** southwards. Gourock is principally a resort town, and the main port for Clyde cruises. Car ferries operate to Dunoon and a passenger service runs to Helensburgh across the estuary to the north-west, and to Kilcreggan directly north.

Greenock is a highly industrialised town with important dockyards and a busy port. Squeezed in between the hills and the Clyde estuary, it forms an elongated strip of built-up area from Gourock to Port Glasgow. If you notice a strange cooking smell it is the sugar refineries, one of the town's main industries with shipbuilding and engineering, worsted mills and wool mills. James Watt, inventor of the steam engine, was born here in 1736. He died in 1819 and some years later his son commissioned Blore to build a memorial house. The James Watt Memorial Building is in Union Street and contains the McLean Museum and Art Gallery with works by the local artist James Guthrie (1859–1930) and many other items of interest. The pirate, Captain Kidd who died in 1701, was also a native of Greenock. The Old West Kirk (1591) is worth visiting, at the eastern end of the esplanade which runs westwards from the town centre. This church has fine stained-glass work by Burne-Jones, Rossetti and Morris, but originally it was on a different site, removed to this one to allow for an urban development project in 1920. It was the first post-Reformation church, and the first Presbyterian church to be confirmed by Parliament. The Memorial above the town on Lyle Hill is to the French sailors lost in the Battle of the Atlantic. (In the Second World War this was the main Free French naval base in Britain.) There are rewarding views from up here.

Port Glasgow was developed in the seventeenth century as the highest point up river with a deep water port, and its main industry is still shipbuilding. Bell's steamer, *The Comet*, was built here in 1812 by

John Wood. As you leave the town you pass Newark Castle on the east side overlooking the Clyde, a remarkably complete sixteenth to seventeenth century turreted mansion with an older tower and attractive dovecot, particularly noticeable in its dreary urban surroundings.

From Port Glasgow there are alternative routes to Paisley, the quicker being that running along Clydeside connecting with the motorway (M898), and also with Erskine Bridge (toll) opened in 1971, superseding the ferry service and creating a neat by-pass around the west of Glasgow. Along this route is Finlaystone House, a museum with interesting exhibits, including an unusual doll collection and Victoriana. The wooded grounds have pleasant walks and a garden centre. The A8 runs across the north of Paisley into Glasgow through **Renfrew** (mainly industrial and shipbuilding) where the Clyde is crossed by a constant car ferry service to Yoker.

The more interesting road to Glasgow from Port Glasgow is the A761 through Paisley, which rapidly ascends as it travels inland presenting refreshing views. The Weaver's Cottage at Kilbarchan is well worth visiting for an instructive look at the cottage industry of handloom weaving, carried out here from the 1700s up to the Second World War, with numerous objects to look at, including looms, and period cottage furniture. At Elderslie, two miles (3 km) west of Paisley on the A737, is the Wallace Memorial as this is where he is supposed to have been born around 1272.

Paisley, synonymous with patterned woven shawls since the nineteenth century, and well-known for its ruined Abbey, is a sizeable town (over 100,000), with some dignified buildings, including the classic Town Hall (late nineteenth century) opposite the Abbey. It is now the largest thread-producing town in the world, but much of its earlier history can be learned from the museum at the other end of the High Street, covering topics ranging from the local prehistory to the Paisley shawl (many fine examples on display), in a well-modernised building (originally 1870). There is also an Art Gallery here, as well as an Observatory and a Weather Station.

Paisley Abbey was founded as a priory, in the twelfth century, gradually increasing in importance to become an Abbey in 1219. Nearly 100 years later the English destroyed it, and it was not repaired until after 1450, when the building you see today was built, now used as Paisley's parish church. During the Reformation the tower was damaged, collapsing onto the choir which was also destroyed, leaving only the lower part of the west front and south wall of the nave, all that now survives of the original church. The nave was re-roofed in 1780, and serious restoration work was undertaken in 1897, completed in the 1920s by Sir Robert Lorimer (who also designed the choir stalls). It is a fine abbey to look around and has a recumbent female effigy which is probably Robert the Bruce's daughter, Marjory, (who died after a hunting accident locally, aged 23, in 1316); there is also the tomb of Robert III. Note the vaulted ceiling of the choir, and the interesting panels in St Mirren's Chapel (late fifteenth century). The Place of Paisley, part of the fifteenth century abbey, adjoins the church, and has some fine timber vaulting, but you can only get in by arrangement.

Part Two
IV: Glasgow

Although only about 45 miles (72 km) from Edinburgh, Glasgow has a population of over 1,000,000 (the largest in Scotland) and its own very distinct identity which has evolved with its enormous industrial growth. The Clyde, whose shipbuilding yards are world famous, flows through the city, spanned by several bridges, and the city centre lies mainly on its north side. The buildings are largely smoke-blackened, but there are good examples of Victorian architecture, as well as older, more elegant buildings. The shopping facilities are excellent, and there is a city underground service (the only one in Scotland) to 15 stations, but it isn't a place that invites you to stroll around at your leisure. Glaswegians are caricatured as whisky-drinking, aggressive, witty, sentimental and resourceful people who are mean with their money (of which all Scots, however generous, are accused) but judging from our experience of Glasgow people none of that applies generally, except the wit. There is a great sense of humour everywhere, and visiting Glasgow for the first time you would probably also notice the friendliness, especially in pubs, which are a vital element of Glasgow life. In a city this size we can only hope to cover its main features, and recommend that, if you plan to spend more than a day or two here, you visit the Municipal Information Bureau in George Square for more detail.

Starting at the top of the High Street in Cathedral Square, which was Glasgow's first nucleus when St Mungo (the city's patron saint) built a church here in the sixth century, there are several places of interest, including Glasgow Cathedral, the city's most important building. Mainly thirteenth century Early English in style, it has survived well and has many fine architectural points, worth spending some time to look around. Not to be missed are the Blacader aisle (founded by Archbishop Blacader, late fifteenth century) and the superb Scottish medieval architecture of the lower church (now parish church of Glasgow), which is the highlight of the cathedral, with lovely proportions, bold vaulting and a row of four chapels. St Mungo's tomb is also here.

Outside the cathedral is the area where, in 1300 at Bell o' the Brae, William Wallace defeated the English governor (Percy) who held the castle. There are statues in Cathedral Square of William III and David Livingstone, and in the north-west corner stands Provand's Lordship, now a museum, which is Glasgow's oldest house, built around 1471 for the priest who ran the nearby hospice of St Nicholas. It is likely that James II, James IV and Mary Queen of Scots stayed here, the latter when she visited her ailing husband Darnley (probably poisoned) in

January 1567, shortly before his murder in Edinburgh (early February). Over the Bridge of Sighs, on the hill behind the cathedral is the Necropolis, a large burial ground laid out in 1833, with many elaborate tombs. One memorial is a Doric column, with John Knox on the head of it (by Robert Forrest) to the memory of the Reformers.

From Cathedral Square, take the road straight down towards the river from the High Street to Glasgow Cross, and Saltmarket to Jocelyn Square. Glasgow Cross, with only a replica of the original medieval Cross, gradually became the centre of the city after Cathedral Square, until the nineteenth century when the centre shifted to George Square, the main square of today. Gallowgate runs east from Glasgow Cross to where the gallows used to be, at the city gate. The weekend 'flea market' known as 'the barrows' is now in this area. Saltmarket is so-called because salt for curing the fish caught locally was sold here, and it leads to Jocelyn Square (formerly Jail Square) which witnessed a public hanging as recently as 1865, in front of some 30,000 spectators. East of the square Glasgow Green stretches along the river bank, on the eastern side of which is People's Palace, a fascinating museum, opened in 1898 as a cultural centre for the residents of this part of the city. The theme is the history of Glasgow over the past 800 years, and special exhibits include Mary Queen of Scots' purse and ring, Archbishop Beaton's bible and the organ that James Watt built. (While in this area, if you wonder what the unexpectedly extravagant Venetian-style building beyond Glasgow Green is, it was Templeton's Carpet Factory, based on the Doge's Palace in Venice!)

At the north-west of Glasgow Green turn off Greendyke Street to see the conspicuous eighteenth century St Andrews Church, with a central steeple and Corinthian pillars adorning its front. Its fine contemporary interior includes rich plasterwork.

George Street crosses the High Street below Cathedral Square, and leads west to George Square, heart of the Glasgow of today, named after George III. The Royal College of the University of Strathclyde (1903) on the right along George Street heading towards George Square, has a year-round programme of exhibitions in its Collins Hall. On the left further along is the City Chambers building, whose front takes up the whole of the east side of George Square. Italian Renaissance in style, it is vastly imposing, with a great 216-foot (66 m) tower, and an interior equally impressive, with two grand staircases, a 110-foot (34 m) banqueting hall (with murals) and a loggia built like a Roman Renaissance church. The building was opened by Queen Victoria in 1888 and demonstrates all the opulence of the city at that time. On the opposite side of the square is the Merchants' House (1874 by John Burnet) which contains the Glasgow Chamber of Commerce, the oldest in Britain. In the centre of the square is the first statue of Sir Walter Scott (wearing the plaid, you will notice, on the wrong shoulder, as was his custom) on top of an 80-foot (24 m) column, originally destined to support George III. Other statues in the square include Queen Victoria and Prince Albert, both by the Italian master, Marochetti, Robert Burns, Gladstone, Peel, and James Watt.

Another Marochetti stands outside the Royal Exchange, at the end of Ingram Street on Queen Street, a remarkably realistic equestrian statue of the Duke of Wellington. The building was once a private residence (1775) but taken on by the Exchange in 1827, when the portico was added. Ingram Street has Hutcheson's Hospital, originally founded in 1641 (as a charity home for orphan boys and poor old men) by two brothers, whose statues stand in niches on the present building which dates from 1803 (built by David Hamilton). Another two brothers, whose initials can be seen on the slabs above their graves which are now part of the pavement outside St David's Church, were R. and A. Foulis, eighteenth century printers, well-known in their day, who founded Glasgow's first School of Art. St David's Church (1824) is known as 'Ramshorn' possibly from an early monastery here. The pavement was part of the cemetary up to 1835.

Queen Street leads down towards Argyle Street (a hectic shopping centre) whose eastern end becomes Trongate, at the point where Stockwell Street and Glassford Street join it. (At this junction is the site of the house where the Young Pretender stayed during his retreat north, though he never managed to muster very much support in Glasgow. A plaque records the visit at the Royal Bank of Scotland here.) Glassford Street runs north from here, and has a Robert Adam building of 1792, the domed Trades House. To the south runs Stockwell Street as far as Victoria Bridge, built by John Walker in 1851–54 on the site of a medieval bridge which had a leper hospital on its south side. Now you can see *S.V. Carrick*, a triple-masted vessel of 1864 moored here, and from Victoria Bridge a pedestrian path leads west along the river.

To the north-west of George Square, beyond Queen Street Station, is Glasgow's well-known Sauchiehall Street, about two miles (3 km) in length, reaching to Kelvingrove Park from Buchanan Street. In Buchanan Street, partly pedestrian precinct, you pass St George's Place on the left as you go north. This has buildings of interest on all three sides: on the south is the Stock Exchange, a 'French Venetian' building by John Burnet of 1877, which has a visitors' gallery, on the west is St George's Tron Church by William Stark of 1807, and on the north is another John Burnet building, of 1888, the Athenaeum, with four stone figures by Mossman, depicting Reynolds, Wren, Purcell and Flaxman. This is the Royal Scottish Academy of Music and Drama. (The first soiree of the Athenaeum when it was still in Ingram Street, was chaired by Charles Dickens.)

Sauchiehall Street is crossed by Hope Street, where you can visit the splendidly restored Victorian Theatre Royal (reopened in 1975 and Glasgow's Opera House), and, further west, by Scott Street which ascends to the outstanding Glasgow School of Art designed by Charles Rennie Macintosh in 1897–1909. At no. 518 you can see the regimental Museum of the Royal Highland Fusiliers, illustrating the history of the

Royal Scots Fusiliers, and the Highland Light Infantry which amalgamated in 1959.

Just off Sauchiehall Street, in North Street near Charing Cross, is the Mitchell Library, founded in 1874. It is the largest public reference library in Scotland, whose one million books include the greatest single collection of Robert Burns' work, as well as rare material on Scottish poetry and Celtic literature. Due north of here, on the Great Western Road, you will find the graceful Cathedral of St Mary, built in 1871–93 by Sir Gilbert Scott and J.O. Scott, beyond which, towards the River Kelvin, is Lansdowne Church (1863), and over the river is Glasgow Academy (where James Barrie, of Kirriemuir, attended). North of this road is Springbank Street on which stands Queen's Cross, a church built by Charles Rennie Macintosh which now houses the Macintosh Society headquarters, and an exhibition of some of his achievements.

Back on the Great Western Road, further out, are the Royal Botanic Gardens, founded in 1817, extending over 40 acres (16 ha) beside the Kelvin. In the glasshouses wonderful orchids and begonias are grown, while in the exeptional Victorian glass 'palace' (Kibble Palace), a memorable sight in itself, tree ferns are grown, among other things, and there is a permanent exhibition entitled 'the plant kingdom' in one of the wings. There is also an inspired herb garden, a systematic garden (botanically grouped in plant families) and 'chronological border' showing the order in which common garden plants were introduced to cultivation in Britian.

Kelvingrove Park, just south of Great Western Road, is very important to the visitor to Glasgow in that it contains the Art Gallery and Museum, and Glasgow University. The University houses the Hunterian Museum, based on an original collection of Dr William Hunter (1718–83), Professor of Anatomy and 'Physician Extraordinary' to Queen Charlotte. He bequeathed his collection of coins, medals, books, antiques, paintings and anatomical preparations in 1807, making this the oldest of Glasgow's museums. Since then the collection has grown out of all recognition and now includes some superb Chinese jade, archaeological and geological items. If you want to see the anatomical/zoological departments, you will need to make special application.

The University building itself, spread over a hill in the north of the park, is an enormous nineteenth century Gothic structure with a 300-foot (90 m) tower and spire, and a frontage of over 500 feet (152 m), built by Sir Gilbert Scott. The University was founded in 1451 at which time its only accommodation was a crypt in the cathedral; it moved to other cramped quarters soon after, in the High Street, where it stayed until the seventeenth century when the Old College buildings were begun; see the plaque in College Street, off High Street. (It was from here that Adam Smith taught, and James Watt experimented.) In 1870 the University moved to this site, and there are now around 10,000 students.

The Art Gallery and Museum are contained within a grand building of red sandstone (1901) designed by Milner Allan and J.W. Simpson.

The Art Gallery is on the first floor, and the pictures are displayed according to category. The British works are hung in the east wing, Continental in the west wing, while water colours, drawings and prints adorn the walls of the corridors. Sculpture, jewellery, silver and ceramics are displayed on the balconies and the entire collection is probably unsurpassed by any municipal collection. The internationally famous works are too numerous to mention individually, including the sculpture, but this is a gallery to rank with the best. The Museum occupies the huge Central Hall (also used for organ recitals and special exhibitions) and its departments include archaeology, armour, engineering, history, prehistory and natural history. There are model reconstructions of Roman and bronze-age structures, with their original contents as they were discovered. It is an excellent and absorbing collection of very varied subject matter. The 85-acre (34 ha) Kelvingrove Park, in which all these treasures are to be seen, is bisected by the Kelvin, on the bank of which is an amphitheatre, where concerts are given regularly in summer.

The Dumbarton road, which runs south of the park, heads west out of the town towards Victoria Park, where you can see the renowned Tree Fossil Grove, which was discovered in 1887 and is now protected within a building. The fossils are of tree stumps and roots from 230 million years ago, formed by mud in the bark making casts (unlike petrified wood). The roots fork symmetrically, showing that they belong to trees the like of which we have never known, and the same trees were eventually to become the coal found in Clydeside.

Glasgow to the south of the river contains several places to visit but the most impressive, for the scale of its exhibits, is the Museum of Transport. It is on Albert Drive, off Pollokshaws Road, and opened in 1964. The premises used to be Municipal Transport works buildings and are necessarily extensive, because on display are forms of transport ranging from bicycles to railway engines, fire engines, horse-drawn vehicles, and the oldest car in Scotland. There is a working model railway and a collection of trams, and in 1978 a shipping gallery was opened.

The Battle of Langside, 13 May, 1568, took place near Queen's Park, at the top of Battlefield Road (memorial pillar), which is by the Victoria Infirmary. After only 11 days of freedom from Lochleven Castle, Mary Queen of Scots suffered her final defeat here, by Moray, her half-brother. She is said to have witnessed the fiasco from Court Knowe (Queen's Knowe) in Linn Park, south of Queen's Park, where there are also the ruins of Cathcart Castle, abandoned in 1750. Following this defeat, Mary had to flee to England, aged 25, little knowing that she was about to embark on nearly 20 years of imprisonment, terminating in her execution in 1587.

Taking the Pollokshaws Road along the west of Queen's Park, Pollok House stands in 360 acres (146 ha) of grounds. Given to the City of Glasgow in 1966, it was built to William Adam's design after his death, by his son, John Adam, for Sir John Maxwell of Pollok. The collection of Spanish paintings on exhibition are considered among the most representative in Britain, including works by El Greco, Goya and Murillo, but there is also some beautiful Spanish glass, as well as very fine silver, porcelain and furniture. The new museum in the grounds is to show the vast Burrell Collection, of around 8,000 works of art, given to the City by Sir William Burrell in 1944. The collection has exotic and exquisite pieces from all over the world including carpets, bronzes, tapestries, stained glass, pottery, stone and metalwork.

North-east of Pollok Park, at 100 St Andrew's Drive is a museum at Haggs Castle, sixteenth century in origin though much altered, which was built by another John Maxwell of Pollok. The museum is of special interest to children, with a reconstructed kitchen and a Victorian nursery, and in the eighteenth century cottage is an activities workshop for participation in crafts such as spinning and weaving, available to children on Saturdays.

Another building in the outer regions of Glasgow worth visiting is Provan Hall, four miles (6 km) east of the city centre on Auchinlea Road, which is one of the most perfect examples of a fifteenth century mansion house in Scotland. Restored by the NTS, Provan Hall has two buildings which are separated by an attractive courtyard. The original has a turret and stepped gable, while the other is a seventeenth to eighteenth century addition. Note the adjoining walled garden.

Crookston Castle, south of the Paisley road, some four miles (6 km) from the city centre, was a fourteenth century stronghold of the Stewarts of Darnley, ancestors of the Darnley who married Mary Queen of Scots, and after their marriage in 1565 the couple spent a few days at this castle.

Finally, sports-minded people visiting Glasgow will like to know of Bellahouston Park, south of the Clyde and three miles (5 km) west of the city centre off the Paisley road, where the 1938 Empire Exhibition was held, it has an outdoor athletic centre, and 120-foot (37 m) dry-ski slope (you can hire the necessary equipment). The nearby Bellahouston Sports Centre has many facilities, including archery, tennis and golf.

Part Three

The northern part of Strathclyde, above Glasgow, has been known as Argyll (coast of the Gaels) for centuries, and though officially absorbed by the new larger region of Strathclyde in the 1975 local government reorganisation, it is unlikely ever to lose its own particular identity, with its fragmented coastline, long peninsulas separated by narrow fingers of sea. These lochs and inlets, straits and sounds make for circuitous motoring, but the ferry services are good from Gourock to Dunoon on the many-pronged Cowal peninsula, and from the islands of Bute and Arran to either Cowal or Kintyre. The roads here need to be enjoyed for their own sake and not regarded as through routes (except perhaps for the A82 along the west bank of Loch Lomond which is a popular road to the Highlands, in summer rather slow going).

The scenery in Argyll varies from the forests of Argyll Forest Park, and farmland, to Highland and broken, rugged coast (few beaches but excellent sailing), making it altogether much more impressive than southern Strathclyde. There are more prehistoric remains in this part of Scotland than in any other. Most of the embarkation points for the Western Isles are on this coast, which has helped to establish it as a tourist attraction over many years.

We describe the roads leading from Glasgow into Argyll, systematically starting with the most south-westerly, in three separate routes (V–VII).

V: Dumbarton – Helensburgh – Dunoon

Leaving Glasgow on the A82 you pass the north end of Erskine bridge as you follow the north bank of the Clyde westwards. In former days the Romans' Antonine Wall ended here, at Old Kilpatrick. There are no traces surviving, but nearby at Duntocher, two miles (3 km) east, you can still see a rampart base of the old wall. Also near here is the Auchentoshan Distillery where guided tours are arranged with a free dram of whisky at the end of the tour.

Dumbarton is a large town with shipbuilding yards, and the historic Dumbarton Castle is built prominently above the Clyde on the isolated Dumbarton Rock, 240 feet (73 m). You have to approach it from the riverside (the landward entrance was destroyed), and you will notice the sundial at the foot of the rock, presented by Mary Queen of Scots who left secretly for France from this castle, aged 5, in 1548. The castle first became a royal stronghold in the thirteenth century but frequently changed hands, at one point being governed by the treacherous Sir John Mentieth, William Wallace's captor, who probably detained Wallace here before packing him off to London, in 1305, to be executed. 'Wallace's Guardhouse', up the steps in the rock cleft, has a rough portrait of Mentieth with his finger in his cheek, a recognised sign of a traitor. 'Wallace's Seat' is the higher of the two summits of the rock, divided by a long cleft. The castle is mostly used as barracks now, but the old dungeon can still be seen, and the twelfth century gateway.

West of Dumbarton, Cardross is where Robert the Bruce died in 1329. Just behind the golf course on the site of an ancient church you can see the finely restored fifteenth century Chapel of Kilmahew (St Mahew was a friend and follower of St Patrick in the sixth century).

Some five miles (8 km) on is **Helensburgh**, named after Helen, wife of Sir James Colquhoun of Luss who planned the old quarter (on the grid system) in the late eighteenth century. It is an active resort town, opposite the tip of the narrow Rosneath peninsula, reached from Garelochhead. (Rosneath Castle was where Churchill and Montgomery met with Eisenhower in 1944 to orchestrate the invasion of France, but the castle has since been demolished.) In Upper Colquhoun Street in Helensburgh you can visit the Hill House (1902), by Glasgow's architect Charles Rennie Macintosh who is also known for his distinctive style of furniture design. J.L. Baird (pioneer of television) was born in Helensburgh in 1888 and is commemorated by a bust, while Henry Bell, who built Europe's first practical passenger steamship (1812) and is buried at nearby Rhu, is commemorated by an obelisk. There are attractive woodland gardens at Rhu, Glenarn Gardens, which overlook the slender stretch of Gare Loch (base of Combined Operations in World War Two). The road runs along the east bank of Gare Loch to Garelochhead, crosses the isthmus and follows the east bank of Loch Long. The scenery improves all the time as the road climbs northwards, with views across the mouth of Loch Goil which penetrates Argyll Forest between densely wooded banks. The forest also descends to the west bank of Loch Long, affording fine views over the loch for its whole length.

Arrochar is at the head of Loch Long where there is a choice of routes and we now continue westwards on the A83. Only two miles (3 km) from Loch Lomond and within easy range of the superb walking and climbing offered by the peaks of the Argyll Forest Park, Arrochar is a popular holiday centre. The Forest Park, created in 1935 as the first Forestry Commission Forest Park, consists of the forests of Ardgarten, Glenbranter and Benmore; Ardgarten Forest Office is just above Loch Long outside Arrochar to the west, with detailed information on the walking possibilities.

The A83 follows the course of Glen Croe through beautiful Highland scenery, and then Glen Kinglas, opening out to moorland as it descends towards Loch Fyne. Near the head of the loch, Strone Gardens has a pinetum with Scotland's tallest tree. Turning left onto the A815, another left turn after a couple of miles (3 km) takes you on to the B839, known as Hell's Glen. (Note the heart-shape of white stones here on the old road, the Argyll tinkers' traditional wedding place, and a quarter of a mile (½ km) south, the stone-age Ardno Cairn.) Hell's Glen climbs steeply through desolate moorland to 719 feet (219 m), then winds abruptly down to Lochgoilhead in its fjord-like setting. There is an interesting restored fourteenth century church here, and a small road leads down the west bank of Loch Goil to fourteenth century Carrick Castle (first recorded in 1511), a great Keep of the Argylls which they also used as a prison. It was burned by the men of Atholl in 1685. The roof was destroyed but the walls are still standing.

The A815 clings to the east bank of Loch Fyne for some six miles (10 km) after the junction with the B839, twisting inland across the Cowal peninsula along Loch Eck and Holy Loch towards Dunoon. After the turn inland, at Strachur you can see interesting sculptured stones from a local chapel built into the walls of the eighteenth century church. Loch Eck is six miles (10 km) long and only a quarter of a mile (½ km) wide at its widest. The Glenbranter estate at the northern end of the loch used to belong to Sir Harry Lauder, the writer, who died in 1950.

To the south of Loch Eck is the well-known Younger Botanic Garden, annexe of Edinburgh's Royal Botanic Garden, which has over 250 species of rhododendrons, flowering from January through to September

(but quite breathtaking in May and June), as well as spectacular conifers, including an avenue of Californian giant redwoods now well over
100 years old.

Holy Loch is supposed to take its name from being the place where a
ship was wrecked on its way back from the Holy Land to Glasgow where
it was delivering a shipload of earth, to be used in the foundations of
Glasgow Cathedral. On the north bank of the loch is an interesting
Arboretum at Kilmun, with a number of signed walks and a Forest
Office. The road then rounds Stone Point leading up the east coast of the
peninsula, passing Ardentinny where you can visit the Forest Nursery,
before heading inland, up Glen Finnart through Larach Pass at 533 feet
(163 m), and back down to Loch Eck.

The A835 travels round the southern bank of Holy Loch to Dunoon. If
you take a slight detour keeping along the coast, you can see the site of a
quarantine station dating from the Napoleonic wars at Lazaretto Point,
and Hunter's Quay, a ferry point for Gourock on the opposite banks of
the Clyde and headquarters of the Royal Clyde Yacht Club. The direct
route takes you past a stone-age burial chamber known as Adam's Cave.

Dunoon is an established holiday resort and regarded as the 'capital'
of Cowal, with many visitors by ferry from Gourock, as well as by road.
In the past it was important for its thirteenth century castle which has all
but disappeared, replaced by the nineteenth century Castle House,
where you can see a variety of old prints and photographs of Dunoon in
the Tulloch Library. The old castle was the scene of a bloody massacre in
1646 by the Marquess of Argyll, of 200 prisoners taken from Toward
Castle (on the south coast of this peninsula, not open to the public)
belonging to his enemies the Lamonts. The victims of the massacre were
thrown into mass graves, which were discovered when the road around
Castle Hill was being built in the nineteenth century. There is now a
memorial to those that died there. The men of Atholl destroyed Dunoon
Castle in 1685, and Dunoon lost its importance until the end of the
eighteenth century when it began to attract tourism. Robert Burns' great
love, 'Highland' Mary Campbell, was born near here and is commemorated with a statue at the foot of Castle Hill. A beacon built by Robert
Stevenson (Robert Louis' grandfather, noted for his lighthouses) marks
the Gantock Rocks offshore. The road south is a dead end, though you
can walk from Knockdow, where it finishes, up to the head of Loch
Striven, by footpath.

To reach the western tongue of the Cowal peninsula, instead of staying
with the A815 through Strachur, stay beside Loch Fyne for about four
miles (6 km) before turning inland and south, or stay with the loch all the
way to Kames, this latter certainly being the one for those interested in
prehistoric remains, as there are several sites not far from the road.
Tighnabruaich is a sailing centre and general resort, beautifully set
overlooking Bute and the western Kyle of Bute, with a nine-acre (4 ha)
Wildlife Centre about two miles (3 km) north, run by the Forestry
Commission. A car ferry operates across the eastern Kyle of Bute from

Colintraive, (where there is a bronze-age burial cairn), on the A886 that runs down the east bank of Loch Riddon. A small road, the B836, branches east off this road near the head of Loch Riddon, and winds across to Holy Loch, passing two more standing stones at Balliemore, and some ruined mills at Clachaig, where gunpowder was manufactured in the last century.

VI: Loch Lomond – Inveraray – Campbeltown

Near Dumbarton the River Leven flows out into the Clyde from Loch Lomond five miles (8 km) up the valley northwards. The A82 follows its course through a landscape which is built-up as far as Balloch, then increasingly beautiful with the island-studded loch on the east and some fine scenery on the landward side. Balloch is a popular holiday resort. At **Renton**, three miles (5 km) south, you will see a monument to Tobias Smollett, the eighteenth century novelist and surgeon, with a latin epitaph partly written by Dr Johnson. The Smollett family home is Cameron House, on the estate of Cameron Loch Lomond, a park with wildlife reserves including bears, bison and yak (seen by car only) as well as a picnic area, an adventure play area, watersports facilities, a wildfowl refuge, a children's zoo and pleasant gardens. The house was extensively rebuilt after fire damage in the nineteenth century and now houses the Smollett Library Museum, a charming Victorian nursery and collection of rare arms.

The A811 bears north-east to Drymen, where a small road leads back to Loch Lomond and continues up its east bank, through Balmaha which is a popular fishing and sailing village, and Balmaha Pass, short and steep (once used by Highland marauders). A group of islands in the loch near here, together with a patch of the mainland, form the Loch Lomond National Nature Reserve. On one of the islands, Inchcailleoch, there is a picnic area and a nature trail. Further up, Rowardennan is both a popular port for the *Maid of the Loch* paddle steamer (last to be built in Britain) from Balloch, and the favourite starting point for walking up Ben Lomond, 3,192 feet (974 m), (which takes five to six hours to the top and back).

Loch Lomond itself is the largest stretch of inland water in Britain and believed by many to be the loveliest, with its 'bonnie, bonnie banks' ranging from gentle pasture to steep sinister crags, its grand setting and pattern of islands. There are some 30 islands in all. The largest, Inchmurrin, boasts ruins of a castle, Lennox Castle, to which the Duchess of Albany retired in distress in 1425 after James I had seen to the execution of her father, her husband (Murdoch Stewart) and her son, in compliance with his resolve to rob the great nobles of their power. The island was also once used as an internment centre for the drunk and insane.

The A82 leads up to Rossdhu, home of the Colquhouns since the twelfth century; in the fifteenth century a castle was built, succeeded by the present building in 1773. Probably designed by Robert Adam, it is a delightful Georgian residence in an idyllic setting, with ruins of earlier buildings in the grounds, as well as a contemporary icehouse. There is a picnic area and bathing beach. Within the house you can see heirlooms, family portraits, a nineteenth century taxidermy collection and period furnishings. Luss is two miles (3 km) north, and Tarbet is up in the middle of the long finger of the loch leading between mountains of over 3,000 feet (915 m), just two miles (3 km) from Arrochar at the head of Loch Long (*see* p. 63).

From here Loch Lomond tapers to a point at Ardlui, the loch's head, while the A82 crosses the boundary to Crianlarich (*see* Central, p. 137 and Tyndrum, where it runs northwards, crossing back into Strathclyde after a couple of miles, towards Glen Coe (*see* Highlands). From Tyndrum the A85 heads west through lonely country towards Loch Awe, a thin string of a loch 23 miles (37 km) long.

Two miles (3 km) south-west of Dalmally is a monument to the 'Burns of the Highlands', Duncan Ban MacIntyre (1724–1812) on Monument Hill, which offers a fine view of Kilchurn Castle at the north-eastern end of the loch. The keep, built in 1440, and the late seventeenth century oblong building beside, can only be seen from the outside. From here the A85 continues west towards Oban through the Pass of Brander where the scenery is particularly striking, while the A819 forks off to the south down to **Inveraray** on Loch Fyne, following Glen Aray for the latter part. Two fine eighteenth century bridges cross the Aray and the Shira rivers entering Inveraray from the north, a product of the re-planning and building of Inveraray which began in the 1750s, leaving a lasting monument to eighteenth century town planning. The project was conceived by the 3rd Duke of Argyll who decided to build not only a new castle (started in 1746) to replace the fifteenth century one, but a new Inveraray to go with it, which finally took over 100 years to complete. The new Inverary Castle is an imposing three-storeyed square building with round towers at each corner and a large central tower, but it is best known for the wonders of its interior, the décor and the treasures. The top floor was destroyed by fire in 1877, rebuilt, then destroyed once more by fire in 1975 (fully restored by 1978). The original building was by Roger Morris with help from William Adam, and it is possible they used sketches made by Vanbrugh. The interior decoration was completed by R. Mylne in 1772–82, with exquisite French-style decorative painting. Among the many fine objects, note especially the porcelain, the tapestry work, the furniture and superb portraits. The castle grounds are extensive, with walks taking you to the pretty little waterfalls on the Aray river, just over three miles (5 km), or, for the less energetic, about a mile (2 km) from the castle, to the Dovecot at Carlunan. You can also walk to the 850-foot (259 m) hill and watch tower of Duniquoich through the grounds.

In the main street of Inveraray the sixteenth century Cross was moved from its earlier site. The Argyll Arms was designed by John Adam in

1750, and just left of it is an avenue that leads past the Episcopalian church with a striking 140-foot (43 m) bell tower with the finest peal of bells in Scotland. Every day the bells are chimed to melodies, and each bell is inscribed with the name of a saint. The Town House is another John Adam design.

About 5½ miles (9 km) south of Inveraray on the A83 is the unusual and informative Auchindrain Museum which gives a clear impression of life on a joint-tenancy farm in the late 1700s, using traditional buildings such as barns, byres, croft houses and blacksmith's forge in which to exhibit the utensils and equipment of the era. There is also a Visitor Centre.

The road rejoins the lochside at Furnace (named after its iron-smelting furnace, long abandoned), then passes Crarae Woodland Gardens with lovely ornamental shrubs, in a picturesque setting. About two miles (3 km) further south is Minard Castle, originally sixteenth century, which has an annual piping contest. Paintings of the Franco-Scottish Royal House can be seen here. **Lochgilphead** (at the head of Loch Gilp, a small arm of Loch Fyne) is a fairly quiet holiday resort with a spacious main street. There is a Burne-Jones' window in the parish church.

The peninsula south of here is Knapdale and is best appreciated by taking the B8024 off the A83 rather than taking the A83 straight down the east side, by Loch Fyne. The west side is bounded by the Sound of Jura, and Loch Caolisport, at the head of which an even smaller road leads round towards Ellary, passing St Columba's Cave after about three miles (5 km). The cave was certainly used by Early Christians, and is traditionally associated with St Columba's arrival from Ireland in the sixth century. Within the cave you can see a rock shelf with an altar, with crosses engraved above it, and a basin which could have been used as a font. Excavations in the nineteenth century proved habitation from an early age here (about 8000 BC) and you can see the fragments of a chapel, possibly thirteenth century, and some dwellings in front of the cave. There is a smaller cave beside it, which has some steps.

Returning to the B8024, it runs down beside the sea with long views across to Jura and Islay, coming to Kilberry in about 10 miles (16 km). Just off the road, towards Kilberry Home Farm, are the Kilberry Stones, a group of early gravestones collected from around the Kilberry estate during the past 100 years. Opposite the Kilberry parish church further south, you can see three standing stones on the other side of the little river.

The B8024 now heads north-east along the bank of West Loch Tarbert up to the A83, and Tarbert village, on the isthmus known as the 'tarbert'. It is a sheltered fishing port and unspoilt village resort. Overlooking East Loch Tarbert is the ruin of a castle once inhabited by Robert the Bruce, by Robert II, and by James IV. Before the Crinan Canal (*see* p. 69) was opened, linking Loch Gilp to Crinan Loch, the 'tarbert' was often witness to boats being manhandled across land, notably by Robert the Bruce's men, to attack Castle Sween around the Knapdale peninsula, near the mouth of Loch Sween, which was far quicker than sailing round.

From Tarbert the A83 runs down the west coast of the Kintyre peninsula as far as Westport, where it crosses over to Campbeltown on the east coast. From Ronachan Point you can often see seals around the offshore rocks, and if you cross over to Gigha Island from Tayinloan, some seven miles (11 km) south of Ronachan, (passenger ferry only), you are also likely to see seals around the rocks of Gigha jetty. The island is about six miles (10 km) long and less than two miles (3 km) at its widest. It has a ruined church, Kilchattan, thirteenth century, and some semi-tropical gardens developed since the 1950s, Achamore House Gardens (the house is not open to the public). The A83 passes the only good stretches of uninterrupted sandy beaches on Kintyre, between the Sound of Gigha and Machrihanish Bay. From Machrihanish, where there is very good golfing, a small road cuts directly east to Campbeltown through the fertile 'hollow' of Kintyre, where it meets the A83.

Campbeltown is Kintyre's main town, and though small has no less than two whisky distilleries! It is a royal burgh named after the Campbells of Argyll. The fifteenth century Campbeltown Cross, standing at the lower end of the main street near the harbour, used to be up beside the Town Hall (moved from there during the Second World War). Nearby is the Campbeltown Library and Museum in Hall Street with useful local historical and archaeological information. Have a good look at the models of vitrified forts for clarification. Above the town, Castlehill Church was the rallying point for Argyll's rebellion in 1685, supporting Monmouth. The founder of the British India Line, Sir William Mackinnon, was born here in 1823, as was the painter, William McTaggart in 1835. Another Mackinnon, Archibald, born in 1854, is remembered for the painting he did of the Crucifixion (1887) in a cave on Davaar Island which stands in Campbeltown Loch. At low tide you can walk out to it along the Dhorlin, a shingle spit which is submerged at high tide. At the age of 80 the artist renovated his picture, the inspiration for which came originally to him in a dream.

Taking the 'Learside' (leewardside) road round the east coast of the lower bulb of the Kintyre peninsula, before reaching the Dhorlin you will see Kilkerran, said to be where St Kieran (forerunner of St Columba) first landed from Ireland. Round the headland at Auchinhoan Head, one of the caves is known as St Kieran's Cave and has a stone table and basin (perhaps Scotland's first Christian chapel). Being 25 feet (8 m) above the high water mark, it is not very easy to enter.

The road leads through Southend, a tiny holiday resort (totally different from its English namesake!) where there once stood a Macdonald stronghold on the headland, Donaverty Castle. Keil is just beyond and is supposedly where St Columba landed on his first mission to Scotland. Imprints of two feet can be seen in a flat rock near the ruined chapel here (possibly founded by the saint), held to be those of Columba as he stood back to look at his native Ireland, to which country he vowed not to return, (later settling on Iona with 12 companions). The island of Sanda, some three miles (5 km) off Southend, is where Robert the Bruce took refuge in 1306, but it also has much earlier associations with St Ninian, after whom the ruined chapel on the island was named.

The drive back up the east coast of Kintyre has several points of interest. South of Saddell is the Ugadale estate which Robert the Bruce gave to the local man who helped him cross the hills when he was fleeing to Ireland. The estate still belongs to the descendants of that man. At Saddell you can see the fragmentary remains of Saddell Abbey, an early thirteenth century Cistercian monastery. Kintyre's highest peak is just north of here, Beinn au Tuirc, 1,491 feet (455 m).

At Carradale, which is a fishing and holiday village, you can visit the ruined Aird Castle and its dungeons, and Carradale House Gardens, with a nineteenth century walled garden, and a wild pond garden. The Forestry Commission Centre at the road junction gives information about walks up the wooded valley of Carradale Water, and by the shores of Kilbrannan Sound. At Claonaig the car ferry crosses to the north part of Arran, at Lochranza, and the road cuts back across the peninsula to join the A83. At Skipness, a couple of miles (3 km) further round the coast (dead end road) there is a ruined castle overlooking the bay with an early thirteenth century curtain wall, and windows which were incorporated from the original Chapel of St Columba.

VII: Crinan Canal – Oban – Lismore

Taking the inland route, the A816, from Lochgilphead, just a mile (2 km) outside the town it is worth stopping to go and look at the particularly good example of cup and ring markings on two flat rock expanses, involving a half-mile (1 km) walk over the field behind Achnabreck Farm. One of the rocks is in a clearing in the wood (beyond the top left corner of the field) and the other is a short distance further on.

The Crinan Canal is a nine-mile (14 km) stretch of water with 15 locks, built in 1793–1801 as a short cut for shipping, now used mostly by pleasure craft. Extending south of it is Knapdale Forest through which little roads lead down to Loch Sween, one on either side. Where these roads divide at the head of the loch, there is a Forest Centre. The Taynish Nature Reserve is on the Taynish peninsula along the west side of Loch Sween, and has fine oakwoods and birches, a substantial remnant of native deciduous woodland, and the environment around this little peninsula encourages the growth of richly varied sponges and seaweeds. The east road down the loch leads to Castle Sween, possibly the oldest stone castle on mainland Scotland, dating from the eleventh or twelfth century. Still amazingly intact, it is well worth seeing, with such details visible as oven recesses in the kitchen, and a rubbish shaft. The MacSweens lost the castle to Robert the Bruce around 1308, after they had turned to the English cause. He handed it to the McNeills of Argyll. Its destruction was brought about by royalists in 1647.

About three miles (5 km) south, off the road is Kilmory Knap Chapel (thirteenth century) with a good collection of sculptured stones, and a decorated fifteenth century cross outside, Macmillan's Cross, with a crucifixion on one side and a hunting scene on the reverse.

Returning to the A816, three miles (5 km) from the canal are the ancient remains of Dunadd Fort, typical of its period and important as the capital of the Dalriada Kingdom, (from the sixth to ninth centuries) founded by Celtic Christians (the Scots) including St Columba, who had crossed over from Ireland to settle in Argyll. The location of the fort takes advantage of the natural hill and rocks and you can see traces of walls, and a rock at the top, which has symbolic markings. Note the footprint, the boar, and deep basin. The original is now covered by a replica (delivered by helicopter in 1979) because of the effects of weathering. It is believed that the first Christian 'coronation' in Britain took place here (in 574), on a stone throne which, according to tradition, was the Stone of Destiny. (The sacred Stone was moved to Dunstaffnage, then to Scone and ultimately to England by Edward I, to sit in Westminster Abbey in London.) St Columba probably officiated at this inaugural ceremony.

About three miles (5 km) beyond Dunadd on the A816, you reach an area unequalled for its wealth of prehistoric evidence, which, during the Stone and Bronze ages must have been of great importance as a ritual centre. There are standing stones, and burial cairns in abundance, all within easy reach, the Nether Largie group being the most impressive, especially Nether Largie Cairn North which has been partly reconstructed and now has a glass roof over the chamber. Kilmartin is a mile (2 km) along the road, and has interesting crosses and slabs in the churchyard, including a ninth century standing cross.

Off the road a further mile or so (2 km) north is Carnasserie Castle built in the sixteenth century by the first Protestant Bishop of the Isles, John Carswell (known for having written the first book published in Gaelic (1567), a translation of John Knox's liturgy). In 1685 the castle was seized during Argyll's rebellion, and part of it blown up.

Near Carnasserie the B840 leads off the A816 to the north-east, along the 23-mile (37 km) stretch of Loch Awe on its east side, into scenery that grows more beautiful the further you go, the loch finally spilling out into the River Awe below the great bulk of Cruachan, with its important hydro-electric power station (and Visitor Centre on the A85). Interestingly, long ago this loch flowed out in the other direction, towards Crinan in the south. A short walk up the path signed to Loch Fyneside to the right, takes you to the ruin of Kilneuair Church, sadly overgrown and derelict, which used to be the main church of the district, noted for the busy market held at its gates. Further along the road is another ruin, Fincharn Castle, perched on a ledge of rock overlooking the loch. Two islets in the loch have ruins, Innis Sherrich Chapel dedicated to St Findoc, (which you can walk out to, with difficulty, on stepping stones at low water) and Ardchonnell Castle, a fifteenth century Campbell stronghold.

There is a less scenic road along the west shore of the loch, which includes an enormous standing stone about a mile (2 km) north of Ford at the head of the loch, and also the Inverliever and Inverinan Forests, with Information Centre, and a choice of nature trails. Just beyond, a narrow road branches west through fine scenery, curving around Loch Avich, to the coast at Kimelford, in places pretty steep. The lochside road heads north away from the loch at Annat, following Glen Nant down to the A85. East of the road, on the headland jutting into Loch Awe, are the Ardanaiseig Gardens, with lovely views over the loch (turn off just north of Annat). The road joins the A85 near Bonawe where there is a restored iron-smelting charcoal furnace (1753–1874), Bonawe Iron Furnace, viewed from the outside only. The Glen Lonan road loops south and west to Oban, passing the attractive Barguillean Garden beside a small loch after about three miles (5 km). The A85 passes through **Taynuilt** where the River Awe runs out into Loch Etive, which reaches the sea eight miles (13 km) west. Taynuilt is an attractive holiday village, and cruises run from here twice a day, sometimes combining with the postman's round. Even in winter he delivers the mail by boat three times a week, taking out-of-season passengers who want to go along. (Observe the grand view from the pier.) Taynuilt was once the iron-smelting centre of the country, using the trees (oak and beech) from the profuse forests all around for its charcoal. Nelson's navy was supplied with cannon and shot produced in Taynuilt, and a monument commemorates his victory at Trafalgar in 1805, erected by local iron-workers who evidently felt they had played their part in the battle.

The A85 reaches Connel at the mouth of the loch about eight miles (11 km) further on. Below the bridge you can see the turbulence caused by the tide meeting the currents of the out-flowing loch, known as the Falls of Lora.

Having turned off the A816 at Carnasserie for Loch Awe, we now take up the route again, leaving Carnasserie. After about five miles (8 km) the road runs down to pass the head of Loch Craignish and on the right there is a single standing stone, with remains of two burial cairns, close to the road. On the peninsula that borders the north-west side of Loch Craignish, is the Lunga Wildlife Reserve, and several miles beyond, on a small promontory, are the notable coastal gardens of Arduaine, with a water garden, a rock garden and a variety of superb flowering shrubs and trees.

The road heads north after rounding the head of Loch Melford, rejoining the coast at Kilninver, where a small road goes west to Clachan Bridge in four miles (6 km). This bridge with its charming hump-backed single arch, was built in 1791 to connect the island of **Seil** to the mainland. On Seil, An Cala Gardens are worth seeing, with a rock garden, a water garden and some fine roses. From the top of the hill above Balvicar the seaward views are outstanding. From Seil a passenger ferry goes to the tiny island of Easdale to the west, and a car ferry to Luing from the southerly tip, at Cuan, each crossing taking about five minutes. These three islands used to quarry slate (including that used on

71

Iona for re-roofing the Cathedral), but now concentrate on farming. There are boat excursions in summer from Cuan to Mill, Lunga, the Garvellochs, and to Scarba and Jura, separated by the Strait of Corryvreckan, and the Corryvreckan Whirlpool, which can be both seen and heard from afar. It is a highly dangerous area for smaller boats, so treat with caution, and don't sail too close!

Oban is a busy and crowded centre, popular as a holiday destination in its own right apart from being the main port for many of the Western Isles. The Tourist Information Centre will give details of ferry services. The harbour is flanked by Railway Quay, George Street and North Pier, with cafes, souvenir shops, pubs etc. strung along the front. Beyond North Pier is Corran Esplanade, with Corran Halls, a centre for traditional Scottish entertainment, but you can expect a 'ceilidh' atmosphere in many establishments in the town, especially as the evening wears on. The odd-looking round building dominating the town is McCaig's Folly, unfinished, built by a wealthy banker in 1897, both as a memorial to his family and as a means of creating local employment. The other uncompleted building on the hill was intended as a hydropathic establishment but ran out of money. Beyond the Esplanade the ruins of Dunollie Castle stand on a rise, a twelfth or thirteenth century MacDougall stronghold of which only the overgrown keep survives intact.

Kerrera is the island that shelters Oban harbour, and a frequent ferry service operates from Gallanach, a couple of miles (3 km) south of the town (the crossing taking less than five minutes). Alexander II died on Kerrera while engaged on an expedition against the Norsemen in the Hebrides in 1249. On their way to Largs in 1263 (and decisive defeat in battle there against Alexander III) Hakon's fleet rested at Kerrera, in Horseshoe Bay. The ruined Gylen Castle on Kerrera was another MacDougall stronghold, but was destroyed by Cromwellians in 1645.

Some four miles (6 km) north of Oban is Dunstaffnage Castle surmounting the mouth of Loch Etive, an impressive thirteenth century structure with three round towers (ruined by fire in 1810) with walls up to 10 feet (3.5 m) thick and over 60 feet (18 m) high in parts, built on a platform of rock over the sea. There is a seventeenth century tower house above the entrance at the south-east corner. Traditionally, the Stone of Destiny was brought here from Dunadd before being removed to Scone, giving Dunstaffnage the status of holding the Court of the early Scots. Kenneth Macalpine was the first king of the merged Scots and Picts, from 843–860, forming the Kingdom of Alba, and he took the sacred Stone (and his Court) to Scone where it remained until 1296. Dunstaffnage was taken by Robert the Bruce in 1308 after he had overwhelmed the MacDougalls in the Pass of Brander. He then made the Campbells 'hereditary captains' of the castle, and their burial place is the little ruined chapel nearby. Hanoverians garrisoned it in 1715 and 1745, and in 1746 Flora Macdonald was held here for 10 days on her way to London as a prisoner, captured for her part in the Young Pretender's escape.

Over the large cantilever bridge at Connel, the Benderoch peninsula stretches north to the Appin peninsula after Loch Creran, both skirted by the A828 up the coast to Ballachulish. Just across the bridge, turn right for the short drive (about three miles (5 km)) to Achnaba, whose church has one of the only two central communion pews in Scotland (the other being on South Uist at Howmore). About three miles (5 km) further is Ardchattan Priory, founded in 1231 by the MacDougalls, and used by Robert the Bruce in 1309 to hold the last parliament meeting to be conducted in Gaelic. In 1654 Cromwellians burned it. The adjoining Ardchattan Gardens are open all summer. Just north of the village of Benderloch is a left turn to Barcaldine Castle (supposed to be haunted) built in 1579–1601, on the shores of Loch Creran, by 'Black Duncan' Campbell.

The A828 loops around Loch Creran and along the Strath of Appin, where several roads lead off south to Port Appin. A ferry service operates here to the slender island of **Lismore** in Loch Linnhe, taking about 10 minutes for the crossing. In the sixth century a Monastery was founded by St Moluag on the island, which, until the thirteenth century, was in the Dunkeld Diocese, then becoming the seat of the Argyll diocese until 1507. There is an eighteenth century church within the choir of the old cathedral, which was minute by cathedral standards, and of which little else remains.

On the slopes of Beinn Churalin is a 418-acre (169 ha) woodland area comprising the Glasdrum National Nature Reserve. The A828 passes picturesque Castle Stalker on an islet off the headland. Early sixteenth century, and well-restored, it was the home of the Stewarts of Appin.

The regional boundary with the Highlands is four miles (6 km) north. Between the boundary and Ballachulish is the James Stewart Tablet, a memorial to 'James of the Glens', wrongly accused of the Appin Murder in 1752, and hanged not far from here. The affair was immortalised by R.L. Stevenson in *Kidnapped*.

The Island of Mull

The crossing from Oban to Craignure takes about three quarters of an hour (there's a catamaran passenger service as well, going to Craignure and Tobermory). From Lochaline on the mainland the crossing to Fishnish takes only five minutes by car ferry, and from Kilchoan to Tobermory, passengers only, takes half an hour.

The word Mull means 'mass of hill' which refers to Ben More, the 3,169 feet (967 m) mountain mass in the west and south part of the island. Ben More is not difficult to climb, taking about 4½ hours to go up and come down, and very rewarding for the sheer breadth of the seaward views all around.

From Craignure it is 22 miles (35 km) to Tobermory, the island's 'capital', in the north. The road follows the coast passing Fishnish after six miles (10 km), then Salen at the narrow 'waist' of Mull, where St

Columba is said to have landed en route for Iona. Just north of Salen, on a promontory over the Sound of Mull, are the striking remains of Aros Castle, once the stronghold of the Lords of the Isles. The pleasant grounds of Aros House are a Forestry Commission Forest Park.

Tobermory literally means the 'well of St Mary', which you can see to the west of the town near a ruined chapel. Tobermory is a very attractive little port on a sheltered bay, a popular destination for yachts and once a thriving fishing village. There is an annual regatta in August. The Mull and Iona Folk Museum is in an old Baptist Church here. Tobermory Bay is where a Spanish galleon took shelter in 1588, its crew coming ashore to receive hospitality and stores for which it didn't intend to pay. Realising this, Donald Maclean went aboard to claim what was the islanders' due, but was locked up by the Spanish. On escaping, he managed to blow up and sink the ship, thereby starting a treasure hunt that still goes on to this day, but apart from some coins and cannon nothing of much value has yet been brought up. Bloody Bay, round the point (but before Ardmore Point) is so-called after a fierce sea battle between father and son in 1439, the 4th Lord of the Isles and his rebellious son Angus.

The west coast is indented with countless creeks and lochs but the road heads straight across the northern peninsula from Tobermory to the tiny village of Dervaig to the west, at the head of Loch Cuan, where cattle used to be brought from the Outer Hebridean islands, using Mull as a stepping stone to the mainland, making it a bustling little port. A mile (2 km) to the south, on the Torloisk Road, the Old Byre Folk Museum is in a converted stone byre, and gives a view of the crofter's life on Mull in the nineteenth century (with audiovisual presentation). Dervaig claims to have the smallest professional theatre in the country, with seating for only 45 people, called the Mull Little Theatre.

From Dervaig the B8073 loops round to the west through Calgary (whence Calgary in Canada got its name), or a smaller road heads south to join it just after Kilninian (where there is a medieval slab depicting a kilted chieftain with broadsword, in the burial ground). A couple of miles (3 km) on, by the shore at Ballygown you can see the remains of a broch. The islands of Gometra and Ulva form the south shore of Loch Tuath. Ulva is the birthplace of General Lachlan Macquarie, 1761–1824, who became the first Governor of New South Wales, and is known as the 'Father' of Australia. You can visit his mausoleum on the Macquarie estate at Gruline House at the head of Loch na Keal, at which point Mull is only three miles (5 km) wide, a road leading northeast across to Salen.

Taking the A849 from Craignure south and then west along the southern peninsula, Ross of Mull, you follow the moorland valley of Glen More as far as the head of Loch Scridain, then follow the south shore of the loch to the point, Fionnphort, where the ferry crosses to Iona. At the outset there are several places to visit. Torosay Castle is 1½ miles (2½ km) south of Craignure, and is set in delightful terraced grounds laid out by Sir Robert Lorimer, with a statue walk and water garden. The house is nineteenth century, by David Bryce, and contains rooms open to the public, with interesting pictures and an unusually good collection of stags' heads including an enormous prehistoric Irish Elk. On the opposite arm of Duart Bay is the magnificently situated Duart Castle, dating from the mid-thirteenth century which, except for a break in the eighteenth century (following Culloden), has always been a Maclean castle. You can see the imposing original keep, and also the prison cell where the Spaniards from the blown-up galleon were held. At the head of Loch Don, just south of Duart Bay, you can see a stone circle.

On the north shore of Loch Scridain, near its mouth, on the Ardmeanach peninsula is an extraordinary 50-foot (15 m) fossilised tree, known as the Burg, which is probably over 50 million years old. You can either see it from the sea, or walk the five miles (8 km) from the road to see it at close quarters, at low tide only. Another natural phenomenom, also entailing a longish walk (three miles/5 km) is the Carsaig Arches, west of Carsaig Bay which is reached by road from Pennyghael. These are great tunnels made by the sea in the basaltic rock, and can only be properly seen at low tide. On the way, note the strange carvings in Nun's Cave, supposed to be the work of nuns from Iona who took refuge here during the Reformation.

Fingal's Cave on **Staffa** eight miles (11 km) west of Mull, must be mentioned, partly because Mendelssohn made it famous and partly because it is exceptionally large, 227 feet (69 m) long, the entrance flanked by great black columns and pillars of rock. Within the cavern the roof is about 65 feet (20 m) above sea level, and the floor is about the same distance below. The word Staffa is derived from the Norse 'staphiey' meaning Island of Pillars, which aptly describes this tiny island.

Iona

Iona is a small, low island one mile (2 km) from Mull across the Sound of Iona. Only three miles (5 km) long, and half as wide, it doesn't take long to explore, but it is interesting for being regarded as the cradle of Christianity in Scotland. In 563 St Columba arrived from Ireland with 12 companions, and founded a monastery (no remaining traces) from which he began the gradual spread of the Christian faith through the country. He died and was buried there in 597, but, in the late eighth century, a Norse raid resulted in the slaughter of 68 monks in Martyrs' Bay, and St Columba's remains were returned to Ireland. The island was a place of pilgrimmage for early Christians and soon became the traditional burial place for kings (until the eleventh century, when it was superseded by Dunfermline).

A new monastery for Benedictine monks was founded in 1203 to replace the earlier one, destroyed by persistent Norse raiding parties since the ninth century. An Augustinian nunnery was founded several years later. The Nunnery Church you can see today, up the path from

Iona abbey, Strathclyde.

the quay, is the thirteenth century building, with fragments of a former cloistered court, a refectory and a chapter house to the south. The Church of St Ronan nearby is fourteenth century and serves as a museum with an interesting collection of stones. Further along the path, take good note of the finely carved fifteenth century Maclean's Cross, 11 feet (3 m) high, and the church built by Telford on the left. The cemetary of St Oran is the oldest Christian graveyard in Scotland, with the graves of many kings (supposedly 48 Scottish kings, 8 Norwegian, 4 Irish and 2 French). Duncan, murdered by Macbeth in 1040, was the last king to be buried here. The little Norman-style chapel is said to have been built by St Margaret in 1080.

The main building of Iona is the Cathedral, dating mainly from the early sixteenth century but with later additions. There are many features of interest so try to give it the time it deserves. Most visitors to Iona arrive and leave on the same day, but hotel accommodation is available if you want to stay longer.

The ferry from Fionnphort on Mull takes about five minutes to cross to Iona and there are special excursions from Oban (no cars).

Access to Sites and Places of Interest

Alloway
Burns Cottage
Apr.–Oct. 0900–1900 Mon.–Sat.; (May, Sep., Oct. 1400–1900 Sun.; June–Aug. 1000–1900 Sun.)
Fee.

Burns Monument
Apr. 1000–1700 Mon.–Sat., 1400–1700 Sun.; May 1000–1800 Mon.–Sat., 1400–1700 Sun.; June–Aug. 0900–1900 Mon.–Sat., 1100–1800 Sun.; Sep. 1000–1800 Mon.–Sat., 1400–1700 Sun.; early Oct. 1000–1700 Mon.–Sat., 1400–1700 Sun.
Fee.

Land o' Burns Centre
1000–1800 daily spring/autumn; 1000–2100 daily summer; 1000–1700 daily winter.
Fee, for audiovisual.

MacLaurin Art Gallery
1100–1300, 1400–1700 Mon.–Sat.

Archattan House Garden
Apr.–Sep. daylight hours, daily.
Fee.

Ardanaiseig Gardens
Apr.–Oct. 1000–2100 daily.
Fee.

Ardnaine Gardens
Apr.–Oct. 0900–dusk, daily.
Fee.

Arran
Brodick Castle
2nd half Apr. 1300–1700 Mon., Wed., Sat.; May–Sep. 1300–1700 Mon.–Sat., 1400–1700 Sun.
GardensDaily all year 1000–1700.
Fee.

Nature Centre
Daily 1000–1800.
Fee.

Auchindrain Museum
Easter–Oct. 1000–1800 Mon.–Sat., 1400–1800 Sun.
Fee.

Auchinleck
Boswell Museum
Apply Mr. Hoyle, 131 Main Street.
(Cumnock 20757)
Donation.

Ayr
Tam o' Shanter Inn
Apr.–Sep. 0930–1730 Mon.–Sat.; Oct.–Mar. 1200–1600 Mon.–Sat.
Fee.

Barcaldine Castle
Easter, July–Oct. 1000–1600 Mon.–Sat.
Fee.

Barguillean Garden
Apr.–Sep. daylight hours, daily.
Fee.

Biggar
Gladstone Court Museum
Easter–Oct. 1000–1230, 1400–1700 daily (closed Sun. am & local holidays).
Fee.

Blantyre
Livingstone National Memorial
1000–1800 Mon.–Sat., 1400–1800 Sun.
Fee.

Bothwell Castle
Standard.

Cameron Loch Lomond
Apr.–Oct. 1030–1800, daily.

Cameron House: Apr.–Oct. 1130–1800, daily.

Campbeltown Museum
1000–1300, 1400–1700, 1800–2000 Mon., Tue., Thur., Fri., 1000–1300, 1400–1700 Sat.

Carradale House Gardens
Apr.–Sep. 1400–1700, daily.
Fee.

Castle Stalker
By arrangement.
(Upper Warlingham 2768)
Fee includes boat.

Craignethan Castle
Standard.

Crarae Gardens
Mar.–Oct. 0800–1800, daily.
Fee.

Crossraguel Abbey
Standard.

Cruachan Power Station
Easter–Oct. 0930–1700 Mon.–Fri. (June–
Aug. 0930–1700 daily).
Fee.

Culzean Country Park
All year. Fee.

Park Centre and Castle
Apr.–Oct. 1000–1800 daily (but closes
1600 in Oct.).
Fee.

Dumbarton Castle
Standard.

Dunstaffnage Castle
Standard.

Findlaystone House
0900–1700 Mon.–Fri., 1400–1700
weekends.
Fee.

Gigha
Achamore House Gardens
Apr.–Oct. 1000–1800 daily.
Fee.

Glasdrum NNR
Permit required NCC (SW region).

Glasgow
Botanic Gardens
0700–dusk daily.
Glasshouses: 1300–1645, 1200–1645 Sun.
Kibble Palace: 1000–1645.
Oct.–Mar. everything closes by 1615.

Calderpark Zoo
0900–1900 or dusk daily.
Fee.

Cathedral
1000–1900 Mon.–Sat. (1730 Oct.–Mar.),
1300–1800 Sun.

City Chambers
1030–1200, 1400–1600 Mon., Tue., Wed.,
Fri.

Crookston Castle
Standard.

Greenbank
Garden: all year, 1000–1700 daily.
Advice Centre: 1000–1700 Mon.–Fri.
(Apr.–Oct. 1430–1700 Sat. & Sun.)
Fee.

Haggs Castle
1000–1715 Mon.–Sat.

Hunterian Museum
0900–1700 Mon.–Fri., 0900–1200 Sat.

Kelvingrove Art Gallery & Museum
1000–1700 Mon.–Sat., 1400–1700 Sun.

Merchants' House
May–Sep. 1400–1600 Mon.–Fri.

Mitchell Library
0930–2100 Mon.–Fri., 0930–1700 Sat.

Municipal Information Bureau
June–Sep. 0900–2100 Mon.–Sat., 1400–
2100 Sun.; Oct.–May 0900–1700.

Museum of Royal Highland Fusiliers
0930–1730 Mon.–Fri.

Museum of Transport
1000–1700 Mon.–Sat., 1400–1700 Sun.

People's Palace
1000–1700 Mon.–Sat., 1400–1700 Sun.

Pollok House
1000–1700 Mon.–Sat., 1400–1700 Sun.

Provan Hall
For opening times inquire at Tourist
Information, *or* 041-771 1538.
Fee.

Provand's Lordship
Apr.–Sep. 1000–1700 Mon.–Sat.; Oct.–
Mar. 1100–1600 Mon.–Sat.
Fee.

Queen's Cross
1200–1730 Tue. & Thur., 1430–1730 Sun.

School of Art
1000–1600 Mon.–Fri.

Stock Exchange
1000–1245, 1400–1530 Mon.–Fri.

Tree Fossil Grove
0800–dusk Mon.–Sat., 1000–dusk Sun.

Glenapp Castle Gardens
Mid Apr.–Sep. 1000–1700, daily except Sat.
Fee.

Greenock
McLean Museum & Art Gallery
1400–2000 Mon., Thur., 1000–1300, 1400–1700 Tue., Wed., Fri., Sat.

Hamilton
Mausoleum
1200–1430, 1500–1 hr. before dusk daily.

Museum
1000–1200, 1300–1700 Mon.–Fri., 1000–1700 Sat.

Helensburgh
The Hill House
Summer 1230–1700 Mon., 1230–1900 Tue., 0930–1700 Wed., 1400–1800 Sat. & Sun.; winter 1230–1700 Mon., Tue., 0930–1900 Wed., 1300–1700 Sat. & Sun.

Hunterston Castle
Early June–Mid Sep. 1400–1700 Wed.–Sun.
Fee.

Inveraray
Castle
Easter–mid June 1000–1230, 1400–1800 Mon.–Sat. (except Fri.), 1400–1800 Sun; mid June–early Oct. 1000–1800 Mon.–Sat., 1400–1800 Sun.
Fee.

Episcopalian Church Bell Tower
Apr.–Sep. 1000–1300, 1400–1700 Mon.–Sat., 1400–1700 Sun.
Fee.

Kelburn Country Centre
May–Sep. 1000–1800, daily.
Fee.

Kilbarchan
Weaver's Cottage
May–Oct. 1400–1700 Tue., Thur., Sat., Sun.
Fee.

Kilmarnock
Dean Castle
Mid May–mid Sep. 1400–1700 Mon.–Fri., 1000–1700 Sat., Sun.

Dick Institute
Apr.–Sep. 1000–2000 Mon., Tue., Thur., Fri., 1000–1700 Wed., Sat.; Oct.–Mar. 1000–1700 Mon.–Sat.

Kay Park Monument
Apr.–Sep. 1300–1700, daily; Oct.–Mar. 1300–1700 Sat., Sun.
Fee.

Kirkoswald
Souter Johnnie's Cottage
Apr.–Sep. 1200–1700, daily (except Fri.).
Fee.

Largs
Skelmorlie Aisle
Standard.

Loch Lomond NNR
Warden, 22 Muirpark Way, Drymen.

Manchline
Burns' House Museum
1000–1900 Mon.–Sat., 1400–1900 Sun.
Fee.

Burns' Memorial Tower
Apr.–Sep., daylight hours.

Millport
Museum of the Cumbraes
June–Aug. 1000–1630 Tue.–Sat.

Minard Castle
May–Oct. 1100–1600 Mon.–Fri.
Fee.

Paisley
Abbey
Apr.–Sep. 1000–1630 Mon.–Sat.; Oct.–Mar. 1000–1530 Mon.–Sat.

Museum
1000–1700 Mon., Wed.–Fri., 1000–2000 Tue., 1000–1800 Sat.

Port Glasgow
Newark Castle
Standard.

Rossdhu
About May–mid Oct. 1030–1700, daily (except Sat).
Fee.

Rothesay
Bute Museum
Apr.–Oct. 1030–1230, 1430–1630 Mon.–
Sat. (June–Sep. 1430–1630 Sun.); Oct.–
Mar. 1430–1630 Tue.–Sat.
Fee.

Castle
Standard.

Rhu
Glenarn Gardens
Mar.–Aug. 0900–2100, daily.
Fee.

Saltcoats
North Ayrshire Museum
1000–1600 Mon.–Sat. (except Wed.).
Fee.

Maritime Museum
Summer.Fee.

Seil
An Cala Gardens
Apr.–Sep. 1400–1800 Thur.
Fee.

Strathaven
John Hastie Museum
May–Sep., 1400–1700 Mon.–Fri., 1400–
1900 Sat.

Strone Gardens
Easter–Sep. 0900–2100, daily.
Fee.

Tarbolton
Bachelors' Club
Apr.–Sep. 1000–1800, daily.
Fee.

Wanlockhead
Scottish Lead Mining Museum
July–Aug. 1300–2000 daily (also by
arrangement).
Fee.

Younger Botanic Garden
Apr.–Oct. 1000–1800.
Fee.

Hotels and Guest Houses

Abbotsinch
Excelisior Hotel,
Glasgow Airport PA3 2TR.
(041 887 1212)

Alloway (Ayrshire)
Belleisle House Hotel,
Belleisle Park KA7 4DU.
(Alloway 42331)

Arrochar
Loch Long Hotel.
(Arrochar 434)

Ayr
Aftrongrange Hotel,
37 Carrick Road.
(Ayr 265679)

Arrandale Hotel,
2–4 Cassillis Street.
(Ayr 264196)

Berkeley Hotel,
Barns Street.
(Ayr 263658)

Craiglea Hotel,
8 Cassillis Street.
(Ayr 269629)

Kylestrome Hotel,
11 Miller Road.
(Ayr 262474)

Richmond Hotel,
38 Park Circus.
(Ayr 265153)

Cragallan Guest House,
8 Queen's Terrace.
(Ayr 264998)

Reynolds Guest House,
74 St Leonards Road.
(Ayr 267450)

Westbourne Guest House,
2 Carrick Road.
(Ayr 265781)

Ballachulish
Ballachulish Hotel PA39 4JY.
(Ballachulish 239)

Balloch
Balloch Hotel G83 8LQ.
(Alexandria 52579)

Ballygrant (Isle of Islay)
Ballygrant Inn.
(Port Askaig 271/680)

Blairmore
Stronchullin Farm Guest House.
(Ardentinny 246)

Catacol (Isle of Arran)
Catacol Bay Hotel.
(Lochranza 231)

Corrie (Isle of Arran)
Corrie Hotel.
(Corrie 273)

Craignure (Isle of Mull)
Craignure Inn.
(Craignure 305)

Crawford
Crawford Arms Hotel,
111 Carlisle Road.
(Crawford 267)

Cumnock
Royal Hotel,
1 Glaisnock Street.
(Cumnock 20822)

Douglas
Douglas Arms Hotel,
54 Ayr Road M11 0PX.
(Douglas 322)

Dunoon
Abbeyhill Hotel,
Dhailling Road,
Kirn PA23 8EA.
(Dunoon 2204)

Enmore Hotel,
Marine Parade PA23 8HH.
(Dunoon 2230)

Duror
Duror Hotel.
(Duror 219)

Ford (By Lochgilphead)
Ford Hotel PA31 8RH.
(Ford 273)

Girvan
Auchendolly Hotel,
30 Louisa Drive.
(Girvan 4289)

Glasgow
Adamson Hotel,
4 Crookston Drive.
(041 882 3047)

Albany Hotel,
Bothwell Street G2 7EN.
(041 248 2656)

Crookston Hotel,
90 Crookston Road.
(041 882 6142)

Hazelcourt Hotel,
232 Renfrew Street.
(041 332 7737)

Kenilworth Hotel,
5 Queen Street.
(041 221 5151)

Park Hotel,
960 Sauchiehall Street G3 7TH.
(041 334 1336)

Reidholme Guest House,
36 Regent Park Square G41 2AG.
(041 423 1855)

Gourock
Grantock Hotel,
Cloch Road PA15 1AR.
(Gourock 34671)

Hollybush
Hollybush House Hotel.
(Dalrymple 214)

Inveraray
Argyll Arms Hotel.
(Inveraray 2466)

Iona
Argyll Hotel.
(Iona 334)

Kames (By Tighnabruaich)
Kames Hotel PA21 2AF.
(Tighnabruaich 489)

Kilmory (Isle of Arran)
The Lagg Hotel.
(Sliddery 255)

Kilmarnock
Broomhill Hotel,
57 London Road.
(Kilmarnock 23711)

Lamlash (Isle of Arran)
Bay Hotel.
(Lamlash 224)

Largs
Burnlea Hotel,
Burnlea Road KA30 8BX.
(Largs 672372/674201)

Glen Eldon Hotel,
2 Barr Crescent KA30 8PX.
(Largs 673381)

Springfield Hotel,
North Bay KA30 8NE.
(Largs 673119)

Lochgilphead
Argyll Hotel.
(Lochgilphead 2176)

Lochranza (Isle of Arran)
Butt Loge Hotel.
(Lochranza 240)

Millport (Isle of Cumbrae)
Millerston Hotel,
West Bay Road.
(Millport 480)

Motherwell
The Old Hill Hotel,
42 Braidhurst Street.
(Motherwell 61418)

North Connel
Lochnell Arms Hotel.
(Connel 408)

Oban
Alexandra Hotel,
Corran Esplanade PA34 5AA.
(Oban 62381)

Caledonian Hotel,
Station Square PA34 5RT.
(Oban 63133)

Corran House Hotel,
Esplanade.
(Oban 62343)

Crathie Hotel,
Duncraggan Road PA34 5DT.
(Oban 62619)

Kings Knoll Hotel,

Palace Hotel,
George Street.
(Oban 62294)

The Royal Highland Hotel,
Breadalbane Street.
(Oban 64520)

Wellpark Hotel,
Esplanade.
(Oban 62948)

Elmbank Guest House,
Croft Road.
(Oban 62545)

Paisley
Broadstones Private Hotel,
17 High Calside PA2 6BY.
(041 889 4055)

Port Appin
The Airds Hotel.
(Appin 236)

Port Askaig (Isle of Islay)
Port Askaig Hotel.
(Port Askaig 245)

Prestwick
Carlton Motor Hotel,
Ayr Road.
(Prestwick 75811)

Queens Hotel,
Esplanade KA9 1RO.
(Prestwick 70501)

Renfrew
Dean Park Hotel,
91 Glasgow Road.
(041 886 3771)

Rothesay (Isle of Bute)
Ardmory House Hotel,
Armory Road,
Ardbeg.
(Rothesay 2346)

Marine House Hotel,
23 Marine Place.
(Rothesay 2551)

Salen (Isle of Mull)
The Craig Hotel.
(Aros 347)

Saltcoats
Stanley Hotel,
Ardrossan Road.
(Saltcoats 68866)

Seamill
Seamill Hydro.
(West Kilbridge 822217)

Tighnabruaich
Chalet Hotel.
(Tighnabruaich 257)

Royal Hotel.
(Tighnabruaich 239)

Tiroran (Isle of Mull)
Tiroran House.
(Tiroran 232)

Tobermory (Isle of Mull)
Ulva House Private Hotel,
Strongarbh PA75 6PR.
(Tobermory 2044)

Troon
Anchorage Hotel,
Templehill.
(Troon 313821)

Sun Court Hotel,
Crosbie Road KA10 6HF.
(Troon 312727)

West Kilbride
Ardenlee Hotel.
(West Kilbride 823076)

Whiting Bay (Isle of Arran)
Cameronia Hotel.
(Whiting Bay 254)

Accommodation for the Young

Abington (By Biggar)
Glengonnar Outdoor Centre ML12 6SG.
(Crawford 340)
Contact: The Secretary,
SNCA Ltd,
57 Melville Street,
Edinburgh.
(031 226 6391)

Alexandria
Loch Lomond Youth Hostel,
Arden G83 8RB.

Inverbeg Youth Hostel,
Luss.

Arrochar
Ardgarten Youth Hostel.

Ayr
Ayr Youth Hostel,
Craigwell Road KA7 2XJ.

Biggar
Wanlockhead Youth Hostel,
Lutus Lodge, Wanlockhead ML12 6UT.

Brodick (Isle of Arran)
Brodick Adventure Camp.
(Brodick 2112)
Contact: County Education Officer,
County Hall,
Newport,
Isle of Wight.
(Newport 524031 Ext. 177)

Dalmellington
Craigmalloch Outdoor Centre,
Craigmalloch,
Loch Doon.
(Dalmellington 550829)
Contact: Mrs S. Hendry,
Community Education Dept,
Regional Offices,
Wellington Square,
Ayr.

Girvan
Lendalfoot Outdoor Centre,
Lendalfoot.
(Lendalfoot 236)
Contact: Mrs S. Hendry,
Community Education Dept,
Regional Offices,
Wellington Square,
Ayr.

Glasgow
Baird Hall,
460 Sauchiehall Street G2 3LN.
(041 332 6415)
Contact: Manager of Residences.

The Queen's College,
Gibson Hall,
Dorchester Avenue G12 0DA.
(041 339 8481)
Contact: The Senior Warden.

University of Glasgow,
Accommodation Office,
52 Hillhead Street G12 8PZ.
(041 339 8855 Ext. 7385 *or* 7459)
Contact: Senior Accommodation Officer.

Glasgow Youth Hostel,
11 Woodlands Terrace G3 6DD.

Hamilton
Jordanhill College of Education (Hamilton Site),
Bothwell Road ML3 0BD.
(Hamilton 282700)

Helensburgh
Ardenconnel,
Rhu G84 8LS
(Rhu 820333)
Contact: Booking Dept,
Countrywide Holidays Association,
Birch Heys,
Cromwell Range,
Manchester M14 6HU.
(061 224 2887)

Inveraray
Inveraray Youth Hostel PA32 8XD.

Iona
Youth Centre Iona PA76 6SN.
(Iona 324)

Lamlash
Altachorvie KA27 8AG.
(Lamlash 286)
Contact: R. Tiano,
The Holiday Fellowship Ltd,
142–144 Gt North Way,
London NW4 1EG.

Loch Awe
Loch Awe House PA33 1AQ.
(Dalmally 263)
Contact: R. Tiano,
The Holiday Fellowship Ltd,
142–144 Gt North Way,
London NW4 1EG.

Lochgoilhead
Scout Activity Centre,
Shelter Park PA24 8AQ.
(Lochgoilhead 217)

Lochranza (Isle of Arran)
Lochranza Youth Hostel.

Tighnabruaich
Tighnabruaich Youth Hostel PA21 2BD.

Tobermory (Isle of Mull)
Tobermory Youth Hostel PA75 6NU.

Whiting Bay (Isle of Arran)
Whiting Bay Youth Hostel.

Camping and Caravanning

Arrochar
Forestry Commission,
Ardgarten Camp Site.
(Arrochar 293)

Auchinleck
Laurienne Camp Site,
Birnieknowe.
(Cumnock 20272)

Ayr
Craigie Caravan Site,
Craigie Estate.
(Ayr 264909)
Booking enquiries:
Director of Parks & Recreation,
Kyle & Carrick Dist. Council,
30 Miller Road.
(Ayr 81511 Ext. 249)

Croft Head Caravan Park.
(Ayr 263516)

Heads of Ayr Caravan Park.
(Alloway 42269)

Ballantrae
Laggan House Caravan Park.
(Ballantrae 229)

Barrhill
Madajosa Holiday Village,
Nr Barrhill.
(Pinwherry 227)

Crawford
Murray Place Caravan Site,
Carlisle Road.
(Crawford 258)

Cumnock
Woodroad Park Caravan & Camping Site.
Booking enquiries: Parks Dept,
48 Townhead,
Cumnock.
(Cumnock 21488)

Dunoon
Cot House Caravan Site,
Cot House, Garage.
(Kilmun 351)

Cowal Caravan Park,
Hunters Quay.
(Dunoon 4259)

Glenbarr
Killegruer Camping Site.
(Glenbarr 241)

Glendaruel
Glendaruel Caravan Park.
(Glendaruel 267)

Hollybush
Skeldon Caravan Park.
(Dalrymple 202)

Inveruglas
Loch Lomond Caravan Park,
Tarbet.
(Inveruglas 224)

Lochgilphead
Castle Sween Bay (Holidays) Ltd,
Ellary.
(Ormsary 232)

Lochgilphead Caravan Site.
(Lochgilphead 2003)

Luss
Camping Club Site,
Luss Camping Site.
(Luss 658)
Booking enquiries: Sites Dept,
Camping Club of GB & Ireland,
11 Lower Grosvenor Place,
London.

Oban
Arduaine Caravan Site,
Arduaine.

Gallanachmore Farm,
Gallanach Road.
(Oban 62425)

Ganavan Caravan Site.
Booking enquiries:
Tourism Leisure & Recreation Dept,
Argyll & Bute District Council,
Kilmory,
Lochgilphead.
(Lochgilphead 2127)

Strachur
Strathlachan Caravan Park.
(Strachur 300)

Tarbert
Clachan Caravan Site,
Clachan.
(Clachan 200)

Taynuilt
Crunachy Caravan and Camping Park,
Bridge of Awe.
(Taynuilt 612)

Self Catering

Acharacle
Mrs M. Cameron,
Ardshealach,
Acharacle PH36 3JL.
(Salen 209)

Achnamara
K. Fenton,
9 George Street,
Hull,
N. Humberside.
(Hull 26026)

Appin
J.S. Fletcher,
Flat 3,
5 Seckford Street,
Woodbridge,
Suffolk IP12 4LY.
(Woodbridge 7680)

Mrs D.E. Hutchison,
Kinlochlaich House,
Appin PA38 4BD.
(Appin 342)

Mrs J. Walker,
Strathappin House,
Appin.
(Appin 357)

Ardbrecknish
Blakes Holidays,
Wroxham,
Norwich NR12 8DH.
(Wroxham 2917)

Ardentinny
Anchorage Boating Centre,
Ardentinny by Dunoon.
(Ardentinny 288)

Ardfern
N.L. Boase,
Ardlarach,
Ardfern by Lochgilphead PA31 8QR.
(Barbreck 270/633)

Mary C. Peterson,
Traighmhor,
Ardfern,
Lochgilphead PA31 8QN.
(Barbreck 228)

Ardgour
Renton Finlayson,
Bank House,
82 Atholl Road,
Pitlochry.
(Pitlochry 2512/3021)

Ardtornish
R.A.M. Coyne,
Ardtornish Estate Office,
Morvern by Oban PA34 5XA.
(Morvern 288)

Aros (Isle of Mull)
R & M Waugh Ltd,
Kintaline,
Aros,
Isle of Mull PA72 6JS.
(Aros 427)

Ayr
Belmar Holiday Flats,
J. & A. Moran,
17 Charlotte Street,
Ayr KA7 1DZ.
(Ayr 82663)

Mrs S. McCartney,
7 St Andrews Street,
Ayr.
(Ayr 265655)

Mrs K. Pickles,
Skeldon Caravan Park,
Hollybush by Ayr KA6 7EB.
(Dalrymple 202)

Ballachulish
Barrow & Allen,
The House in the Wood,
Glenachulish,
Ballachulish.
(Ballachulish 379)

Ballantrae
Frank Panter Ltd,
Theal House,
3 & 5 High Street,
Theal,
Reading,
Berks RG7 5AH.
(Reading 302223 & Ballantrae 229)

Balvicar
Mr and Mrs A. MacAskill,
Balvicar Farm,
Balvicar by Oban PA34 4TE.
(Balvicar 221)

Barrhill
Mrs Agnew,
Ward Farm,
Barrhill,
Girvan.
(Barrhill 289)

Benderloch
A.H. James,
24 Cairnmuir Road,
Edinburgh EH12 6LP.
(031 334 4256)

E.T.F. Spence,
Dun-na-Mara,
Ledaig,
Connel.
(Ledaig 233 & Oban 2536)

Biggar
Mrs M. Curtin,
Libberton Mains Farmhouse,
Carnwath,
Lanark.
(Carnwath 532)

Blackwaterfoot
J.P. Boscawn,
Strathtay Estate Office,
Boltachan,
Aberfeldy.

V. Lutz,
The Harbour Shop,
Blackwaterfoot,
Isle of Arran.
(Shiskine 215)

Campbeltown
Blakes Holidays,
Wroxham,
Norwich NR12 8DH.
(Wroxham 2917)

Mrs N.S. Stalker,
Marchwood,
Glenramskill,
By Campbeltown PA28 6RD.
(Campbeltown 3246)

Carradale
R. Galbraith & Mrs M. Galbraith,
The Barnes,
Carradale.
(Carradale 274)

Carsaig (Isle of Mull)
Mrs A. McLean,
Pier Cottage,
Pennyghael,
Carsaig,
Isle of Mull.
(Pennyghael 216)

Coylton
Sundrum Holiday Park,
Coylton by Ayr.
(Ayr 61464 & Lowestoft 62292)

Crinan
N.L. Boase,
Ardlarach,
Ardfern by Lochgilphead PA31 8QR.
(Barbreck 270 & Ormsary 237)

Crosshill
R. Houldsworth,
Kirkbride,
Crosshill,
Maybole.
(Crosshill 202)

Dalmally
Mrs D. Fellowes,
Inistrvnich,
Dalmally PA23 1BQ.
(Balmally 256)

Mrs R.W. Fellowes,
Cladich by Dalmally PA33 1BQ.
(Dalmally 246)

C.S. McFarlane Barrow,
Craig Lodge,
Dalmally PA33 1AR.
(Dalmally 216)

Dervaig (Isle of Mull)
Miss Jill Bristow,
Thorncroft,
Lilliesleaf,
Melrose,
Roxburghshire TD6 9JD.
(Lilliesleaf 424/425)

Mrs Galbraith,
Croig,
Dervaig,
Isle of Mull.
(Dervaig 219)

Quinish Estate,
Dervaig,
Isle of Mull.
(Dervaig 223)

Mr and Mrs D. Stewart,
Achnadrish Lodge,
Dervaig by Tobermory,
Isle of Mull PA75 6QF.
(Dervaig 287)

Dunoon
Abbot's Brae Hotel,
West Bay,
Dunoon.

Mr and Mrs A.B. Garner,
Cowal Caravan Park,
Hunters Quay,
Dunoon PA23 8JY.
(Dunoon 4259)

David and Mary Lax,
Stratheck Caravan Park,
Inverchapel,
Loch Eck by Dunoon PA23 8SG.
(Kilmun 472)

Mr & Mrs F. Noakes,
Claymore,
Wellington Street,
Dunoon.
(Dunoon 2658)

Duror
Mrs E. Malcolm,
Cuilbay,
Duror,
Appin.
(Duror 259)

Easdale
Mrs S.P. Coates,
Old Schoolhouse,
Kilmore by Oban.
(Kilmore 247)

Mrs Barbara Nathan,
The Old Inn,
Easdale by Oban.
(Balvicar 209)

Galston
Mrs J. Walker,
Millside Farm,
Galston KA4 8NQ.
(Galston 820274)

Girvan
Miss Andrew,
The Bungalow,
Rowanston,
Maybole.
(Crosshill 205)

Mrs Moyra M. Hay,
50 Dalrymple Street,
Girvan KA26 9BT.
(Girvan 2378/4421)

H. Killin,
142 Maxwelton Avenue,
East Kilbride,
Lanarkshire.
(East Kilbride 43705)

Mr Russell,
Jeancroft Caravan Park,
Dipple by Girvan.
(Turnberry 288)

Mrs H. Ware,
33 Henrietta Street,
Girvan KA26 9AL.
(Girvan 2543)

Glasgow
D.E.C. MacDonald,
Park Court Hotel,
28 Balshgray Drive,
Glasgow G11 7DD.
(041 339 2143)

Mangr of Residents & Conferences,
University of Strathclyde,
Baird Hall of Residence,
460 Sauchiehall Street,
Glasgow G2 3LN.
(041 332 6415)

The Senior Warden,
The Queens College,
Gibson Hall,
183 Dorchester Avenue,
Glasgow.
(041 339 8481)

Gruinart, Isle of Islay
Mr and Mrs G. Archibald,
Craigens,
Gruinart,
Isle of Islay PA44 7PW.
(Port Charlotte 256)

Inveraray
The Trustees of The Tenth Duke of Argyll,
Cherry Park,
Inveraray PA32 8XE.
(Inveraray 2203)

Bell-Ingram Durn,
Isla Road,
Perth PH2 7HF.
(Perth 21121)

Kilberry
N.L. Boase,
Ardlarach,
Ardfern by Lochgilphead PA31 8QR.
(Barbreck 270 & Ormsary 237)

Kilbirnie
Mr and Mrs J. Dickson,
North Dykes,
Kilbirnie KA25 7LQ.
(Kilbirnie 2187)

Kilchoan
Mrs J. Cameron,
Millburn,
Kilchoan by Ardnamurchan PH36 4LH.

Killundine
William Lauder,
Higher Longcombe,
Totnes,
Devon TQ9 6PN.
(Totnes 863059)

Kilmarnock
Blakes Holidays,
Wroxham,
Norwich NR12 8DH.
(Wroxham 2917)

Kilmore
Mrs D. Brown,
Glenfeochan House,
Kilmore,
Oban PA34 4QR.
(Kilmore 273)

Largs
Clyde Flats,
Westwinds,
Skelmorlie,
(Wemyss Bay 520786)

Mrs Nordbo,
Springfield Hotel,
Esplanade,
Largs.
(Largs 673119)

Lochgoilhead
Mrs O'Malley,
Ben Arthur,
Lochgoilhead.
(Lochgoilhead 325)

Machrie (Isle of Arran)
Mr and Mrs J. Anderson,
Hillcrest Farm,
Machrie,
Brodick,
Isle of Arran KA27 8DZ.
(Machrie 240)

S.C. Gibb,
Estate Office,
Dougarie,
Machrie,
Isle of Arran.
(Machrie 229/259)

Machrie/Sliddery (Isle of Arran)
Machrie House Holiday Homes,
47 Henry Street,
Langholm DG13 0AR.
(Langholm 80272 & Machrie 223)

Mrs Stewart,
Kingston,
Machrihanish by Campbeltown.
(Machrihanish 343)

Maidens
Mrs Finlay,
Rocklea,
21 Ardlochan Road,
Maidstone.
(Turnberry 303)

Mauchline
Mrs Templeton,
Syke Farm,
Mauchline.
(Mauchline 51252)

Morvern
Mr and Mrs J.M. Hornsby,
Rahoy Cottage,
Rahoy,
Morvern PA34 5XE.
(Morvern 287)

Laudale Estate,
Ardgour by Fort William.

Muasdale
Mrs A. Taylor,
Bridge House,
Muasdale,
Tarbert PA29 6XD.
(Glenbarr 271)

North Connel
Mrs Campbell,
Druimbhan,
North Connel.
(Connel 424)

Mrs M. McIntyre,
Eilean Beag,
South Ledaig,
Connel.
(Connel 597)

Mrs C. Scott,
Santana Lodge,
North Connel.
(Connel 380)

Oban
Ach-na-Mara Hotel,
Esplanade,
Oban.
(Oban 62683)

Miss Jill Bristow,
Thorncroft,
Lilliesleaf,
Melrose TD6 9JD.
(Lilliesleaf 424/425)

Cologin Homes Ltd,
Cologin,
Lerags, by Oban PA34 4SE.
(Oban 64501)

Esplanade Court,
The Esplanade,
Oban PA34 5PW.
(Oban 62067)

C. & K. Hunter,
Lerags House,
Lerags, by Oban.
(Oban 64876)

J.D. Ledwidge,
4 Miller Road,
Oban PA34 4DU.
(Oban 63330)

Mrs MacLeod,
Woodlands,
Rockfield Road,
Oban PA34 5DQ.
(Oban 62827)

Mr Stein,
Ardentallen House,
By Oban.
(Oban 62029)

D. Tye,
Oban Divers Ltd,
Laggan Farm,
Glenshellach,
Oban PA31 4QJ
(Oban 62755)

J. Wyse,
Gallanachmore,
Oban.
(Oban 62425)

Otter Ferry
Mrs Miller,
38 Kessington Road,
Bearsden,
Glasgow GC1 2HJ.
(041 942 0559)

Peninver
Blakes Holidays,
Wroxham,
Norwich NR12 8DH.
(Wroxham 2917)

Pirnmill (Isle of Arran)
Mr and Mrs J. Anderson,
Hillcrest Farm,
Machrie,
Brodick,
Isle of Arran KA27 8DZ.
(Machrie 240)

Port Charlotte (Isle of Islay)
Mrs D. Clark,
Craigfad,
Port Charlotte,
Isle of Islay PA4 7UE.
(Port Charlotte 244)

Mrs S. Roy,
Lorgba House,
Port Charlotte,
Isle of Islay PA48 7UD.
(Port Charlotte 208)

Port Ellen (Isle of Islay)
Mrs Carmichael,
61 Frederick Crescent,
Port Ellen,
Isle of Islay.
(Port Ellen 2225)

Jack Prentice,
Bank House,
Main Street,
Bowmore,
Isle of Islay.
(Bowmore 555)

Portsonachan
Mr and Mrs E. Crawford,
Blarghour Farm,
By Dalmally.
(Kilchrenan 246)

Salen, Aros (Isle of Mull)
Richard Greeves,
Salen Pier,
Aros,
Isle of Mull.
(Aros 411)

Mrs F. Lucas,
Glenleedle,
Salen,
Aros,
Isle of Mull PA72 6JC.
(Aros 343)

Salen (Isle of Mull)
D.H. & E.M. McEwan,
Tigh na Creagan,
Salen PH36 4JN.
(Salen 270)

Shiskine (Isle of Arran)
Mrs Currie,
Birchburn,
Shiskine,
Isle of Arran.
(Shiskine 221)

Mrs J. McAllister,
Shedock,
Shiskine,
Isle of Arran.
(Shiskine 261)

Skelmorlie
Mrs Campbell,
Auchengarth Farm,
Skelmorlie.
(Wemyss Bay 520179)

Mrs M. Stirrat,
Mains Caravan Site,
Skelmorlie PA17 5EW.
(Wemyss Bay 520794)

Strontian
Mrs Douglas Clifford,
Bellsgrove Lodge,
Strontian,
Acharacle PH36 4JB.
(Strontian 2152)

L. Madden,
Dunlachlan,
Strontian,
Acharacle PH36 4HY.
(Strontian 2375)

Tavool (Isle of Mull)
Mr Savage,
Tavool,
Isle of Mull.
(Tiroran 207)

Taynuilt
Mrs Baird,
Bonawe House Holiday Flats,
Taynuilt.
(Taynuilt 309)

Mrs R. Campbell-Preston,
Inverawe Fisheries,
Taynuilt.
(Taynuilt 262)

Mrs R. Cameron,
Nant Bank,
Taynuilt.
(Taynuilt 697)

H.M. and Miss S.J. Grant,
Lonan House,
Taynuilt PA35 1HY.
(Taynuilt 253 & Guests 219)

Mrs E. Major,
Fir Cottage,
Ightham,
Kent TN15 9AR.
(Borough Green 883167)

Tighnabruaich
Miss Jill Bristow,
Thorncroft,
Lilliesleaf,
Melrose TD6 9JD.
(Lilliesleaf 424/425)

Mrs J. Thomson,
Ravenswood,
Tighnabruaich PA21 2EE.
(Tighnabruaich 207)

Tobermory (Isle of Mull)
Anderson and Sims,
59 Church Road,
Epsom,
Surrey.
(Epsom 28525)

M.G. Kelliher,
Eastend Farm,
Carmunnock,
Clarkston,
Glasgow G76 9ET.
(East Kilbride 20415)

J.R.E. Nelson,
Glengorm Castle,
By Tobermory,
Isle of Mull.
(Tobermory 2321)

Toberonochy (Isle of Luing)
Lt Col H.M. MacNicol,
Fidgetts,
Crescent Road,
Burgess Hill,
Sussex.
(Burgess Hill 42555)

Troon
Mrs McLean,
The Borgie,
34 Greenlees Road,
Cambuslang,
Glasgow.
(041 641 1903)

Whiting Bay (Isle of Arran)
Mrs G.W. Crawley,
Largiemhor House,
Whiting Bay,
Isle of Arran KW27 8QP.
(Whiting Bay 310)

J. Haluch,
Whiting Bay Hotel,
Whiting Bay,
Isle of Arran KA27 8QJ.
(Whiting Bay 247)

T.E. Langmuir,
Carraig Mhor,
Lamlash,
Isle of Arran.
(Lamlash 453)

Mr and Mrs D. Murray,
Craigielea Hotel,
Whiting Bay,
Isle of Arran.
(Whiting Bay 245)

Silver Hill Chalets,
Whiting Bay,
Isle of Arran.
(Whiting Bay 371)

Golf

Ayr
Belleisle and Seafield Golf Courses.
(Alloway 41258)

Barassie
Kilmarnock (Barassie) Golf Club,
Hillhouse Road.
(Troon 311077)

Barrhead
Fereneze Golf Club,
Ferenze Avenue.
(041 881 1519)

Bearsden
Bearsden Golf Club,
Thorn Road.
(041 942 2351)

Beith
Beith Golf Club.
(Beith 3166)

Caldwell
Caldwell Golf Club.
(041 221 8395)

Carradale
Carradale Golf Course.
(Carradale 624)

Coatbridge
Coatbridge Golf Club,
Townhead Road.
(Coatbridge 28975)

Corrie (Isle of Arran)
Corrie Golf Club.

Craignure (Isle of Mull)
Craignure Golf Club,
Scallastle.
(Craignure 370)

Dunoon
Cowal Golf Club.
(Dunoon 2216)

Glasgow
Alexandra Park Golf Course,
Sannox Gardens.
(041 556 3711)

Bishopbriggs Golf Club,
Brackenbrae Avenue.
(041 772 1810)

Cathcart Castle Golf Club,
Mearns Road,
Clarkston G76 7YL.
(041 638 9449)

Cawder Golf Course,
Cadder Road,
Bishopbriggs.
(041 772 7101)

Cowglen Golf Club,
301 Barrhead Road G43.
(041 632 0556)

Haggs Castle Golf Course,
70 Dumbreck Road.
(041 427 0480)

Keir Golf Course,
Cawder Golf Club.
(041 772 7101)

Kings Park Golf Club.
(041 637 1066)

Lethamhill Golf Course.
(041 770 6220)

Pollok Golf Club,
90 Barrhead Road.
(041 632 4351)

Innellan
Innellan Golf Course.
(Innellan 242)

Lanark
Lanark Golf Course,
The Moor.
(Lanark 3219)

Largs
Largs Golf Club,
Irvine Road.
(Largs 673594)

Oban
Glencruitten Golf Course,
Glencruitten Road.
(Oban 2868)

Prestwick
Old Prestwick Golf Course.
(Prestwick 77404)

Prestwick St Cuthbert Golf Club.
(Prestwick 77101)

Troon
Lochgreen Course.
(Troon 312464)

Darlel Course.
(Troon 312464)

Royal Troon Golf Course and Royal Troon
Golf Club,
Craigend Road.
(Troon 311555)

Turnberry
Turnberry Golf Club.
(Turnberry 393)

Horse Riding

Appin
Lettershuna Riding and Boating Centre,
Lettershuna House.
(Appin 227)

Blackwaterfoot (Isle of Arran)
Cairnhouse Pony Trekking Centre,
Cairnhouse.
(Blackwaterfoot 256)
Accommodation can be arranged near
centre.

Lochgoilhead (Argyll)
Corrow Trekking Centre,
Corrow Farm.
(Lochgoilhead 283/320)
Accommodation can be arranged at centre.

Sea Angling

Ayr
Flounder, dab, cod, dogfish, and conger
from the shore.
Spurdog, cod, pollack, whiting, dogfish,
thornback, ray and conger from boats.
Boats: Available from Mrs M. Johnston,

93

59 Woodlands Crescent, Ayr.
(Ayr 81638)
T. Medina, 44 Fort Street, Ayr.
(Ayr 85297)

Prestwick
Shore: cod, flounder, plaice, dab, coalfish,
dogfish and mullet.
Boat: as above plus tope and rays,
thornbacks and mackerel, except mullet.
Boats: 14 ft skippered boat available from
Prestwick Sea Angling Club and boats can
also be chartered from Troon and Ayr.
J. Wilson,
27 Wallace Avenue,
Barassie,
Troon, Ayrshire.

Troon
Shore: cod, plaice, flounder, coalfish, rays,
dogfish, conger, whiting, pollack.
Boat: as above plus thornback, gurnard
and very occasional tope.
Boats: There are numerous boats available.
'Dusky Maid' – J. Wilson,
27 Wallace Avenue,
Barassie, Troon.
(Troon 313161)
Further information from: Glacier Angling
Club: Mr M. Lindsay,
5 Ayr Road, Kilmarnock.

Irvine
Flounder and cod from the shore. Cod,
flounder, dogfish, rays, conger, haddock,
whiting, coalfish and very occasional tope
from boats.
Boats: 33 ft Aqua Star *'Talisman'* – Hugh
Paterson, A1 Angling,
46 Cambusdoon Place, Kilwinning.
(Kilwinning 57209).
J. Wilson.
(Troon 313161)
Further information from: J.G. Macnab,
27 Wilson Avenue, Irvine.
(Irvine 76886)

Saltcoats and Ardrossan
Cod, rays, flounder, coalfish, dogfish,
conger, whiting and pollack from shore,
plus haddock, dab, gurnard and thornback
from boats.
Boats: Available from Andrew Gibson,
1 Fleck Avenue, Saltcoats.

(Saltcoats 64918)
A. McPhillimey,
12 Donaldson Avenue, Stevenston.
(Stevenston 62707)
A.S. Wass,
22 Templeland Road, Dalry.
(Dalry 3724)
There are no professional hirers at
Ardrossan but private owners are willing to
help.

Isle of Arran
Lamlash
Cod, haddock, whiting, coalfish, pollack,
conger, rays, flatfish, mackerel, dogfish.
Boats: Dinghies are available from the
Arran Sea Angling Centre,
Brodick.
(Brodick 2192)
N.C. McLean, Torlin Villa, Kilmory.
(Sliddery 240)
Johnston Bros, Old Pier Shop, Lamlash.
(Lamlash 333)
Further information from: N.C. McLean,
Torlin Villa, Kilmory. (Sliddery 240)

Lochranza
Cod, conger and haddock from the shore.
Cod, conger, haddock from boats.

Inveraray
Cod, mackerel, pollack, coalfish, ling,
dogfish, conger eel, hake and plaice.
Boats: 46 ft MFV *'Boreas'*, 24 ft fibreglass
boat with inboard engine, 3 rowing boats
based at Inveraray Pier available from
Dugald Cameron,
McCulloch Buildings,
Lochgilphead.
(Lochgilphead 2773)

Tarbert (Loch Fyne)
Cod, mackerel, coalfish, and sea trout from
the shore.
Mackerel, cod, coalfish, rays, haddock and
whiting from boats.
Boats: Evening out with the boats of the
herring fleet can be arranged.
Boats available from Dugald Cameron,
McCulloch Buildings,
Lochgilphead.
(Lochgilphead 2773)

J.W. Cresswell,
Quay Houses, Tarbert.
(Tarbert 667)
Johnsons Newsagent.
(Tarbert 494).
John Hunt,
Kintyre Electrical, Tarbert.
Loch Fyne Cruiser,
Tarbert.
J.W. Cresswell runs scheduled daily
summer short trips service.

Firth of Clyde

Tighnabruaich

Mackerel and coalfish from the shore, plus
cod, haddock, flatfish, whiting and dogfish
from boats.

Rothesay

Shore: cod, pollack, plaice, mackerel,
wrasse.
Boat: cod, pollack, plaice, mackerel,
conger, spurdog, thornback, coalfish,
wrasse and whiting.
Boats: Peter McIntyre (Clyde) Ltd,
Port Bannatyne.
MacLeod Marines, Montague Street,
Rothesay Pier, (charter trips only, sleeping
and catering aboard).
Keith Todd,
Carleol,
Alma Terrace, 1 fishing cruiser and
boarding house.
Advance booking necessary.

Kilchattan Bay

Cod, pollack, plaice, mackerel, conger,
dogfish, wrasse, whiting.
Boats: C. Kay,
St Blanes Hotel,
Kilchattan Bay,
Isle of Bute.

Millport

Shore: mackerel, pollack, cod, conger and
coalfish.
Boat: cod, haddock, coalfish, pollack,
dogfish and mackerel.
Boats: S. McIntyre (five boats).
A. Wright (Millport 579) (one boat).
Mr Wilson (Millport 784).
A considerable number of rowing boats are
available for hire, and drive-yourself motor
boats.

Further information from: F.A. Mapes,
4 Guildford Street, Millport.
(Millport 444).

Largs

Cod, pollack, haddock, mackerel, coalfish,
dogfish.
Boats: Mitchell Hotel Services,
78 Greenock Road,
Largs.
(Largs 672044)

Gourock

Codling, whiting, pouting, conger, flatfish,
mackerel and rays from boat and shore.
Bait: Lug, rag, mussels, cockles and crabs
are easily obtainable from the shoreline.
Boats: Doug Nicol (Helensburgh 2707).
John Fishwick (Clynder 445).
Archie Campbell (Greenock 21082).
Doug Crockett (041 332 1041).
Danny Watt (Greenock 83069).
W. Irvine (Gourock 33686).
Larry Green (Kilcreggan 2436).
Mr Woods (Dumbarton 31665).
Robert Wilson (Gourock 36864).
Mr Bell (Dumbarton 63937).
Mr Glover (Dumbarton 64629).
Mr Ramage (Alexandria 56450).
Mr Taylor (Alexandria 53873).
Ian McLennan (Duntochar 78614).
Bob Colquhoun (Dunfermline 27233).
Tom Allison (Alexandria 72812).
Season for fishing: all year.

West Coast Mainland

Oban

Boat: mackerel, dogfish, rays, pollack and
occasionally cod and haddock. Heavy
catches (mainly dogfish) have been taken
in the entry to Loch Feochan during the
past two seasons.

Kyle of Lochalsh

Conger, coalfish, pollack and whiting from
the harbour.
Pollack, cod, coalfish, mackerel and
whiting from boats.
Further information from: Wester Ross
Tourist Information Centre, Kyle of
Lochalsh.

Poolewe and Aultbea

Shore: pollack, coalfish, dab, codling.

Boat: haddock, cod, codling, gurnard, skate, whiting, mackerel, flat fish.
Boats: A. Wiseman, 40 Mellon Charles.
(Aultbea 349).
T. Newton, Poolewe.
(Poolewe 257).
F. Wiseman, Mellon Charles,
Mrs I. & R. Grant, Isle of Ewe,
Aultbea.

Lochinver
Cod, haddock, whiting, saithe, gurnard, ling, pollack, mackerel, wrasse, conger, skate. Coalfish, pollack, cod and mackerel from the shore.
Boats: N.A. MacAskill, *'Petrel'*.
Wm Hutchison,
Valhalla,
Inverkirkaig by Lochinver,
J. McKenzie,
Torran Cottage, Lochinver.
(Lochinver 338)
J. Crookes, Lochinver. *'Dolphin'*

Isle of Islay
Boat: cod, haddock, whiting, coalfish, pollack, mackerel, gurnard, dogfish, spurdog, plaice, flounder, tope, ling, conger, skate and rays.
Boats: A 20 ft motor boat from Port Charlotte Hotel; organised fishing parties catered for.

Isle of Mull (Salen)
Coalfish, pollack, cod, wrasse, flounder, mullet, sea trout and mackerel from the shore. Ray, skate, ling, pollack, coalfish, cod, spurdog, tope, conger and gurnard from boats.
Further information from: Duncan Swinbanks, Tackle and Books,
10 Main Street, Tobermory.
(Tobermory 2336)

Isle of Mull (Tobermory)
Tope, skate, rays, pollack, coalfish, ling, conger, gurnard, spurdog, cod, haddock, flatfish (plaice, dabs, and turbot) and whiting from boats. Coalfish, pollack, cod, wrasse, flounder, grey mullet, sea trout, conger, thornback and mackerel from the shore.
Boats: Brian Swinbanks, 8 Main Street, Tobermory, has a purpose-built 32 ft sea

angling boat for fishing parties with boat rods and reel available.
There are 14–16 ft dinghies for hire for fishing in and around the bay.

Isle of Coll
Mackerel, coalfish, pollack, cod, conger, haddock, skate and flounder.
Boats: Dinghies with or without outboard engines can be hired from local lobster fishermen.
Further information from: Alistair Oliphant of Coll Hotel. (Coll 334)

Game Fishing

Annick River
Salmon, sea trout, brown trout.
Permits: Currie Sports Shop,
Townhead,
Ayrshire.

Annick Water
Salmon, sea trout, brown trout.
Permits: Dreghorn Angling Club:
W. Gibson,
23 Dunlop Crescent,
Dreghorn, Irvine,
Ayrshire.

Alexanders Fishmongers,
10 Bank Street,
Irvine.

Ardtornish Estate
Salmon, sea trout, brown trout.
Permits: Ardtornish Estate Office,
Morvern by Oban.
(Morvern 288)
Charges on application.

Ascog Loch
Brown trout, rainbow trout.
Permits: Kyles of Bute Angling Club, and several shops in Kames and Tighnabruaich.

Assopol Loch
Salmon, sea trout.
Permits: Argyll Arms Hotel,
Bunessan,
Isle of Mull.
(Fionnphort 240)

Awe Loch
Sea trout, brown trout.
Permits: Chief Forester, Forest Office,

Dalavich by Taynuilt.
(Lochavich 258)

Brown trout, salmon.
Permits: Portsonachan Hotel,
by Dalmally.
(Kilchrenan 224)

Salmon, trout.
Ford Hotel,
Ford.
(Ford 273)

Ayr River
Salmon, sea trout, brown trout.
Permits: Director of Finance,
Town Buildings,
Ayr.

Arthur Allan,
25 Kyle Street,
Ayr.

Gamesport,
60 Sandgate,
Ayr.

Salmon, sea trout, brown trout.
Permits: Auchinleck Angling Association:
J. McColm, Secretary,
21 Milne Avenue,
Auchinleck,
Ayrshire.
(Auchinleck 21953)

Salmon, sea trout, brown trout.
Permits: Linwood & Johnstone,
Newsagent,
The Cross,
Mauchline,
Ayrshire.

Mr and Mrs Preston,
Post Office,
Main Street,
Ochiltree.

Barnluasgan Loch
Permits: Chief Forester, Forest Office,
Knapdale Forest,
Cairnbaan,
Lochgilphead.
(Lochgilphead 2304)

Mrs Robertson,
Barnluasgan,
Lochgilphead.

Burnock Water
Salmon, sea trout, brown trout.
Permits: Linwood and Johnstone,
Newsagents,
The Cross,
Mauchline,
Ayrshire.

Mr and Mrs Preston,
Post Office,
Main Street,
Ochiltree.

Carse Burn
Sea trout.
Permits: Head Forester,
Torinturk,
West Loch,
Tarbert.
(Tarbert 251)

Cessnock Water
Brown trout.
Permits: Linwood & Johnstone,
Newsagents,
The Cross,
Mauchline,
Ayrshire.

Mr and Mrs Preston,
Post Office,
Main Street,
Ochiltree.

Clyde River
(Except Lanark and Lamington Angling
Club's Waters), main tributaries and
Springfield Reservoir by Carluke.
Brown trout, grayling.
Permits: Most tackle dealers in Glasgow,
Edinburgh and main West of Scotland
towns;
or United Clyde Angling Protective
Association Ltd,
Robert C. Sharp,
20 Cunningham Street,
Motherwell,
Lanarkshire.

Coll Estate
Various small lochs on Coll estate within 2
miles (3 km) radius of Arinagour (locations
from factor)

Brown trout.
Permits: Factor, Coll Estate House,
Arinagour,
Isle of Coll.
(Coll 367)

Coyle River
Brown trout, grayling, late salmon, sea
trout.
Permits: Sundrum Castle Hotel,
Sundrum, by Ayr.
(Joppa 253)

Salmon, sea trout, brown trout, grayling.
Permits: Drongan Youth Group Angling
Club;
A. Kennedy, Treasurer,
1 Craig View,
Coylton,
Ayrshire.

Doon River
Salmon, sea trout, rainbow trout, brown
trout.
Permits: Hollybush House Hotel,
Hollybush,
Ayrshire.
(Dalrymple 214)

Euchar River
Salmon, sea trout, brown trout.
Permits: Mrs Mary McCorkindale,
Glenann,
Kilninver, by Oban,
Argyll.

Forsa River
Salmon, sea trout.
Permits: Tackle & Books,
Main Street,
Tobermory,
Isle of Mull.

Salmon, sea trout.
Permits: Glenforsa Hotel, by Salen,
Isle of Mull.
(Aros 377 and 379)

Fyne River
Tidal water.
Salmon, sea trout.
Permits: (Alternate weeks)
Ardkinglas Estate Office,
Cairndow,
Argyll.

(Cairndow 217 and Cairndow Estate,
Cairndow 284)

Irvine River
Salmon, sea trout, trout.
Irvine and District Angling Club,
Robert Gilmour,
58 Muir Drive,

Permits: Currie's Sports Shop,
Townhead,
Ayrshire.

Lomond Loch
Salmon, trout, brown trout.
Permits: Ardlui Hotel,
Ardlui,
Loch Lomond, by Arrochar.
(Inveruglas 243)

Lussa Loch
(North of Scotland Hydro-Electric Board)
Trout.
Permits: Officials of Kintyre Fish
Protection and Angling Club:
Secretary, Rev. J. McFie,
Lochend Manse,
Campbeltown.
(Campbeltown 2605)

Machrie Water
Salmon, sea trout.
Permits: J.T. Boscawan,
Strathtay Estate Office,
Killiechassie,
Aberfeldy,
Perthshire.

Mishnish, Aros Lochs
Trout.
Permits: Tobermory Angling Association:
c/o Brown's Shop,
Tobermory,
Isle of Mull.

Mishnish Lochs
Trout.
Permits: Western Isles Hotel,
Tobermory,
Isle of Mull.
(Tobermory 2012)

Prestwick Reservoir
Brown trout, rainbow trout.
Permits: Prestwick Angling Club,

The Wheatsheaf Inn,
Main Street,
Monkton,
Ayrshire.

James Graham,
Newlands Cottage,
Monkton,
Prestwick,
Ayrshire,

J.B. Gibson,
67 Seaforth Road,
Ayr.

Special Interest Holidays

Arden
Kilmelford Yacht Haven,
Kilmelford by Oban.
(Kilmelford 248)
Self-sail yachts.

Brodick (Isle of Arran)
Allandale Guest House,
Brodick.
(Brodick 2278)
Walks: wild flower, archaeological,
geological and hill-walking weeks
arranged.

Isle of Arran Field Studies,
Woodside,
Glen Sannox.
(Corrie 207/282)

Carsaig (Isle of Mull)
School of Painting,
Inniemore Lodge,
Carsaig,
Isle of Mull.
(Pennyghael 201)

Cullipool
Ru'A Fiola,
Cullipool,
Oban.
(Chapelknowe 240)
Sailing, mountain and natural history
expeditions.

Galston (Isle of Mull)
Little Cessnock Estate,
Galston.
(Galston 820 888)
Stag stalking.

Cessnock Estate.
Roe stalking.

Largs
Inverclyde and Cumbrae National Sports
Training Centre.
(Largs 672468)
Golf, badminton, sailing.

Taynuilt
St Just Marine Charters Ltd,
Lochavich,
Taynuilt.
(Lochavich 212)
Crewed charters and cruises.

Tobermory (Isle of Mull)
Erray Estate,
Tobermory,
Isle of Mull.
(Tobermory 2052)
Fishing, golf, archery and pony trekking.

Troon
Sub and Surface Sea Sports Ltd,
The Harbour,
Troon.
Contact: Hebridean Holidays Ltd,
2 Upper Dean Terrace,
Edinburgh EH4 1NU.
(031 225 9531)
Sea cruises and charters.
This company also arranges walking,
climbing, cruises and diving on Isle of
Mull.

Cycling

Brodick (Isle of Arran)
Mrs D. Glen,
Hillshore,
Alma Road.
(Brodick 2444)

Howie Hires,
Roselynn.
(Brodick 2460)
Contact: Andrew Howie.

Coll, Isle of
Coll Hotel Enterprises Ltd,
The Hotel.
(Coll 334)
Contact: A.P. Oliphant.

Around Scotland

Colonsay
Isle of Colonsay Hotel.
(Colonsay 316)
Contact: Kevin Byrne.

Dunoon
Argyll Hotel,
Argyll Street.
(Dunoon 2059)
Contact: L.M. Fletcher.

Glasgow
Dale's (Cycles) Ltd,
26–30 Maryhill Road.
(041 332 2705)
Contact: James Houston.

David Rattray & Co Ltd,
261 Alexandra Parade.
(041 554 3757)

Scottish Youth Hostels Association,
11 Woodlands Terrace.
(041 332 3004)

Lamlash
Mrs J. Hislop,
Park Cottage.
(Lamlash 441)
Contact: Mrs Joan Hislop.

Millport
Bremner's Stores,
13 & 17 Cardiff Street.
(Millport 309/707)
Contact: G.M. Stark.

F.V.G Mapes & Son,
3–5 Guildford Street.
(Millport 444)
Contact: Frances Arthur Mapes.

A.T. Morton,
4 Mount Stuart Street,
(Millport 478)
Contact: A.T. Morton.

Tobermory (Isle of Mull)
William Harley,
21 Main Street.
(Tobermory 2460 night;
Tobermory 2020 day)
Contact: William Harley.

Whiting Bay (Isle of Arran)
Stanford Hires,
Stanford Shore Road.
(Whiting Bay 313)
Contact: J. Ritchie.

Where to Eat

Ardentinny (Nr Dunoon)
The Ardentinny Hotel.
(Ardentinny 209)

The Heron Tea Room.
(Ardentinny 237)

Brodick (Isle of Arran)
Kingsley Hotel.
(Brodick 2226)

Biggar
Toftcombs Hotel ML12 6QX.
(Biggar 20142)

Bute, Isle of
Glenburn Hotel,
Glenburn Road,
Rothesay.
(Rothesay 2500)

Dunoon
Enmore Hotel,
Marine Parade,
Kirn PA23 8HH.
(Dunoon 2230)

Glasgow
Kensington's Restaurant,
164 Darnley Street.
(041 424 3662)

North British Hotel,
George Square.
(041 332 6711)

Poachers Restaurant,
Ruthven Lane.
(041 339 0932)

Ubiquitous Chip,
12 Ashton Lane.
(041 334 5007)

Kames (By Tighnabruaich)
Kames Cottage.
(Tighnabruaich 259)

Lochgoilhead
Bouquet Garni Restaurant.
(Lochgoilhead 206)

Stewarton
Chapeltoun House.
(Stewarton 82696)

Car Hire

Abbotsinch
Godfrey Davis (Car Hire) Ltd,
Glasgow Airport,
7 Marchfield Avenue,
Paisley.
(041 889 8359/60)

Hertz Rent-a-Car.
(041 887 2451)

Swan National Car Rental,
Phoenix House,
Inshinan Road,
Paisley.
(041 889 0033)

Airdrie
Budget Rent-a-Car,
Watsons Bros (Airdrie) Ltd,
28–48 High Street.
(Airdrie 54651/2)

Ayr
Budget Rent-a-Car,
(Prestwick Airport and Ayr)
196 Prestwick Road.
(Ayr 61631/64087)

Dalblair Motors,
127 Prestwick Road.
(Ayr 69123)

Drew Dodds (Car Hire) Ltd,
84 Prestwick Road.
(Ayr 81938)

McKnight Motors,
146 Prestwick Road.
(Ayr 67456/7)

Wellington Motors Co. (Ayr) Ltd,
Parkhouse Street.
(Ayr 63291/2)

Brodick (Isle of Arran)
Arran Transport & Trading Co Ltd,
Pier Head.
(Brodick 2121)

Bunessan
Robert McCallum,
The Garage,
Ardenfaig.
(Fionnphort 206)

Coll, Isle of
Isle of Coll Hotel,
Arinagour.
(Coll 334)

Glasgow
Andersons of Newton,
Mearns,
268 Ayr Road,
Newton Mearns.
(041 639 2271)

Avis Rent-a-Car,
161/169 North Street.
(041 221 2827)
(Range Rovers available)

Budget Rent-a-Car,
(Appleyard),
65 Springkell Avenue.
(041 424 0833)

Godfrey Davis (Car Hire) Ltd,
556 Pollokshaws Road.
(041 423 5661/2/3/4)

Hertz Rent-a-Car,
106 Waterloo Street.
(041 248 7733)

International Car Rental,
Waterloo Street Service Station,
Waterloo Street.
(041 248 6591)

Kenning Car Hire,
10 Abbey Drive,
Jordanhill.
(041 954 9191)

Mitchells Self Drive,
Multi Storey Car Park,
Mitchell Street.
(041 221 8461)

Around Scotland

SMT Self Drive Hire,
39 West Campbell Street.
(041 248 4533 or 041 204 0176)

Swan National,
Car Rental,
Buchanan Street Bus Station.
(041 332 8896)

Lochgilphead
Fyneside Service Station,
Paterson Street.
(Lochgilphead 2229)

Oban
Argyll Motor Services (Oban) Ltd,
Amsol,
Shore Street.
(Oban 3519, after hours: Connel 357)

Hazelbank Motors,
Lochside Street.
(Oban 3463)

Mogil Motors (Oban) Ltd,
Soroba Road.
(Oban 3061/2)

Western Garage (Oban) Ltd,
Dunollie Road.
(Oban 3717)

Wilson's Garage Ltd,
Aird's Place.
(Oban 3173/4)

Prestwick
Arran View Filling Station,
Ayr Road,
Auchengate,
Irvine.
(Prestwick 311221)

Avis Rent-a-Car,
Prestwick Airport.
(Prestwick 77218)

Douglas Car Hire Ltd,
Towans Hotel.
(Prestwick 77831)

Godfrey Davis Ltd,
14 Kirk Street.
(Prestwick 70566)

Hertz Rent-a-Car,
Prestwick Airport.
(Prestwick 70666/7)

Kenning Car Hire,
Adamton House Hotel,
Monkton.
(Prestwick 75507)

Swan National Car Rental,
Prestwick Airport.
(Prestwick 76517/8)

Renfrew
Europcar,
Normandy Hotel,
Inchinnan Road.
(041 885 1554/5)

Rothesay (Isle of Bute)
Bute Motor Company,
Union Street.
(Rothesay 2330)

Lothian

Lothian is the area flanking Edinburgh to its west, south and east, about 50 miles (80 km) wide and 12–15 miles (19–24 km) deep, occupying most of the south bank of the Firth of Forth. Though not noted for its scenery, there is a wealth of interesting places to see, with a history that spans over 4,000 years. Mary Queen of Scots lived here for about seven years of her life, and it is the places with which she is associated that have the strongest appeal to visitors.

From the Borders region, six main roads lead to Edinburgh, which we describe from east (the coast) to west. Section IV travels into Strathclyde (Glasgow) and Central regions and the routes are described from Edinburgh.

I: Dunbar – Haddington – Musselburgh

The boundary between Borders and Lothian runs across a wide stretch of lonely upland country known as Lammermuir, with the Lammermuir Hills on its north side, and reaches the North Sea at Cockburnspath, on the A1. The round beacon tower of the church here is sixteenth century, and a mile (2 km) to the north is the fine fifteenth century Dunglass Collegiate Church, in the pleasant setting of Dunglass House grounds. It has been partly restored and has unusually good detail to see both outside and in.

Dunbar, about seven miles (11 km) north, is a historic royal burgh with a port, and a picturesque ruined castle at the mouth of the harbour. It is a rapidly expanding holiday resort. The lower quarter, around the harbour, and castle promontory, is the most attractive part of the town. Dunbar Castle, once a forbidding fortress, is now a mere fragment but it is still of interest as the place where Mary Queen of Scots took refuge with Darnley, after he had murdered her Italian secretary Riccio in Edinburgh in 1566. She was here again with Bothwell in 1567, firstly when he carried her off from Edinburgh, then shortly after their marriage. The following year the castle was destroyed by Moray, Mary's half-brother, when he became Regent after Mary's defeat at Carberry Hill. Cromwell added to its destruction in 1650 by taking its stones to reinforce the harbour walls. Much earlier, after Robert the Bruce's victory at Bannockburn in 1314, his adversary Edward II fled to this port and escaped by sea. His father, Edward I, had triumphed over the Scots here in 1295 when his vassal King, John Balliol, revolted. In the wide High Street of the busy town centre there is Lauderdale House designed by Robert Adam, and a seventeenth century Town House (probably the oldest Scottish civic building to have been in constant

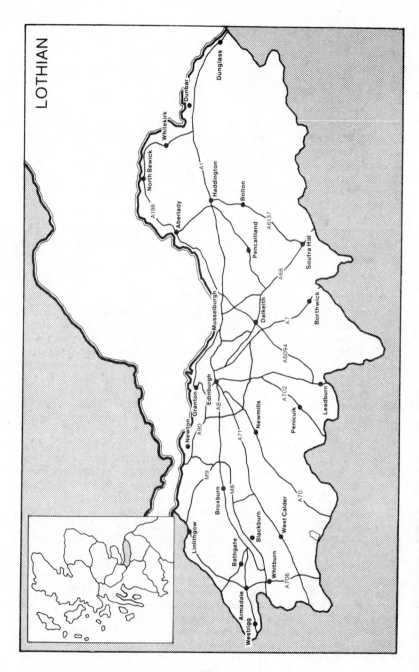

LOTHIAN

Dunglass
Dunbar
Whitekirk
North Berwick
Aberlady
A198
Haddington
A1
Bolton
Pencaitland
A6137
Soutra Hill
A68
Musselburgh
Dalkeith
A7
Borthwick
A6094
Granton
Edinburgh
Newton
A90
A8
A71
Newmills
A702
Penicuik
Leadburn
M9
Broxburn
M8
West Calder
A70
Linlithgow
Blackburn
Bathgate
Whitburn
A706
Armadale
Westrigg

Lothian

use). At Castle Park there is a branch of the Myreton Motor Museum of North Berwick.

After Dunbar the A1 leaves the coast, heading east. The A198 follows the coast (*see* Route II). Before reaching East Linton, a mile (2 km) north of the road are Tyninghame House Gardens, with walled garden, rose garden, terraces and a ruined Norman church. East Linton is best known for its attractive old water mill, Preston Mill (now NTS) which is still in working condition, and functioned commercially until 1957. There is a museum here, with exhibits of agricultural equipment, and nearby is John Rennie's Phantassie Doocot (dovecot) which is also NTS. Rennie was born at Phantassie mansion in 1761, and became a respected engineer and architect. (See his memorial on the by-pass.) Just south of the A1 is the site of a discovery (in 1919) of fourth century silver, pagan and Christian, now to be seen in Edinburgh, at the National Museum of Antiquities. The site is on the distinctive hill of Trapain Law, which had a settlement from prehistoric times at least until the eleventh century.

Outside East Linton the A1 passes Hailes Castle a mile (2 km) to the south, which retains many of its thirteenth century features, particularly the masonry, and a sixteenth century chapel. Note the gruesome prison pits in the towers, where you can relive in your imagination the horror of being imprisoned, if you want to climb down the ladders provided for the purpose. On their flight between Borthwick and Dunbar in 1567, Mary Queen of Scots and Bothwell rested here as he owned the castle at that time.

About five miles (8 km) south of Haddington, east of the A6137 is the compact seventeenth to eighteenth century village of Gifford, in a pretty setting, with a church that was bodily shifted to this site from its previous site a mile (2 km) away in 1708. It contains a seventeenth century pulpit and an ancient bell. The Reverend John Witherspoon, the only cleric to sign the American Declaration of Independence, and the first President of Princeton University, was born here in 1723 (memorial plaque near the church).

North of Gifford, on the B6369 about a mile (2 km) from Haddington is Lennoxlove House, a seventeenth century mansion named after a beautiful woman who was Charles II's mistress before running away with the Duke of Richmond and Lennox, Charles Stuart, and marrying him. As Duchess of Lennox she was known as 'La Belle Stuart'.

North of the A1 off the B1343, is the village of Athelstaneford where a pictorial plaque at the church tells the story of how the white St Andrew's Cross on a blue ground became the Scottish flag, from a battle here in the tenth century between the Scots (and Picts) and the Northumbrian English, under Athelstane. The flag now flies here at all times.

East Fortune aerodrome is not far away, off the B1377, and is well known as the starting point for the airship's first double Atlantic air crossing in 1919. The Museum of Flight (part of the Royal Scottish Museum in Edinburgh) has aircraft on display which include a 1934 autogiro, a Spitfire, the Fairey Delta (world speed record holder in

1956), and jet fighters. The Blue Streak missile heads the rocket section. Just south of the B1377 is a very good example of an iron-age fort, known as the Chesters, where you can see fragments of its former multiple ramparts.

Haddington forms a centre for the sites described above, and is a historic town, made a royal burgh by David I (Alexander II was born here in 1198). Its Town House was built by William Adam in 1748, but you can't see much of the original structure now. There is a planned walk around the town indicated on the wall of the building, which takes you past the most interesting of Haddington's well-preserved buildings in about half an hour. The Church of St Mary is fourteenth to fifteenth century (restored), and the Pleached Alley from St Mary's Gate leads towards St Mary's Pleasance, the delightful seventeenth century gardens of Haddington House. The Court House (built by William Burn in 1833) is where the Palace used to be, and the Knox Memorial Institute of 1879 is where the school used to be, that was attended by John Knox, the sixteenth century reformer who was born here in 1505. Haddington's Museum is housed in the nineteenth century Public Library, formerly the Meeting House, and has a local history exhibition.

The A1 continues east, but it is worth taking the B6363 after about five miles (8 km), to Winton House, a superb Renaissance building of 1620 with especially fine chimneys and ceilings. Beyond, the village of Ormiston is unusually pretty, with a fifteenth century Market Cross in the broad main street. You can rejoin the A1 from here by the B6371.

As you enter **Musselburgh** you pass Pinkie House, seventeenth century with later additions, which has notable plasterwork and a fine painted gallery, of about 1625. Musselburgh is beside the Firth of Forth with a waterfront much enjoyed by bird watchers, and a nice sixteenth century bridge, Esk Bridge, and Tolbooth close by, though otherwise it is a largely modern and noisy town. The golf links to the north-east have existed for over 500 years.

To the south of the town, Inveresk is a peaceful village where there was a Roman camp, as this was the end of the road they built, Dere Street. For those with small gardens in search of inspiration, visit the Inveresk Lodge Gardens here, now run by the NTS. Just south again, you can see Carberry Hill where Mary Queen of Scots surrendered to the rebel lords under Moray in 1567 (where her husband and supposed ally Bothwell galloped off, the last she was ever to see of him).

II: A198 – North Berwick – Prestonpans

The A198 leaves the A1 northwards some four miles (6 km) west of Dunbar. Whitekirk is about three miles (5 km) up, and has an interesting sixteenth century double-storey tithe barn, beside the church. The barn was originally used by the monks of Holyrood Abbey (behind the Palace of Holyroodhouse in Edinburgh) as a grain store. The church spire, on its great tower, is made of wood and was damaged in 1914 by

Suffragettes, now restored.

Where the road reaches the coast the huge ruin of Tantallon Castle is impressively perched on the cliffs with a sheer drop to the sea on three sides. This mighty red sandstone Douglas stronghold was built around 1375 with walls up to 14 feet (4 m) thick, remaining impregnable until 1651, when General Monk bombarded it for 12 days on Cromwell's behalf, finally destroying it. The central tower is still here, and flanking towers linked by ramparts. The well was cut through the rock to a depth of 100 feet (30 m).

From Tantallon Castle you can see the prominent island of Bass Rock about 1½ miles (2.5 km) off shore. It is about a mile (2 km) in circumference and 350 feet (107 m) high. Now a sanctuary for vast numbers of sea birds (the third largest gannetry in the world), it was once a prison island for Covenanters (after 1671). In 1691 the fort was seized by Jacobite prisoners who held it for three years, until granted an amnesty, soon after which the fort was dismantled. There are several other sea bird islands off shore to the west of Bass Rock – Craigleith (with a colony of puffins), Lamb, Fidra and Eyebroughty.

North Berwick, a royal burgh since around 1400, has been a popular holiday resort for over 100 years and has good beaches, and an interesting harbour and waterfront area, with the ruined Auld Kirk, below a busy town center. The Borough Museum is on the upper floor of an old school in School Road, and has good local collections of natural history and archaeology, (note the display of relics from the scant ruin of the 'abbey', a twelfth century nunnery, which is in the grounds of The Abbey house). North Berwick Law is the 612-foot (187 m) hill behind the town, with a tower built as a lookout for Napoleonic invaders, and also a curious archway constructed from the jawbones of a whale. The views from up here are impressively long.

To the west of the town is the village of Dirleton, often said to be the prettiest in Scotland. There is a ruined castle dating from about 1225, destroyed by Cromwell in 1650, which still has very attractive features. Additions to the castle include a hall in the fifteenth century, and a magnificent Renaissance mansion in the seventeenth century. In the grounds is a seventeenth century bowling green surrounded by yew trees, and a seventeenth century dovecot in the eastern corner (housing up to 1,100 doves' nests). The coastline is fringed with sand beaches to the west of Dirleton at Gullane Bay, which is a centre of the Dune Control Scheme. The village has the Muirfield championship golf course.

Just before you enter Aberlady note the ruined sixteenth century Luffness Castle, whose thirteenth century keep is on the site of an ancient Norse camp, with traces of fortifications and a moat. The Myreton Motor Museum is on the eastern edge of the village and has a wide-ranging collection of motor, horse-drawn and military vehicles. Aberlady Bay is a nature reserve mainly known for its great variety of birds (some 200 different species have been recorded, including all five types of tern). You can best watch the birds by crossing the footbridge and walking to the headland.

At the southern end of Gosford Bay you will see the fifteenth to sixteenth century Seton Collegiate Church, off the road, which consists of choir, transepts and stone spire (truncated). The 5th Lord Seton, who was killed at Flodden in 1513 fighting for James IV, is probably buried here. Seton Castle, not open to the public, is on the site of Seton Palace, where Mary Queen of Scots came with Darnley after Riccio's murder, and with Bothwell after Darnley's murder, Lord Seton being one of her staunchest supporters.

The neat and elegant village of Preston, with some distinguished buildings from the fifteenth century onwards including a superb seventeenth century Market Cross, is just inland from **Prestonpans**. East of here is the Battle Cairn commemorating the Young Pretender's triumphant victory over the Government troops in 1745. After a surprise attack at dawn on 20 September, which lasted only 10 minutes, he had claimed the lives of 400 of the enemy, losing only 30 of his own.

At Prestongrange Colliery, now closed after 800 years of recorded activity, is the unique Prestongrange Mining Museum with a vast Beam Pumping Engine on display (operational from 1874–1954) as well as steam excavators and locomotives. The old Power House is now an exhibition hall for mining exhibits and photographs.

III: Dalkeith – Penicuik – Pentland Hills

This route includes the southerly approaches to Edinburgh – the A68, A7, A703 and A70.

The A68 approaches Edinburgh from the south-east, crossing the Borders/Lothian boundary at Soutra Hill (1,130 feet/345 m), which commands extensive open views from the road. Some five miles (8 km) beyond, a left turn takes you to the village of Crighton, where there is an important castle, well positioned on the side of a peaceful green valley. Crighton Castle grew from a plain tower house (fourteenth century) to an elaborately decorated mansion (sixteenth century). The Italianate stonework was added around 1585 by the 5th Earl of Bothwell, who had been to Italy. Note the particularly striking high wall with diamond bosses, which is in stark contrast to the horrible secret dungeon. Beyond the castle, the other building is an unusual ruined defended stable. To reach the castle, park near the church and take the footpath along the side of the valley, taking 5–10 minutes. The open setting in quiet countryside adds to the pleasure of the visit. The small church, with conspicuous tower, is Crighton Collegiate Church (1499), which is still in use and sits in a well-tended graveyard. It is noted for its barrel vaulting.

Dalkeith is a busy little town at the junction of several roads. Dalkeith Palace is of interest, though not open to the public. It was a twelfth century castle when the 2nd Duke of Buccleugh bought it in 1651 but his daughter, Anne, had the existing Palace built around it (by James Smith) about 50 years later. Her coffin is in the Collegiate Church of St Nicholas, which also has the tombs of Sir James Douglas, 1st Earl of Morton, (the Douglases of Morton being the previous owners of the castle) and his Countess Joanna, daughter of James I, who was deaf and dumb. Dalkeith Palace Park, in the extensive palace grounds, has woodland walks and nature trails, a bridge by Robert Adam, rock tunnels, an adventure playground and an orangery. The Dalkeith Arts Centre has an outdoor area for sculpture exhibitions and an indoor gallery. Newbattle Abbey was founded by David I, but destroyed by the English under Hertford in 1544. The remains are now incorporated in a College.

Craigmillar Castle, one of Mary Queen of Scots' best-loved residences, is still an impressive and dignified complex (dating from the fourteenth to seventeenth centuries) despite the encroachment of urban development. Damage inflicted by Hertford in 1544 resulted in the construction of the triple-storey apartments on the east wall of the courtyard during Mary's reign. The west wall buildings are mid-seventeenth century, and differ from the rest in that architecture was by then less concerned with defence. The original L-shaped tower house has a great hall on the second storey, approached by four separate staircases. The north-east corner tower (fifteenth century,) has gunports which serve as one of the earliest examples in Scotland of this sort of defence. The plot to murder Darnley took shape at Craigmillar in 1566, probably with Bothwell as its ringleader. Though Mary Queen of Scots was in residence at the time, whether she was involved or not is unknown. From the entrance to the castle, the view across the Forth is crowded with modern development, but it takes little imagination to visualise the untamed landscape that past residents enjoyed.

The A7 crosses the Borders/Lothian boundary some five miles (8 km) west of the A68 and 16 miles (26 km) south of Edinburgh. The only important site to mention on this road is Borthwick Castle, at Borthwick, the first village you reach on the Lothian side. It is well-known as the place to which Bothwell brought Mary Queen of Scots after their unfortunate marriage in 1567, and from which they both had to flee, the Queen disguised as a page boy, when they found that their enemies had surrounded the castle. It was built around 1430 and is one of the largest and most robust tower houses in Scotland, with twin oblong towers dominating the approach beneath a stone arch. The church here has a fifteenth century aisle and some nice Norman detail.

The A703 crosses the Borders/Lothian boundary at Leadburn and reaches **Penicuik** in three miles (5 km). The Edinburgh Crystal Works are based here, and demonstrations can be seen, by prior arrangement, of how top-quality crystal glass is produced.

A couple of miles (3 km) out of Penicuik a right turn leads to Roslin village, important for its beautiful chapel, founded in 1466. The carving in Roslin (or Rosslyn) Chapel is outstanding, especially the highly decorated Prentice Pillar at the east end of the south aisle. Roslin Castle existed before the chapel but was extended by William Sinclair, founder of the chapel. In 1544 Hertford destroyed it and over the next 100 years it was slowly rebuilt as the fortified house you can see today. There are some passages and dungeons partly built into the cliff face surviving from the older castle, and notice the chute from the lower castle down into the moat, designed as an emergency escape route.

The upland area between the A702 and the A70 is the Pentland Hills about 5 miles (8 km) wide running south-west of Edinburgh for about 16 miles (27 km). Scaldlaw is the highest point at 1,898 feet (579 m). The east slopes are the more varied and scenic. Castlelaw Fort, reached by a small road off the A702 south of Flotterstone, is an iron-age fort which has an earth house inside it, with a passage and chamber. At Hillend, in the north Pentlands, there is a ski centre with chairlift, and Britain's longest dry-ski slope.

From the A70, the views of the Pentlands are not as good, as the slopes are more gradual. In Balerno, just off the road, are attractive shrub gardens at seventeenth century Malleny House (NTS; not open to the public, but the gardens are) some 7½ miles (12 km) from Edinburgh. There are many interesting plants, but shrub roses are a feature.

IV: A8 – Bathgate – A90 – Cramond

Leaving Edinburgh on the A8 (Corstorphine Road) you reach the Scottish National Zoological Park, or Edinburgh Zoo, which is one of the best and largest in the British Isles, spread over 70 acres (28 ha) on Corstorphine Hill. It was founded by the Royal Zoological Society of Scotland in 1913 and is perhaps best known for its marvellous breeding colony of Antarctic penguins, which file out daily in summer for the renowned Penguin Parade, (mid-afternoon). The Carnegie Aquarium is one of the finest in Britain.

Beyond Corstorphine, just after the railway, turn left at the sign for Suntrap, a mile (2 km) off the road. This is an NTS Gardening Centre with instruction courses, especially for those with small gardens. Edinburgh Airport is a little further along the A8, and then Ingliston Showground, scene of the Royal Highland Show every June, and one of the best showgrounds in Europe, with the MacRobert Pavilion as its centrepiece.

Niddry Castle, to which Mary Queen of Scots rode after escaping from Lochleven Castle in 1568, is up a small road a mile (2 km) out of Broxburn on the A89. When Mary came here it was a keep belonging to Lord Seton, and it is said that the following morning she rushed out to salute the local people before even arranging her hair, which flowed in auburn tresses over her shoulders, in her eagerness to enjoy freedom after nearly a year's captivity. Now Niddry is a dark and unkempt ruin in a landscape of slag heaps.

At **Uphall** on the A899, turn left for Mid Calder, reached in three miles (5 km), on the A71. The choir of the church here was restored in

1932, but originates from 1541. In 1848 Chopin stopped here on his tour of Britain, and it was here that John Knox administered the first Protestant Communion in 1556.

Off the A71 at East Calder is the Almondell Country Park, an attractive wooded valley with the River Almond flowing through, criss-crossed by paths (and bridges) made by Enterprise Youth with young people of many nationalities.

Return to the A89 for **Bathgate**, a sprawling industrial town where James Simpson, pioneer of anaesthesia, was born (he used chloroform for the first time in 1847). North of the town are the Bathgate Hills, one of which is a prehistoric ritual and burial site, probably in use in 2500 BC, called Cairnpapple Hill. The site has been painstakingly and imaginatively reconstructed, though much of the original work can still be seen. There is a model for greater clarification on the site, and tape-recorded commentary within the large cairn. This large cairn was built over earlier structures used for ritual purposes, in the Bronze Age, as a major burial site. There are outstanding views from Cairnpapple Hill.

The other side of the hill is the village of Torpichen on the B792, where the Knights of St John of Jerusalem founded their preceptory in 1153. What you can see today is part of the thirteenth century ruins, and the sixteenth century parish church which is built over the nave of the earlier church, and the site is worth visiting as a fine example of how, in the fifteenth century, even religious buildings had to be defensively constructed. The exhibition here describes the history of the Knights.

A mile (2 km) north of Torpichen is the Lothian boundary with Central, and four miles (6 km) beyond Bathgate is its boundary with Strathclyde.

The A90 leaves Edinburgh westwards running parallel to the south shore of the Firth of Forth. About four miles (6 km) from the city centre at Cramond Road South, is Lauriston Castle overlooking the Forth. It was built by Sir Archibald Napier (whose son invented the logarithm) in about 1590 and was later inhabited by John Law (1671–1728), founder of the first Bank of France, during his childhood. The castle was much enlarged in the nineteenth century and is now an elegant house with fine contents including furniture, tapestries, paintings and some lovely Blue John ware.

You can walk from Lauriston Castle along the Forth to **Cramond** on one of the prettier stretches of the Forth's south shore (very built-up around Edinburgh), where the River Almond flows out. Cramond has some attractively restored eighteenth century houses and a quiet atmosphere. Beside the seventeenth century church you can see the foundations of a Roman fort, built in 142 AD to watch over the harbour. (Excavations yielded many Roman finds, which you can see in Edinburgh, at Huntly House Museum.) The fifteenth century tower to the east of the fort probably belonged to the bishops of Dunkeld at one time.

A mile (2 km) south Cramond Old Bridge (1619), spans the Almond where an older bridge used to be, on which James V was attacked by robbers. He was discovered and rescued by the local miller, Jack Howieson, who brought him a ewer of water. In gratitude the King granted lands to his family, on the condition they should always have a basin and ewer of water in readiness to offer passing royalty. The tradition has held, and the miller's descendants have fulfilled their side of the bargain several times, with George IV in 1822, Queen Victoria in 1842, George V in 1927, and the present Queen in 1952.

Dalmeny is just off the A90 and is well worth visiting for its superb little Norman church, one of the best for detail in all Scotland. Built in the twelfth century, the west tower fell after some 300 years, and has been rebuilt, but the stone-vaulted choir and apse are in their original condition, with two elaborately carved round arches and there is typical chevron patterning on the round-shaped windows. In 1671 an addition was built on to the north side of the nave for a loft for the Roseberry family who own Dalmeny House.

V: Edinburgh

Edinburgh acquired its name in the sixth century at a time when Lothian had been subjugated by the Angles of Northumbria. A fortress already existed on the great crag here called Dun Eadain 'fortress on the slope'. When the Northumbrian King Edwin rebuilt the fortress for his own defence, it quickly became known as Edwin's Burgh, and gradually Edinburgh. For hundreds of years Edinburgh was little more than its fortified rock, the ramifications of a town only just beginning in the eleventh century, and helped considerably in the twelfth century by the foundation of Holyrood Abbey, by David I, at the foot of the slope from the fortress. In 1329 Robert the Bruce made it a royal burgh (officially) and in the middle of the fifteenth century it became Scotland's capital, instead of Perth, since when its history has been colourful, and its enormous development cultural rather than commercial.

The first part of the town established itself along the back of the hill sloping from the Castle to the Abbey, known as Old Edinburgh or the Royal Mile. This is now a warren of characterful streets, passages and buildings. Immediately south of the castle there is a sheer drop to the valley and the area of Grassmarket and Greyfriars, less picturesque but historically worth exploring. The third main area of interest to the visitor is that to the north of Old Edinburgh, which starts with Princes Street.

Edinburgh is ranked as one of the finest capital cities in Europe, both for its unusual site and for the state of preservation of its best architecture. No other capital has a main street more attractive than Princes Street, open to the south side to views across gardens and trees along the floor of the valley to the steep ridge of the old town, culminating in the impressive 400-foot (122 m) Castle Rock.

Princes Street, with Waverley Railway Station at its east end, has most of the important shops, stores, hotels, banks, travel and tourist information offices, with wide roads leading onto it from George Street and Queen Street which run parallel to it along the ridge to its north. This is the area known as New Town, dating from the eighteenth and nineteenth centuries, a dignified residential and professional area with generous squares and crescents, and exceptionally wide streets.

Taking the three main areas one at a time, the most we can hope to do in this book is outline the most important places to be seen for the visitor passing through, or spending a day or two here. There is so much of historical and artistic merit that even devoting a fortnight to exploring it scarcely does it justice. For anyone planning to base their holiday here we advise you to make use of the central Tourist Office, at Waverley Station, and the Scottish Tourist Board.

Edinburgh's annual three-week Festival of Music and Drama takes place at the end of August and first half of September, when the city is invaded by thousands of spectators, avid to see as varied a programme of live performances as they can. The **Edinburgh Festival** is far from being a spontaneous affair, the entire programme now carefully planned and organised well in advance and it has become so popular since it started soon after the Second World War that you now need to book your accommodation, as well as tickets to shows, well ahead of the event. A film festival is also an integral part of the international festival. The official festival programme is accompanied by the ever-growing 'fringe', which encompasses a wide spectrum of the performing arts, in every available space in the city – schoolrooms, pubs, clubs, halls – are all taken over for the duration of the festival, and some performances start first thing in the morning. One of the recognised highlights of the Festival is the Military Tattoo at night on the Castle Esplanade in front of the floodlit castle. The Festival Office supplies details of all programmes, and will also help with reservations and places to stay.

Focussing now on the **Royal Mile**, or **Old Edinburgh**, the obvious starting point is the Castle. The buildings of the Castle seen today comprise a massive structure, whose smooth defensive walls grow straight up from the face of the precipitous cliff, high western edge of the great sloping volcanic rock on which Old Edinburgh was built. The approach is through an outer arched gateway from the Esplanade, the wide parade ground which is the scene of the ancient ceremony of Beating the Retreat, as well as the Military Tattoo during the Edinburgh Festival. The Esplanade has a number of memorials, mainly military, and statues of Robert the Bruce and William Wallace flanking the castle entrance. There is a great deal to see within the walls of the castle but one of the most delightful is the chapel, dedicated to St Margaret, Queen of Malcolm Canmore, who probably built the chapel in 1076, to be founded in her honour by her son David I, who founded so many momentous religious houses in the Lowlands during his reign. This is the oldest building in Edinburgh, though restored on several occasions. Queen Margaret died here in 1093 during a seige, and her body had to be secretly lowered down the cliff to be conveyed to Dunfermline across the River Forth for burial.

On the way to Crown Square in the Castle, you pass the impressive Scottish National War Memorial by Sir Robert Lorimer (1927). In the Crown Room, within the Old Palace you can see the Scottish Regalia, (including the crown, sword and sceptre) saved from Dunnottar Castle in 1652. In 1707, on the Union of the Parliaments, they were put in a chest and forgotten, only to be rediscovered at the instigation of Sir Walter Scott in 1818. On the south side of Crown Square is the Old Parliament Hall, now housing a collection of armour and weapons. Originally early fifteenth century, it was much rebuilt by James IV. There are dungeons below here. In Queen Mary's Apartments you can see the little room in which she gave birth to James VI (19 June, 1566) – note the initials of them both on the ceiling.

On the west and east of Castle Square is the important Scottish United Services Museum, opened 1931, covering the three armed services (the first such museum to be established in Britain). Mons Meg is the castle's fifteenth century cannon, removed to London in the eighteenth century but restored to Edinburgh on the insistence of Sir Walter Scott in 1829. Near Foog's Gate you can see the Regimental Museum of the Royal Scots, Britain's oldest infantry regiment.

Leaving the Castle, the walk down the Royal Mile is full of interest. The painter Allan Ramsay lived in Ramsay Lodge (1740), and the Witches' Well indicates where over 300 witches were burned between 1480 and 1722. One of the first buildings at the top of Castle Wynd steps is Cannonball House (1630) directly connected with the castle, as the cannon ball embedded in its west gable wall below the central window is supposed to have been fired from the castle, aimed at Holyroodhouse when the Young Pretender was briefly in residence there in 1745, but fortunately misfired, doing no damage, even at such close range.

On the opposite side of Castle Hill is Outlook Tower, which contains a camera obscura reflecting actual scenes of Edinburgh, explained by a guide (enabling you to make a sort of tour of the sites, without getting sore feet!). The church opposite is Tolbooth St John, where services are still conducted in Gaelic (also known as the Highland Church). Here Castle Hill becomes Lawnmarket, so-called as the place where lawn and linen sellers had their booths. Gladstone's Land (NTS) is an unusual building on the left, early seventeenth century with an outside staircase, and arcade at street level. (Inside you can see the original sixteenth century exterior wall with window, and well furnished rooms in seventeenth century style.) Note the restored shop booths on the street.

A short close a little beyond leads to Lady Stair's House, an early seventeenth century house, now a literary museum devoted to Scotland's great men, Robert Burns, Walter Scott and R.L. Stevenson. (Stevenson's inspiration for *Dr Jekyll and Mr Hyde* was Deacon Brodie, a cabinet maker and town councillor by day, and a thief by night, who used to live opposite Lady Stair's House at Brodie's Close. Deacon Brodie's Tavern along from this house is a good spot to take some refreshment.) Lady Stair was a society figure who died in 1731.

The Royal Mile here changes from Lawnmarket to High Street. After the crossroads, St Giles Cathedral dominates Parliament Square on the right. In Parliament House, on the south of the square you can see Parliament Hall, a superb Gothic chamber with a magnificent window (of James V's Court of Session, 1532) and open timber roof. Outside, the equestrian statue of Charles II is the only statue made in lead in Scotland.

On the east side of the square is the Mercat Cross on the site of the original city centre. St Giles Cathedral, or High Kirk of Edinburgh, has its original fifteenth century square tower supporting the distinctive Crown of St Giles, though it has lost many of its finer architectural features through constant alterations and restorations. At one time it was converted into four separate churches. There are many historic associations with the church as can be seen from the monuments and memorials to famous Scots that it contains, so allow time to study these. John Knox became minister here in 1559–72, and had discussions with Mary Queen of Scots during this period. His statue overlooks the site of his grave outside the south-west corner of the church. The Chapel of the Order of the Thistle in the south-east corner, built by Sir Robert Lorimer, opened in 1911, has elaborate canopies over the oak stalls, heraldic windows and a groined roof. Outside the west door of St Giles is a heart-shaped design in the cobbles, the Heart of Midlothian, marking the entrance to the Old Tolbooth (prison), famous for being stormed in 1736 in the Porteous Riots. Unfortunately this interesting building was demolished in 1817.

A little further down on the right is the Edinburgh Wax Museum, Scotland's challenge to Madame Tussaud's. Just past the Festival office, with tableaux of Scottish history, models including Mary Queen of Scots, the Young Pretender, Robert Burns and William Wallace, plus a chamber of horrors, including Burke and Hare, Deacon Brodie, and a fairytale section for children.

At the corner of South Bridge is the Tron Church, to this day the traditional gathering place for Hogmanay. A tron is a public weighing beam, one of which stood here for merchants' use (and if their weights were inaccurate, they were nailed to the beam by the ears!) Further down the High Street on this side is the intriguing Museum of Childhood, aimed at adults but equally popular with children, and the first of its kind anywhere, showing the composition of children's lives in former days. Opposite is John Knox House (and next door Moubray House, probably the oldest house in the City still in private occupation). Knox might never have lived here, but it is likely that he did, on the second floor, from 1561 until he died, 11 years later. Anyway, that he might have been its occupant saved the house from demolition long ago, and it is one of the most attractive old houses in Edinburgh, now containing a museum of Knox and his times.

Just below is the site of the main gate of the old walled city, Netherbow Port, through which the Young Pretender's Highlanders stormed at 2 in

Dean Village in Edinburgh, Lothian.

the morning, to take the city, when it was opened to allow a city deputation to pass, returning from a meeting with the Young Pretender. At this point the Royal Mile becomes Canongate. The fine sixteenth century Canongate Tolbooth (the building with the projecting clock) down on the left, has a permanent collection of tartans, as well as temporary exhibitions, forming part of the Huntly House Museum (the City Museum) on the other side of Canongate. The interior has good features (panelling, fireplaces, a painted ceiling) and the local history exhibits are well displayed through a series of pleasant rooms that have been both a single town house, and a group of dwellings. Next door is Acheson House (1633, restored in 1937), now the Scottish Craft Centre with a shop and craft exhibitions.

Canongate Church (1688) is beside the Tolbooth, and has the Canongate Mercat Cross in its churchyard. Adam Smith, the economist, is buried here. Behind the church you will find Dunbar's Close Garden, laid out as a typical seventeenth century Edinburgh garden. White Horse Close in the seventeenth century had a coaching station with the White Horse Inn, where stagecoaches departed for London. Now private houses, it has been beautifully reconstructed and succeeds in conveying the atmosphere of its time.

At the end of the Royal Mile stands the vast **Palace of Holyroodhouse**, the Royal residence of today. Holyrood Abbey, whose ruins lie behind the Palace, is the older building, founded by David I in 1128. Though it twice suffered damage by Hertford in the 1540s, the main cause of its ruination was the roof falling in after rebuilding work which proved too heavy for the structure, in 1768. Its history is rich with royal connections, for Kings were born, married and buried here. Mary Queen of Scots married Darnley here, and in 1633 Charles I was crowned here. The only fragment of the original twelfth century Abbey is a solitary Norman arch behind the royal vault. Most of the remains are thirteenth cetury.

The Palace of Holyroodhouse was started in 1500 by James IV, and additions were made by James V but it suffered severe damage at the hands of Hertford in 1544 and 1547. Mary Queen of Scots arrived in 1561 from France, and the six years she spent here are still those that stand out in the palace's long history. The seventeenth century enlargement to its present scale was during Charles II's reign, by the Duke of Lauderdale (who cheerfully demolished part of the Abbey Church to accommodate his extensions). In 1745, from 17 September to 31 October, the Young Pretender held his court here (under constant threat of canon fire from the Castle up the hill), but since James VI took his crown and his court south in 1603, no British monarch has been resident here for any length of time.

The interior can only be seen by guided tour, taking about three quarters of an hour. The Historical Apartments are perhaps the most interesting, in the sixteenth century tower, Mary's and Darnley's rooms connected by a private staircase in the wall. Of Mary's rooms, her little supper room is where, in 1566, Darnley burst in with accomplices, seized Riccio who was one of several dining with Mary, dragged him through the bedroom to the audience chamber, and left him dead, stabbed 56 times. The rest of the tour includes the picture gallery, 150 feet (46 m) in length, with 111 portraits of Scottish kings. They were all painted by Jacob de Wet, as a job-lot commissioned by the Government, in 1684–86. The State Apartments are those used to this day by the sovereign when in residence, and have some fine paintings, tapestries and seventeenth century ceilings. Holyrood Park is the natural moorland area on the south side of the Palace, with an 822-foot (251 m) hill, known as Arthur's Seat, commanding superb city views, three small lochs and Salisbury Crags.

From Old Edinburgh we now turn to **New Town**, already described as an area famous for its architecture, particularly Georgian, but which also contains some of the city's most important buildings. When work on the New Town began about 200 years ago, a great deal of debris had to be disposed of, so it was dumped in the valley between Princes Street and the Royal Mile, effectively forming a bank across it, known as the Mound with gardens now on either side of it. A road sweeps over, passing on the east side the National Gallery of Scotland, built in 1845–58 with an extension in 1978, and the Royal Scottish Academy, founded in 1826. The National Gallery has an enormous permanent exhibition of paintings and sculpture, drawings and prints, by many of the most important artists in the world. The large Scottish collection in the New Wing includes works by Henry Raeburn, Allan Ramsay and David Wilkie, and is altered from time to time. The main building contains the rest of the British and the European works, displayed in chronological order through a series of 23 rooms on the ground and first floors, ranking with the major galleries of the world, with masterpieces far too numerous to itemise here. The Royal Scottish Academy, for the promotion of the fine arts in Scotland, has annual and Festival exhibitions through the summer months. The gardens on either side of the Mound are East Gardens and West Gardens. In the East Gardens you will immediately notice the Scott Monument, with Sir Walter Scott and his dog standing below a 200-foot (61 m) spire, with various characters from his writings in the niches, erected in 1840.

Just east of here the bridge crosses to Market Street, which runs parallel to the upper end of the Royal Mile and has several art galleries worth visiting. At no. 29 you will find the Fruit Market Gallery, (constantly changing exhibitions), with the New 57 Gallery, and the Printmakers Workshop Gallery, above it. The City Art Centre is in an important building (nos. 1–4 Market Street) by Findlay and Dunn (1899), note particularly the façades, and it houses an important art collection of over 3,000 pieces. In the West Gardens there are two churches, St John's with a 'Gothic revival' nave built by William Burn in 1817, and St Cuthbert's, founded in the seventh century but rebuilt in 1894 by Hippolyte Blanc, (tower dates from 1789). There are also memorials in these gardens to the Scottish American War (by R. Tait McKenzie of Philadelphia) and to the Royal Scots Greys. The colourful Floral Clock is an unusual feature in the north-east corner by Princes Street, where a cuckoo announces every quarter hour, amidst imaginative designs of flowering plants. There is an open-air theatre in the gardens, too, the Ross Theatre, which is a summer attraction.

Princes Street runs along both gardens, becoming Waterloo Place at North Bridge, near Waverley Station and continuing round the south edge of Calton Hill. The Post Office in Waterloo Place houses the British Philatelic Bureau with stamp exhibits and a collectors' service, and opposite is the Scottish Record Office, Register House, in a fine building designed mainly by Robert Adam. Calton Hill (350 feet/107 m) is unmistakable, with its unfinished Parthenon building (in honour of the victims of the Napoleonic wars but abandoned through lack of money), its Nelson Monument (108 feet/33 m) and old Observatory buildings. None of these are of special interest or beauty in themselves, but the high setting gives another angle on Edinburgh. You can walk up the steps from the Waterloo Place and Regent Road corner, or drive up. Further along Regent Road you will see the Royal High School, where such names as Robert Adam, Alexander Graham Bell, James Boswell and Walter Scott are listed among the former pupils. Along a bit further is the 1830 Burns Monument by Thomas Hamilton, and a path leads down to Tolbooth Wynd and the lower end of the Royal Mile.

Hanover Street crosses both George Street and Queen Street, and becomes Dundas Street, and at no. 13A you will find the New Town Conservation Centre with a library, exhibition, and guided walks. For a comprehensive appreciation of the area, start here; but to take in the most impressive aspects of the quarter on your own, go to Charlotte Square with its unsurpassed north side frontage designed by Robert Adam (who died before it was completed). Nos. 5–7 belong to the NTS, with no. 5 as its Headquarters, no. 6 as the official residence of the Secretary of State for Scotland, and no. 7, Georgian House, fully furnished in the manner of a wealthy Georgian home. The Scottish Arts Council gallery is at no. 19, on the west side of the square, with West Register House in the former St George's Church (1810–14), which holds the more recent documents of the Scottish Record Office, and has a permanent historical exhibition. On the south side, no. 19 is where Alexander Graham Bell, inventor of the telephone, was born (1847–1922).

West of Charlotte Square is Randolph Crescent, where streets lead off to St Mary's Cathedral, built in 1874–1917 by Sir Gilbert Scott (one of the largest post-Reformation Gothic churches), and to Easter Coates House, an elegant early seventeenth century country house now used as a Music School. From Randolph Crescent, Queensferry Street leads over the Water of Leith (100 feet/30 m below) to picturesque Dean Village, an ancient grain milling centre, by way of Dean Bridge, built by Telford in 1832. Ann Street, north-east of here, leading out of Dean Terrace along the river, is also very attractive.

On Queen Street, at the east end, is the National Museum of Antiquities, with the Scottish National Portrait Gallery in the same building. The Museum includes all sorts of objects at one time used in Scotland, from ancient to modern times, from simple domestic utensils to bronze-age gold and medieval silver, brought together here from throughout the country and its islands, making an extremely valuable and interesting collection. The Portrait Gallery is a historical record of Scotland through the medium of portraits of its most significant figures, many painted by world-celebrated artists.

Also in Queen Street, no. 9 is the Royal College of Physicians (1845), by Thomas Hamilton, and no. 8 by Robert Adam. 32 York Place is where Sir Henry Raeburn lived and worked, and in the Church of St Paul and St George here, Walter Scott's pew is preserved. York Place becomes Picardy Place, where Sir Arthur Conan Doyle (of Sherlock

Holmes fame) was born, and Picardy Place leads into Leith Walk, off which are two museums, the Braidwood and Rushbrook Fire Museum, and the Transport Museum, the first concerned with old uniforms, equipment and engines from the 1920s onwards, and the second with full-scale and model exhibitions of Edinburgh's varied transport over the years. George Street forms a broad band along the top of the ridge, with many dignified eighteenth and nineteenth century buildings (including the Music Hall, 1784–87, by J. Henderson and William Burn). Sir Walter Scott lived at no. 107 for a while, and there are statues of George IV and William Pitt in the street (by Chantrey).

The area to the south-east of the Castle around **Grassmarket and Greyfriars** has a number of interesting features, if lacking the splendour of New Town and the quaint charm of Royal Mile. Grassmarket is a long broad stretch at the east end of which is the site of the old gallows where a Cross now stands. It was to here, in 1736, that Captain Porteous, city guard commander, was dragged from the old Tolbooth by the people and hanged when he was reprieved from the charge of murder (for having ordered his men to fire on a potentially unruly mob, so causing the deaths of several innocent people). On the north side of Grassmarket is an old inn favoured by William Wordsworth as well as Robert Burns, the White Hart. Another historical connection is with the murderers Burke and Hare, who had their den just off here, and who were found guilty of murdering 18 people from 1827–28, the motive being money as they sold the bodies for medical research. In West Bow you will find the well-known experimental theatre, the Traverse Theatre Club, in an eighteenth century building. Another theatre, the Royal Lyceum in Grindlay Street west of here, is a Victorian theatre that has recently been well-renovated.

Cowgate heads towards the Palace of Holyroodhouse, parallel to Canongate in the Royal Mile, with Magdalen Chapel, founded in 1547, near its west end. This was once also a charity home for pensioners, and it has an original stained glass window well worth seeing. Further along, St Cecilia's Hall, built by Robert Mylne as a concert hall in 1762, now houses an unusual collection of early keyboard instruments. Greyfriars Church is south of here, on the site of a Franciscan friary, and dates from 1612 though considerably restructured since then. This is where, in 1638, the National Covenant was signed (in blood in some instances) giving it great significance in religious history. In the churchyard there are a variety of elaborate tombs. Opposite Greyfriars is a statue of a little Skye terrier called Bobby, or Greyfriars Bobby, commemorated thus for his loyalty to his master whose grave he guarded stoically for 14 years, from his master's death in 1848. (He was granted a special licence collar by the city provost in order not to be mistaken for a stray.)

Just south-west is Lauriston Place and the impressive seventeenth century George Heriot School. Heriot was a jeweller and banker to James VI (in Scott's novel *Fortunes of Nigel*, the Jingling Geordie is based on him), and he endowed the school before his death in 1624. Heriot-

Watt University is on the left up Chambers Street heading north-east from Greyfriars, and Edinburgh Univesity is on the right further along, after the Royal Scottish Museum, which has one of the most varied collections imaginable, covering art, archaeology, natural history and technology. The 'Old College' is a William Adam building (1789) that W.H. Playfair completed in 1834, with a splendid pillared portico, and a dome that was added in 1884, surmounted by a Youth (by Hutchison). It was very near here that Darnley met his death in 1567 when Kirk o'Field, where he was staying, was blown up, and he was found in the garden, showing signs of strangulation. The Talbot Rice Arts Centre is a gallery with permanent and changing exhibitions, part of the University. The New University Buildings were designed by Rowland Anderson in 1884, and there are more buildings of the university in George Square, a little to the south.

On George IV Bridge (road) you will find the National Library of Scotland on the right heading towards the city centre. Founded in 1682 it is one of the largest libraries in Britain, with a unique collection of books and papers, amongst which you can see Mary Queen of Scots last letter (written the night before she was beheaded), and the original order for the Glen Coe Massacre. There are also letters and papers of Burns, Boswell, Carlyle, Scott, Hume and Stevenson.

Further from the centre, the Royal Botanic Garden, north of the Water of Leith, has a famous rock garden and various plant houses in the grounds of a small eighteenth century mansion, Inverleith House. This has been the temporary home of the National Gallery of Modern Art before moving to new premises on Belford Road. The gallery contains the work of many celebrated twentieth century artists, including Picasso, Braque, Kokoschka, Matisse, Giacometti, and sculptures by Moore, Hepworth, Epstein and Butler.

To the east of the city centre the Meadowbank Sports Centre was opened in 1970 to hold the Commonwealth Games that year, offering facilities for over 30 different sporting activities. (Visitors can apply to the Centre for temporary membership.)

Finally, before you leave Edinburgh, if you want to treat yourself to a delicious meal in a lovely seventeenth century house set in fine parkland, Prestonfield House is only 10 minutes by car from the centre. Since it was built by William Bruce in 1687, the house has been graced by such as the Young Pretender, James Boswell, Samuel Johnson and Benjamin Franklin. The food these days is the very best of Scottish combined with superb French cuisine, accompanied by fine wines, but it is perhaps the atmosphere, and the setting, which will live in your memory. Also a hotel, there are a very limited number of rooms, all delightfully furnished. Prices are not exorbitant.

Access to Sites and Places of Interest

Aberlady
Myreton Motor Museum
Easter–Oct. 1000–1800 daily; Nov.–Easter
Sat. & Sun. only.
Fee.

Cairnpapple Hill
Apr.–Sep. standard; Oct.–Mar. apply:
Custodian, Torphichen Preceptory.

Castlelaw
Apply Crosshouse Farm.

Craigmillar Castle
Standard.

Dalkeith
Arts Centre
1000–1230, 1400–1630, 1800–1930 Mon. &
Thur., 1000–1230, 1400–1630 Wed. & Fri.,
1000–1230 Sat.

Palace Park
Easter–Oct. 1100–1800.
Fee.

Dirleton Castle
Standard

East Fortune
Museum of Flight
July & Aug. 1000–1600.
Fee.

Edinburgh
Acheson House
1000–1700 Mon.–Sat.

Braidwood & Rushbrook Fire Museum
By arrangement.
(031 229 7222)

Castle
May–Oct. 0930–1800 Mon.–Sat., 1100–
1800 Sun.; Nov.–Apr. 0930–1715 Mon.–
Sat., 1230–1630 Sun. No adm. from 45 min.
before closing time.
Fee for Historic Apartments and Scottish
Services Museum.

City Art Centre
For opening times inquire at Tourist
Information.

City Museum (Huntly House,
Canongate Tolbooth)
1000–1800 Mon.–Sat. (to 1700 Oct.–May);
also 1400–1700 Sun., during Festival.

Fruit Market Gallery
1000–1730 Mon.–Sat.

Georgian House
Mid Apr.–mid Oct. 1000–1700 Mon.–Sat.,
1400–1700 Sun.; late Oct.–Jan. 1000–1630
Sat., 1400–1630 Sun.
Fee.

Gladstone's Land
For times inquire at Tourist Information.

Holyrood Palace & Abbey
May–Oct. 0930–1800 Mon.–Sat., 1100–
1800 Sun.; Nov.–Apr. 0930–1715 Mon.–
Sat., 1230–1630 Sun. No adm. from 45 min.
before closing time. Palace may be closed
for Royal or State visits.
Fee.

John Knox House
1000–1700 Mon.–Sat.
Fee

Lady Stair's House
1000–1800 Mon.–Sat. (to 1700 Oct.–May);
also 1400–1700 Sun. during Festival.

Magdalen Chapel
1000–1600 Mon.–Fri.

Museum of Childhood
1000–1800 Mon.–Sat. (to 1700 Oct.–May);
also 1400–1700 Sun. during Festival.
Fee.

National Library of Scotland
Reading Room: 0930–2030 Mon.–Fri.,
0930–1300 Sat.
Exhibition: 0930–1700 Mon.–Fri., 0930–
1300 Sat.

National Gallery
1000–1700 Mon.–Sat. (to later during
Festival), 1400–1700 Sun.

National Gallery of Modern Art
1000–1800 Mon.–Sat. (or in winter to one
hour before sunset), 1400–1800 Sun. (but
in winter 1300–1600 or one hour before
sunset).
Parking in Arboretum Road.

National Museum of Antiquities
1000–1700 Mon.–Sat. (to 1800 during
Festival), 1400–1700 Sun. (1100–1800
during Festival)

National Portrait Gallery
1000–1700 Mon.–Sat. (to later during Festival), 1400–1700 Sun.

Nelson Monument
1000–1800 Mon.–Sat. (to 1500 Oct.–Mar.). Fee.

New 57 Gallery
1030–1730 Mon.–Sat.

New Town Conservation Centre
0900–1700 Mon.–Fri.

Outlook Tower
0930–1800 daily.
Fee.

Parliament Hall
1000–1630 Mon.–Fri.

Philatelic Bureau
0900–1630 Mon.–Thur., 0900–1600 Fri., 0900–1230 Sat.

Printmakers Workshop Gallery
1000–1730 Mon.–Sat.

Register House (Exhibition)
1000–1600 Mon.–Fri.

Royal Botanic Garden
0900–dusk daily (1100, but 1000 during Festival, Sun.). Plant houses open at 1000 (1100 Sun.).

Royal Scottish Academy
1000–2100 Mon.–Sat., 1400–1700 Sun. Only open during exhibitions.
Fee.

Royal Scottish Museum
1000–1700 Mon.–Sat., 1400–1700 Sun.

Scott Monument
0900–1800 Mon.–Fri. (to 1500 Oct.–Mar.). Fee.

Scottish Arts Council
1000–1800 Mon.–Sat., 1400–1800 Sun. Occasional fee.

St Cecilia's Hall
1400–1700 Sat.
Fee.

St Giles Cathedral
1000–1700 Mon.–Sat.
Fee for Thistle Chapel.

Talbot Rice Arts Centre
1000–1700 Mon.–Sat.

Transport Museum
1000–1700 Mon.–Fri.

Wax Museum
1000–1900 (to 1700 Oct.–Mar.).
Fee.

West Register House
1000–1630 Mon.–Fri.

Zoo
0900–1900 daily (to 1700 Oct.–Mar.).
Fee.

Haddington Museum
1000–1900 Mon., Tue., Thur., Fri., 1000–1200 Wed., 1000–1600 Sat.

Hailes Castle
Standard.

Hamilton House
By arrangement.
(Prestonpans 811035)

Inveresk Lodge Garden
1000–1630 Mon., Wed., Fri., 1400–1700 Sun., when house is occupied.
Fee.

Lauriston Castle
Apr.–Oct. 1100–1300, 1400–1700 daily (except Fri.); Nov.–Mar. 1400–1600 Sat. & Sun.
Fee.

Lennoxlove House
Parties only, by prior arrangement.
(Haddington 3720)
Fee.

Luffness Castle
By arrangement.
(Aberlady 218)

Malleny House Gardens
May–Sep. 1000–dusk daily.
Fee.

Musselburgh
Pinkie House
Only during Loretto School term time. 1400–1600 Tue.

North Berwick Museum
June–Sep. 1000–1300, 1400–1700 Mon.–Sat., 1400–1700 Sun.

Preston Mill
Apr.–Sep. 1000–1230, 1400–1930 Mon.–
Sat., 1400–1930 Sun.; Oct.–Mar. as above,
but closes 1630.
Fee.

Prestongrange Mining Museum
0830–1600 Mon.–Fri., 1030–1530 Sun.,
Sat. by arrangement.
(031 661 2718)

Roslin Chapel
Easter–Oct. 1000–1300, 1400–1700 Mon.–
Sat.
Fee.

Seton Collegiate Church
Standard.

Suntrap (NTS)
Garden: 0900–dusk daily.
Advice Centre: 0900–1700 Mon.–Fri. (Also
Mar.–Oct. 1430–1700 Sat. & Sun.)
Fee.

Tantallon Castle
Standard.

Torpichen Preceptory
Standard.

Tyninghame House Gardens
May–Sep. 1400–1630 Mon.–Fri.
Fee.

Winton House
Parties only, or individuals with special
interest, by appointment.
(Pencaitland 340222)
Fee.

Hotels and Guest Houses

Bathgate
Bridge Castle Hotel.
(Armadale 30228)

Currie
Glenburn Hotel,
Blinkbonny.
(031 449 3236)

Dalkeith
Buccleuch Hotel,
20 Buccleuch Street.
(031 663 4725)

Edinburgh
Abercraig Hotel,
2 Picardy Place EH1 3JT.
(031 556 6257)

Allison Hotel,
17 Mayfield Gardens EH9 2AX.
(031 667 8049)

Avon Hotel
1–2 Spence Street EH16 5AG.
(031 667 8681)

Braid Hills Hotel,
134 Braid Road EH10 6JD.
(031 447 8888)

Clans Hotel,
4 Magdala Crescent EH12 5BE.
(031 337 6301)

Colroy Hotel,
7 Hopetoun Crescent EH7 4AY.
(031 556 6469)

Dean Hotel,
10 Clarendon Crescent EH4 1PT.
(031 332 0308)

Edward Hotel,
58 Great King Street EH3 6QY.
(031 556 1154)

Fox Covert Hotel,
187 Clermiston Road EH12 6UG.
(031 334 3391)

Glenorchy Hotel,
22 Glenorchy Terrace EH9 2DH.
(031 667 5708)

Gordon Hotel,
7–9 Royal Circus EH3 6TL.
(031 225 3000)

Hanover House Hotel,
26 Windsor Street EH7 5JR.
(031 556 1325)

Kildonan Lodge Hotel,
27 Craigmillar Park EH16 5PE.
(031 667 2793)

Ladbroke Dragonara Hotel,
Belford Road.
(031 332 2545)

Malcolm Hotel,
2 West Coates EH12 5JQ.
(031 337 2173)

Myrim Hotel,
1 Royal Circus EH3 6TL.
(031 225 5332)

Old Waverley Hotel,
43 Princes Street EH2 2BY.
(031 556 4648)

Prestonfield House Hotel,
Priestfield Road.
(031 667 8000)

Rothesay Hotel,
8 Rothesay Place EH3 7SL.
(031 225 4125/6)

Salisbury Hotel,
45 Salisbury Road EH16 5AA.
(031 667 1264)

Suffolk Hall Hotel,
10 Craigmillar Park EH16 5NE.
(031 667 4810)

West End Hotel,
35 Palmerston Place EH12 5AU.
(031 225 3656)

Guest Houses (Edinburgh)
Abileen Guest House,
46 Minto Street EH9 2BR.
(031 667 8995)

Amaragua Guest House,
10 Kilmaurs Terrace EH16 5DR.
(031 667 6775)

Ashdene Guest House,
23 Fountainhall Road EH9 2LN.
(031 667 6026)

Awhirk Guest House,
15 Mayfield Road EH9 2NG.
(031 667 7691)

The Beaumont Guest House,
113 Willowbrae Road EH8 7HN.
(031 661 3823)

Brucefield Guest House,
8 Park Road EH6 4LF.
(031 552 3846)

Clarin Guest House,
4 East Mayfield Street EH9 1SD.
(031 667 2433)

Dargil Guest House,
16 Mayfield Gardens EH9 2BZ.
(031 667 6177)

Gil Dun Guest House,
9 Spence Street EH16 5AG.
(031 667 1368)

Granville Guest House,
13 Granville Terrace EH10 4PQ.
(031 229 1676)

International Guest House,
37 Mayfield Gardens EH9 2BX.
(031 667 2511/9833)

Kiloran Guest House,
17 Leamington Terrace EH10 4JP.
(031 229 1789)

Kinneil Guest House,
1 Bonnington Terrace EH6 4BP.
(031 554 4107)

Lindsay Guest House,
108 Polwarth Terrace EH11 1NN.
(031 337 1580)

Meriden Guest House,
1 Hermitage Terrace EH10 4RP.
(031 447 5476)

The Park Lodge Guest House,
13–15 Abercorn Terrace EH15 2DE.
(031 669 9325)

Ravensneuk Guest House,
11 Blacket Avenue EH9 1RR.
(031 667 5347)

Rosebank Guest House,
5 Upper GIlmore Place EH3 9NL.
(031 229 4669)

Rowand Guest House,
7 Hermitage Terrace EH10 4RP.
(031 447 4089)

Southside Guest House,
8 Newington Road EH9 1QS.
(031 667 5650)

Tania Guest House,
19 Minto Street EH9 1RQ.
(031 667 4144)

Villa San Monique Guest House,
4 Wilton Road EH16 5NY.
(031 667 1403)

Gorebridge
Middleton Hall Conference Centre.
(Gorebridge 20661)

Haddington
Browns Hotel,
1 West Road.
(Haddington 2254)

Linlithgow
St Michael's Hotel,
High Street.
(Linlithgow 2217)

North Berwick
Brentwood Private Hotel,
Clifford Road EH39 4PP.
(North Berwick 2783)

Nether Abbey Hotel,
Dirleton Avenue.
(North Berwick 2802)

Bayview Guest House,
22 Melbourne Road.
(North Berwick 2859)

South Queensferry
Forth Bridges Lodge EH30 9SF.
(031 331 1199)

Hawes Inn.
(031 331 1990)

Accommodation for the Young

Edinburgh
Allison House Hotel,
15/17 Mayfield Gardens.
(031 667 8049)

Arden Hotel,
18–20 Royal Terrace.
(031 556 8688)

Bonaly Camping & Training Centre,
Colinton.
(031 441 1878)

Bruntsfield Youth Hostel,
7 Bruntsfield Crescent EH10 4EZ.

Heriot-Watt University,
Leonard Horner Hall,
19 Great King Street.
(031 449 5111)

Pollock Halls,
18 Holyrood Park Road EH16 5AY.
(031 667 1971)

The Trefoil Holiday & Adventure Centre
for the Handicapped,
The Trefoil Centre,

Gogarbank EH12 9DA.
(031 339 3148)

YWCA New Town Residence,
2 Randolph Crescent.
(031 226 3842)

YMCA,
14 South St Andrew Street EH2 2AX.
(031 556 4303)

YWCA,
Frances Kinnaird Hostel,
14 Coates Crescent EH3 7AG.
(031 225 3608)

Camping and Caravanning

Dalkeith
Fordell Caravan & Camping Site,
Lauder Road.
(031 663 2451)

Edinburgh
Little France Caravan Site,
219 Old Dalkeith Road.
(031 664 4742)

Muirhouse Camping Site,
City of Edinburgh Dist. Council,
27 York Place.
(031 225 2424 Ext. 6311)

Haddington
Monksmuir Caravan Site.
(East Linton 340)

Linlithgow
Binns Caravan Club Site,
Queensferry Road.
(Philipstoun 772)

North Berwick
Gilsland Caravan Site.

Rhodes Caravan Site,
Lime Grove.

Self Catering

Aberlady
Mr Binnie,
Kilspindie House Hotel,
Aberlady.
(Aberlady 319)

Dunbar
Mrs Hall,
Bourhouse,
Dunbar.
(Dunbar 62293)

W.H. Henderson,
Pleasants,
Dunbar EH42 1RE.
(Dunbar 63737)

Edinburgh
Baronscourt Guest House,
7 Milton Road East,
Edinburgh EH15 2ND
(031 669 6900)

Mrs Connie Bedford,
Schiehallion,
64 Maidenhead Road,
Stratford-upon-Avon,
Warwickshire CV37 6XU.
(Stratford-upon-Avon 293710)

Mrs Bothwell,
19 Cammo Road,
Edinburgh EH4 8EF.
(031 339 6101)

Mrs Cox,
26 Minto Street,
Edinburgh EH9 1SB.
(031 667 0880)

Mrs S. Cruickshank,
7 Hillpark Terrace,
Wormit-on-Tay,
Fife.
(Newport-on-Tay 794)

Grays Apartments,
5/7 Abercorn Terrace,
Edinburgh EH15 2DD.
(031 669 1044)

Mrs Hayward,
Wards End Farm,
Moss Lane,
Glazebury,
Warrington,
Cheshire WA3 5PH.
(Warrington 4087 *or* 031 441 3295)

Keyplan Service Flats,
21–31 Causewayside,
Edinburgh EH9 1QR.
(031 667 7500)

Mrs D. Martin,
Park Lodge,
13/15 Abercorn Terrace,
Portobello,
Edinburgh EH15 2DT.
(031 669 9325)

National Trust for Scotland,
5 Charlotte Square,
Edinburgh EH2 4DU.
(031 226 5922)

Mrs C.J. Raven,
30 Great King Street,
Edinburgh EH3 6QH.
(031 556 2912)

E.G. Riley,
Teviotdale Guest House,
53 Grange Loan,
Edinburgh EH9 2ER.
(031 667 4376)

Mr and Mrs F. Westbury,
116 Braid Road,
Edinburgh EH10 6AS.
(031 447 3695)

Mrs Sheila Wood,
24 Shandon Street,
Edinburgh EH10 1QH.
(031 337 5487)

Gifford
Mrs Jackson,
Newlands Farm,
Gifford.
(Gifford 259)

Gullane
Mrs Milligan,
Lawhead,
East Linton.
(East Linton 277)

Heriot
Mrs M. Clamp,
Borthwick Hall,
Heriot
(Heriot 206)

Scottish Country Cottages,
20 Churchill Way,
Bishopbriggs,
Glasgow G64 2RH.
(041 772 5920)

Golf

Bathgate
Bathgate Golf Course,
Edinburgh Road,
(Bathgate 52232; booking: 630505)

Bo'ness
The West Lothian Golf Club,
Airngath Hill.
(Bo'ness 2330)

Edinburgh
Baberton Golf Course.
(031 441 1061 club house;
031 441 2511 secretary)

Braid Hill Golf Courses,
Braid Hills Approach.
(031 447 6666)

The Bruntsfield Links Golfing Society.
(031 336 2006)

Craigmillar Park Golf Club,
1 Observatory Road.
(031 667 0047)

Kingsknowe Golf Course,
326 Lanark Road.
(031 441 1144)

Prestonfield Golf Club (Private),
6 Priestfield Road North.
(031 667 1273; bookings: 031 667 8597)

Ratho Park Golf Club,
Ratho New Bridge.
(031 333 1752)

Silverknowes Golf Course.
(031 336 3843)

Sea Angling

Dunbar
Cod, haddock, flounder, mackerel.
(Further information: Tourist Information
Centre, Dunbar.)

Edinburgh
Cramond, Seafield and Portobello areas.
Flatfish, cod, mackerel.
(Further information: 031 661 5546)

North Berwick
Cod, haddock, mackerel.
Boats: Mr F. Marr,
Victoria Road.

Game Fishing

Bonaly Reservoir
Brown and rainbow trout.

Clubbied, Crosswood and Fruid Reservoirs
Brown trout.

Crosswood Reservoir
Brown trout.

Permits for above: Lothian Regional
Council,
Comiston Springs,
55 Buckstone Terrace,
Edinburgh EH10 6XH.
(031 445 4141)

Hopes Reservoir
Brown trout.
Permits: Lothian Regional Council,
Dept. of Water Supply,
Haddington.
(Haddington 2109)

Where to Eat

Dunbar
Bayswell Hotel,
Bayswell Park.
(Dunbar 6225)

Edinburgh
Albany Hotel,
Maridors Restaurant.
(031 556 0397/8)

Cramond Inn,
Cramond Village.
(031 336 2035)

The Howtowdie,
27A Stafford Street.
(031 225 6291)

Prestonfield House Hotel,
Priestfield Road.
(031 667 8055)

Rules Restaurant,
19–21 Dundas Street.
(031 556 1752)

Car Hire

Edinburgh
Alexanders of Edinburgh Ltd,
Self Drive Dept,
Semple Street.
(031 229 3337)

Avis Rent-a-Car Co Ltd,
100 Dalry Road.
(031 337 6363/4/5/6)

Belfords Car Hire,
40 Craigmount View.
(031 339 5314)

Budget Rent-a-Car,
Carlaw Baxter Ltd,
Comely Bank.
(031 332 5054)

Budget Rent-a-Car,
Craigmount Service Station,
136 Glasgow Road.
(031 334 2214/2375)

Capital Car Hire, (Edinburgh) Ltd,
26A Russell Road,
Roseburn.
(031 346 1110)

Peter Carnie & Son Ltd,
Windyvale Garage,
Meadow Place Road.
(031 334 1919/9206)

Peter Carnie Ltd,
Craighall Garage,
Craighall Road.
(031 552 5521)

Cascade Hire Drive,
17 Poplar Lane,
Leith.
(031 554 0461)

Charlie's Chauffeur Driven Cars,
High & Lowland Tours etc.,
28 Dean Park Avenue,
Balerno.
(031 449 4954)

Kenning Car Hire,
40/44 Duff Street.
(031 337 8145/4585)

Mitchell's Self Drive Cars,
32 Torphichen Street.
(031 229 5384)

Newington Chauffeur Drive,
8 Merchiston Mews.
(031 229 8666)

Ross Rent-a-Car,
4/40 Ratcliffe Terrace.
(031 667 6984)

Scothire Chauffeur Drive Ltd,
15 Station Road.
(031 334 9017)

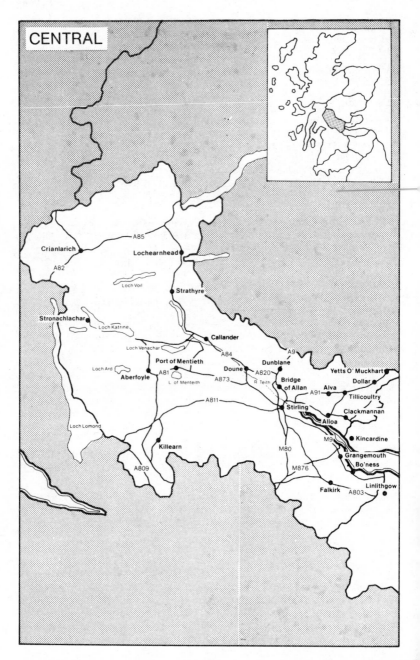

CENTRAL

Crianlarich
A82
A85
Lochearnhead
Loch Voil
Strathyre
Stronachlachar
Loch Katrine
Loch Venachar
Callander
A84
A9
Loch Ard
Port of Mentieth
A81
Doune
A820
Dunblane
Yetts O' Muckhart
Aberfoyle
L. of Mentieth
A873
R Teith
Bridge of Allan
Dollar
A91
Alva
Tillicoultry
A811
Stirling
Clackmannan
Alloa
Loch Lomond
Killearn
M80
M9
Kincardine
Grangemouth
A809
M876
Bo'ness
Linlithgow
Falkirk
A803

130

Central

Central Region is sandwiched between Strathclyde and Tayside, Loch Lomond running along its western boundary and the River Forth penetrating on its eastern boundary with the ancient and prominent town of Stirling at the head of the river. Most routes in Central radiate from Stirling, and we describe first the approach from the south-east travelling along the south bank of the Forth. The Forth bridges and South Queensferry are included in the Fife section, so this route will start just east of the Central boundary, with Hopetoun House.

I: Hopetoun – Linlithgow – Falkirk – Bannockburn

Both inside and out Hopetoun is an outstanding mansion in beautiful parkland which is stocked with rare four-horned black sheep (St Kilda) and a deer herd. One mile (2 km) north of the M9 it is superbly sited overlooking the Forth. Hopetoun House was built around 1700, but it was the work carried out between 1721 and 1854 by William Adam and his sons that has elevated it into a category of its own amongst the great Scottish mansions. The interior is mainly attributable to John and Robert Adam, and of special note are the yellow drawing room, the carved staircase and the ballroom. There is a fine collection of paintings (Titian, Rubens, Rembrandt, Canaletto, Van Dyck, and Gainsborough among many others), a museum and a roof terrace with views across the Forth. In the stable block is an enterprising exhibition called 'Horse and Man in Lowland Scotland', and a nature trail takes you around the grounds.

About two miles (3 km) west is the stark fifteenth century fortress of Blackness Castle jutting out onto the Forth, and on the same road leading off the A904 is the House of Binns, historic home of the Dalyells (of which family Thomas (or Tam) Dalyell is best known, 1599–1685, a royalist and general who raised the Scots Greys, now the Royal Scots Dragoon Guards, and is buried at Abercorn nearby). Built as a fortress in the fifteenth century, it was converted to a family residence in the seventeenth century, when the lovely Italian moulded ceilings were added (in preparation for a proposed visit by Charles I); the main fronts were altered in the early nineteenth century.

Linlithgow, on the A9 just south of the M9, is one of David I's royal burgh towns with a magnificent ruined fortified palace. The town has a number of historic houses and a fountain (1807) copied from an earlier one dating from James V. The Canal Museum describes the story of the Union Canal, opened in 1822. Linlithgow Palace was a royal residence at least from David I's reign though nothing of this survives. The oldest part to be seen now is the tower at the south-west angle that was built in 1302 by Edward I; architecturally the sixteenth century south and east sides of the quadrangle are the most interesting, dating from James V's reign around the time that his daughter, Mary Queen of Scots was born here (1542). His own parents, James IV and Queen Margaret were here when he was born in 1512, just a year before Flodden, and his father's death. Queen Margaret's Bower, an octagonal turret of the north-west tower, is traditionally where the queen awaited in vain the return of her husband after Flodden. The quadrangle is the nucleus of the palace, with the main apartments on the first floor. The elaborate fountain in the middle was James V's wedding present to his second French wife, Mary of Guise, on which occasion it is said to have issued not water but wine. The great hall along the east side is 94 feet (29 m) long with tall windows facing the inner court, and though now open to the elements many of these rooms are not badly ruined, with fireplaces and walls mainly intact. The royal apartments, on the west side, include the presence chamber with a peculiar horizontal window, the king's hall and bedchamber.

Beside the palace stands the largest pre-Reformation parish church in Scotland, the church of St Michael where Mary Queen of Scots is thought to have been baptised and where, just before Flodden her grandfather James IV saw an apparition that warned him against war with England (appearing to him in 'St Catherine's aisle', the south transept).

North of here, see Kinneil House, off the A904, and Bo'ness Museum in **Bo'ness** (short for Borrowstounness). Though the great shell of Kinneil has some fine sixteenth century wall paintings and decorated ceilings it is known better as the place where James Watt developed the steam engine (in an outhouse in the grounds) in 1765, sponsored by the owner of the Carron Ironworks who lived at Kinneil at that time. The Bo'ness Museum, in converted seventeenth century stables, has an interesting exhibition of local industrial history.

Grangemouth, just west of here, is Scotland's major petro-chemical centre, with extensive docks. For detailed explanations of the technology of the new oil industry, visit the BP Information Centre here, in the north-east of the town, which also has an audiovisual account of James Young, the nineteenth century pioneer of commercial oil nicknamed 'Paraffin' Young from his company Young's Paraffin Light and Mineral Oil Company. A 'Paraffin' Young Heritage Trail of 40 miles (64 km) begins from the BP centre here.

Smeaton's Forth-Clyde Canal (1768–90) was constructed approximately following the Roman Antonine Wall which led from Bo'ness to Old Kilpatrick on the Clyde. The wall was built 10 years later than Hadrian's Wall, and was a turf rampart on solid stone foundations, with a military road south of it, a ditch on the north side and forts about every two miles (3 km). The sculptures, inscription and measurement slabs, and other finds from the wall are now in Edinburgh and Glasgow

(National Museum of Antiquities, and Hunterian Museum, respectively).

Falkirk is now an industrial town, but is famous for two battles, first when Edward I defeated William Wallace in 1298, and second when the Young Pretender threw off pursuing Government troops in 1746 (before Culloden). The town has good access points to the Antonine Wall, and two good museums, Falkirk Museum with Roman finds from the wall, medieval pottery, Victoriana and industrial archaeology, and the Scottish Railway Preservation Society Depot in Wallace Street, which has railway workshops, historic locomotives and much more to delight the train enthusiast.

There are several more good Roman traces of the wall in the area, examples of which are visible at Watling Lodge (Camelon), at Callendar Park housing estate; at Seabegs Wood on the B816 there is also a stretch of rampart and military road. This last is two miles (3 km) west of Rough Castle which is the best preserved fortified site along the wall.

Approaching Stirling, two miles (3 km) to the south on the A80 is the NTS Bannockburn Memorial and Information Centre commemorating the historic battle, fought somewhere to the east of this site in 1314, between the Scots under Robert the Bruce and English under Edward II, when the English were defeated despite far superior numbers, and Scotland's independence was secured. The 'Forging of the Nation' is an audiovisual presentation here describing the events preceding the battle, and the tactics Bruce employed to win it. The heroic bronze equestrian statue of Bruce by Pilkington Jackson was erected in 1964 as the official memorial.

Roughly a mile (2 km) to the south-west is another famous battleground, Sauchieburn, where James III was defeated by rebel lords in 1488. Fleeing on horseback the king was thrown and knocked unconscious, then carried to a mill for shelter. In the guise of a priest offering him the last sacrament, one of his enemies was able to get close enough to stab him fatally. He was buried at Cambuskenneth Abbey a mile (2 km) east of Stirling, as was his queen, Margaret of Denmark. (Interesting to note that in 1864 their skeletons, in two coffins, were unearthed here, and on the instructions of Queen Victoria were re-interred at the site of the high altar beneath a memorial.) The Abbey was founded in 1140 by David I, and given to the Earl of Mar in 1604. He built Mar's Wark, his palace in Stirling, from the Abbey's stones thereby reducing it to a total ruin. The fourteenth century tower has two rooms (with a dug-out canoe, discovered in the Forth, and some worked stones).

II: Stirling – Dollar – Clackmannan

Stirling occupies an appropriately prominent position at the head of the Forth on a gradual hill, culminating in the dramatic Renaissance castle at 340 feet (104 m), around which the ground falls steeply away. There is much to describe in the town but its historical significance revolves inevitably around Stirling Castle, so it is up there that we begin, overlooking a vast panorama of central Scotland (especially fine from Queen Victoria's Look-out at the north-west corner of the ramparts. Note the little hole in the wall, traditionally made to enable Mary Queen of Scots to peep through when she was a small girl before leaving for France at the age of 5, where she stayed for the next 13 years). The view is also very good from the Esplanade, now mostly used as a car park, which is adorned with another heroic statue of Robert the Bruce. On the right as you approach the Esplanade, Landmark has a Visitor Centre (recently changed hands) which illustrates some 700 years of Stirling's history with an audiovisual presentation. This is well worth watching to enrich your appreciation of the castle. Most of the buildings date from the fifteenth and sixteenth centuries but there has been a castle on this site since much earlier times. Alexander I died here in 1124 and William the Lion in 1214. When it fell to the English in 1296, William Wallace retook it in 1297 following the Battle of Stirling Bridge. In 1304 it fell once more to the English after a fierce and furious seige under Edward I, the last place in Scotland to hold out against him. Bannockburn was the next milestone in 1314 after which Robert the Bruce dismantled the castle as was his custom. The Stewarts favoured Stirling as a royal residence. James II was born here (1430), as was James III (1451). James V came here for safety after Flodden (1513) and spent much time here later (often going out amongst the townsfolk in disguise, by the Sally-Port, still there, beneath the ramparts), his daughter, Mary, in her turn was crowned Queen of Scots here (aged 9 months) in 1542 in the Chapel Royal, and her son, James VI grew up here. The drum towers of the Gatehouse were built by James III, as well as the Prince's Tower (which served as schoolroom for James VI and his tutor George Buchanan). The Palace, on one side of the Upper Square (which also has Parliament Hall, the Chapel Royal and the King's Buildings), was completed by James V. There is a great deal to capture your interest here but with our limited space we can only recommend you to allow plenty of time to explore the great complex on your own.At the castle look out for the Argyll and Sutherland Highlanders Regimental Museum with many exhibits of military interest. (The Portcullis Hotel outside the castle holds the atmoshere of the castle, especially the dining room, and is a lot more comfortable to sleep in!)

In the town, buildings to look out for are the Municipal Buildings which show the town's history in stained glass (Corn Exchange Road), Smith Art Gallery and Museum, recently restored, in Albert Place, Cowane's Hospital (built 1639–49 by John Cowane) off St John Street nearing the castle, the beautiful Gothic Church of the Holy Rude just above the 'hospital', Mar's Wark (already mentioned with Cambuskenneth Abbey) beyond the church and never completed, Argyll's Lodging (now YHA) just opposite, and the Tolbooth (1701, by Sir William Bruce) in Broad Street which also has the Cross. (It was here that Archbishop Hamilton was tried and hanged all in one day for his part in the murder of Henry, Lord Darnley in 1571, the unpopular husband of Mary Queen of Scots.) The Macrobert Arts Centre Gallery is at the University of Stirling and has very varied and unusual changing exhibitions.

The Old Bridge, still used as a footbridge, was built around 1400, and was the only route to the north out of Stirling for James I and all successive monarchs till Charles I's reign. The bridge of the Battle of Stirling Bridge was a different, wooden bridge above this one. Between the Old Bridge and the castle the old Beheading Stone is on Gowan Hill.

The A91 heads out of Stirling towards Kinross and the M90, crossing from Central to Tayside at Yetts o' Muckhart. The first place of interest on this road is the restored sixteenth century Menstrie Castle, its main interest being in that Sir William Alexander, who became James VI's Lieutenant for the Plantation of Nova Scotia (commonly regarded as Founder of Nova Scotia), was born here in 1567. The solid castle sits squarely in Menstrie, and has a Nova Scotia Exhibition Room (NTS) displaying the coats of arms of over 100 Nova Scotian Baronets.

Just beyond is **Alva**, a small weaving town dominated to the north by Ben Cleuch which is the highest of the Ochil Hills, at 2,363 feet (721 m). Above **Tillicoultry** you can take the Mill Glen Nature Trail to enjoy the scenery better than from the road. **Dollar** is also under the lee of the Ochils and on a steep slope above, in Dollar Glen, sits Castle Campbell commanding long views over the plains of the Forth. Set in 600 acres (243 ha) of NTS woodland you can reach the castle by paths up through the Glen over foot bridges or by car within a quarter of a mile (½ km). Built towards the end of the fifteenth century it was burned by Cromwell in 1654 leaving it the ruin you see today, with an impressive ribbed barrel-vault roof (early 1600s) still intact on the third floor of the tower, whose first floor was the great hall. At one time the castle was known as 'Castle Gloom', since it is amidst the glens of 'Care' and 'Sorrow', by the waters of 'Grief' in the parish of 'Dolour' (Dollar), though history doesn't relate how these places earned their names!

Just east of the A91 beyond Dollar is Rumbling Bridge, where the River Devon falls through a ravine, spanned by three bridges, with the spectacular waterfalls of Devil's Mill and Caldron Linn.

At Yetts o' Muckhart the A823 crosses the A91 and follows Glen Devon up towards Glen Eagles (*see* Tayside, p. 157).

The A907 leaves Stirling on the north bank of the Forth, known here as Links of the Forth, a very fertile area through which the river twists and curves its way for 12½ miles (20 km) (only 5½ miles/9 km as the crow flies). At **Alloa** in the lower part of the town is Alloa Tower, once a Mar stronghold, where Mary Queen of Scots spent part of her infancy, as did both her son and her grandson. She came back as an adult in 1566 to visit the tower with Lord Darnley.

About a mile (2 km) east is **Clackmannan** which means Stone of Mannan and refers to the stone you can see mounted on a shaft in the town square, supposed to have been sacred to Mannan the pagan god. Also in the square is the seventeenth century Cross, and the Tolbooth, which was once 40-feet (12 m) longer incorporating a court, goal and goaler's lodge. The fourteenth century tower on the hill west of the town is Clackmannan Tower, the remains of a substantial residence.

A mile (2 km) east the A907 crosses the A977 which leads to Kincardine on the Forth at the north side of Kincardine Bridge, 1936, over half a mile (1 km) long.

III: Dunblane – Doune – Callander – Aberfoyle

The A9 heads north out of Stirling to Bridge of Allan, a couple of miles (3 km) up, passing the new University buildings, pleasantly landscaped into the Airthrey estate park which is open to the public.

North-west of Bridge of Allan, off the B824, Lecropt Church (with its Keir Loft, 1826) marks the entrance to Keir House where, during the time of Sir William Stirling Maxwell, 1818–78, Chopin was a guest in the year 1848. It is now noted for its gardens which are open to the public, with an unusal yew tree house, water garden and prolific flowering shrubs.

Further up the River Allan, in an attractive situation is **Dunblane**, about seven miles (11 km) from Stirling. Well known for its very beautiful Cathedral and Cathedral Close, with mostly seventeenth to nineteenth century houses, Dunblane was made a bishopric by David I, who founded the cathedral in the mid-twelfth century. After the Reformation the building fell into neglect, (the nave roof collapsed in the late sixteenth century) but the choir was still usable as parish church for 300 years. The nave's total restoration in 1893 was followed in 1914 by the restoration of the choir (by Lorimer), and the end result is an intriguing mix of period and style which is quite lovely. The Cathedral Museum is in Dean's House, one of the seventeenth century close houses (1624), and the Scottish Church House, with a partly underground chapel and comprising eighteenth century houses, is also in the Cathedral Close.

Sheriffmuir is several miles (4 km) east of Dunblane on the west slopes of the Ochil Hills, and is known as the 1715 battleground of the Earl of Mar (for the Old Pretender) and the Duke of Argyll, who was ultimately the victor.

Several miles (6 km) west of Dunblane is **Doune**, a pleasant town with three places of particular attraction, Doune Castle, Doune Motor Museum, and Doune Park Gardens. The castle is exceptional even amongst Scottish ruins, built impressively on a triangular site for natural protection (bordered by two rivers and a moat) with a lot of very nicely preserved medieval detail within. It was built by the Duke of Albany and his son in the late fourteenth and early fifteenth centuries, but handed over to the Crown after his death in 1419 and his son's execution in 1425, eventually conferred back onto the Earls of Moray (related to the Dukes of Albany), now bearing the title Lord Doune. There are so many good features to take in here that we recommend you buy the *Castle Guide*. You should try to allow an hour or so and notice the exterior (the gatehouse tower is nearly 100 feet/30 m tall) as much as the interior.

The Motor Museum is about a mile (2 km) north of Doune off the A84 and is the Earl of Moray's personal collection of vintage and post-vintage motor cars, mostly in running order. Half a mile (1 km) further away you will find the entrance to the 60-acre (24 ha) Doune Park Gardens laid out originally in the nineteenth century by the 10th Earl of Moray to provide a setting for his new home, Doune Park, finished in 1802. The gardens have a fine walled garden, a pinetum planted in the 1860s, beautiful woodland walks and the gardener's cottage with abundant flowering shrubs (late spring is best for these).

For another open air diversion locally, visit the Blair Drummond Safari Park (Scotland's Safari Park) two miles (3 km) south of Doune off the A84 where there is a very good wild animal collection and in summer boat trips are arranged around Chimp Island and the Hippo Pool.

Callander is some seven miles (11 km) west of Doune on the A84, and may seem immediately familiar to some television viewers, as it is where the series 'Dr Finlay's Casebook' was filmed. It is a bustling town, popular as a holiday centre being close to the Trossachs (*see* p. 137). Beyond Callander the narrow Pass of Leny has to accommodate the A84, the tumbling river and the old railway line, all of which manage to squeeze through to come out at the foot of Loch Lubnaig ('bent loch'). At the north end of the loch there is the Forestry Commission Centre of Strathyre with ample picnic area, and ask at the information office for advice on trails and walks from here. An imaginative display at the Centre illustrates a working forest and other aspects of Scottish forestry.

Off the A84 at King's House Hotel two miles (3 km) north of Strathyre, turn left for Balquhidder to visit Rob Roy's tomb, where lies Scotland's romanticised 'Robin Hood' figure, together with members of his family, in the churchyard beside the ruins of two churches. The existing church is mid-nineteenth century, the older ones thirteenth and seventeenth century, partly sharing the same site.

The A84 joins the A85 at Lochearnhead (*see* Tayside, p. 137), which continues north-west, then south-west over lonely and often desolate country. (For Killin *see* Tayside, p. 000.) Crianlarich is a railway junction for the Oban and Fort William lines from Glasgow, an isolated little village.

The turning south off the A84 at the Pass of Leny is the A821 that heads along the north shore of Loch Venachar into the Trossachs, a wild and wooded gorge leading to Loch Katrine from the beautiful overgrown little Loch Achray with mountains on either side.

The Trossachs represent an area known through the novels of Sir Walter Scott (*Rob Roy* and *The Lady of the Lake*) and of consequent interest to Scott's readers, but it is also of great natural beauty with its tangled tree-clad mountains and sparkling lochs. Loch Katrine is best enjoyed from the water, and the steamer *Sir Walter Scott* cruises to Stronachlachar up to four times daily in summer, though there is a road along the north shore. (The view from the Silver Strand is described in *The Lady of the Lake* and the island you see from here is named after that Lady Ellen's Isle, once used by the MacGregors as a secret store and cattle pen for their ill-gotten cattle herds.) There is a seven-mile (11 km) drive through Achray Forest (a part of the Queen Elizabeth Forest Park) revealing lovely scenery. David Marshall Lodge is a viewpoint and picnic area just north of Aberfoyle.

Aberfoyle, also featured in Scott's *Rob Roy*, is a rambling village on the A81, beside which is the Lake of Mentieth. On an island in the lake are the superbly situated ruins of Inchmahome Priory, founded in the thirteenth century by Walter Comyn, Earl of Mentieth. In 1547 Mary Queen of Scots was conveyed here, aged 5, for safe-keeping after the Scots' defeat at the Battle of Pinkie, before she embarked for her long stay in France from Dunbarton. Earlier, in 1362, David II was married at the thirteenth century church here, the choir and some arches still remaining. A ferry visits the island from near Port of Mentieth. There are two smaller islands, Inch Talla with the ruin of the Mentieth's castle, and Dog Island, at one time used for kennels.

Some 11 miles (18 km) southwards on the A81 from Aberfoyle is Killearn, a village situated about a mile (2 km) east of the road on the A875 and worth seeing only for the Obelisk commemorating George Buchanan (1502–82) tutor to James VI at Stirling Castle, and noted historian and humorist, who was born near here, at Moss.

Where the A81 meets the A875 you can visit the Glengoyne Distillery if you make arrangements beforehand.

West of the A809 near the Devil's Pulpit a path leads to the place from which Queen Victoria had her first sight of Loch Lomond in 1879.

Access to Sites and Places of Interest

Achray Forest Drive
Early Apr.–Sep. 1000–1900 daily.
Fee (50p coins required for machine).

The Binns
Easter–Sep. 1400–1730 daily except Fri.
Park is open 1000–1900.
Fee.

Blackness Castle
Standard.

Blair Drummond Safari Park
Mid Mar.–Oct. 1000–dusk daily.
Own car or safari bus.
Fee.

Bo'ness Museum
1000–1700 Mon.–Sat.

Cambuskenneth Abbey
Standard, but closed in winter.

Castle Campbell
Standard.

Doune
Castle, Motor Museum, Doune Park Gardens
(Apr.–Oct. 1000–1630 daily (June, July, Aug. to 1800). (Castle is closed Thur. in Apr. & Oct.)
Fee.

Dunblane
Cathedral
Standard, but closes 1700 on Sun. in summer.

Dean's House (Museum)
Mid May–Oct. 1030–1230, 1430–1600 Mon.–Sat.
Donation.

Falkirk
Museum
1000–1700 Mon.–Sat.

Museum and Scottish Railway
Preservation Society
1100–1700 Sat. & Sun.
Fee.

Grangemouth BP Information Centre
Apr.–Sep. 0900–1700 Mon.–Fri.

Hopetoun House
Easter, May–late Sep. 1100–1730 daily.
Fee.

Inchmahome Priory
Apr.–Sep. 0930–1900, Oct.–Mar. (weather
permitting ferry) 0930–1600.
Fee.

Keir Gardens
Apr.–Oct. 1400–1800 Tue.–Thur.
Fee.

Kinneil House
0930–1900 Mon.–Sat., 1400–1800 Sun.
Fee.

Linlithgow
Canal Museum
Mid Mar.–mid Sep. 1400–1700 Sat. & Sun.
Fee.

Palace
Standard.

David Marshall Lodge
Mid Mar.–mid Oct. 1100–1900 daily.

Menstrie Castle (Nova Scotia Exhibition)
May–Sep. 1430–1700 Wed., Sat., Sun.

Stirling
Castle
Apr., May, Sep. 0930–1815 Mon.–Sat.,
1100–1800 Sun.; June–Aug. 0930–2000
Mon.–Sat., 1300–1600 Sun.; Oct.–Mar.
0930–1600 Mon.–Sat., 1300–1600 Sun.
Fee.

Landmark
0900–1700 normally daily.
Fee.

Museum of the Argyll & Sutherland
Highlanders
Late Mar.–Sep. 1000–1800 Mon.–Sat.,
1200–1800 Sun.; Oct. 1000–1600 Mon.–
Fri.
Donation.

Smith Art Gallery & Museum
1400–1700 daily.

Hotels and Guest Houses

Alloa
Crown Hotel,
Bank Street FK10 1HP.
(Alloa 723871)

Bridge of Allan
Royal Hotel,
Henderson Street FK9 4HG.
(Bridge of Allan 832284)

Crianlarich
Crianlarich Hotel,
FK20 8RW.
(Crianlarich 272)

Dennyloanhead
The Crown Hotel.
(Bonnybridge 2453)

Glendevon
Tormaukin Hotel,
FK14 7JY.
(Glendevon 252)

Stirling
Golden Lion Hotel,
8 King Street FK8 1BD.
(Stirling 5351)

Station Hotel,
Murray Place FK8 2BX.
(Stirling 2017)

Neidpath Guest House,
24 Linden Avenue FK7 7PQ.
(Stirling 4840)

Strathblane
Country Club Hotel,
G63 9AH.
(Blanefield 70491)

Accommodation for the Young

Blanefield
Auchengillan Scout Camp,
Auchengillan Camping & Training Estate
G63 9AU.
(Blanefield 70256)

Dollar
Glendevon Youth Hostel,
Glendevon FK14 7JY.

Stirling
Loch Ard Youth Hostel,
Kinlochard FK8 3TL.

Stirling Youth Hostel,
Argyll Lodging,
Castle Wynd.

Camping and Caravanning

Auchenbowie
Auchenbowie Caravan Site.
Booking Enquiries: Robert Forsyth,
Easterton, Denny.
(Denny 822141/2)
Nearest town: Stirling.

Balmaha
Camping Club Site,
Millarochy Bay.
(Balmaha 236)
Booking Enquiries: Sites Dept.,
Camping Club of GB & Ireland,
11 Lower Grosvenor Place,
London.

Dollar
Riverside Caravan Park,
Dollar.
(Dollar 2896)

Stirling
Cornton Caravan & Camping Park,
Stirling.
(Stirling 4503/5504/62481)

Self Catering

Auchenbowie
R. Forsyth,
Easterton Service Station,
Glasgow Road,
Denny.
(Denny 822141/822142)

Stirling
Bell-Ingram,
Durn, Isla Road,
Perth PH2 7HF.
(Perth 21121)

Mrs S. MacKenzie,
48 Barnton Street,
Stirling FK8 1NA.
(Stirling 61031)

Vacation Letting Officer,
University of Stirling,
Administration Building,
Stirling FK9 4LA.
(Stirling 3171)

Golf

Alva
Alva Golf Club,
Beauclere Street.
(Further details on application)

Balmore
Balmore Golf Course,
Torrance.
(Balmore 240)

Bonnybridge
Bonnybridge Golf Club,
Larbert Road.
(Bonnybridge 2822)

Drymen
Buchanan Castle Golf Club.
(Drymen 369)

Stirling
Stirling Golf Course,
Queen's Road.
(Stirling 3801)

Game Fishing

Achray Loch
Trout.
Permits: Loch Achray Hotel,
The Trossachs by Callander FK17 8HZ.
(Trossachs 229)

Allan Water
Sea trout, brown trout, grilse.
Permits: D. Crockart & Son,
King Street, Stirling.

Allanbank Hotel,
Greenloaning,
Dunblane.
(Braco 205)

Banton Loch
Brown trout.
Permits: Kilsyth Fish Protection
Association,
S. Gillies, Secretary,
24 Kingston Flats,
Kilsyth.
or
P. Brown,
Colzium Sales & Service Station,
Stirling Road,
Kilsyth.
(Kilsyth 2003)

Forth River
Salmon, brown trout.
Permits: Messrs D. Crockart & Son,
15 King Street,
Stirling.
(Stirling 3443)

Loch Lomond
Salmon, trout.
Permits: Inversnaid Hotel,
Inversnaid.
(Inversnaid 223)

Teith River
(Blue Banks)
Salmon, trout.
Permits: D. Crockart & Son,
15 King Street,
Stirling.
(Stirling 3443)

Cycling

Stirling
Stewart Wilsons Cycles,
35 Baker Street.
(Stirling 5556)

Fife

I: Firth of Forth – Dunfermline – Kirkcaldy

Fife has, for hundreds of years, been known as the Kingdom of Fife, and is a self-contained touring district well worthy of a few days' diversion. It is one of the smaller Scottish counties (total area 505 square miles (130,795 ha) but it has 120 miles (193 km) of coastline, the variety of which is one of the county's great features: ancient but still active harbours and fishing villages, castles and ruins veiled in vivid history, long stretches of sandy beach and some of the best golfing in the world (*see* St Andrews, p. 147).

Access has been much simplified for the motorist by the opening of the Forth and Tay road bridges, though the Forth has had a railway bridge since 1890, at that time the longest cantilever bridge in the world. The road bridge, spanning the river less than a mile (1 km) west of the railway, was the longest suspension bridge in the United Kingdom when it was built (1964) which gave rise to the expression '. . . like painting the Forth road bridge'. The river traffic beneath includes heavy oil tankers from the North Sea oil fields that unload at the Grangemouth refineries further up the estuary, and dozens of small sailing boats. **South Queensferry** and North Queensferry were once busy ferryports but now have the dejected air of places whose purpose has gone. There is a museum at South Queensferry, Dalmeny House, which contains a collection of Rothschild antiques.

To the east the ever-widening estuary is dotted with islands, each with its own legends, romances or history. Inchgarvie, the closest inland, serves as a stepping stone for the railway bridge, though it once boasted a fortified castle, and has been used as a detention centre. The Isle of May, the furthest seaward and the largest of the group (about one mile by a quarter of a mile (1½ × ½ km) is now a National Nature Reserve and is a seabirds' paradise. Fulmars, kittiwake, guillemots, gannet, shag, eider-duck, tern, razorbills, puffins and many others have these islands largely to themelves, while the flora includes a wide variety of flowering plants and seaweeds. With their cliffs and caves, neolithic standing stones (Inchmickery), ruined chapels and monastery (Inchcolm), and vital lighthouses, these islands have served many purposes, from prisons, and quarantine stations for plague ships, to oysterbeds, and barracks in the Second World War.

There are also plenty of attractions inland, and towns like **Dunfermline**, no more than half an hour's drive from Edinburgh, are interesting on a number of counts. Dunfermline was once the capital of Scotland, and home of the Scottish kings after Malcolm III (1057–93)

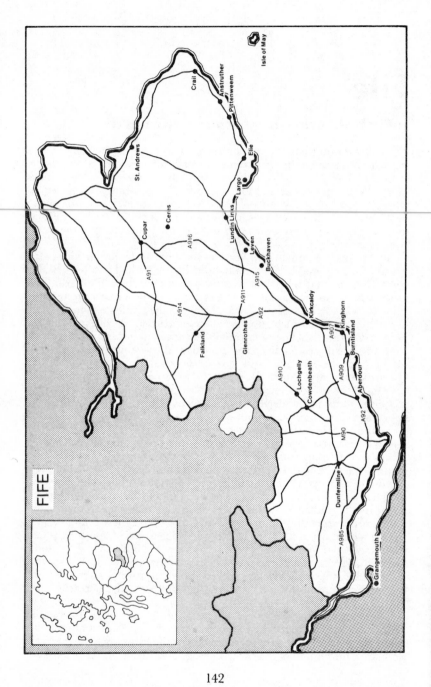

FIFE

Isle of May

Crail
Anstruther
Pittenweem
St. Andrews
Elie
Largo
Ceres
Lundin Links
Cupar
Leven
A916
Buckhaven
A91
A915
A914
A911
A92
Kirkcaldy
Glenrothes
Kinghorn
Falkland
A907
Burntisland
A910
A909
Aberdour
Lochgelly
Cowdenbeath
A92
M90
A985
Dunfermline
Grangemouth

and Queen Margaret built their palace here. This now lies in ruins beside Dunfermline Abbey, founded 900 years ago by the sainted Queen Margaret. Once a great Benedictine house, and imposingly situated above Pittencrieff Park, the Abbey contains numerous royal graves, including that of Robert the Bruce, who died of leprosy in 1327 and is now buried in the choir, marked by a modern brass. Across the street is the Abbey Tavern which is an unusual and picturesque pub, refreshingly unmodernised. The Dunfermline Museum, Viewfield, has exhibits of the linen and weaving industries that were founded in Dunfermline during the last century.

Pittencrieff Park, known as the Glen, represents one of many gifts bestowed on Dunfermline by Andrew Carnegie (1835–1919), well-known local philanthropist and self-made millionaire. Son of a weaver, he grew up humbly in Moodie Street, emigrated to Pennsylvania and made his fortune in iron and steel. The Moodie Street cottage is now a museum, and the Memorial Hall next door houses some interesting personal relics. Pittencrieff House, also bought by Carnegie, stands in the ornamental park and is now a gallery and museum. The Carnegie Central Library, Guildhall Street, was built in 1883, the first of nearly 3,000 libraries he donated all over the world. This one houses a collection of Burns relics. Beside the Glen gates at the end of the High Street, the townsfolk have erected an imposing statue of their great benefactor. The Glen itself has formal rose gardens, trees and steeply winding paths, lawns, an aviary, a menagerie of small animals, hot houses, tea rooms, a bandstand and the usual playground apparatus, which makes it a very pleasant place to while away a couple of hours with the family. First thing in the morning, when there are few people about, is our favourite time, followed by fresh baps and coffee in one of the High Street bakeries.

Some seven miles (11 km) west of Dunfermline off the A985 on Torry Bay in the Firth of Forth, is another place of historical, and architectural interest, the royal burgh of **Culross**, which is a perfect example of a restored medieval township. The small 'palace' was built around 1600 by Sir George Bruce who developed the seagoing trade in salt and coal here, and other important buildings to visit are the Study, the Town House (housing the Tourist Information Centre), the Ark and the Nunnery. Its dramatic setting, olde-worldliness, and flag-stoned streets make it a popular choice for period film sets. It is also the birthplace of St Mungo, patron saint of Glasgow, and the ruins of a chapel built in 1503 survive to denote the exact spot. For a good pub, go to the Dundonald Arms right in the heart of old Culross, which has a friendly and unspoilt atmosphere.

Following the A985 west along the firth for a quarter of a mile (½ km), nineteenth century Dunimarle Castle is south of the road and has some notable paintings and furniture. The road continues to **Kincardine**, known mainly for its bridge crossing the neck of the River Forth, just west of the Fife/Central regional boundary. Kincardine Bridge was built

The Study, Culross, Fife.

in 1936, is over half a mile (1 km) long and has a central swing-span of 100 yards (91 m).

Travelling up the east coast from the Forth, on the A92, the A915, the A921 and the A917, several of the small seaside towns are worth visiting before you reach the East Neuk (or 'corner') which begins at Lundin Links, near Largo (where Alexander Selkirk, better known as Robinson Crusoe, was born in 1676), and continues along the coast beyond Crail. Between the East Neuk and Aberdour there are roughly 20 miles (32 km) of sandy beaches punctuating the rugged coastline. Development of the 'best' beaches is evident around Aberdour, Burntisland, Kinghorn, Kirkcaldy, Buckhaven and Leven.

Aberdour nestles attractively between wooded cliffs, with its harbour, historic castle, church and dovecot, but those drawn to Scotland for tranquillity may want to avoid it as, being within easy reach of Dunfermline and Kirkcaldy, its famous 'silver sands' make it a very popular resort. **Burntisland** is still noisier, with all the elements of a thriving resort. (The name derives from the custom of setting land alight for improvement, but it is not in fact an island.) It had the first ever rail ferry in the world, and details can be learned at the small museum in the High Street. The octagonal church, with outside staircase to a sailor's loft and eighteenth century tower, is a notable example of a post-Reformation church.

Kinghorn, a couple of miles (3 km) further up the coast, is best known for the fact that Alexander III met his death just south of the town (a monument marks the spot) in 1286. Riding towards his royal residence at Pettycur at night his horse stumbled and they were both killed falling over the cliff, which event had curiously enough been prophesied at his wedding a year earlier.

Once known as the 'lang toun' because it was simply one long street from Invertiel to Dysart, **Kirkcaldy** is nowadays the biggest and busiest shopping centre in Fife. It has a recently converted theatre, named after Adam Smith, economist and author of *The Wealth of Nations* who was born here. Other famous men connected with Kirkcaldy include the architects Robert and James Adam, 'man of letters' Thomas Carlyle, and McDouall Stuart, the explorer. There is a Library, Museum and Art Gallery which houses material on the history and landscape of the district, a large collection of pottery with pieces of Wemyss ware, and important paintings, in the agreeable setting of the War Memorial Gardens. Outdoor facilities at Ravenscraig Park and Beveridge Park include bowling greens, tennis courts, picnic areas, boating lake and play areas. Kirkcaldy is the home of linoleum, and it was the production of this in the last century that first brought prosperity to the town. This has now declined but other industries, like furniture-making, have expanded.

On the A910 west of Kirkcaldy it is worth calling at **Lochgelly** (or 'bright water') for any water-skiing enthusiasts, as there is an established centre beside the loch. Lochgelly and **Cowdenbeath** used to be thriving coal-mining towns, but since coal resources ran out new industries have taken hold, and the man-made landscape of the 'bing' (or slag-heap) has been adapted for recreational use.

II: Glenrothes – Cupar – Leuchars

Several miles north of Kirkcaldy, the Balbirnie Craft Centre, on the A92 towards **Glenrothes** and on the outskirts of the new town, demonstrates a range of crafts for sale and in the making, in an eighteenth century coach house complex. Set in a public park, there is a prehistoric stone circle (moved from its original site nearby to make way for the new road), play areas and pleasant walks.

About five miles (8 km) from here is the small town of **Falkland** on the A912, an ancient royal burgh amidst rolling hills commanding fine views over countryside that was once rich in deer and boar, making Falkland a centre for royal hunting parties in the fifteenth and sixteenth centuries. Its very name means 'land of falconry', and Falkland Palace, described as 'the finest monument to the auld alliance', was a favourite residence of King James V. Only its south wing has been preserved, but it contains valuable tapestries, ceiling panelling and stained glass. The French influence from James V's second wife, Marie de Guise (mother of Mary Queen of Scots), can be seen on the façades of the inner court, for it was her dowry that financed the renovations to this and a number of other royal Scottish residences, which have the look of Renaissance 'chateaux'. The gardens were faithfully restored in the 1940s on the plan of an early seventeenth century engraving. The original royal tennis court (1539) is the oldest court still in use in Britain. The whole setting is romantic and the town is yet unspoilt – a strongly recommended port-of-call. The Tourist Information Centre and shop adjoin the palace grounds.

Continuing on the A912, you can head east at **Strathmiglo** for **Cupar**, where the extraordinary gardens at Dalgairn House are worth seeing. Unlike most 'public' gardens, these are not formal or landscaped but a profusion of wild flowers, edible weeds and poisonous herbs – a rare and instructive wild garden.

The Fife Folk Museum at **Ceres**, three miles (5 km) south-east is a 'must' for those with any curiosity about our domestic and agricultural past over the last 100 years. The collection is housed in a seventeenth century Weigh House, recently extended, near the medieval bridge. Note also the early nineteenth century church with its unusual horseshoe gallery. On the A916, 2 miles South of Cupar is *Hill of Tarvit*, an NTS mansion house, originally seventeenth century but largely rebuilt in 1906 by Sir Robert Lorimer. Within you can see some lovely porcelain, tapestries and furniture, and paintings including works by Raeburn and Ramsay. Nearby is *Scotstarvit Tower*, the late sixteenth century home of Sir John Scot, (1585–1670) the geographer, cartographer and scholar.

From Cupar, link up with either the A914 towards the Firth of Tay or the A92. A couple of miles (3 km) west of the Tay railway bridge is a ruined Cistercian abbey, founded in the thirteenth century by Alexander II. Overlooking the Tay and opposite Dundee, Balmerino Abbey is an interesting ruin with a fine cloistral entrance, though it can only be viewed on the outside.

The shape of Fife has been compared to the profile of a dog's head, the Firth of Tay forming the back of the neck, the north-eastern peninsula the ear, Fife Ness the tip of the noe, and St Andrews the eye. Take the road from Newport on Tay eastwards to Tay Port, then down to Leuchars with Tentsmuir Forest stretching to the sea, rich in wildlife and with lovely woodland walks. Leuchars is noted for its twelfth century church, with some of the most superb fragments of Norman work in Britain. South of Leuchars the road connects with the A91 which leads into St Andrews from the east.

III: St Andrews – The East Neuk

Named after the patron saint of Scotland, **St Andrews** is the oldest university in Scotland, founded in 1412 by Bishop Wardlaw, who educated James I. The twelfth and thirteenth century Cathedral, now in magnificent ruins, was Scotland's largest church, though now only parts of the east and west gables, the south wall of the nave and the choir and south transept survive. The Cathedral Museum has displays of Celtic and medieval monuments, pottery, glasswork and even a unique sarcophagus (stone coffin) among other interesting relics. Access to St Rule's (Regulus') Tower, beside the cathedral, is from the museum, and on a clear day the view from the top of this stark 108 feet (33 m) high tower amply repays the effort of the climb. It was named after a Greek monk who is supposed, in 345, to have had a vision about the remains of the Apostle Andrew.

The castle, in a strategic position overlooking the sea, was founded in 1200 (rebuilt within 200 years) and has borne witness to events of bloody and dramatic significance in Scotland's history. Its sinister Bottle Dungeon, in the Sea Tower, is hewn 24 feet (7 m) deep into the solid rock, and the underground tunnels are worth seeing as a rare example of medievel seige technique. A comprehensive guide to the castle is available in situ.

In the picturesque 'old quarter' of St Andrews, a well-restored eighteenth century cottage in North Street is the site of the St Andrews Preservation Trust, which has a small local history museum with interesting exhibits. The old city of St Andrews is approached from Pends Road through the West Port Arch which is the best surviving example of a burgh gate in Scotland. The churches and college buildings, some dating from the fifteenth century, generate an atmosphere of timeless tranquillity even as they mingle with the bustle of a modern university town, with restaurants and wine bars, cinemas and coffee shops.

There is a small harbour with a robust stone pier, used to this day by lobster and crab fishermen. Walk to the end of the pier for a different perspective on St Andrews, and notice how clear the sea here can be. There are long sandy beaches, and of course excellent golfing facilities, for which St Andrews is renowned the world over. In 1754 a number of 'noblemen and gentlemen, being admirers of the ancient and healthful exercise of the golf' founded the Society of St Andrews Golfers, to become the Royal and Ancient Golf Club. The Club House, built in 1854, is now the headquarters of the world game (open to members only). Scotland as a whole, but St Andrews in particular, can ably justify its claim to be the 'Home of Golf'. There are over 400 courses and clubs throughout the country, mostly in superb settings; the oldest is the Old Course at St Andrews, which makes the most of the expanses of beach to hand. There is an interesting Golf museum at St Andrews, with a collection of golfing relics, photographs, clubs and balls, called Auchterlonie's Golf Museum.

St Andrews is fortunate in having its own theatre, in Abbey Street. The Byre Theatre which takes its name from the old cattle byre in which the original theatre was formed 50 years ago, hardly a stone's throw from the new site, is a modern theatre with a reputation for high standards of production. The Crawford Centre for the Arts in North Street has exhibition galleries and drama studios.

So to the East Neuk, either south-east via Kingsbarns, on the A917, or south-west to Largo on the A915. Fife's greatest tourist attraction, the East Neuk is the shelf of coastline that represents the dog's lower jaw. Fishing is the traditional industry in these parts, and all the villages have decorative harbours, working fishing boats, the constant scream of gulls, and the smell of fish and seaweed. Taking the road from Largo, Elie is strung out along the very edge of the sea, with sands where garnets can be found, if you look hard enough! Lady's Tower, east of the harbour, is so called after a local beauty who used to bathe here, Lady Janet Anstruther. At **St Monans** (sometimes 'Monance') there is a firm of boat-builders that has been making fishing boats since 1747, and a large model sailing ship is suspended in the transept of the fourteenth century parish church. This distinctive kirk is a national treasure, and a vital landmark, perched perilously close to the edge of the sea on a rocky outcrop where it has weathered many a violent storm. One of the few churches left in Scotland to have been in regular use over six centuries, St Monans Kirk is a good example of medieval Gothic architecture perfectly adapted to the environment, with relatively squat tower and octagonal steeple surmounting the crossing of the choir and transepts. Experience the contrast in stepping from the bright, blowy churchyard lashed by waves on the sea front, into the calm and spacious interior of a very unusual church. St Monans has two harbours, once so busy that it was usual to cross from one to another by walking over the closely moored boats. The houses here, like many in the East Neuk, are built of mellow stone with an outside stone 'forestair' leading to the front door at first-floor level, with decorative crow-stepping on the gable ends. The ground floor was originally storage space for fishermen or craftsmen.

Out on a small headland to the west is a good example of a beehive dovecot, at Newark Castle, while a couple of miles (3 km) eastward is **Pittenweem** (or 'the place of the cave' in the language of the Picts). Not far from the lively harbour, currently the home of the East Neuk Fishing Fleet, is St Fillan's Cave which has long had its place in history; used by Augustinian monks in the twelfth century, worship is even now carried on once in a while. After exploring the caves and the wee town, a pub on the quay called the Larachmor Inn, named after a ship wrecked off this coast) is a friendly place to relax in, have a snack and sample the malts, before setting off to look around Kellie Castle, off the B9171 above Pittenweem. This sixteenth century castle is now the home of sculptor Hew Lorimer (grandson of Professor James Lorimer, the architect who restored the castle about a hundred years ago) and is a fine example of domestic architecture, set in 16 acres (6 ha) of attractive grounds, well worth visiting.

Anstruther is the focal point of the East Neuk, and contains the inspired Scottish Fisheries Museum (also Tourist Information Centre). The museum, in a group of buildings known as St Ayles, is right at the harbourhead of the old fishing port which is still very active, and gives a comprehensive view of fishing through the centuries in Scotland, imaginatively displayed. Note the 'Fifie', the local traditional fishing boat. In the harbour is an unusual floating museum, the North Carr Lightship, stationed off Fife Ness till 1975, and now refurbished to demonstrate life aboard. Buckie House, on the High Street, is an art gallery interesting for its exhibitions of painting, pottery and craftwork, and also for the building itself, part of which is late seventeenth century.

Crail, a few miles along the coast, is a picturesque village and harbour. The discovery of bronze-age burial urns here signify a long past, and to the south-west are caves, Caiplie Caves, decorated with the carved crosses of early Christian missionaries. Another cave, towards Fife Ness, is known as Constantine's Cave because King Constantine II is said to have been slain here at the hands of the Danes in 875. Crail harbour is enclosed by two piers. Robert Louis Stevenson's grandfather designed the second pier in the early 1800s to increase the harbour's safety, and when necessary the harbour entrance can, apparently, still be closed, with massive wooden beams. Lobster and crabs (or 'partans') are brought ashore here, and can be eaten freshly cooked from Pat Reilly's stand at the harbour. Salt herrings and Crail capons (smoked or dried haddock) used to be exported from Crail and if you look closely at the weather vane on the Town Hall (or Tolbooth) tower, Marketgate, you will see a gilded capon instead of the familiar weather cock. The tower has the oldest bell in Fife, cast in Holland in 1520, and still rung at 10 pm daily to summon decent and sober citizens to bed. The red pantiled roofs of the houses are typical of the Scottish east coast, as pantiles used to arrive as ballast in trading vessels from the Low Countries. Crail Museum, 62 Marketgate, has some interesting exhibits including a 'marriage lintel', the beam over the front door, carved with the initials of the first man-and-wife occupants. The original twelfth century structure of Crail kirk has been much altered, and the present building was founded in 1517. There is an eighth century Pictish cross slab in the entrance.

Access to Sites and Places of Interest

Aberdour Castle
Standard.

Anstruther
Scottish Fisheries Museum
Apr.–Oct. 1000–1230, 1400–1800 Mon.–Sat.; 1400–1700 Sun.; Nov.–Mar. 1430–1630 daily (excl. Tue.)
Fee.

Buckie House
1030–1230, 1430–1730 Mon.–Sat. (excl. Wed.), 1430–1530 Sun.

North Carr Lightship
Apr.–Oct. daily 1000–1700 (to 1900 in June–Aug.)
Fee.

Balmerino Abbey
No adm. but closely seen from grounds.

Burntisland Museum
Apply Curator.
(Kirkcaldy 60732)

Ceres
Fife Folk Museum
Apr.–Oct. 1400–1700 Mon.–Sat. (excl. Tue.), 1500–1800 Sun., 1400–1700 in Oct.
Fee.

Culross

Palace
Standard

The Study
Late Oct.–Mar. 0930–1230, 1400–1600 Sat., 1400–1600 Sun.; other times by prior arrangement (4 days' notice).
Donation.
Town House
Easter–mid Oct. 0930–1230, 1400–1730 Mon.–Sat., 1400–1730 Sun.
Fee.

Cupar
Dalgairn House Garden
June–Aug. 1400–1830 Sat. & Sun.
Fee

Dunfermline

Abbey Church
Standard, but closed during services.
Carnegie Museum
1100–1300, 1400–1900 (to 1700 in winter) Mon.–Sat., 1400–1800 Sun.

Museum
1100–1700 Wed.–Sat., 1300–1700 Sun.

Pittencrieff Museum
May–Oct. 1100–1700 Wed.–Sun.

Dunimarle Castle
Apr.–Oct. 1400–1800 Wed., Thur., Sat., Sun.
Fee.

Falkland Palace
Apr.–Oct. 1000–1800 Mon.–Sat., 1400–1800 Sun.; no entry after 1715.
Fee.

Inchcolm Abbey
Standard. Boat from Aberdour.

Kellie Castle
Castle: Easter–Sep. 1400–1800 daily except Mon. & Tue.
Gardens: Easter–Sep. 1000 to dusk.
Fee.

Kirkcaldy

Industrial Museum
May–Sep. 1400–1700 Mon.–Sat.
Museum & Art Gallery
1100–1700 Mon.–Sat., 1400–1700 Sun.

John McDouall Stuart Museum
(May–Sep. 1400–1700 daily.

South Queensferry Museum
Mon.–Fri. Apply Burgh Chambers during working hours.

St Andrews
Auchterlonie's Golf Museum
By arrangement.

Castle
Standard.

Cathedral
Standard.
Fee for museum and church tower.

St Fillan's Cave
1000–1230, 1400–2000 daily.
Fee.

Hotels and Guest Houses

Aberdour
Forth View Hotel,
Hawkcraig Point KY3 0TZ.
(Aberdour 860402)

Burntisland
Inchview Hotel,
69 Kinghorn Road KY3 9EB.
(Burntisland 872239)

Cowdenbeath
Marchmont Guest House,
91 Broad Street KY4 8JR.
(Cowdenbeath 510823)

Dunfermline
Brucefield Hotel,
Woodmill Road KY11 4AD.
(Dunfermline 22199)

Pitreavie Guest House,
3 Aberdour Road KY11 4PB.
(Dunfermline 24244)

Elie
Golf Hotel,
Bank Street KY9 1EF.
(Elie 3302091)

Glenrothes
Balgeddie House Hotel,
Leslie Road.
(Glenrothes 742511)

Kirkcaldy
Dunnikier Huse Hotel,
Dunikier Way KY1 3LP.
(Kirkcaldy 66630/68393)

St Andrews
Ardgowan Hotel,
2 Playfair Terrace,
North Street,
(St Andrews 72970)

Rusacks Marine Hotel.
(St Andrews 74321)

Argyle Guest House,
127 North Street.
(St Andrews 73387)
(St Andrews 73319)

Number Ten Guest House,
10 Hope Street KY16 9HJ.
(St Andrews 74601)
(St Monans 215/564)

Accommodation for the Young

Falkland
Falkland Youth Hostel,
Bank Wynd KY7 7BX.

Hillend by Dunfermline
Fordell Firs Scout Camp,
Fordell Estate.
(Inverkeithing 412704)

Camping and Caravanning

Anstruther
Anstruther Holiday Camp.
(Anstruther 310484)

Crail
Ashburn House Caravan Site.
(Crail 314)

Balcomie Links Caravan Park.
(Crail 383)

Sauchope Links Caravan Site.
(Crail 460)

Cupar
Tarvit Mill Farm Caravan Park.
(Cupar 52009)

Elie
Kincraig and Shell Bay Caravan Park.
(Elie 330283)

Ladybank
Annsmuir Caravan Park.
(Ladybank 30551)

Leuchars
Almar Bank Caravan Park.
(Leuchars 303)

Lower Largo
Bay View Caravan Site.
(Lundin Links 320469)

Lundin Links
Woodland Gardens Camping and Caravan
Site.
(Upper Largo 319)

Around Scotland

Pittenweem
Grangemuir Caravan Site.
(Anstruther 311213)

St Andrews

Clayton Caravan park,
(Balmullo 242)

Craigtown Meadows Holiday Park,
(St Andrews 75959)

Cairnsmill Farm Caravan Site,
(St Andrews 73604)
Kinkell Braes Caravan Site.
(St Andrews 74250)

St Monans
The Common.

Tayport
East Common.
(Tayport 2334)

Golf

Anstruther
Anstruther Golf Club,
Marsfield.
(Anstruther 310387)

Burntisland
Dodhead Golf Course,
Burntisland Golf House Club.
(Burntisland 873247)

Crail
Balcomie Links Golf Course,
Balcomie Clubhouse,
Fifeness KY10 3XN.
(Crail 278/686)

Dunfermline
Canmore Golf Club,
Venturefair.
(Dunfermline 24969)

Dunfermline Golf Club,
Pitfirrane House,
Crossford.
(Dunfermline 23534)

Pitreavie (Dunfermline) Golf Club,
Queensferry Road.
(Dunfermline 22591)

Elie
Earlsferry Thistle Golf Club,
Melon Park.
(Anstruther 310053)

The Golf House Club.
(Elie 330301/330327)

Glenrothes
Glenrothes Golf Course,
Golf Course Road.
(Glenrothes 758686)

Kirkcaldy
Dunnikier Park Golf Course,
Dunnikier Way.
(Kirkcaldy 61599)

Kirkcaldy Golf Club,
Balwearie Road.
(Kirkcaldy 260370)

Leuchars
St Michael's Golf Club.
(Leuchars 365)

Lochgelly
Lochgelly Golf Course,
Lochgelly Golf Club,
Cartmore Road.
(Lochgelly 780174)

St Andrews
Royal & Ancient Golf Club.
(St Andrews 72112/3)

St Andrews Old Course.

St Andrews New Course.

St Andrews Eden Course.

St Andrews Jubilee Course.

St Andrews Balgove Course.
(St Andrews 75757)

Tayport
Scotscraig Golf Club,
Golf Road.
(Tayport 2515)

Painting Holidays

St Andrews
Kincale House.
(Strathkinness 217)

Riding School

Raith Riding School,
off Forres Drive,
Kirkcaldy.
(Kirkcaldy 60000)

Sailing

South Queensferry,
Port Edgar.
(031 331 3330)

East Neuk Charters
(Tayport 2339)

Water Ski-ing

Fife Water Ski-ing,
Lochgelly,
Fife.
(Kirkcaldy 4222)

Sea Angling

Anstruther
Cod, coalfish, haddock, flounder and
wrasse from the shore, plus ling and conger
from boats.
Boats:
'*Hilda Ross*' Capt. Anderson; '*Seagull*': N.
Newlands; '*Quest*': D. Lorimer; and '*quarius*:
Miss Peters.
(Kirkcaldy 52242)

Crusoe Hotel,
Lower Largo, Fife.
(Lundin Links 320759)

Pittenweem
Cod, haddock, coalfish, wrasse and
flounder, from shore. Cod, haddock,
coalfish, wrasse, flounder,ling and conger
from boats.
Boats: Mr R. Imrie,
66 Pickford Crescent, Cellardyke.
(Anstruther 310805)

A.G. Marsh,
14 Mid Shore, Pittenweem.
(Pittenweem 611)

Tayport
Cod, flounder and plaice from shore, with
occasional sea trout (permit required).

Game Fishing

Cameron Reservoir
Brown trout.
Permits: St Andrews Angling Club.
54 St Nicholas Street,
St Andrews,
Fife KY16 8BQ.
(St Andrews 76347/Peat Inn 236)

Clatto Loch
Brown trout.
Permits: Crawford Priory Estate,
Mr Colombo, West Lodge,
Crawford Priory Estate,
Cupar, Fife.
(Cupar 2678)

Eden River and Ceres Burn
Salmon, sea trout, brown trout.
Permits: Eden Angling Association,
J. Fyffe,
67 Braehead,
Cupar, Fife.
(Cupar 3588)
or
J. Gow & Sons,
Union Street,
Dundee.

Fitty Loch
Brown trout, rainbow trout.
Enquiries: Game Fisheries,
Loch Fitty, Kingseat,
Dunfermline, Fife.
(Dunfermline 23162)

Ore Loch
Brown trout.
Permits: Fishing Lodge,
Lochore Meadows Country Park,
Crosshill, Lochgelly,
Fife.

Kelty Co-operative,
Chemist Branch,
Kelty, Fife.

Lochgelly Centre
David Street,
Lochgelly, Fife.

Sports Shop, High Street,
Cowdenbeath, Fife.

Where to Eat

Anstruther
The Cellar,
22–24 East Green.
(Anstruther 310)

Dunfermline
East Port Bar,
East Port Street.

Around Scotland

Elie
Golf Hotel,
Bank Street.
(Elie 330209)

Falkland
Kind Kyttocks Kitchen,
Cross Wynd.
(Falkland 477)

Freuchie
(nr Glenrothes)

Lomond Hotel
Parliament Square.

Car Hire

Dunfermline
Mackay Bros & Co.,
14/16 Grieve Street.
(Dunfermline 31891/2)

Kirkcaldy
Drysdales Fife Ltd,
Ford Rent-a-Car,
Mitchelston Industrial Estate.
(Kirkcaldy 52771)

Economy Self Drive,
JVS Hub Garage,
Hendry Road.
(Kirkcaldy 201160)

Mackay Bros Car & Van Hire,
Nicol Street,
Service Station.
(Kirkcaldy 65482

St Andrews
Methven Self Drive,
Greyfriars,
Bridge Street.
(St Andrews 72494)

Tayside

Tayside occupies a large irregular area of East Central Scotland with Perth and Dundee as the main centres, and most routes radiating from Perth. Within the boundaries of Tayside, only the routes north of Perth are described starting out from Perth. The three major routes towards Perth from the south and west, the A90 (M90), A9 and A85, are described with Perth as the destination, linking with Fife and Central.

I: Kinross – Glen Eagles – Loch Earn – Crieff

The M90 motorway goes from the north side of the Forth up to Perth and is excellent for fast motoring, but for sightseeing take the side roads, branching off at Exit 5 to visit the Vane Farm Nature Reserve and make the trip around Loch Leven just across the Fife boundary. Loch Leven is best known for having had Mary Queen of Scots imprisoned on one of its islands for 11 months from June 1567, locked in the round tower of a fourteenth to sixteenth century castle, under the unkindly auspices of Lady Douglas, who inhabited the main tower. After many abortive attempts wee made to free her, she eventually escaped on 2 May, 1568, with the cooperationof 18-year-old William Douglas, who secured the gaoler's keys while everyone was at prayers, got Mary into a boat, locked up again, and threw the keys overboard. In those days the Loch was about four times its present size, (the deeper water making the island much smaller), but she was safely received at the loch-side and conveyed to Niddry Castle, west of Edinburgh. You can visit Loch Leven Castle by ferry from Kinross, north-east of the town beside the caravan site.

The Vane Farm Nature Reserve has Britain's first Nature Centre in a well-converted farm building. The numerous displays explain the nature of the area and binoculars are supplied for bird observation as it is a favourite feeding place for wild geese and duck during the winter months. The Loch Leven National Nature Reserve is the most important freshwater area for breeding and migratory wildfowl in Britain. On the east side of the loch, Bishop Hill is a gliding centre (Portmoak Airfield). **Kinross** is on the west side of the loch, and has an interesting local history museum in the High Street with exhibits on peat and linen. The seventeenth century Tolbooth was repaired in the eighteenth century by Robert Adam. Kinross House was built by William Bruce in 1692, and he also laid out the decorative formal gardens, which are still here today.

Travelling on the A90 towards Perth, turn off to Abernethy on the A913. Though now just an ordinary large village with little trace of its former status, this was once a Pictish capital, and centre of the Scotic Church in 862–87. Now only the ancient Round Tower, 74 feet (22.5 m)

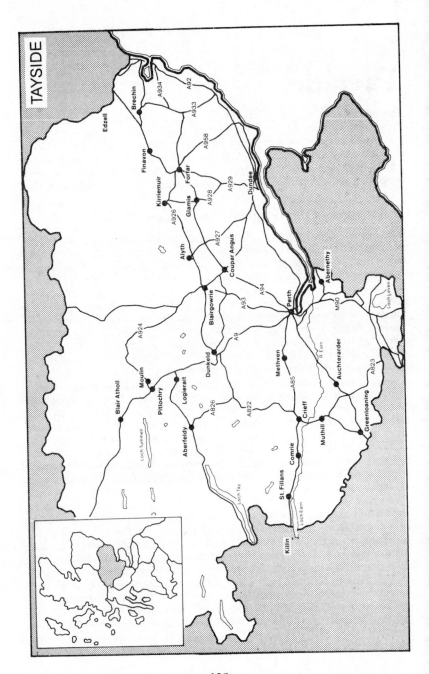

TAYSIDE

high, remains to be seen, the lower part of which is probably ninth century, the upper part eleventh or twelfth century. In 1072 William the Conqueror and Malcolm III are said to have met here.

Turn off the A90 again four miles (6 km) south of Perth to visit Elcho Castle beside the River Tay, a well-preserved Wemyss stronghold mostly dating from about 1530.

The Central/Tayside regional boundary crosses the A9 several miles (4 km) north of Dunblane. At Greenloaning the road forks, the A9 proceeding to Auchterarder and thence to Perth, while the A822 travels north to Crieff, via Muthill where there is an interesting fifteenth century ruined church (with twelfth century tower typical of this part of Scotland), and passing the site of an impressive Roman station built to house up to 40,000 men, Ardoch Roman Camp, east of the road within a mile or two (2 km) of Greenloaning.

Glen Eagles (from 'eaglais' meaning 'church') runs down from the Ochil Hills to meet the A9 about a mile (1 km) south of Auchterarder. Gleneagles Hotel, internationally known for its golf courses, and tournaments, is just north of here. As non-residents of the hotel are made welcome, it is an ideal place to stop for a coffee or traditional afternoon tea. Note the distinctive indoor swimming pool, amongst numerous other facilities. (Though often regarded as an exclusive hotel, Gleneagles now offers excellent value 'package' holidays, not only for golfers, as there are plenty of other diversions locally, and the food is of unusually high standard. Some holidays also include golfing instruction.)

Gleneagles House, built in 1624 from the stones of the former castle, is at the north end of the Glen, with a twelfth century chapel. The house, seat of the Haldane family for over eight centuries, is not open to the public, but you can visit the chapel (which contains many Haldane memorials) by appointment.

The A9 leads on to **Auchterarder**, a royal burgh which was burnt to the ground by the Earl of Mar in 1715 after the battle of Sheriffmuir, but is now a lively centre. Within three miles (5 km) (north-west) just off the A823 is the fifteenth century Tullibardine Chapel, a collegiate chapel well worth seeing for its completeness (note especially the detailed heraldry).

For aircraft enthusiasts, the Strathallan Air Museum is about three miles (5 km) out of Auchterarder on the Crieff Road, B8062 (follow road signs to the airfield) and has a varied collection of vintage military and civil aircraft. Those that are airworthy are often flown in displays during the summer. The Scottish Parachute Club is also based at this airfield.

From Auchterarder the A9 continues due north-east about 13 miles (21 km) into Perth.

Strathearn is the beautiful valley of the River Earn and is said to be the very middle of Scotland, where the Lowlands meet the Highlands, and where travellers between the two areas have traditionally taken their rest. Loch Earn is on the east of the Central/Tayside boundary, with the A85 skirting its north shore from Lochearnhead, and continuing all the way to Perth. A small road skirts the south shore to St Fillans at the easterly point of the loch. St Fillans is a centre for water sports and sailing, as the loch provides a delightful setting for both, at the foot of magnificent wooded mountains. On the site of the cell of St Fillan you can see the ruins of a chapel (about 1500) the burial place of the Stewarts of Ardvorlich. It was at Ardvorlich, on the south shore of Loch Earn, that the MacGregors are remembered for having avenged themselves, in the late sixteenth century, on the king's forester (against whom they had complaint) by beheading him and presenting his head, on a platter, with a crust of bread between his teeth, to his poor sister.

Leaving this lovely loch, **Comrie** is only a few miles (7 km) east on the A85, and is a charming village (note the unusual elegance of the old parish church's castellated steeple). The Museum of Scottish Tartans (Scottish Tartan Society) in Drummond Street is a truly comprehensive museum with over 1,300 tartans and an enormity of related information, from dyeing and weaving (demonstrations), to records of every known tartan.

Crieff, a further six miles (10 km) on, is an attractive, popular centre surrounded by picturesque places, such as Sma' Glen up the A822 northwards (through which the Young Pretender retreated in 1746) and Drummond Castle and gardens, two miles (3 km) south (west of the A822). Lord Drummond founded this castle in 1491 but it was damaged by Cromwell, and in 1745 partly dismantled by the owners (staunch Jacobites) to avoid Hanoverian occupation. Now rebuilt in the old style, only the square tower is actually original. Superb features are the formal Italian gardens, and multiple sundial, designed by John Milne in 1630.

James Square is the centre of **Crieff**, and the Town Hall, East High Street, has the old stocks at the entrance, and an octagonal Cross of 1688. The Mercat Cross nearby is tenth century. The Knock is a tree-covered hill (911 feet/278 m) about a mile (2 km) out of Crieff beside the A85, also a public park. Gallows Hill to the south was where raiding High-landers were hanged in the eighteenth century.

Several miles (5 km) on, Fowlis Wester is a small village just north of the A85, whose Church of St Bean is of considerable historic interest. Also, Alan Bean, the astronaut, took some McBean tartan to the moon with him, a piece of which now hangs in this church.

Continuing towards Perth, Methven is close to the place where Robert the Bruce was defeated by the English in 1306, and also to Methven Castle (not open to the public) where James IV's widow, Margaret Tudor, died in 1541.

Very close to Perth, stop for a look around Huntingtower Castle with its fifteenth century towers, connected by a seventeenth century building, all in good condition.

II: Perth – Dunkeld – Pitlochry – Blair Atholl

Perth, with main roads converging on it from seven directions, is often called the 'Gateway to the Highlands'. With a population of about 42,000, the centre is not too large to explore on foot and is situated beside an attractive stretch of the Tay, spanned by a fine bridge built by Smeaton in 1773. It is an ancient royal burgh whose history has been colourful and varied, (it was the capital of Scotland until the mid fifteenth century, and an important religious centre with several great monasteries, now disappeared). A 100-acre (40 ha) park, North Inch, is just north of the centre, banking the river and offers a wide range of sports facilities, (the large modern domed building is Bell's Sports Centre). At the southern end of the park in Charlotte Street is the Fair Maid's House, built on the site of the house where the 'fair maid's' father lived (of Scott's novel *The Fair Maid of Perth*). In Rose Terrace also overlooking the park is the Old Academy with its classical façade, now the county library. (Painter John Ruskin, 1819–1900, spent many childhood years in this street.) The Scottish Baronial Balhousie Castle, off Hay Street, is the Regimental Museum of the Black Watch (Royal Highland Regiment) presenting a history of the famous regiment. Another classical façade is that of the Art Gallery and Museum, near Perth Bridge with exhibitions of Perth's history, and fine art collections. There is a third museum at the Perth Ice Rink and Football Ground on Dunkeld Road, the Royal Caledonian Curling Club Museum.

The Church of St John, founded in 1126 (rebuilt in the fifteenth century) in St John Street gave the burgh the name of St Johnstoun in its earlier history. It has a wealth of incident to record, including visits from numerous kings of Scotland, and the Scottish reformer John Knox preached his famous sermon here in 1559. Notable aspects of the church include the vaulting of the north porch (the base of the old tower), the war memorial chapel by Sir Robert Lorimer, the original wooden roof of the choir, Strachan's great east window, the 'Cellini Cup', and the baptismal basin (one of Scotland's oldest).

The Round House, near the railway bridge over the Tay, is now the Information Centre but it was built in 1832 as the waterworks. South Inch is the open green area beside the river on the south side of the town, and a path from here leads over the railway bridge and crosses the island in the river (Friarton, or Moncrieffe Island) which has the King James VI golf course. Over the river on the Dundee Road is the outstanding Branklyn Garden, with impressive collections of plants (alpines in particular). For a superb view of the Tay countryside, go up Kinnoul Hill just south east of the town.

The A9 is one of the busiest roads out of Perth as it has been a popular north–south route for centuries. General Wade built a road here between 1726 and 1733, Telford improved it in 1830 and in 1925 work began on its reconstruction. The countryside leaving Perth is gently undulating at first, then more densely wooded between cliffs on each side of the road towards Dunkeld. Amongst these woods was Birnam Wood, of Shakespeare's *Macbeth* fame. Some of the ancient trees on Terrace Walk, along the bank of the Tay below Birnam village (opposite

Dunkeld), are thought to have been a part of the original Birnam Forest.

Dunkeld, an early seat of Scottish sovereignty and Celtic Christianity, is 15 miles (24 km) from Perth, and is a delightful small town (less than 1,000 inhabitants) in a perfect setting beside the Tay, here spanned by a graceful Telford bridge of 1809. Dunkeld Cathedral stands on smooth grass sloping to the river. Parts of it are twelfth century but in the main the building dates from the fourteenth and fifteenth centuries. Most of the roof was destroyed by Reformation damage in 1560, and the nave and aisles have stayed open to the sky ever since, but the choir was restored and is now used as the parish church. Note the finely traced windows of the nave, and the great west window, which is oddly off-centre. Other features of interest include fifteenth century wall paintings, graves and tombs, memorials, and a recumbent armoured effigy of the 'Wolf of Badenoch'.

Cathedral Street is a great attraction in itself, with its 'little houses' beautifully restored by the NTS and Perth County Council, that were fortunate in only suffering damage in 1689, when the rest of the town was gutted in a battle between 1,200 Cameronian Covenanters, and 500 Highlanders fighting for the cause of James VII/II. The cause was lost when the Covenanters fired the town, and the Highlanders retreated. Old Dunkeld is the part of the town that survived (being held by the Cameronians), and here you will find the Visitor and Information Centre, attractive craft shops, Stanley Hill park (through the archway beside the Visitor Centre), friendly pubs (try the 10-year-ld Tamdhu Whisky at the Perth Arms Hotel for a very smooth drink), and a first-rate grocery, Robert Menzies, on the corner with a great range of the best in traditional foods. In the square you will also find the Regimental Museum of the Scottish Horse.

Outside Dunkeld, visit The Hermitage, an eighteenth century folly built above the River Braan overlooking the tumbling waters two miles (3 km) to the west, and two miles (3 km) to the north-east is Loch of Lowes, off the A923, a Scottish Wildlife Trust reserve with Visitor Centre where you can watch ospreys from a hide.

Leaving Dunkeld the A9 continues through superb scenery. A detour can be made (about 20 miles/32 km more) by following Strath Braan west along the A822, turning north at Cablea for Aberfeldy which is at the junction with the A827 in Strath Tay. The A827 leads from Ballinluig to Killin, at the westerly end of the scenic Loch Tay, 14½ miles (23 km) long. **Killin** is a quiet village with the Falls of Dochart tumbling over the rapids around two small islands midstream, where it is spanned by the old bridge. The overgrown and neglected ruin of Finlarig Castle is on a mound just north of Killin concealed by trees. There is not much to see, but if you bother to scramble up, note the shallow pit beside the ruin that was used as a beheading pit by Black Duncan of the Cowl, a cruel Clan Campbell chief.

At **Aberfeldy** the Tay is crossed by Wade's Bridge, generally regarded as his best, and certainly seen to advantage in a setting of such natural beauty. In Mill Street visit the Oatmeal Mill to learn how oatmeal is processed.

On the A827 returning to Ballinluig on the A9, note St Mary's Church (sixteenth century), towards Grandtully, with its interesting contemporary painted ceiling. Logierait, just before Ballinluig, is where Rob Roy escaped from gaol in 1717, the same gaol used by the Young Pretender to hold 600 of his captives from Prestonpans nearly 30 years later. The detour ends here.

Now following the River Tummell, the A9 leads into **Pitlochry** which is at the heart of some of the most magnificent scenery in the British Isles, combining the grandeur of heavily wooded valleys and wide stretches of bright water backed by dark mountains, with lovely walks, cascading waterfalls and small winding roads. Pitlochry's Festival Theatre, now on the banks of the River Tummell, moved to its new premises in 1980, and if you plan to spend any time here it is well worth looking at the summer programme and booking ahead as the standard of production is generally very high. The Highland Games, held in September (second Saturday) every year are another attraction, and many of the visitors to the area enjoy the Highland Nights down by the Tay, twice weekly in summer (with musicians, singers and dancers.) Pitlochry has a new Tourist Information Centre which will supply any information you could possibly require, and is geared to handle up to 280 bookings a day at the height of the season. Despite the varied organised entertainments, Pitlochry's main allure is undoubtedly the physical beauty of its surrounding country, into which you can make a number of excursions: following the road along the north shores of Loch Tummell and Loch Rannoch past Queen's View; taking the path from Moulin up to Craigower (NTS) or Ben Vrackie for the views; witnessing the salmon leaping up the Fish Pass on Loch Faskally where there is also an observation chamber, and Hydro-Electric Exhibition; walking a mile and a half (2 km) to the Black Spout waterfall in the woods; visiting the battlefield at the Pass of Killiecrankie, to name but the most obvious excursions. On your way to Loch Tummell pause at Garry Bridge for the sheer magnificence of the scenery. At Bonskeid, just before Queen's View, there is a YMCA which must be one of the most beautifully situated in Scotland. Rather than backtrack, you can take the B847 which joins the A9 at the tiny village of Struan, and is an unspoilt meandering road bordered by a lot of bracken, and sheep, and scant signs of human habitation.

Blair Atholl lies between Struan and the Pass of Killiecrankie, another of Queen Victoria's favourite spots, famous for the battle of 1689 when the Jacobites overwhelmed the English troops of King William (only to be defeated at Dunkeld three weeks later). There is a very good Visitor Centre (NTS) providing a clear background to the battle. Blair Atholl has the very imposing Blair Castle, an enormous baronial turretted mansion, gleaming white with slate grey roofs approached by an avenue of lime trees. Dating from 1269 (Cumming's Tower, built by

John Comyn of Badenoch), it has been consistently altered and enlarged, the latest building work in 1904. It is the last castle in Britain to be besieged (albeit unsuccessfully, by the Jacobites, under Lord George Murray, just before Culloden when Cumberland held the castle). It is also the headquarters of the only private army in Britain, the Atholl Highlanders. The contents of the castle are fascinating and varied, including arms, toys, china, furniture, tapestry and paintings. There is an equally imaginative natural history museum, not to mention notable architectural features. All in all, allow plenty of time to wander about because there's a lot to see.

From Blair Atholl the A9 follows Glen Garry upwards, through increasingly bleak scenery with isolated forest patches. The road is fast dual-carriageway.

III: Scone – Blairgowrie – Glamis – Brechin

Leaving Perth on the A93, you are distracted almost at once by Scone Palace (Scone pronounced 'scoon') only two miles (3 km) out, and just left of the road, standing in pretty woodland (which includes a pinetum with some very rare and old trees). This building is early nineteenth century, and is chiefly of interest for its contents (especially the ivories, French furniture, and some of Mary Queen of Scots' own needlework), but the historic interest centres around much earlier times when the Stone of Scone lent supreme importance to the place. This stone was traditionally carried here by Kenneth Macalpine in the ninth century because it bore sovereignty, and accordingly Scone became the seat of Government in Pictish times. At the end of the thirteenth century, Edward I took the stone off to London (Westminster Abbey) but that didn't prevent Scone being used for the coronation of subsequent kings of Scotland (including Robert the Bruce, James IV and Charles II). In 1716 the Old Pretender kept regal state here for several weeks, then his son spent a night here in 1745.

Some eight miles (13 km) north at Meikleour, after the Bridge of Isla, the sudden dense green wall running beside the road for 580 yards (530 m) is the remarkable ancient Beech Hedge, planted in 1746 and now nearly 100 feet (30 m) high, (striking at all times but particularly in autumn.)

Due west of here about three miles (5 km) (via the A984, then a track) are the remains of Roman ramparts and ditches, built 1,900 years ago, as the Inchtuthill Roman Camp. A dig here in 1961 brought to light 7 tons (7 tonnes) of unused Roman nails.

Back on the A93, **Blairgowrie** is a compact small town in the heart of farming and fruit-growing land (noted for its exceptional raspberries – which we can vouch for as a close relation of ours makes an annual expedition here just to pick the fruit for jam-making). It is a pleasant place for a short stop with a choice of tempting tea shops. A mile (2 km)

Glamis Castle, Tayside.

out of Blairgowrie on the A923 is sixteenth century Ardblair Castle (built on twelfth century foundations), seat of the Jacobite family of the Oliphants, and containing Jacobite relics.

The A93 north of Blairgowrie follows Glen Shee between high moorland landscapes on each side. Spittal of Glenshee is probably the site of an old hospice for travellers of this lonely road, which is 1,125 feet (343 m) at this point, and very popular as a summer centre for pony trekking and walking, and a winter base for skiing from Cairnwell Pass (*see* Grampian, p. 163).

The A94 runs north-east from Perth through mostly farming country. The B953 leads off at Balbeggie six miles (10 km) north, towards the hills which include Dunsinane, made known by Shakespeare in *Macbeth*. There is an ancient ruined fort on top of the hill, 'Macbeth's Castle' where according to Shakespeare (if not actual history) Macbeth was slain.

Coupar Angus, on the junction of the A94 and the A923, has a local history museum, and an eighteenth century Tolbooth. There was once a Cistercian Abbey here, founded by Malcolm IV in 1164, but it was destroyed in 1559 and its only trace is a fragment beside the A923 to Dundee.

Further along the A94, Meigle is worth stopping at for its particularly interesting museum with a unique collection of early Christian carved stones, all found locally. **Alyth**, a couple of miles (3 km) north-west on the A927, is a very attractive small town with its burn flowing through it beside the main street. There is a Folk Museum in Commercial Street, with local domestic and agricultural bygones. Turning right at Alyth you can continue to Kirriemuir on the A926, then drop back down to Glamis on the A94 (by making this detour the only interesting site you would miss is the fine sculptured stone at Eassie, between Meigle and Glamis).

Kirriemuir is noted chiefly for its associations with Sir James Barrie who was born here in 1860, and died in 1937 (buried in the cemetary), well known for his novels and plays (such as *A Window in Thrums*, *Peter Pan* and *Quality Street*), he lived at the weaver's cottage, 9 Brechin Road which is now a museum run by the NTS, and here you can find out which places in the locality relate to his writings.

Down the A928 towards **Glamis**, the famous Glamis Castle (mentioned by Shakespeare in *Macbeth*) is off to the left. It is a striking building with turrets and battlemented parapets dating mainly from the seventeenth century though parts of it are a lot older and it is known that there was an important building here in early times. (Malcolm II is supposed to have been murdered here in 1034.) In 1537 the burning of Lady Glamis as a witch meant the Castle passed to the Crown, but when it was later proved that she had been wrongly accused her son retook possession, and his descendant, Patrick Lyon, became Earl of Strathmore in 1677. The Old Pretender held his court here in 1715, and, in the first years of the twentieth century, Queen Elizabeth the Queen Mother spent her childhood here. In 1930 her second daughter, Princess Margaret, was born here. Both the castle and its grounds offer very varied interest, the grounds with an Italian garden, a formal garden, and an unusual Baroque sundial. The interior of the castle has many intriguing features in its numerous public rooms, including a beautiful arched plasterwork ceiling (1671) and a very fine fireplace in the drawing room (where there is also a group of portraits), Mortlake tapestries in the billiard room, and a Family Exhibition.

In Glamis village, just south, is the Angus Folk Museum (NTS) which has a superb collection covering local life (agricultural and domestic) in the last century and before, contained within the delightful row of Kirkwynd Cottages.

Forfar is about five miles (8 km) on from Glamis and is a bustling town at the junction of six A-roads at the east end of Loch of Forfar. At the Meffan Institute in the High Street there is a Museum and Art Gallery with local and natural history exhibits. One curious item is the Forfar Bridle, used as a gag for witches, whose persecution in these parts was merciless. The Art Gallery includes a work by Landseer, but is mostly of local interest, with works by J.W. Herald.

The A94 passes through Finavon about 6 miles (10 km) on, where you can see one of the largest dovecots in Scotland, with well over 2,000 nests. Finavon Castle was sixteenth century on earlier foundations, but, undermined by a watercourse, fell down in 1712.

The more interesting road to Brechin is the B9134 which runs a mile (2 km) or so to the south-east of the A94 and includes Restenneth Priory to the east of the road, believed to have been founded twice over, first in 710 by the Pictish King Nechtan, and again by Malcolm IV in the mid twelfth century. Except for the distinctive tower (the base of which is older) most of the ruins are twelfth century. Aberlemno is mid-way between Forfar and Brechin. Stop and have a look at the Aberlemno Pictish Stones in the village (one in churchyard) for their well-defined carving.

The royal burgh town of **Brechin** is best known for its small Cathedral which is now in use as the parish church. Founded by David I in 1150, parts of it were wrecked by the Reformation and not repaired until 1902. Inside you can see some early tombstones. Attached to the Cathedral is a round tower, one of only two such towers on the Scottish mainland, built by Irish clergy between 990 and 1012, and showing unusual stone carving. Brechin Museum (mainly local history) is in St Ninian's Square in the public library.

The nineteenth century Kinnaird Castle stands in 1,300 acres (526 ha) of deer park to the south-east of Brechin. You can ask at the Estate Office for permission to drive through the park, but there is no admission to the castle; another castle on the estate is Farnell Castle (sixteenth century), now an old people's home. To the north-west you can visit the White Caterthun and the Brown Caterthun, two iron-age hill forts on a ridge.

Now reaching the border with Grampian, a couple of miles (3 km) inland along the border is Edzell Castle, a mile (2 km) from **Edzell** on the B966, whose most memorable feature is the Pleasance, or walled garden, by Sir David Lindsay, Lord Edzell, in 1604, whose walls are intricately decorated in low relief. Foundations of a bath house in the south corner indicate a degree of luxury, as bathing was certainly not the norm in 1604! The summer house has a small stair-turret, and a closet with twin privies, but the box hedge in the garden's centre is relatively recent, and has been planted so as to read: 'Dum spiro spero' ('While I breathe I hope'), the family motto. The castle has a tower house built in the early sixteenth century, to which the elegant mansion was added in 1580.

IV: Dundee – Arbroath – Montrose

If you take the A85 out of Perth, the main coast road to Dundee, you will pass the flat, fertile strip that separates the Sidlaw Hills from the Firth of Tay, Carse of Gowrie, which is noted for strawberry growing. The grounds of Megginch Castle, off the A85, have some ancient yew trees, and are open to the public, but the castle is not. The great tower of Huntly Castle is five miles (8 km) on, near Longforgan, and was built in 1452 by Lord Gray of Fowlis, who also built the Church of St Marnan as it stands today, about three miles (5 km) north of Longforgan.

Dundee, capital city of Tayside, is a large commercial city with a lively history and its own university. Much of old Dundee has gone, so today's city is a combination of the preserved old buidings and modern-style architecture. Made a royal burgh around 1190, it grew into a major town, but changed hands repeatedly during the wars with the English suffering varying degrees of destruction. The population today is around 193,000, and the city supports industries which include shipbuilding and engineering.

The most interesting buildings are mainly around the central City Square, to the east of the complex of roads that lead to the Tay Road Bridge. The Albert Institute is in Albert Square, which connects to City Square by Reform Street and is a handsome building with a Burns statue in front (by Steell). Prominently sited, it houses the Central Museum and Art Gallery, with various collections including archaeological material and two exceptional exhibits are a bronze-age spearhead adorned with gold, and the oldest astrolabe in existence (1555). The Howff (meaning 'meeting place') lies between Albert and City Squares and was Dundee's principal cemetary for over 300 years from 1564, when it was given to the town by Mary Queen of Scots, until 1857. Before this it was the orchard of a Franciscan monastery, destroyed in 1548. On the north side of Nethergate leading west from City Square are the City Churches, three parish churches under the same roof, with the fine old steeple of St Mary's dominating them all. At the end of the eighteenth century, despite repeated earlier attacks, there were four churches here – St Mary's, St Clement's, St Paul's and St John's – but in 1841 they were destroyed by fire and when they were rebuilt St John's congregation was provided for elsewhere. Further west on Nethergate, on the opposite side, is St Andrew's Roman Catholic Church (with a 1963 Walter Pritchard mosaic reredos) and beyond that is the University of Dundee, formerly a part of St Andrew's University, but independent since 1967. You can see exhibitions from the university collections at Bonar Hall. In City Square you can't fail to notice Caird Hall with its row of Doric columns, covering an area of two acres (1 ha), built as a city hall and council chambers (from a bequest by Sir James Caird) between 1914 and 1923. Where the old castle was, you now find St Paul's Episcopal Cathedral, and in Cowgate is St Andrew's Church by Samuel Bell (1774); just beyond which is the town's only surviving gate, Wishart Arch, built in 1591 and restored in 1877.

Not far from the Howff, on the corner of Barrack Street, is the Barrack Street Museum which has exhibits on shipping and natural sciences. To the north-west Barrack Road leads to Dudhope Park. Dudhope Castle was built after Bannockburn to replace the earlier Dundee Castle which was on the site of the present St Paul's. It is closed to the public, but in the past has served as woollen mill, barracks, and college of technology. The Dundee Repertory Theatre is up here, in Lochee Road, housed in a converted church.

At Victoria Dock, beside the harbour on the Tay, the frigate *Unicorn* is being restored as a floating museum. Built in 1824 and in use until 1968, it is the oldest ship afloat in Britain. Before leaving Dundee there is a choice of parks around the town worth mentioning. Caird Park is north of the city and has a ruined sixteenth century castle to explore, while Balgay Hill (continuing along Lochee Road from the theatre) has the Mills Observatory with a 10-in. refractor telescope and various other smaller telescopes for detailed appreciation of the broad views from here. Finally Camperdown Park, further out to the north-west, is a big area (600 acres/243 ha) with rare specimens of trees, a zoo for children, nature trails, a golf course and the Spalding Golf Museum, as well as Camperdown House (1824) built by William Burn.

The A930 leaves Dundee by the coast, first skirting the harbour, then reaching **Broughty Ferry** on the eastern outskirts. Broughty Castle is prominently positioned by the sea where it has stood for about 500 years, and there is a museum with exhibits of whaling, and also on the ecology of the Tay. Nearby the Orchar Gallery in Beach Crescent has exhibitions of Scottish paintings. At the crossroads north of here on the A92 and B978 there is an example of an undamaged Z-plan tower house, Claypotts Castle, late sixteenth century, with two round towers and complete roof with crow-stepped gable ends. **Carnoustie**, 12 miles (19 km) out of Dundee, is probably best known for having one of the toughest championship golf courses in the world, but it is also a thriving seaside resort in summer.

Arbroath is a sizeable town a further eight miles (13 km) up the coast, which heralds some picturesque red sandstone cliff scenery for several miles to the north (Cliffs Nature Trail will particularly interest bird-watchers). The town has been a royal burgh since 1559 and has a startling ruined Abbey, lovely in its glowing sandstone. The Abbey was founded in 1178 by William the Lion, and dedicated to Thomas à Becket, whose recent murder at Canterbury by Henry II of England had led to William I's capture at Alnwick in 1174. On his release he founded Arbroath priory, but because of setbacks in the construction work it wasn't actually completed until nearly 20 years after he died (1214). William was buried before the high altar and the effigy, without head and with feet placed against a lion, which you can see in the museum in the Abbot's House, is thought to be a monument to him, by virtue of the lion. The Priory became an Abbey in 1285. In 1320 the important Declaration of Arbroath took place here, acknowledging Robert the Bruce as King of Scotland, independent from the English. The ruin still has very beautiful features, though it was neglected and sabotaged for building stones from the seventeenth century onwards. There is a circular window in the south transept called the Round O of Arbroath which used to be lit from within, beaming seawards for the benefit of night sailors. The vaulted structure beside the south transept was probably the sacristy, and has extraordinary acoustics. There are more fine vaults in the kitchen of the Abbot's House, as well as some of the original thirteenth century tiles in the hall. This is now a museum with some fine Scottish medieval works of art. In the Guest House adjoining there is a reconstructed vault.

Apart from the Abbey's museum, there is an Art Gallery in Arbroath at the library, containing two works by Breughel as well as local art, and a local museum at Signal Tower, which was once the shore base for Bell Rock, 11 miles (18 km) out to sea. Also called Inchcape Rock, this was a hazard to ships until the lighthouse was built in 1807–11, being submerged at high tide, and the cause of many a shipwreck, lying as it does in the fairway of the Tay. The lighthouse was built by John Rennie and Robert Stevenson, (R.L. Stevenson's grandfather). Another important museum here is St Vigean's Museum in a converted cottage in the north-west outskirts of the town, with a remarkable collection of ancient sculptured stones, all beautifully displayed.

Two miles south-west of Arbroath is Kellie Castle, a partly twelfth century tower house, much restored towards the end of the seventeenth century and now delightfully adapted as a modern dwelling. Part of the castle is a Gallery of Scottish Arts. A final footnote on Arbroath – if you are doing your own cooking, try 'Arbroath Smokies' as a tasty alternative to ordinary kippers while you are in this area.

The A92 heads north out of Arbroath to Montrose, 14 miles (23 km) on. On the way you pass close by Red Castle overlooking the scenic Lunan Bay, a conspicuous red sandstone fifteenth century ruin that replaced the twelfth century stronghold of William I, who probably stayed here while supervising the construction of Arbroath Priory. Treasure hunters may like to browse on the pebbled beach about three miles (5 km) south of Montrose, as it is not uncommon to discover semi-precious stones here such as onyx, amethyst and cornelian.

Montrose is on the strip of land between the sea and Montrose Basin, a two mile (3 km) square tidal basin, now a Scottish Wildlife Trust nature reserve. The museum is behind the Old Town Hall, and has good local collections, including maritime exhibits, and the William Lamb Memorial Studio in Market Street has some fine examples of the work of this well-known local artist. The length of stonework lying in a Museum Street garden is from the old Montrose suspension bridge (1828–1928). Montrose's old castle has long disappeared, destroyed by the fierce Scottish patriot William Wallace in 1297 after its occupation by Edward I. The 1715 Rebellion ended at Montrose in 1716, when the Old Pretender finally embarked, secretly, with the Earl of Mar on 4 February.

Access to Sites and Places of Interest
Arbroath
Abbey
Standard.

Art Gallery
0930–1800 Mon.–Sat., 0930–1700 Sun.

St Vigean's Museum
Standard (closed Sun.).

Signal Tower Museum
0930–1300, 1400–1700 Mon.–Sat.

Ardblair Castle
By arrangement.
(Blairgowrie 2155)
Fee.

Blair Castle
Easter Sun. & Mon. in Apr. & May–mid
Oct. 1000–1800 Mon.–Sat., 1400–1800
Sun. No adm. after 1730.
Fee.

Brechin Museum
0930–1800 Mon.–Fri., 0930–1700 Sat.

Broughty
Castle Museum
July–Oct. 1100–1300, 1400–1700 Mon.–
Thur. & Sat., 1400–1700 Sun.

Orchar Gallery
July–Oct. 1100–1300, 1400–1700 Mon.–
Thur. & Sat., 1400–1700 Sun.

Claypotts Castle
Standard.

Comrie
Museum of Scottish Tartans
1000–1300, 1400–1700 Mon.–Sat., 1400–
1700 Sun.
Fee.

Coupar Angus
Museum
May–Sep. 1300–1700 Mon.–Fri.

Drummond Castle Gardens
Apr.–Oct. 1400–1800 Wed. & Sat.
Fee.

Dundee
Barack Street Museum 1000–1700 Mon.–
Sat.

Bonar Hall
0900–1200, 1330–1500 Mon.–Fri.

Central Museum & Art Gallery
1000–1730 Mon.–Sat.

Mills Observatory
Apr.–Sep. 1400–1900 Mon.–Fri., 1400–
1600 Sat.; Oct.–Mar. 1400–2200 Mon.–
Fri., 1400–1600 Sat.
Fee.

Spalding Golf Museum
Easter–Oct. 1300–1700 Mon.–Thur. &
Sat.; July–Oct. 1400–1700 Sun.

'Unicorn'
1000–1700 Mon.–Sat., 1400–1700 Sun.
Fee.

Dunkeld
Cathedral
Standard.

NTS Information Centre
Easter–Sep. 1000–1800 Mon.–Sat., 1400–
1800 Sun.

Museum of the Scottish Horse
Easter–Sep. daily.
Fee.

Edzell Castle
Standard.

Elcho Castle
Standard.

Finavon Dovecot
1000–1800 daily.
Fee.

Forfar
Meffan Institute
0930–1900 Mon.–Sat. (to 1700 Thur. &
Sat.).

Glamis
Angus Folk Museum
May–Sep. 1300–1800 daily. (No entry after
1730.)
Fee.

Castle
Easter. May–Sep. 1300–1700 Sun.–Thur.
(& also Fri. in July–Sep.)
Fee.

Huntingtower Castle
Standard.

Kellie Castle
May–Sep. 1000–2000 daily; Oct.–Apr.
1100–1630 daily.
Fee.

Killiecrankie Visitor Centre
1000–1800 Mon.–Sat. (July & Aug. 0930–
1800), 1300–1800 Sun.
Fee.

Kinross
Kinross House Gardens
May–Sep. 1400–1900 daily.
Fee.

Museum
May–Sep. 1300–1700 Mon.–Fri.

Kirriemuir
Barrie's Birthplace
May–Sep. 1000–1230, 1400–1800 Mon.–Sat., 1400–1800 Sun.
Fee.

Loch Leven
Castle
May–early Oct. 1000–1800 Mon.–Sat., 1400–1800 Sun.
Fee includes ferry.

National Nature Reserve
Access confined to Kirkgate Park, Findatie, Burleigh Sands, and Loch Leven Castle. Permission necessary elsewhere. (NCC, SE Region.)

Vane Farm Nature Reserve
Apr.–Oct. 1000–1700 daily except Fri.; Nov.–Mar. 1000–1630 Sat. & Sun.
Fee.

Loch of Lowes
Visitor Centre
Apr.–Sep. 1030–dusk.
Donation.

Meigle Museum
Standard, but closed Sun.

Montrose
William Lamb Memorial Studio
June–Sep. 1400–1700 Sun.

Museum
0930–1300, 1400–1700 Mon.–Sat.

Perth
Art Gallery & Museum
1000–1300, 1400–1700 Mon.–Sat., 1400–1600 Sun.

Balhousie Castle (Black Watch Museum)
1000–1200, 1400–1630 Mon.–Fri. (to 1530 Oct.–Apr.).

Branklyn Gardens
Mar.–Oct. 1000–sunset daily.
Fee.

Fair Maid's House
1000–1700 Mon.–Sat. Closed Wed pm, except July–Sep.

Pitlochry Hydro-Electric Exhibition
Easter–Oct. 1000–1830 daily.
Fee.

Scone Palace
Easter. End Apr.–early Oct. 1000–1800 Mon.–Sat., 1400–1800 Sun. No adm. after 1730.
Fee.

Strathallan Air Museum
1000–1700 daily.
Fee.

Tullibardine Chapel
Standard.

Accommodation for the Young

Aberfoyle
Dounans Outdoor Centre.
(Aberfoyle 291)
or Write: The Secretary,
SNCA Ltd,
57 Melville Street,
Edinburgh.
(031 226 6391)

Craggan
The Boys Brigade Outdoor Centre.
(Killin 545)
Bookings: Kirk House,
7 Victoria Terrace,
Edinburgh.
(031 225 4095)

Crieff
St Ninians Centre,
Comrie Road.
(Crieff 3766/7)

Dunblane
Scottish Churches House,
Kirk Street.
(Dunblane 823588)

Dundee
University of Dundee.
(Dundee 23181 Ext. 240)

Dunkeld
Dalguise Centre.
(Dunkeld 339)

Enochdhu (Blairgowrie)
Kindrogan Field Centre.
(Strathardle 286)

Glenshee
Compass Ski & Outdoor Centre,
Glenshee Lodge,
By Blairgowrie.
(Glenshee 209)

Lochearnhead
Lochearnhead Scout Station.
(Lochearnhead 256)

Meigle
Belmont Outdoor Centre.
(Meigle 275)

Perth
Kinfauns Castle.
(Perth 25587)

Pitlochry
Atholl Baptist Centre,
Atholl Road.
(Pitlochry 3044)

Pitlochry Youth Hostel,
Knockard Road.

Port-of-Menteith
Dykehead Residential Centre.
Contact: Scottish School Boy Club,
38 Lansdowne Crescent,
Glasgow.
(041 334 5649)

Camping and Caravanning

Aberfoyle
Forestry Commission Cobleland Campsite.
(Aberfoyle 392)

Aberfeldy
Aberfeldy Caravan Site,
Dunkeld Road.
(Aberfeldy 20475)

Abroath
Seaton Estate.
(Arbroath 74762)

Birnam
Erigmore House Caravan Park Ltd.
(Dunkeld 236)

Blair Atholl
Blair Castle Caravan Site.
(Blair Atholl 263)

Bridge of Cally
Corriefodly Caravan Site.
(Bridge of Cally 236)

Strathardle Leisure Park,
Ballintuim House Hotel.
(Bridge of Cally 276)

Callander
Callander Holiday Park,
Invertrossachs Road.
(Callander 30265)

Gart Estate Caravan Park.
(Callander 30002)

Calvine
Struan Inn Caravan Park.

Cargill
Beech Hedge Restaurant & Caravan Park.
(Meikleour 249)

Carnoustie
Woodlands Caravan Park,
Angus District Council,
12 Hill Terrace,
Arbroath.
(Arbroath 76221)

Crieff
Crieff Holiday Village,
Turret Bank.
(Crieff 3513/2236)

Crook of Devon
Drum Caravans,
Fossoway.
(Fossoway 246)

Dundee
Camperdown Park,
Liff Road.
(Dundee 23141)

Dunkeld
Inver Mill Farm Caravan Site,
Inver Mill.
(Dunkeld 217)

Kenmore
Kenmore Caravan & Camping Park.
(Kenmore 226)

Killin
Cruachan Caravan Site.
(Killin 302)

High Creaggan Caravan Site,
Morenish.
(Killin 449)

Kinloch Rannoch
Forestry Commission Kilvrecht Caravan
Site.
(Kinloch Rannoch 335)

171

Kinross
Gairney Bridge Farm Caravan Site.
(Kinross 62336)

Loch Leven Caravan Site,
Sandport.
(Kinross 63560)

Turfhill Camp Site.
(Kinross 63123)

Monifieth
Riverview Caravan Park.
(Dundee 2837)

Perth
Cleeve Caravan Site,
Parks & Recreation Dept,
Marshall Place.
(Perth 25662)

Windsor Caravan Site,
Windsor Terrace.
(Perth 23721)

Pitlochry
Faskally Home Farm.
(Pitlochry 2007)

Milton of Fonab Caravan Site.

Scone
Camping Club Site,
Scone Racecourse.
(Scone 52323)

Strathyre
Camping & Activity Centre,
Immervoulin Farm.
(Strathyre 287)

Thornhill
Mains Farm.
(Thornhill 605)

Tummel Bridge
Tummel Valley Holiday Park.
(Tummel Bridge 221)

Tyndrum
Pine Trees Caravan Park.
(Tyndrum 243)

Self Catering

Aberfeldy
Miss Jill Bristow,
Thorncroft,
Lilliesleaf,
Melrose,
Roxburghshire TD6 9JD.
(Lilliesleaf 424/425)

Mrs J. MacDiarmid,
Mains of Murthly,
Aberfeldy,
Perthshire PH15 2EA.

Mr and Mrs Middlemass,
Aberfeldy Country Cottages,
Moness Farm,
Aberfeldy,
Perthshire PH15 2DY.
(Aberfeldy 20851)

Aberfoyle
Dr Duncan J.M. Ferguson,
Kumalo,
14 Cromarty Crescent,
Bearsden,
Glasgow.

Alyth
Renton Finlayson,
Bank House,
82 Atholl Road,
Pitlochry,
Perthshire PH16 5BL.
(Pitlochry 2512/3021)

Arbroath
Mrs O. Faleur,
Woodfield,
Abroath,
Angus DD11 3RB.
(Arbroath 74444)

Warden, Seaton Estate Caravan Site,
Seaton Road,
Arbroath,
Angus.
(Arbroath 73762)

Auchterarder
Mrs Bayne,
Castlemains,
Auchterarder,
Perthshire PH3 1DX.
(Auchterarder 2475)

Bell-Ingram,
Durn,
Isla Road,
Perth PH2 7HF.
(Perth 21121)

Tay Valley Properties,
230 Oakbank Road,
Perth PH1 1HD.
(Perth 27478)

J. Watt,
171 High Street,
Auchterarder,
Perthshire PH3 1AD.
(Auchterarder 2197)

Balquhidder
Mrs M.M. Ellesley,
Coshnachie,
Balquhidder,
Lochearnhead,
Perthshire FK19 8NZ.
(Strathyre 258)

Mr Hopper,
Stronvar House,
Balquhidder,
Lochearnhead,
Perthshire.
(Strathyre 688)

Bankfoot
Hoseasons Holidays,
Sunway House,
Lowestoft,
Suffolk.
(Lowestoft 62292)

Blairgowrie
Altamount Chalet Park,
Coupar Angus Road.
(Blairgowrie 3324)

Brechin
Mrs B.M. Booth,
Old Station House,
Farnell by Brechin.
(Farnell 208)

Bridge of Cally
Patrick Dean Ltd,
Mere Hall,
Bracebridge Heath,
Lincoln.
(Lincoln 791209)

Callander
Neil and Fiona Snow,
Invertrossachs by Callander.
(Callander 30010)

Calvine
C.S. Chisholm,
Struan Inn,
Calvine.
(Calvine 208)

Comrie
P.J. Bickmore,
Millside,
Nurses Lane,
Comrie,
Perthshire PH6 2DZ.
(Comrie 640)

Mrs J.D.B. Mitchell,
Coneyhill,
Comrie,
Perthshire PH6 2LR.
(Comrie 248)

Coupar Angus
Renton Finlayson,
Bank House,
82 Atholl Road,
Pitlochry,
Perthshire PH16 5BL.
(Pitlochry 2512/3021)

Jas W. King & Co. Ltd,
5 Atholl Place,
Perth.
(Perth 26178)

Crieff
Alan Colquhoun,
Loch Monzievaird Chalets,
Ochtertyre,
Crieff.
(Crieff 2586)

Dundee
Student Services,
Duncan of Jordanstone College of Art,
Dundee.
(Dundee 23261)

Accommodation Officer,
University of Dundee,
Perth Road.
(Dundee 23181)

Dunning
D.M. Howie,
Mill House,
Yetts Road,
Dunning,
Perth.
(Dunning 233)

Fearnan
M.C. Leighton,
Tighnachoille,
Fearnan,
Aberfeldy.
(Kenmore 259)

Glen Lyon
Renton Finlayson,
Bank House,
82 Atholl Road,
Pitlochry.
(Pitlochry 2512/3021)

Glenfarg
Mrs S.R. Christie,
Rossie Ochil,
Forgandenny,
Perthshire.
(Glenfarg 307)

Kenmore
Renton Finlayson,
Bank House,
82 Atholl Road,
Pitlochry.
(Pitlochry 2512/3021)

Kirkmichael
Mrs J. Brodie,
Balvarran Estate,
Bridge of Cally,
Perthshire.
(Strathardle 248)

Kirriemuir
Mrs F.M. Fleming,
Easter Peep,
Lintrathen by Kirriemuir,
Angus.
(Lintrathen 205)

Perth
G. & M. Associates,
8/10 Inchaffray Street,
Perth PH1 5RX.
(Perth 33875 (office hours))

Margaret Ritchie,
Whitehouse,
3 Huntingtower,
Perth.
(Perth 35270)

Pitlochry
Renton Finlayson,
Bank House,
82 Atholl Road,
Pitlochry PH16 5BL.
(Pitlochry 2512/3021)

Strathtay
A.J. Bell,
Tighantuir,
Strathtay,
Perthshire.
(Strathtay 254)

Strathyre
Forestry Commission Forest Holiday
Bookings,
231 Corstorphine Road,
Edinburgh EH12 7AT.
(031 334 0066)

Riding Schools

Glenfarg
Glenfarg Riding School,
Smiddyhill.
(Glenfarg 262)
Accommodation can be arranged near
centre.

Pitlochry
Blair Castle Trekking Centre,
Blair Atholl.
(Blair Atholl 263)
Camping and Caravanning facilities
nearby.

Sea Angling

Arbroath
Cod, coal fish, mackerel, flounder, conger,
plaice, haddock, pollack.
Boats: C. Ferrier,
34 Newton Avenue,
Arbroath.
(Arbroath 73360)

Dundee
Cod, flat fish from shore; cod, haddock
plaice from boats.
Information: Frank Doyle,

174

Ross's Angling Club,
29 Haldane Crescent,
Dundee.
(Dundee 812064)

Game Fishing

Ardle River
Trout, salmon.
Permits: Corriefodly Hotel,
Bridge of Cally.
(Bridge of Cally 236)

Bridge of Cally Hotel.
(Bridge of Cally 231)

Log Cabin Hotel,
Kirkmichael.
(Strathardle 288)

Loch Rannoch
Brown trout.
Permits: Dunalastair Hotel,
Kinloch, Rannoch.
(Kinloch Rannoch 323)

Loch Tay
Salmon, trout.
Permits: Ardeonaig Hotel,
By Killin.
(Killin 400)

Ben Lawers Hotel,
By Aberfeldy.
(Killin 436)

Killin Hotel.
(Killin 296)

Tay River
Trout salmon.
Permits: Dunkeld House Hotel.
(Dunkeld 243)
Director of Finances Offices,
Perth.
No Sunday fishing.
Season: Mid Jan.–mid Oct.

Salmon, trout, grayling.
Permits: Logierait Hotel,
Ballinluig,
Perthshire.
(Ballinluig 253)

Trout
Permits: Post Office,
Dunkeld & Birnam,
R. Scott Miller,

The Tackle Shop,
Atholl Street,
Dunkeld.
(Dunkeld 556)

Salmon, brown trout, grayling.
Permits: Grandtully Hotel,
Strathtay,
Perthshire.
(Strathtay 207)

Within boundaries of City of Perth.
Salmon, sea trout, brown trout.
Permits: Director of Finance,
Perth & Kinross District Council,
1 High Street,
Perth.
(Perth 21161) (not Saturday)

Kercock & Delvine beats.
Salmon, trout.
Permits: Kinloch House Hotel,
Dunkeld Road,
Blairgowrie,
Perthshire.
(Essendy 237)

Salmon, trout.
Permits: Weem Hotel by Aberfeldy.
(Aberfeldy 381)

Kercock & Delvine beats.
Salmon, brown trout, sea trout.
Permits: Muirton House Hotel,
Essendy Road,
Blairgowrie.
(Blairgowrie 2113)

Salmon.
Permits: Salmon beats are let by Messrs
P.D. Malloch (Field Sports) Ltd,
Tackle Manufs,
24 Scott Street,
Perth.

Hotels for Shooting and Stalking

Ballinluig
Logierait Hotel.
(Ballinluig 253)
Game shooting/stalking.

Dunning
Kippen House Hotel.
(Dunning 447/450)
Game shooting.

Kirkmichael
The Log Cabin Hotel,
Glen Derby.
(Strathardle 288)
Game, rough shooting, stalking.

Special Interest Holidays

Alyth
Titletod Farm Camp,
Leroch Farm,
Alyth,
Perthshire.
(Alyth 2496)
Fruit picking with dormitory facilities.

Ballintuim by Blairgowrie
Scottish (Tayside) Cycling Holidays.
(Bridge of Cally 201)
Cycling.

Crieff
Loch Monzievaird Lodges,
Ochtertyre,
Crieff,
Perthshire.
(Crieff 2586)
All year. Sailing, golf, pony trekking, fly fishing, sailing, water skiing, skiing.

Kenmore
Sailing School,
South Loch Tayside,
Kenmore,
Perthshire.
(Kenmore 236)
Sailing, canoeing, golf, pony trekking.

Kinfauns Castle
Booking Dept, CMA,
Birch Heys,
Cromwell Range,
Manchester M14 6HU.
(061 224 2887)
Hill walking.

Lochearnhead
Glenogle Sailing Centre,
Mansewood House,
Lochearnhead,
Perthshire.
(Lochearnhead 213)
Sailing, water skiing, canoeing.

Loch Rannoch
School of Adventure,
Kinloch Rannoch,

Pitlochry,
Perthshire.
(Kinloch Rannoch 325)
Cross country, skiing, mountaineering, canoeing, sailing, fishing.

Portmoak Airfield
Scotlandwell,
Kinross.
(Scotlandwell 543/243)
Gliding.

St Fillans Sailing School
Dalvreck House,
Crieff,
Perthshire.
(Crieff 2292/St Fillans 257)
Sailing.
Accommodation can be arranged.

Strathallan Airfield
Auchterarder,
Perthshire.
Parachuting.

Cycling

Aberfeldy
McKercha & MacNaughton,
2 Bank Street.
(Aberfeldy 567/8)

Blairgowrie
A. Fender & Son,
65 Perth Street.
(Blairgowrie 2422)

Callander
Trossachs Youth Hostel,
Brig O' Turk.
(Trossachs 227)

Dundee
Broughty Bikes,
80 King Street,
Broughty Ferry.
(Dundee 737005)

Where to Eat

Blair Atholl
Blair Castle Restaurant.
(Blair Atholl 207)

Blairgowrie
Stormont Lodge Hotel,
Kirk Wynd.
(Blairgowrie 2853)

Callander
Dalgair House Hotel,
113–115 Main Street.
(Callander 30283)

The Lade Inn,
Trossachs Road,
Kilmahog,
nr Callander.
(Callander 30152)

Crieff
Murraypark Hotel,
Connaught Terrace.
(Crieff 3731)

Golf

Aberfeldy
Aberfeldy Golf Course,
Taybridge Road.
(Aberfeldy 535)

Alyth
Alyth Golf Course,
Pitcocknie.
(Alyth 2268)

Arbroath
Arbroath Golf Course,
Elliot.
(Arbroath 75837)

Auchterarder
Auchterarder Golf Club,
Orchil Road.
(Auchterarder 2804)

Gleneagles Hotel Golf Courses,
Gleneagles Hotel.
(Auchterarder 3543/4/5)

Barry
Panmure Golf Club.
(Carnoustie 53120)

Blair Atholl
Blair Atholl Golf Course.
(Blair Atholl 407)

Blairgowrie
Rosemount & Lansdowne Golf Course,
Blairgowrie Golf Club.
(Blairgowrie 2383)

Brechin
Brechin Golf Club,
Trinity.
(Brechin 2383)

Carnoustie
Burnside Golf Course,
Links Parade.
(Carnoustie 53249)

Dalhousie Golf Club.
(Forfar 5101)

Mercantile Golf Club.
(Forfar 5101)

Carnoustie Medal Golf Course.
(Carnoustie 53249)

The Carnoustie New Taymouth Golf Club,
9 Taymouth Street.
(Carnoustie 52425)

Comrie
Comrie Golf Club.
(Comrie 230/773)

Crieff
Crieff Golf Club,
Ferntower.
(Crieff 2397)

Dundee
Caird Park Golf Course.
(Dundee 451147)

Camperdown Golf Course.
(Dundee 645457, 23141, Ext. 413)

Downfield Golf Course.
(Dundee 825595)

Killin
Killin Golf Club.
(Killin 312)

Kenmore
Taymouth Castle Golf Course.
(Kenmore 228)

Perth
Craigie Hill Golf Course.
(Perth 22644)

King James VI Golf Club.
(Perth 25170)

Royal Perth Golfing Society.
(Perth 22265)

Pitlochry
Pitlochry Golf Course.
(Pitlochry 2114)

St Fillans
St Fillans Golf Club.
(St Fillans 312)

GRAMPIAN

Grampian

I: Braemar – Ballater – Peterculter

The A93 crosses the Tayside/Grampian boundary at Cairnwell Pass, the highest main road pass (2,199 feet/670 m) in Britain. Popular with skiers in winter, there is a 1,000-foot (305 m) chairlift at the pass to the summit of Cairnwell (3,059 feet/932 m), and a dry ski run, open all year. It is also a hang gliding centre. The zig-zag road approaching the pass, Devil's Elbow, is now by-passed by a new road, then follows Glen Clunie down to the River Dee at **Braemar**, nine miles (14 km) to the north. Braemar is an attractive small ski resort in winter, and busy in summer because of its scenic location. Braemar Castle, built in 1628, has a colourful history, . The star-shaped defensive curtain wall, loopholed for muskets, was built after the '45 Rebellion. Note the central round tower, vaulted halls, prison pit and iron gate. The other castle, Kindrochit, is a mere fragment of a fourteenth century hunting lodge beside the car park by Cluny Bridge. On behalf of the Old Pretender the Earl of Mar raised his standard of rebellion here in 1715, making this the historic rallying place for the '15 Rebellion, (the exact spot is now beneath the Invercauld Arms hotel, indicated by a plaque within). The attempt failed, ending in defeat at Sheriffmuir, through the lack of promised support from France, or from the Lowlands, a similar sorry story to be re-enacted 30 years later, in the name of the Young Pretender. The Braemar Royal Highland Gathering, is perhaps the best-known such event in Scotland. The Invercauld Festival Theatre, used for certain events of the festival, was once a church. It now has an open stage, Elizabethan-style, and some very impressive murals. The house opposite is where R.L. Stevenson's *Treasure Island* was written (1881). The countryside around, deeply wooded and mountainous, invites walking and climbing, but check locally before embarking that your itinerary isn't too ambitious (or over private land) and that it isn't the deer stalking season, as certain restrictions exist. (See the *Braemar Official Guide* for information about walks.) The little road west of Braemar to the Linn of Dee is picturesque, at the bridge the river cascading through a rocky cleft, and you can return by the opposite bank (about 13 miles/21 km round trip).

Leaving Braemar on the A93 Balmoral lies seven miles (11 km) on, best known for the Castle, still used by the Royal Family, which was built for Queen Victoria and Prince Albert in 1853, their having bought the estate the previous year. It is a Scottish baronial mansion of white granite, described by Victoria as 'this dear Paradise'. Prince Albert had rare trees planted in the grounds, and his Queen bought the neighbouring Ballochbuie Forest to extend the estate with native Caledonian pine trees up to 200 years old. George VI extended it again in 1947 by buying the Bachnagairn Estate. The compact granite church of 1895 is Crathie Church where the Royal Family worship when in residence.

A further seven miles (11 km) on the A93 takes you to **Ballater**, a beautifully situated little town whose existence is owed to an old woman, and a Jacobite prisoner exiled in London for 20 years after Culloden. Hearing, during his absence, of the old lady's cure from scrofula by bathing in the water below Pannanich Hill, on his return to Scotland he built Pannanich Lodge as a spa. The railway, long used by Royalty visiting Balmoral, ends here at Queen Victoria's wish. Note the Royal Bridge, opened in 1885 by Queen Victoria, originally one of four. Glen Muick, south of Ballater, runs for 10 miles (16 km) with a road that also branches back to Balmoral. A cairn stands just outside Ballater, where Queen Victoria met a battalion of Gordon Highlanders in 1899 and reviewed them before they embarked for South Africa. Birkhall Mansion two miles (3 km) up the west bank of the Muick, is where Florence Nightingale lived as a tenant of the Queen, in 1856. (Encouraged by the Queen, from here she persuaded the Army to form what is now the Royal Army Medical Corps.) 'The Hut' is a shooting lodge, much used by Victoria and Albert, beside the bridge leading across to Spital of Glenmuick on the west bank of the River Muick. Just west of Ballater is the McEwan Gallery, housed in the unusual 1902 building by Swiss artist Rudolphe Christen, exhibiting many Scottish works of art. The foot of Culblean Hill, north of the road between Ballater and Dinnet, was the scene of an important battle in 1335 (memorial beside the Tarland road). Loch Davan and Loch Kinord both have crannogs (man-made islands), and were the sites of castles that played a part in the battle.

Muir of Dinnet is a 3,497-acre (1,416 ha) National Nature Reserve, and Dinnet Oakwood is a separate reserve of 33 acres (13 ha), with some of the best surviving examples of oakwood in the area. Passing through lovely woodland scenery, the A93 continues east, with various offshoots of interest. South of Aboyne, a pleasant centre in summertime, visit the Braeloine Visitor Centre with exhibitions of local wildlife, farming, forestry and information on local walks. North of the road four miles (6 km) north-west of Aboyne, a smaller road leads to the remains of Tomnaverie Stone Circle, an example of a recumbent stone circle of about 1800–1600 BC, and near Tarland on the B9119, is the well-preserved Culsh earth house. About one mile (2 km) off the A980, Peel Ring of Lumphanan is where Shakespeare's Macbeth made his last stand against Malcolm Canmore, and Macbeth's Cairn (three quarters of a mile (1 km) north of Lumphanan, on the slope north of the A980) is a small ring of trees, where Macbeth is supposed to have been slain.

Just off the A980 north of Lumphanan is Craigievar Castle, a beautifully preserved tower house, completed in 1626 and scarcely altered from that day to this. It still has the original seven-storey tower, crow-stepping, turrets and steeply angled roofs, and inside a marvellous Renaissance ceiling adorns the hall which still has a minstrels' gallery above. (Over the huge fireplace the motto reads 'Doe not vaiken sleiping dogs'.) This is now a NTS property, and well worth seeing, as a piece of untouched seventeenth century architecture, and for the treasures it contains.

Banchory, at the junction with the A93 and the A980, is delightful to visit as it is a lavender growing centre, with a lavender distilling factory, where visitors are made welcome. There is a local interest museum which occupies a room in the old Council Chambers. Just south of the town, at the Bridge of Feugh, where the river forms rapids, salmon may be seen leaping. Beyond Banchory, on the A93 Crathes Castle and Gardens (575 acres/233 ha) certainly merit seeing. The castle, originally sixteenth century with seventeenth and nineteenth century additions, has well-known features of painted ceilings in three chambers, and an oak-panelled ceiling in the long gallery which is unique in Scotland. In the outstanding gardens there are four nature trails leading through the rare collection of trees and shrubs. (Some of the yew hedges have been here since 1702.) The grounds also include a base camp with accommodation for school parties etc. The A93 now bears north-east, and about five miles (8 km) from Crathes Castle is Drum Castle which is a battlemented tower (1272) with a seventeenth century mansion attached. Robert the Bruce gave it to his trusty armour bearer in 1324, in whose family it remained until bequeathed to the NTS in 1976. The castle has a fine library, well-furnished rooms and a 400-acre (162 ha) estate which includes part of the ancient Caledonian pine forest, and a seventeenth century family chapel.

At **Peterculter**, a paper mill town, the statue seen from the bridge overlooking the Leuchar Burn is of Rob Roy (1671–1734), the traditionally amiable outlaw (who in fact was just a cattle-lifter and freebooter). Peterculter and Maryculter were named after St Peter's Chapel, and St Mary's Chapel when the Culter district was divided, by the donation of the south bank of the district (Maryculter) to the Knights Templar in the late twelfth century. The Roman Catholic St Mary's College (founded 1827) has some notable treasures which include a portrait of Mary Queen of Scots found hidden at Douai after the French Revolution. Aberdeen is eight miles (13 km) from here.

II: Johnshaven – Inverbervie – Stonehaven

After the Tayside/Grampian regional boundary, St Cyrus is the first village on the A92 heading north along the east coast. There is an active salmon fishery here, on the broad sands below the village, and a nature reserve, noted for its wide variety of plant life. **Johnshaven**, several miles on, was a prospering port until the Second World War, but now has only one fishing vessel working from the harbour, for cod in winter, crab and lobster in summer. These days though, it is the base of one of the largest lobster dealers in Britain, and you can see tanks of circulated sea water by the harbour containing the lobster stocks. One mile (2 km) before Inverbervie the attractive village of Gourdon clusters along the shore. There are still 12 active boats here, and it is the last remaining centre in Scotland where the long line is used for haddock fishing (involving a laborious process of baiting and preparing the line). Try to catch the lively fishmarket on weekday afternoons. Hercules Linton, designer of the famous wool and tea clipper, *Cutty Sark*, was born at **Inverbervie**, and there is a memorial at the north end of the main street. There are flax and rayon mills here. At Bervie Brow on the north side of the river, Craig David is the promontory where David II landed in May 1341, swept ashore in a storm while escaping the English, after nine years' exile in France. King's Step is the rock on which his foot is supposed to have first touched Scottish soil after his voyage, with his Queen Johanna.

Along the B967, just north of here, Arbuthnott is worth a visit, about three miles (5 km) inland. Arbuthnott House is sixteenth to eighteenth century with a seventeenth century Renaissance frontage and terraced gardens in the grounds, as well as an eighteenth century bridge. The chancel of Arbuthnott Church is of the original building (1242), while the rest is sixteenth century.

Back on the A92, take the small coast road to Kinneff, about a mile (2 km) north of Inverbervie. The church here, Old Kinneff, once concealed the 'regalia' of Scotland (crown, sceptre and sword), when the Minister's wife courageously smuggled them out of the besieged Dunnottar Castle in 1652, and hid them from the Cromwellians below the church floor under the pulpit, until the Restoration. A monument here commemorates the action of this Mrs Grainger, who saved the Honours of Scotland. Keeping on the minor coastal road, a mile (2 km) beyond the cliff-top lighthouse at Tod Head, you turn right for Catterline, one of the best-preserved cliff-top villages on the east coast, (the subject of much of the Scottish artist Joan Eardley's work, and where she spent her later years). Crawton, a mile (2 km) to the north, is a fishing village that was abandoned 50 years ago because of its inhospitable site and the changing fishing conditions. A path leads from the deserted houses to a shingly beach below vertical cliffs, and it makes a good spot for a picnic.

Returning to the A92, Dunnottar Castle is on a great crag surrounded by sea on three sides, and by a cleft on the fourth side, formed when the crag split from the main cliff. These extensive ruins are certainly some of the most dramatically sited in Scotland. Resembling a fortified township more than a simple castle, they sprawl over the entire crag and have some outstanding features to visit, including the well, the gatehouse, the drawing room (with modern ceiling, painted and carved), the domestic rooms (kitchen, bakery, wine vault and brewery) and the Whigs vault, a grim dungeon, open to the sea. The great square tower and chapel are the oldest remains, from the late fourteenth century. A stronghold of the Earls Marischal of Scotland, it was abandoned in 1716 when the Jacobite 10th Earl Marischal had to forfeit the estate. Don't leave without experiencing the view from the Marischal suite, high above the sea.

Stonehaven, comprising cluttered Old Stonehaven round the harbour, and orderly New Stonehaven (nineteenth century) above it, is a busy tourist resort in summer with a lively port. The harbour is the best between Arbroath and Aberdeen, so was important during the herring boom of the nineteenth century, but is unsuitable for the larger vessels of today which use Aberdeen's facilities. Note the Tolbooth built by the Earl Marischal as a storehouse in the late sixteenth century, on the quay, now a local history museum. Stonehaven's large outdoor heated swimming pool is reckoned to be one of the best open-air pools in Scotland. (From Stonehaven a road known as the 'Slug Road' (A957), opened in 1800, leads north-west to Deeside and passes an interesting standing stone, the Auquhollie, with clear inscriptions. To find it, take a right turn opposite Ricarton House entrance, then a left, and the stone is on the right just beyond the first farm.)

The village of Cowie on the north side of Stonehaven, was a thriving fishing community, when it was wiped out by a plague of cholera brought ashore by the survivors of a Swedish shipwreck in 1864.

About five miles (8 km) up the A92 from Stonehaven, at Muchalls, the modest castle is worth noting, as a good example of a typical seventeenth century Scottish laird's house which is still lived in. Muchalls village was built as a 'model' fishing village in 1865, and played its part in the fishing heritage of this coast before the decline of the herring industry and the immense growth of Aberdeen. Very little fishing is now done from any of these villages, but they are picturesque to visit set on the grassy 'heugh heid' (cliff top) above a steep drop to pebbly beaches, broken now and again by sheltered coves. Findon is the place where the curing process for haddock was discovered, smoking the fish in 'peat reek', hence the name 'finnan haddock'.

III: Aberdeen – Peterhead – Banff – Elgin

Aberdeen or the 'Granite City' because of the abundance of granite, one of the city's main exports, is a broadly spread, dignified centre comprising the harbour, Old Aberdeen, the main city and the outer city. At the harbour hundreds of tons of fish are landed daily and it is still Scotland's largest fishing port, but oil and gas industrial development in the North Sea, using Aberdeen as service and supply base, has brought many changes, and of course increased prosperity to the area. The harbour is easily accessible by car and on foot, but you have to get there by 7.30 am if you want to catch the clamour and bustle of the morning fish auction. Footdee, or 'Fittie', by the head of the North Pier, was built in the early nineteenth century specifically for the fisherfolk, with cottages strictly laid out in three squares, now undergoing restoration and modernisation.

Old Aberdeen is the quieter district, north of the Dee, near the River Don, with St Machar Cathedral and King's College, separated by St Machar Drive. The Cathedral of St Machar was founded in 1157 but the earliest remaining stonework is fouteenth century (sandstone). Granite was used for most of the later building though the two sandstone steeples on the west towers were added in 1522, by Bishop Dunbar, whose flat-panelled oak ceiling is a feature of the interior. With Marischal College, King's College forms Aberdeen University. King's was founded in 1495, a century before Marischal, and was then called St Mary of the Nativity, only assuming the present name during the reign of James IV, in his honour. The chapel, built in 1500, is the most interesting building here, with a double row of canopied stalls and elaborate carving in the main chapel (note the pulpit with the heads of Scottish kings from James I–VII).

The Brig o' Balgownie is the oldest medieval bridge in Scotland, (less than a mile (1 km) from the High Street of Old Aberdeen), with a 62-feet (19 km) wide Gothic arch spanning a pool of the River Don. It was commissioned by Robert the Bruce around 1320 (repaired 1606) and an odd prophecy was made about it at the time: that should an only son, riding a mare's only foal, ever cross the bridge it would fall. (Either such an event has never occurred or the prophet got it wrong, for the bridge still stands!)

The compact main city has a striking City Cross (with a unicorn on a decorated hexagonal base, which has medallion heads of Scottish kings), in Castle Street at the east end of Union Street. The Old Town House of 1886 incorporates the tower and spire of the Tolbooth (1615–27) outside which executions took place up until 1867 and is on the corner with Broad Street. Off Castle Street in King Street is St Andrew's Episcopal Cathedral, mother church of the Episcopal Church in America, with a striking interior. The arms on the ceiling of the north aisle are of all the American states, and those in the south aisle are of all the Aberdeenshire families loyal to the Jacobites in the eighteenth century. St Nicholas House in Broad Street is a modern building, with municipal offices and tourist information, that does nothing to improve Aberdeen's skyline. It dwarfs the Provost Skene's House, which is sixteenth century (used by Cumberland, the 'butcher', for some weeks prior to Culloden) and is now a fine museum, with superb period furniture, seventeenth century painted ceilings and woodwork (the chapel) and a small but interesting display on the evolution of Aberdeen. Marischal College has a magnificent pinnacled façade, and is considered as one of the most beautiful granite buildings in the world, opened in 1906. The hall has a window illustrating the history of the college, and there is a portrait gallery, and museum (with local, classical, Egyptian and Chinese antiquities, and an ethnographic collection). There is an Art Gallery on Schoolhill with notable collections, especially of Aberdeen silverware, and upstairs the Macdonald Collection, with includes self-portraits by many famous artists. The War Memorial Hall of Memory is part of the ground floor, and opposite James Dun's House Museum, which has exhibitions of particular interest to children including natural history, geology, and local history.

Her Majesty's Theatre is near the Art Gallery, and opposite statues of Wallace and Prince Albert (seated). Another statue of Edward VII is on the corner of Union Terrace and Union Bridge, with the Music Hall (1820) to the west on Union Street, and St Mary's Roman Catholic Cathedral (1880) beyond, in Huntly Street. Further west on Union Street is Christ's College (1851).

Leaving Aberdeen on the A92 towards Newburgh, the Ythan estuary marks the edge of a 1,774-acre (718 ha) nature reserve comprising one of the largest, most untouched dune systems in Britain, with foreshore, dunes, estuary spit as well as heath, rough pasture, and cliff. Famous for wintering wildfowl and for nesting colonies of different kinds of tern, it is also of botanical interest. (Beneath the dunes, foundations have been found of a bronze-age village, and of a medieval village signifying that the area was engulfed in dunes relatively recently.)

Up-river five miles (8 km) on the Ythan, **Ellon** also has ancient origins (though now a dormitory town of Aberdeen). A remnant of the old castle can be seen on the north terrace over the river, and two miles (3 km) west off the A920 is a neglected medieval tower called Esslemont. Continuing the diversion from the coast road, also off the A920 is Pitmedden Garden on the outskirts of the village, a seventeenth century 'great garden' laid out by Sir Alexander Seton in 1675 and recreated by the NTS. With four formal gardens (three based on Holyrood Palace gardens in Edinburgh, the fourth a heraldic design based on Seton's coat of arms) and two look-out towers, or 'thunder houses' which are rare in Scotland, it is best viewed from the lawn above. Set in 100 acres (40 ha), there are pleasant woodland walks on the estate, which has Highland cattle and a picnic area. Udny Castle is just south of here, a noticeable turretted, four-storey battlement which is not open to the public.

From Udny, take the B9000 back to the A92 at Newburgh, and head north skirting the dune reserve past Collieston. The Old Castle of Slains is 1½ miles (2 km) north of here on a promontory. Now only a fragment of a tower remaining, it was given to the Earl of Errol (by Robert the Bruce) in the fourteenth century, but blown up by James VI when the 9th Earl rebelled, in 1594. Pardoned in 1597, the Earl returned from exile to build the new Slains Castle about four miles (6 km) north, whose ruins now sprawl over the cliff top beside the sea.

The Bullers of Buchan is the name given to the extraordinary 200-foot (61 m) chasm in the cliff, a couple of miles (3 km) north of Slains Castle. This is particularly worth visiting in rough weather when the sea pounds in, under the natural arch of rock, but a good spectacle in all weathers (Dr Johnson said, in 1773 '. . .no man can see (it) with indifference'). Boddam is another ex-fishing village whose heyday was ended by the damaging storms of 1898 which wrecked many of the boats in harbour and at sea.

Peterhead is about two miles (3 km) further along this dramatic coastline, and one's arrival here is heralded by the vast sweep of the harbour's south bay, enclosed by great breakwaters built by prisoners from Peterhead Prison, known as the Harbour of Refuge. A solidly built, pink granite town, it is a North Sea oil and gas service and supply base, and it is not uncommon to see an oil rig moored in the south bay for repairs and maintenance work. It is also the principal fishing port in Europe, with from 6,000–14,000 boxes of fish handled here daily. Go to the West Pier at midnight on Sundays to see the seine-net boats racing for the fishing grounds. The Arbuthnot Museum and Art Gallery commemorates the herring boom here, and the fact that earlier, in the nineteenth century it was a busy whaling port. (Note the Arctic exhibits.)

Peterhead was founded by the 5th Earl Marischal in 1593, but the 10th (last) Earl and his brother were exiled from here in 1716 for secretly allowing the Old Pretender to land. The brother, James Keith, became a marshal in the army of Frederick the Great of Prussia. A statue of him was presented by William I of Prussia in 1868, and now stands before the Town House (built in 1788). Just north of Peterhead, the late sixteenth century Inverugie Castle is where James Keith was born, now a neglected overgrown scant ruin, abandoned since the two brothers were exiled in 1716.

West of Peterhead for 12 miles (19 km) on the A950 after it crosses the A92, you will find the fragmentary remains of Deer Abbey, founded in 1219 for Cistercian monks. At Old Deer, nearby, there was once a seventh century Celtic monastery.

Further north of Peterhead, to the east of the A952, is the Loch of Strathbeg which was connected to the sea until 1720 when a bad storm blocked the channel with sand. It is now a freshwater bird sanctuary, with many swans. The lighthouse at Rattray Head oversees long sands and a shelving shore, with a fast tide that can prove dangerous, so be careful bathing. The bright flare south of the lighthouse is the North Sea gas terminal at St Fergus. On the road to Rattray at the southerly end of the loch are the remnants of an early tenth century chapel, and on the southern slopes of Mormond Hill (768 feet/234 m) you can see a white horse and a white stag etched onto the hillside by exposing the quartzite; the horse attributed to a Fraser commemorating his charger that was killed in battle, and the stag dating from 1870. North of Mormond Hill, on the A981 at Memsie, is a bronze-age burial cairn, without entrance passage.

Inverallochy (a twin village with Cairnbulg), on the eastern point of Fraserburgh Bay, has a row of low fishermen's cottages, worth visiting, with the stark fragment of Inverallochy Castle to the south, by the road to St Combs. Cairnbulg castle, restored a century ago, is not open to the public but can be seen from the B9033. It was a Comyn stronghold, later belonging to the Frasers, (who founded Fraserburgh in 1546).

Fraserburgh has no special features, but is an important centre for fishing with several major fish factories. The harbour is the base for a large fleet of purse-netters, which circumnavigate the British Isles in search of mackerel and herring (when permitted). Many fishermen from the declining villages around now work out of this harbour. From Fraserburgh, the A98 loops inland with nothing of particular interest to see, so take the coastal route, which is slower but more scenic, with some steep hills. The ruins of fifteenth to sixteenth century Pitsligo Castle are on a small road leading south from Rosehearty near the old Pitsligo Church, also ruined, and the new Pitsligo Church. The coast road climbs to command long views, then drops down to the shore at Aberdour Bay, near New Aberdour, and St Drostan's Well. St Drostan was the founder of the celtic monastery at Old Deer (*see* p. 186) and is said to have landed here. Just east of **Macduff**, the old spa town of Tarlair has a beautifully situated open-air swimming pool. The hill behind Macduff has a 70-foot (21 m) War Memorial tower, worth climbing up to for the view. **Banff**, on the west shore of the mouth of River Deveron, is a royal burgh town with an ancient past, now a lively little port, whose harbour periodically becomes silted up. Duff House, next to the golf links in the south of the town is a Georgian baroque house designed by William Adam (there is an exhibition which helps to interpret it). In the town, which has an olde-worlde atmosphere with its winding streets and paths, the castle (1750) is now a public building. Opposite the post office in the old cemetary you can see a remnant of the aisle of St Mary's Church (pre-Reformation). Where the gallows used to be, Biggar Fountain now stands. The town museum has an exhibition of British birds and of locally crafted silver.

From Banff the A98 heads inland before regaining the coast at **Portsoy** a little fishing port that is no longer active, famed for the lovely serpentine marble that is found here. (The French much admired this marble, and used it in the Palais de Versailles.) Marble souvenirs can be bought from the local workshops, converted from fish warehouses. Outside Portsoy, Sandend is one of the prettiest cluster of houses along this coast, huddling between the sea and a grassy brae. On the west side of Sandend Bay, with rocks at the ends of the beach, a path leads to Findlater Castle, now a ruin on the rocks but once an Ogilvy and Gordon stronghold. Cullen Bay has extensive white sands and three conspicuous red sandstone rocks, the Three Kings of Cullen. A railway viaduct, now disused, divides **Cullen** into upper and lower towns, the upper town built in 1822–30 to replace Old Cullen, an ancient royal burgh. Robert the Bruce founded the Old Church, and Alexander Ogilvy of Findlater made it collegiate in 1543. His huge baroque tomb survives from this period, with his effigy beneath the canopy clad in armour. In Deskford Church, five miles (8 km) south, there is a rather smug inscription in the sacrament house (1551) stating that it was provided by the same Alexander Ogilvy and his wife.

From Cullen you can take the coast road beside the sands of Spey Bay, to **Buckie**, some six miles (10 km) west of Cullen. Buckie Maritime Museum has an exhibition of the fishing industry. From here the A98 leads through Speymouth Forest where there are fine walks, down to **Fochabers** on the east bank of the Spey. The town was lifted bodily from its former site, just north, near Gordon Castle, and rebuilt in 1776 to the plan of John Baxter. The Cross is still on the original site. Gordon Castle, not open to the public, is surrounded by 1,300 acres (526 ha) of wooded parkland, and has long been a Gordon estate now belonging to the Duke of Richmond and Gordon. **Kingston**, at the mouth of the Spey estuary, was developed by two Yorkshiremen who came up here in 1786 to buy timber from the Gordon estate and stayed to establish a shipbuilders yard, naming the place after Kingston-on-Hull. Their yard was active until 1815, and wooden ships continued to be built in the village until 1890.

Garmouth, on the B9015 on the west bank of the Spey, is where Charles II landed in 1650 after signing the two covenants. The village harbour is constantly shifting with the flooding of the Spey. South of Garmouth on the A96 is the Old Baxter Shop, a replica of Baxter's original famous establishment in Fochabers. There is a Visitor Centre and restaurant.

Elgin is not only interesting in its own right, but is in an area worth exploring so forms a useful base for touring. An ancient royal burgh on the south bank of the Lossie, Elgin's ruined Cathedral is amongst the loveliest in the whole of Scotland, described in the fourteenth century as 'the ornament of the district, the glory of the kingdom, and the admiration of foreigners' by Bishop Barr. The terrorising 'Wolf of Badenoch', natural son of Robert II, avenged himself for his excommunication by the Bishop of Elgin following a bad quarrel, by burning down the cathedral and two thirds of the town in 1390. The cathedral was rebuilt. In the mid sixteenth century it was desecrated by a murderous brawl between the Dunbar and Innes families (known as Bloody Vespers), then within 12 years the roof lead was stripped to raise money for paying the troops (to no avail since the ship laden with all the plunder subsequently sank) and the cathedral fell into decay. The tracery of the west window was smashed by Cromwellians in 1650. A curious tale connected with the cathedral ruins is that of Gilzean Anderson, a soldier's widow who was half mad, and came back to her native Elgin in 1748 taking up residence with her baby son in the cathedral's lavatory, using the piscina as a cradle. Her son grew up to enlist in the Honourable East India Company and rose to Lieutenant General, amassing a substantial fortune. He bequeathed part of his fortune to his home town. The lavatory of his infancy can still be seen between the north aisle of the choir and the octagonal chapter house. Rebuilt after 1390, the chapter house is in better repair because it was used as a Courthouse up until 1731. The lady chapel (or south choir aisle) still with its fifteenth century vault, was the former burial place of the Gordons. The tomb at the east end is the Bishop of Winchester's (who died in 1460) and in the middle is the tomb of the 1st Earl of Huntly who died 10 years later.

Elgin's High Street still has some old arcaded houses (note no. 46) and a hotel now occupies Thunderton House, on the south side, where the Young Pretender stayed for 11 days, before his Culloden fiasco in 1746.

Elgin abbey, Grampian.

The museum, at the east end of the High Street, has a notable collection of fossils, and prehistoric pieces. The library is in Cooper Park at Grant Lodge which is a Georgian mansion. In the middle of the High Street, St Giles' Church (1828) stands beside the old Tower Hotel (1624), with the Muckle Cross at its east end, rebuilt in 1888. Elgin Academy replaces a school which was recorded in 1489. The inventor of the telephone, Alexander Graham Bell, was a pupil teacher and then resident master at Weston House Academy here. Before leaving Elgin, go to Greyfriars House Gardens on Queen Street, where there are hundreds of flowering trees.

The area around Elgin suggests two round tours, to the north and west, and to the south and west. The northerly tour includes first Spynie Palace off the A941 two miles (3 km) from Elgin, which can only be viewed from the outside but is the most impressive ruined bishop's palace in Scotland. From 1205–1686 it served as the palace of the bishops of Moray, and its most remarkable remaining feature is David's Tower, begun by Bishop David Stewart as protection from the Gordons, whose chief he had excommunicated. During Mary Queen of Scots' campaign against the Gordons she stopped here in 1562.

The A941 continues north to **Lossiemouth** with an attractive harbour and beautiful beaches. This was the birthplace of Ramsay MacDonald (1866–1937), the first Labour prime minister, and you can still see his house. Heading west on the B9040, then south on the B9012 you pass Gordonstoun School (where the Prince of Wales, and his father, went to school) on the left, then Duffus Castle which is a weathered fourteenth century tower. Built on an ancient earth motte, the great stone castle has subsided, splitting the tower. Note the otherwise well-preserved moat, with water. David I stayed here while Kinloss Abbey was under construction, near Forres. To extend the tour, at New Duffus, instead of turning south on the B9012, head west along it as far as Burghead, now a fishing village but once the site of iron-age and Norse forts. In the iron-age fort is the Burghead 'Roman well' cut into natural rock and fed by a spring which is somewhat mysterious, though probably an early Christian baptistry, because of the steps down into the water, the basin and the pedestal. Every January an ancient ceremony is conducted at Burghead of carrying a lighted tar barrel through the streets to scare off any evil spirits, called 'Burning the Clavie'. From here you can return to the A96 on the B9013 and back to Elgin.

The southerly route includes the ancient church at Birnie, and the dramatically contrasting Pluscarden Abbey, on the small road off the B9010, six miles (10 km) from Elgin. Birnie Kirk is probably the oldest church in continuous use in Scotland, and is built on a site used for pre-Christian worship, as is indicated by a standing stone of a pre-Christian ritual at the Minister's Gate, with others built into the wall of the churchyard. A Celtic church stood here around the year 500, and the present church was built in 1140. A local saying is that to be prayed for three times at Birnie Kirk 'will either mend ye or end ye'! Pluscarden Abbey was sadly decaying when it was given to Benedictine monks from England in 1943, since when the monks have been busily restoring it. Founded in 1230 by Alexander II, it was damaged by Edward I in the early fourteenth century, only to be badly damaged again, by fire in 1390, caused by the 'Wolf of Badenoch' during the destructive quarrel mentioned earlier. This is now a great and prospering Abbey, and visitors are welcome at most reasonable times. The lady chapel, which has a great deal of the original masonry, will be opened on request.

Heading west on the A96, **Forres** is an ancient royal burgh, witnessing many a royal slaying. Macbeth and Banquo were on their way here in the early eleventh century to Duncan's Court, when they met the 'weird sisters' on the 'blasted heath' (Hardmuir, or Macbeth's Hill), three of the witches for whom Forres was famous, but whether Macbeth murdered Duncan here, or at Cawdor, or at Inverness (as Shakespeare had it) is not certain. The Falconer Museum in Forres High Street has a good collection of local fossils, and the Nelson Tower (1806) is a fine viewpoint. Just outside the town Sueno's Stone is on the B9011, and is a 23-foot (7 m) Pictish, early Christian sandstone shaft, well worth visiting to see its intricate carvings. Further along this road is the meagre ruin of Kinloss Abbey, once an important Cistercian foundation of David I.

Kincorth House Gardens, a couple of miles (3 km) north-west of Forres, specialises in roses. Brodie Castle, rebuilt (after its seventeenth century destruction) in the eighteenth and nineteenth centuries, now houses superb paintings.

IV: Kintore – Inverurie – Huntly – Keith

The A96 is the direct route all the way to Fochabers from Aberdeen, but various detours on the route are recommended to encompass sites of special interest, such as the Maiden Stone and Leith Hall on the B9002.

Kintore is a small town, made a royal burgh in 1506, with a quaint eighteenth century Town House, and a decorated sixteenth century sacrament house in the church. The churchyard has a Pictish stone with symbols both pagan and Christian.

A couple of miles (3 km) north-east, seventeenth century Balbithan House has an unusual collection of Scottish kitchen antiques in its small museum, and a fine old-world garden. Just north of here on the road to Fintray is Kinkell church, early sixteenth century, whose parson in those times was Alexander Galloway, a leading artistic thinker on sacrament houses, and the one here bears his initials and the year 1524. At Kinmuck, two miles (3 km) east towards Dyce, you can see the Meeting House and Schoolhouse of the first Quaker community in Scotland.

Inverurie is another royal burgh town, probably given its status by Mary Queen of Scots (and not David I) who visited the twelfth century castle here in 1562. The castle has long disappeared but it was on the site of the Bass, a 60-foot (18 m) high motte on the B993 just out of town. In the cemetary alongside are Pictish sculptured stones (one with a boisterous figure of a pony). Inverurie has a museum with a collection of local archaeology. The Brandsbutt Stone is on the north side of town off the A96, and has early eighth century Pictish symbols.

Pitcaple Castle, with its two round towers, is a delightful fifteenth to sixteenth century castle, still used as a family house. Mary Queen of Scots visited it in 1562, and a tree at the front is growing where an older tree once grew, beneath the branches of which the Queen is supposed to have danced. There is a family museum here. About a mile (1½ km) north is the Loanhead Stone Circle, a good example of the local 'recumbent stone' style. The mass of smaller stones were once a burial cairn, and are encircled by erect stones, with other stone and earthworks alongside.

From Pitcaple take a southerly turn off the A96 towards Chapel of Garioch for about two miles (3 km) to see the ruined tower of Balquhain (1530). Apparently, when Cumberland ordered it to be burned in 1746, one of the Leslies to whom it belonged bribed Cumberland's men to use damp straw to start the fire to reduce the damage. About six miles

(10 km) from Inverurie off the A96 is the Maiden Stone, 10-foot (3 m) high, generally accepted as one of the best of Scotland's Early Christian monuments, with a Celtic cross and Pictish symbols. (The name comes from the comb and mirror carved at the base.) Just west of here a forest walk has been laid out by the Forrestry Commission, with car park. Off the B9002 two miles (3 km) beyond Insch is the 'Picardy Stone', a seventh or eighth century whinstone monolith with Pictish symbols. The B9002 then leads to Leith Hall which is approached up an elegant avenue and stands in interesting grounds with rock gardens, herbaceous borders, a bird observation hide and pond walk, nature trails and a flock of the small hardy Soay sheep. The mansion was built in 1650 around a central courtyard and from this period the tower house, with turrets and gables, survives. The Young Pretender presented a writing case on the eve of the fateful Battle of Culloden, which can be seen in the exhibition room, as well as the official pardon granted to Andrew Hay, who fought at Culloden with the Young Pretender.

The B9002 ends at the A97 which follows the course of the River Bogie north of Huntly, with Clashindarroch Forest along the high ground to the west (the largest Forestry Commission forest in this area), making good walking country, with access roads for walkers up the valleys towards the slopes of the forest.

Huntly is an attractive eighteenth century planned town with an intriguing ruined castle (known as Strathbogie Castle until 1544) that overlooks the Deveron Water and has a motte beside it, (as well as a long and complicated history involving the Scottish royalty). The main part of the existing building is the sixteenth to seventeenth century palace. Note the beautiful row of oriel windows (1602) the panel of heraldic ornamentation above the main doorway (probably the finest heraldic doorway in Britain) and the fireplaces. There is a grim fifteenth century vaulted dungeon below the palace, with ancient graffiti on the walls, possibly the work of the dungeon guards. The museum in Huntly is in the Library in the pleasant main square, and the Adamston Agricultural Museum (with over 450 farm implements from this area of Scotland) is two miles (3 km) south, off the A96.

North on the A96 is **Keith** on the River Isla, where the Strathisla Whisky Distillery has been since 1786, the oldest established in Scotland. The façade of the Roman Catholic Church (1830) is copied from Santa Maria de Angelis in Rome, and the picture hanging over the altar was presented by the Emperor Charles X of France to this church.

(Interesting to note that at Auchinhove, four miles (6 km) east, the northernmost traces of Roman penetration into Scotland were discovered.)

V: Castle Fraser – Dufftown – Tomintoul

An alternative route to Elgin is the A944 leaving Aberdeen, joining the A97 at Mossat, and the A941 at Rhynie.

To visit the Lapidary Workshops at Garlogie, some seven miles (11 km) from Aberdeen, take the B9119 off the A944 to Garlogie, south of Loch of Skene. You can see demonstrations of stone cutting and polishing. Where the small road north rejoins the A944, cross over to take the road to Castle Fraser, about a mile (1½ km) north of the main road. This NTS castle was built between 1575 and 1636 but incorporates earlier building. One of the master masons involved in the building was Thomas Lieper (also of Tolquhon Castle), and another was J. Bel, whose signature can be seen on the great heraldic panel, north side. There is an exhibition off the courtyard, on the Castles of Mar, of which Castle Fraser is perhaps the most impressive. Beyond here, off the B993, at the little village of Monymust, 20 miles (32 km) from Aberdeen, is Monymust House, once a thirteenth century priory, then part of a castle, before becoming a mansion house. It is not open to the public. Just east of the house, Robert the Bruce is supposed to have camped in Camp Field, on the way to battle at Barra Hill near Old Meldrum in 1307. One mile (1½ km) north beside the River Don is the restored Pitfichie Castle which demonstrates how a round tower attached to the corner of a keep offered defensive command along the length of two sides.

To reach Alford you can drop back down to the B993, then the A944 or you can continue on the unclassified road that roughly follows the course of the Don, which takes you past nineteenth century Castle Forbes on the left, occupied by the lords Forbes, whose sixteenth century tower house, the restored Balfluig Castle, is just south of Alford. In Alford, which was the scene of a battle, won by Montrose against Covenanters in 1645, there is a short section of 2-foot gauge railway track in the grounds of Murray Park, which is being extended to Alford station.

When you reach the junction with the A97 at **Mossat**, you have a choice of routes to Grampian's north coast, but we describe places of interest on the most direct route first, via Dufftown and Rothes, the alternative route joins the Highlands route at Grantown-on-Spey, via Tomintoul (*see* p. 195). Heading north from Mossat on the A97 you pass the ruin of St Mary's or Auchindoir Church, which is still a good example of a thirteenth century Scottish medieval parish church, with a fine sacrament house, transitional door (with semi-circular arch and dog-tooth moulding) and lancet window in north wall. Just west of this ruin is Craig Castle which is open by appointment only. The keep here is dated 1528 though possibly earlier, and the Courthouse is worth seeing. **Rhynie** is the village where you turn left onto the A941 for Dufftown, and about half a mile (1 km) east is Druminnor Castle (a Forbes mansion built in 1577 with the original fifteenth century tower of the lords Forbes), which has a museum, and rooms open to the public. The A941 runs below Tap o' Noth, which is 1,851 feet (564 m) high. It has a pointed summit with a vitrified fort and a 15-foot (5 m) rampart, as well as a Forestry Commission fire look-out. The road then crosses moorland country before descending to Glen Fiddich from where there is an excellent view of Auchindoun Castle, a dramatic yet austere ruin on a rise (reached by a track 1½ miles (2 km) south of Dufftown off the A941). Some of the stones of this castle, including the tailored corner-stones, were used in the construction of Balvenie Castle in Dufftown. The lonely ruin is surrounded by prehistoric earthworks.

Dufftown, founded in 1817 by James Duff, 4th Earl of Fife, is the centre of the whisky distilling industry, and the Glenfiddich and Balvenie distilleries demonstrate the malting, mashing, fermenting, distilling, maturing and bottling of the stuff. The town has an attractive central clock tower (also a museum), a twelfth century church (Mortlach Church half a mile (1 km) south of the town) and on the north side the extensive ruins of Balvenie Castle. Originally thirteenth century, it was much rebuilt in the fifteenth and sixteenth centuries when the tower house was added altering its character from a fortress to a nobleman's mansion. The heavy wrought-iron gate of the arched entrance is original. Visitors over the centuries include Edward I (1304), Mary Queen of Scots (1562), and Cumberland (1746), whose troops were stationed here.

At **Craigellachie**, the head of Strathspey, a new bridge now spans the river that was spanned by Telford's elegant single-span bridge from 1815 to 1973, with decorative stone towers at each end. **Rothes** is noted principally for its Glen Grant and Caperdonich distilleries.

The southerly route from Mossat on the A97 passes Kildrummy Castle founded in the early thirteenth century on Alexander II's orders, but considerably altered by Edward I of England when it fell to him at the end of that century. The history of this castle is as impressive as the remains that now stand over an extensive area. The wife and children of Robert the Bruce were sent here for safe-keeping in 1306 when he fled to Rathlin, but were betrayed by an avaricious blacksmith, to whom the English promised as much gold as he could carry if he set fire to the castle. Though Bruce's family escaped, the castle's defenders had to surrender, and the blacksmith is said to have been rewarded by having molten gold poured down his throat! The castle came under siege again in 1335, saved by the battle at Culblean. The son of the 'Wolf of Badenoch' kidnapped the Countess of Mar here in 1404, forcing her to marry him, for her title. By 1715 it was the seat of the Erskines of Mar and the plans for the '15 Rebellion were laid here for the Old Pretender. After the failure of the rebellion the castle was forfeited and dismantled, but what is left is certainly worth seeing, as are the castle gardens, with Japanese water gardens, and shrub and alpine gardens in the old quarry.

Several miles (5 km) further, the Glenkindie earth-house is amongst the trees on the left of the drive from the westernmost lodge gate of Glenkindie House. It is worth stopping for as it differs from other earth houses in having only a short passage, but a second chamber leading from the main chamber through a confined hole. It is well-preserved, but take a torch if you have one.

Beyond, a mile or so (2 km) on the A97 is Glenbuchat Castle, a late sixteenth century Gordon tower that later became the seat of John

Gordon, known as 'Old Glenbucket of the '45' who was a staunch Jacobite but died in France, penniless, after the Culloden defeat. (Over the door is the apt inscription 'No thing on arth remains bot fame'.) A pleasant example of a small Highland parish church is Glenbuchat Church, originally fifteenth century but reconstructed in the seventeenth and eighteenth centuries. It is no longer in use but note the box pews (with moveable partitions), the belfry and the laird's loft (1828). Towards the end of August every year the Lonach Highland Gathering is held at Bellabeg, well-known for its March of the Clansmen from Inverernan, two miles (3 km) west. The graceful Poldullie Bridge over the Don near Bellabeg, with a 70-foot (21 m) single arch, was built in 1715 by Jack Forbes of Inverernan who died the following year, a victim of the '15 Rebellion.

Corgarff Castle is a sixteenth century tower converted into unattractive fortified barracks by the Hanoverians. It was garrisoned from 1745 to control the military road here (the Lecht Road), and continued as a military station, for the inhibition of smuggling, until about 1830. The earlier history of Corgarff Castle includes a gruesome episode during the feud between the Gordons and the Forbes, when in 1571 Adam Gordon besieged the tower while Alexander Forbes was away. Rather than surrender, his wife and children and entire household burned to death when the castle was set alight. The Lecht Road, a section of the Hanoverian military route, rises steeply to the summit pass at 2,100 feet (640 m), where the scenery is bleak moorland with sweeping vistas. This area is renowned for heavy snowfalls and ski tows serve the slopes on both sides of the road, before it descends towards **Tomintoul**, at 1,160 feet (354 m) the highest village of the Highlands. In summer Tomintoul is a fairly busy centre, especially enjoyed for the local fishing despite its exposed position. The local museum has a reconstruction of a farm kitchen.

From here it is some five miles (8 km) on the B9008 to Glen Livet, where, in 1594 James VI personally defeated the rebel earls of Huntly and Errol. The Glenlivet Distillery has a Visitor Centre, and exhibition, and offers distillery tours.

Across the Grampian/Highland regional boundary, **Grantown-on-Spey** stands at the crossing of several important roads for touring (*see* Highlands, p. 205). It is a popular yet reasonably unspoiled eighteenth century town, founded by Sir James Grant in 1776, with attractions for both summer and winter visitors, since it is a base for winter sports. In its parish church note the striking black oak pulpit.

VI: Dyce – Old Meldrum – Turriff

The direct route to Banff from Aberdeen is not the most interesting, but there are places not to be overlooked on the route.

Outside Aberdeen on the A947 is Dyce airport that serves Aberdeen. A mile (2 km) south of **Old Meldrum** is Barra Hill, where Robert the

Bruce defeated John Comyn, Earl of Buchan in 1307. East of Old Meldrum is Pitmedden Garden, (*see* p. 185), and a couple of miles (3 km) north is Tolquhon Castle, a remarkable mixture of fortress exterior and domestic inner court, in attractive setting. Despite the impression it gives of a defensive stronghold, (or even because of it?) Tolquhon has never apparently suffered from anything worse than neglect (since the mid nineteenth century), there being no evidence of hostile attack during its history. There were various owners since the fourteenth century, but in 1584 it belonged to William Forbes, an educated gentleman, who employed Thomas Lieper, the master mason, to help him extend the castle. (Lieper was also responsible for the elaborate Gothic tomb of William Forbes and his wife, Elizabeth Gordon, in the parish church at Tarves.) The estate had to be sold in 1716, and the castle continued to be occupied until the middle of the last century.

North of here again, is Haddo House (NTS) a William Adam masterpiece of 1731, set in a great park with an elegant central section whose balcony at first floor level is reached by two great curving flights of stairs. Symmetry is a feature of the building, which also contains superb antique furniture and portraits, arrayed in the graciously proportioned rooms. The chapel, 1880, was the last work of architect G.E. Street, and has a Burne-Jones stained-glass window (east). The Haddo Choral Society has it own theatre in the grounds and, as one of Scotland's leading musical bodies, produces first-rate opera and concerts with internationally acclaimed artists. (For details of performances, contact the Choral Secretary of the Haddo House Choral Society.)

To return to the A947, take the road, unclassified, from Haddo to Fyvie where there is a thirteenth century castle, not open to the public, but one of the grandest castellated mansions in Scotland. There is also a church which has Celtic stones built into its gable, and seventeenth century panels inside.

Turriff is the next small town going north on the A947, and is best known for the 'Trot of Turriff' of 1639 (the first skirmish of the Civil War). 1½ miles (2 km) east of Turriff is Delgatie Castle, a tower house, and home of the Hays for nearly 700 years, with additions made to the building in 1570. In 1562 Mary Queen of Scots stopped here for three days (her portrait hangs in the room she used), but the ceilings painted in 1590 are the main feature of the interior. The castle is as impressive L-plan structure, well viewed from the small road beside the grounds.

Rejoining the A947, leave it again immediately to visit Craigston Castle, also about 1½ miles (2 km) east of the road, on the B9105, four miles (6 km) from Turriff. Since it was built, 1604–07, it has been the seat of the Urquhart family.

There is a remnant of a tower of Eden Castle to the west of the A947 several miles (5 km) further north. Built in 1676, its downfall is attributed to the powerful curse of a mother, who asked the laird to control her wayward son. This he did with awful efficiency, by drowning the lad in the river, never to be forgiven by the grief-stricken mother.

Access to Sites and Places of Interest

Aberdeen
Art Gallery & Museum
1000–1700 Mon.–Sat. (1000–2000 Thurs.),
1400–1700 Sun.

Cathedral of St Machar
0900–2100 daily (closes 1700 in Oct.–Mar.).

James Dun's House Museum
1000–1700 Mon.–Sat.

Fish Market
Auction Mon.–Fri.
Best visited 0730–0930.

King's College
0900–1700 Mon.–Sat.

Marischal College Museum
0900–1700 Mon.–Fri.

Provost Ross's House
For times inquire at Tourist Information.

Provost Skene's House
1000–1700 Mon.–Sat.
Fee.

Arbuthnott House
By arrangement. (Inverbervie 226)
Fee.

Balbithan House By arrangement.
(Kintore 2282)

Ballater
McEwan Gallery
1000–1800 daily.

Balmoral Castle
Grounds only. May–July 1000–1700
Mon.–Sat.
Not open when Royal Family in residence.
Fee.

Banchory Museum
June–Sep. 1400–1700 Wed., Fri., Sat., Sun.

Banff
Duff House
Standard, but only open Apr.–Sep.

Museum
June–Sep. 1400–1700 Wed., Fri., Sat., Sun.

Braeloine Visitor Centre
Easter–Sep. 1000–1800 daily.
Donation.

Braemar Castle
May–early Oct. 1000–1800 daily.
Fee.

Brodie Castle
For times inquire at Tourist Information,
Forres.
Fee.

Buckie Maritime Museum
May–Sep. 1400–1600 Mon., 1000–1200,
1400–1600 Tues.–Fri., 1000–1200 Sat.

Burghead Roman Wall
Standard.

Castle Fraser
Castle: May–Sep. 1100–1800 Mon.–Sat.,
1400–1800 Sun. No adm. after 1715.
Grounds: All year 0930–sunset.
Fee.

Corgarff Castle
Standard, but only open Apr.–Sep.

Craig Castle
Summer, by appointment.
(Lumsden 202)

Craigievar Castle
Castle: May–Sep. 1400–1900 daily except
Fri. No adm. after 1815.
Grounds: All year 0930–sunset.
Fee.

Craigston Castle
By arrangement. (King Edward 228)

Crathes Castle
Castle: May–Sep. 1100–1800 Mon.–Sat.,
1400–1800 Sun. No adm. after 1715.
Gardens & grounds: all year 0930–sunset.
Fee.

Deer Abbey
Standard, but open only Apr.–Sep.

Delgatie Castle
By arrangement. (Turriff 3479)
Fee.

Dinnet Oakwood
(NNR)
Permission required. (NCC, NE Region)

Drum Castle
Castle: May–Sep. 1100–1800 Mon.–Sat.,
1400–1800 Sun. No adm. after 1715.
Grounds: All year 0930–sunset.
Fee.

Druminnor Castle
June–Aug. 1430–1730 Sun.
Fee.

Dufftown Museum
June–Sep. 1000–1300, 1400–1900 daily,
(Sep. to 1800, June to 1600).

Dunnottar Castle
0900–1800 Mon.-Sat., 1400–1800 Sun.;
Nov.–Mar. closed Sat.
Fee.

Elgin
Cathedral
Standard.

Museum
Mid Mar.–mid Oct. 1000–1230, 1400–1700
Mon., Wed.-Sat., 1000–1300 Tue; mid
Oct.–mid Mar. 1000–1200 Wed. & Sat.
Fee.

Forres
Falconer Museum
Mid May–Sep. 1000–1300, 1400–1700
daily, (June & Sep. to 1800, July & Aug. to
1900).

Glen Farclas Distillery
0900–1630 Mon.–Fri.

Glen Fiddich & Balvenie Distilleries
1000–1230, 1400–1630 Mon.–Fri.

Glen Grant & Caperdonich Distilleries
1000–1200, 1400–1600 Mon.–Fri. Closed
mid July–end Aug.

Glenlivet Distillery
May–Sep. 1000–1600 Mon.–Fri.

Haddo House
Easter–Sep. 1100–1800 Mon.–Sat., 1400–
1800 Sun. No adm. after 1715.
Fee.

Huntly
Adamston Agricultural Museum
All reasonable times. Donation.

Castle
Standard.

Museum
0900–1700 Mon.–Sat.

Inverurie Museum
1400–1700 Mon.–Fri., 1000–1200 Sat.

Kincorth House Gardens
June–Aug. 0900–2100 daily.
Fee.

Leith Hall
Hall: May–Sep. 1100–1800 Mon.-Sat.,
1400–1800 Sun. No adm. after 1715.
Grounds: All year 0930–sunset.
Fee.

Maryculter
St Mary's College (Blairs)
By appointment.

Muir of Dinnet
(NNR)
Permit required for camping, boating &
fishing. (NCC, NE Region)

Peterhead
Arbuthnot Museum & Art Gallery
1000–1200, 1400–1700 Mon.–Sat.

Pitcaple Castle
Apr.–Oct. 1100–1800 if convenient, daily.
Fee.

Pitmedden Garden
0930–sunset daily.
Fee.

Strathisla Distillery
1000–1600 Mon.–Fri.

Tolquhon Castle
Standard.

Tomintoul Museum
June–Sep. 1000–1300, 1400–1800 daily,
(July & Aug. to 1900).

Hotels and Guest Houses

Aberdeen
Aberdeen Airport Hotel,
Skean Dhu, Argyll Road,
Dyce AB2 0DU.
(Aberdeen 725252)

Ashley House Hotel,
1 Kings Gate.
(Aberdeen 636382)

Caledonian Hotel,
Union Terrace.
(Aberdeen 29233)

Ferryhill House Hotel,
169 Bon-Accord Street.
(Aberdeen 50867)

Holiday Inn Aberdeen Airport,
Riverview Drive,
Farburn,
Dyce.
(Aberdeen 770011)

Kittybrewster Hotel,
75 Powis Terrace AB2 3PY.
(Aberdeen 46574)

Northern Hotel,
1 Great Northern Road AB9 2UL.
(Aberdeen 43342)

Scotts Private Hotel,
165 Crown Street.
(Aberdeen 26911)

Tree Tops Hotel,
161 Springfield Road AB9 2QH.
(Aberdeen 33377)

Ashgrove Guest House,
9 Forest Avenue AB1 6TU.
(Aberdeen 36226)

Ashgrove Guest House,
34 Ashgrove Road.
(Aberdeen 44861)

Bracklinn Guest House,
348 Great Western Road.
(Aberdeen 37060)

Ravenscraig Guest House,
69 Constitution Street.
(Aberdeen 56912)

Ballater
Alexandra Hotel,
Bridge Street.
(Ballater 376)

Aspen Hotel,
Braemar Road.
(Ballater 486)

Craigendarroch Hotel.
(Ballater 217)

Darroch Learg Hotel.
(Ballater 443)

Deeside Hotel,
Braemar Road.
(Ballater 420)

Glen Lui Hotel.
(Ballater 402)

Loirston Hotel,
Victoria Road.
(Ballater 413)

Ravenswood Hotel,
Braemar Road.
(Ballater 539)

Tullich Lodge Hotel.
(Ballater 406)

Banchory
Banchory Lodge Hotel.
(Banchory 2625)

Burnett Arms Hotel,
25 High Street.
(Bancory 2545)

Banff
Banff Springs Hotel.
(Banff 2881)

The County otel.
High Street.
(Banff 5353)

Dunvegan House Hotel.
(Banff 2374)

Braemar
Braemar Lodge Hotel.
(Braemar 617)

Callater Lodge Hotel.
(Braemar 275)

Mar Lodge
(Braemar 216)

Moorfield Hotel,
Chapel Brae.
(Braemar 244)

Buckie
Cluny Hotel,
2 High Street.
(Buckie 32922)

St AndrewsHotel,
St Andrews Square.
(Buckie 31227)

Cullen
Bay View Hotel,
57 Seafield Street.
(Cullen 40260)

Grant Arms Hotel,
Grant Street.
(Cullen 40243)

Royal Oak Hotel,
43–45 Seatown.
(Cullen 40252)

Three Kings Inn,
21 North Castle Street.
(Cullen 40538)

Elgin
Eight Acres Hotel,
Sheriffmill.
(Elgin 3077/8)

Grove Hotel,
Pluscarden Road.
(Elgin 2958)

Sunninghill Hotel,
Hay Street.
(Elgin 7788)

Torr House Hotel,
8 Moss Street.
(Elgin 2661)

South Bank Guest House,
36 Academy Street.
(Elgin 7132)

Fochabers
Gordon Arms Hotel,
High Street.
(Fochabers 820508/9)

Forres
Carlton Hotel,
65 High Street.
(Forres 72531)

Glenlivet
Blairfindy Lodge Hotel.
(Glenlivet 376)

Huntly
Castle Hotel.
(Huntly 2696)

MacDuff
Deveron House Hotel,
25–27 Union Street.
(MacDuff 32309)

Newburgh
Udny Arms Hotel.
(Newburgh 444)

Tomintoul
Glenavon Hotel,
The Square.
(Tomintoul 218)

Camping and Caravanning

Aberdeen
Garthdee Caravan Site,
Garthdee Road,
Aberdeen District Council,
Dept of Leisure & Recreation,
St Nicholas House,
Broad Street.
(Aberdeen 23456)

Aberlour on Spey
Aberlour Gardens Caravan Park.
(Aberlour 586/Dufftown 461)

Aboyne
Aboyne Loch Caravan Park,
Dinnet Estates, Enterprises Ltd,
Old Station.
(Dinnet 341)

Alford
Haughton House Caravan Park,
Montgarrie Road.
(Alford 2107)

Banchory
Campfield Caravan Site,
Glassel by Banchory.
(Torphins 250)

Banff
Banff Links Caravan Site,
Banff & Buchan District Council,
Church Street,
MacDuff.
(MacDuff 32861)

Burghead
Red Craig Hotel & Caravan Park.
(Burghead 663)

Elgin
North Alves Caravan Park.
(Alves 223)

Riverside Caravan Park,
West Road.
(Elgin 2813)

Findhorn
Findhorn Bay Caravan Park.
(Findhorn 2203)

Findhorn Sands Caravan Site.

Fochabers
Burnside Caravan Site.
(Fochabers 820362)

Forres
Old Mill Inn Caravan Site.
(Brodie 244)

Lossiemouth
Holts Leisure Parks Ltd,
Silver Sands Leisure Park,
Covesea West Beach.
(Lossiemouth 3262/3099)

Muirton House Caravan Site.
(Lossiemouth 3177)

MacDuff
Myrus Camping Caravan Site,
Myrus.
(Banff 2845)

Peterhead
Lido Caravan Site,
South Bay.
(Peterhead 3358)
Bookings: Banff & Buchan District
Council,
Church Street, Macduff.
(Macduff 32861)

Rosehearty
Municipal Caravan Site,
Sea Front.
Bookings: Banff & Buchan District
Council,
Church Street, Macduff
(Macduff 32861)

Skene
Mains of Keir.
(Skene 282)

Turriff
Kinnaird House Caravan Site,
Banff Road.
(Turriff 2550)

Self Catering Accommodation

Aberlour
Bell-Ingram,
Durn, Isla Road,
Perth.
(Perth 21121)

Auchterless
Blakes Holidays,
Wroxham, Norwich,
Norfolk.
(Wroxham 2917)

Ballater
Mr & Mrs Nimmo,
Morvada Guest House,
Ballater.
(Ballater 501)

Banff
Mrs H. Massie,
Wardend Farm,
By Banff.
(Banff 2201)

Braemar
Mrs A. Normand,
Seamews,
Gullane,
East Lothian.
(Gullane 842106)

Craigievar
National Trust for Scotland,
5 Charlote Square,
Edinburgh.
(Edinburgh 226/5922)

Cullen
Mrs Grant,
Earlsfield, Kennethmont,
Insch, Aberdeenshire.
(Kennethmont 207)

Blantyre Holiday Homes,
West Bauds,
Findochty Buckie,
Banffshire.
(Buckie 31773)

Drum
National Trust for Scotland,
5 Charlotte Square,
Edinburgh.
(Edinburgh 226/5922)

Dufftown
Mrs J. Smart,
Errolbank,
134 Fife Street,
Dufftown.
(Dufftown 20229)

Fochabers
Christies (Fochabers) Ltd,
The Nurseries,
Fochabers,
Moray.
(Fochabers 820362)

Forres
W. Scott,
Whiterow,
Forres, Morray.
(Forres 72718)

Glenlivet
Mr Davidson,
Riverstone,
Ballindalloch, Banffshire.
(Glenlivet 219)

Huntly
Mrs Gordon,
Tillyminate,
Gartley by Huntly,
Aberdeenshire.
(Gartly 207)

Kennethmont
Mrs S. Grant,
Earlsfield,
Kennethmont by Insch,
Aberdeenshire.
(Kennethmont 207)

Lossiemouth
R. Grant,
Relugas, Old Post Office,
Dunphail by Forres,
Moray.
(Dunphail 233)

Pitmedden
National Trust for Scotland,
5 Charlotte Square,
Edinburgh.
(Edinburgh 226/5922)

Rothiemay
Mrs A.D. Williams,
Mayen,
Rothiemay, Huntly,
Aberdeenshire.
(Rothiemay 276)

Tomintoul
Mrs M.H. Grant,
Badnafrave,
Tomintoul, Banffshire.
(Tomintoul 268)

Golf

Aberdeen
Auchmill Golf Course
(Aberdeen 714577)

Nigg Bay Golf Club,
St Fittick's Road
(Aberdeen 871286)

Bon Accord Golf Club,
19 Golf Road.
(Aberdeen 633464)

Caledonian Golf Club,
Kings Links.
(Aberdeen 224431)

Deeside Golf Club.
(Aberdeen 47697)

Kings Links Golf Course.
(Aberdeen 23456, Ext. 232)

Links Golf Course,
Links Road.
(Aberdeen 52269)

Royal Aberdeen Golf Club.
(Aberdeen 29151)

West Hill Golf Club.
(Aberdeen 740364)

Aboyne
Aboyne Golf Club.
(Aboyne 2328)

Tarland Golf Club.
(Tarland 413)

Banchory
Banchory Golf Club.
(Banchory 2365)

Banff
Duff House Royal Golf Club,
The Barnyards.
(Banff 2062)

Buckie
Buckpool Golf Club,
Barhill Road.
(Buckie 32236)

Braemar
Braemar Golf Course.
(Braemar 618)

Elgin
Hardhillock Golf Course,
Birnie Road.
(Elgin 2338)

Huntly
Huntly Golf Club,
Cooper Park.
(Huntly 2643)

Inverallochy
Inverallochy Golf Course,
45 Main Street.
(Inverallochy 2544)

Keith
Keith Golf Course,
Fife Park.
(Keith 2469)

Kemnay
Kemnay Golf Club.
(Kemnay 228)

Newburgh-on-Ythan
Newburgh-on-Ythan Golf Course,
Ellon.
(Newburgh 397)

Peterhead
Craigewan Golf Course.
(Peterhead 2149)

Spey Bay
Spey Bay Golf Club.
(Fochabers 820424)

Stonehaven
Stonehaven Golf Course,
Cowie.
(Stonehaven 62124)

Tarland
Tarland Golf Club.
(Tarland 413)

Torphins
Torphins Golf Club,
26 Beltie Road.
(Torphins 493)

Turriff
Turriff Golf Club,
Rosehall.
(Turriff 2745)

Horse Riding

Aberdeen
Hayfield Riding School,
Hazlehead.
(Aberdeen 35703)

Forres
Kinloss Riding Stables,
Old Schoolhouse.
(Kindhorn 2218)
Accommodation can be arranged.

Stonehaven
Stonehaven Riding School,
Cowton,
Rickarton, Stonehaven,
Kincardinshire.
(Stonehaven 63360)

Tomintoul
Tomintoul Stables,
By Ballindalloch,
Banffshire.
(Tomintoul 233)

Sea Angling

Buckie
Cod, pollack, mackerel, haddock, whiting,
flat fish.

Lossiemouth
Sea trout, conger, haddock, cod and plaice
from boats.
Permits: Angling Centre,
Moss Street, Elgin.

Game Fishing

River Dee
Salmon, Sea trout.
Permits: Banchory Lodge Hotel,
Banchory, Kincardineshire.
(Banchory 2625)

Ardoe House Hotel,
Banchory, Kincardineshire.
(Aberdeen 47355)

River Deveron
Salmon, sea trout, brown trout.
Permits: Castle Hotel,
Huntly.
(Huntly 2696)

Forbes Arms Hotel,
Rothiemay,
Huntly.
(Rothiemay 248)

Turriff Angling Association,
I. Mason, 14 Main Street, Turriff.
Aberdeenshire.
(Turriff 2428)

River Don
Salmon, brown trout.
Permits: Kemnay House,
Kemnay,
Aberdeenshire.
(Kemnay 2220)

Kildrummy Castle Hotel,
Kildrummy,
Aberdeenshire.
(Kildrummy 288)

River Don (Kinclune, Kildrummy)
Permits: T. Hillary,
Stonecircle, Glenkindie,
Aberdeenshire.
(Glenkindie 335)

River Don
Permits: Colquhonnie Hotel,
Strathdon,
Aberdeenshire.
(Strathdon 210)

Cycling

Aberdeen
Aberdeen Cycle Centre,
188 King Street.
(Aberdeen 24542)

Alford
W. & K. Mathers,
Haughton Garage.
(Alford 2331)

Braemar
Joseph Grant & Co.,
Castle Garage.

Huntly
Gartly Cycles,
Station Holiday Cottage,
Gartly.
(Gartly 277/343)

Where to Eat

Aberdeen
Aberdeen Airport Hotel,
Skean Dhu,
Argyll Road, Dyce.
(Aberdeen 725252)

Alford
Kildrummy Castle Hotel,
Kildrummy.
(Kildrummy 288)

Buckie
The Mill Motel,
Tynet.
(Clochan 233)

Elgin
Park House Restaurant,
South Street.
(Elgin 7695)

Pennan
Pennan Inn,
nr Fraserburgh.
(Aberdour 201)

Rothes
Rothes Glen Hotel,
nr Elgin.
(Rothes 254)

Car Hire

Aberdeen
Avis Rent-a-Car,
Aberdeen Airport.
(Aberdeen 722282)

Godfrey Davis (Car Hire) Ltd,
121 Causewayend.
(Aberdeen 63571)

Aberdeen Airport.
(Aberdeen 732404).

Highlands

The Highlands covers a vast area of Scotland, and since the days of 'the clearances', roughly between 1780 and 1860, when the indigenous crofters and clansmen were forced out, it has always been the least populated. It has its own tourist authority separate from the STB, the Highlands and Islands Development Board (HIDB) and can be naturally divided into three areas: the northern Highlands with the great lonely mountains, the glens, lochs and burns; Inverness and the densely populated strip to the north of Inverness; and the far north – barren undulating moorland and peat bog.

I: Aviemore – Grantown-on-Spey – Nairn

Approaching the Highlands on the A9 coming up from Tayside, **Dalwhinnie** is the first village after the county boundary, at the northerly tip of Loch Elricht, which is now part of an HEP scheme. (On its west bank is Cluny's Cave, where the Young Pretender and Cluny Macpherson hid after the battle of Culloden.) Dalwhinnie is a bleak place in the midst of wild country, which made it a popular rallying place with the Highlanders, who could hold their own even when vastly outnumbered, in bygone days. Deer herds can be seen here in spring and autumn. Following the A9 northwards up the Spey valley, the Monadhliath mountains straddle the country between this route, and Loch Ness and the Great Glen (the string of connected lochs that form a geological split clean across northern Scotland). They are roadless and uninhabited mountains, the tops at 1,500 feet (457 m) often obscured by low cloud, bare but for occasional areas of forest, and with much of Scotland's bloody history attached to them.

The road up to **Newtonmore** is fast dual-carriageway, and Newtonmore is a good base from which to explore the rugged and untamed scenery. The Clan Macpherson House and Museum, Main Street, is worth visiting here (note the 'black chanter'). The Newtonmore Highland Games, and Clan Macpherson Rally are held on the first Saturday of August every year. Just up the road, **Kingussie** (pronounced 'Kinyewssie') has an excellent museum, the Highland Folk Museum, opened in 1935, with outdoor exhibits, reconstructed dwellings, a clack mill and a kailyard. Over the river are the ruins of Ruthven Barracks, built in 1718, extended in 1734 (by General Wade) and blown up by Prince Charles' Highlanders when they assembled here after their defeat at Culloden. James Macpherson, 1736–96 poet and 'translator' of the Ossianic poems, was born at Ruthven village. His monument, and the mansion he built, Balavil, a couple of miles (3 km) further on are beside the A9.

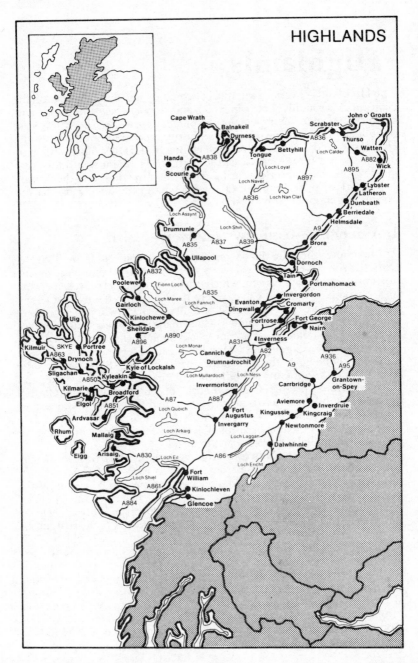

HIGHLANDS

Kincraig has a drive-through Highland Wildlife Park well-stocked with deer, wildcat, bison, lynx, brown bear, wolf (Scotland's last wild wolf was killed in 1742 nearby at Badenoch), and others, all live in natural habitat, and some are usually visible from the car. North-east of Kincraig, three miles (5 km) south of Aviemore, is a beautifully situated loch, Loch-an-Eilean, fringed with pine trees and encircled by a nature trail. There is a ruined castle (origins fifteenth century) on an island, all of which is very picturesque. The Visitor Centre is a converted croft (with exhibitions relating to the native pines).

Aviemore lies to the west of the spectacular Cairngorm mountains, the highest mountain mass in Britain with six peaks over 4,000 feet (1,219 m) (though none as high as Ben Nevis) and to the east of the Monadhliath range, on the Spey, which makes it a very popular and attractive centre for tourism throughout the year, with unique winter sporting facilities, including a chairlift to 3,600 feet (1,097 m) up Cairngorm mountain. Easily accessible by road, rail and air (Inverness airport) there is probably something for everyone here, with accommodation at all levels from luxury modern hotels, to self-catering chalets, bed-and-breakfast and caravans. Entertainments are equally broadly ranged, with theatre, films, exhibitions, discos, Clan Tartan Centre (with computerised tracing of clan links), Highland Craft Village, sports facilities (swimming pool, saunas, squash courts, dry-ski slopes and much more) and 'Santa Claus Land' with activities to amuse children for hours on end. There are shops and restaurants (mostly of the fast-food variety though some of the larger hotels have higher eating standards) and within the vicinity there is much to see. The Craigellachie National Nature Reserve occupies 642 acres (260 ha) to the immediate west of Aviemore, with extensive birchwood and moorland rising to 1,700 feet (518 m), and with a scenic nature trail planned through it. In summer the mountain scenery provides a wide range of excursions and activities.

East of Aviemore on the A951 is Glenmore Lodge, a national outdoor training centre which offers a variety of courses related to mountaineering and skiing, details from the Scottish Sports Council. The Glenmore Forest Park covers 12,000 acres (4,860 ha) of the north-west slopes of Cairngorm and is ideal for hill walking, forest trekking, animal and bird watching from hides, and climbing. Guided tours are organised, and of course there is good skiing most winters. It can be reached by the Ski Road, past Loch Morlich, which has a caravan park and camp site, beach, canoes and sailing boats for hire (motor boats not allowed). Aviemore has winter sports schools, and package holidays are available at hotels and boarding houses with transport and instruction inclusive. Details of all attractions and amenities are available at the Aviemore Centre. Special entertainments can be arranged to order, with Scottish dancers, pipers, fiddlers and dance bands, by contacting the Entertainment Manager (Aviemore 810624). Only ten minutes walk from the centre of Aviemore, Spey Bridge Park provides interesting wildlife as well as peace and quiet.

Approaching from the south, at Inverdruie is a trout farm fed by the Druie, which collects water from the north face of Cairngorm's melting snows, and drainage from moor and peat areas, so has clean, fast water all year, to raise Canadian rainbow trout which grow at twice the rate of brown trout. At the Inverdruie fisheries you can feed the trout, and fish for them in the neighbouring loch. Also at Inverdruie is the unique Cairngorm Whisky Centre and Museum, open since 1981, where you can learn about the history of whisky drinking (such as: at Flora Macdonald's death 300 gallons (1,365 l) of neat whisky were consumed by 3,000 mourners, i.e. one-tenth of a gallon average (½ litre) per head!), the modern industry (there are now 117 malt whisky distilleries in Scotland), and the differences between the full range of whiskies. You can also sample a selection of the best malt whiskies from an impressive choice of almost 100 labels. Be careful if you're driving!

North of Aviemore the A9 leads up through lovely birches and conifers growing in tangles of heather and bracken to the Landmark Visitor Centre, just off the road south of Carrbridge. Landmark, opened in 1970, was the enterprising concept of David Hayes who sought to present the natural history of the Highlands in an intelligible and stimulating manner, and the result is very warmly recommended to visit. Housed in a modern complex, designed by architect John Paterson, it incorporates a multivision theatre, exhibition, craft and book shop, restaurant (good food) and bar. Outside in the forest (remnant of the ancient Caledonian pine forest which covered most of northern Scotland for 8,000 years) is a broad-walk nature trail with information points at intervals, a sculpture park, giant woodland maze, balancing trail and tree top trail. Near the car park is a heather centre where plants can be bought.

At **Carrbridge** note the graceful arch of the old bridge over the Dulnain Water, built in 1717, flood-damaged in 1829. At Boat of Garten off the A95, 6½ miles (10 km) from Aviemore, you can see where volunteers have been working since 1972 to restore the railway line and station, closed in 1965. A limited steam service operates, and a museum shows interesting railway bygones. Eight miles (13 km) north-east of Aviemore, off the B970, the Loch Garten Nature Reserve is worth visiting as from the observation post through binoculars you can see the eyrie of the osprey that returned here to breed in 1959, having been extinct in Scotland.

From Boat of Garten the A95 goes on to **Grantown-on-Spey**, 'capital' of Strathspey and a pleasant, unspoilt tourist centre winter and summer alike (*see* p. 208). Along the 23 mile (37 km) stretch of Strathspey there are several whisky distilleries, notably the Glen Farclas distillery (which produces one of the most potent whiskies on the market – beware!) and the Tamdhu distillery, and further up at Rothes the Glen Grant and Caperdonich distilleries. At Dufftown, south-west of Strathspey, are the Glenlivet and Balvenie distilleries. The Tomatin distillery is on the A9 north-east of Strathspey. Many of the best-known whiskies come from

Speyside, and any of the above distilleries are instructive and enjoyable to visit.

On the A939 to Nairn there are two sites to take in, Lochindorb and Ardclach Bell Tower. Lochindorb (or trout loch) has an island supporting a historic ruined castle, built in the thirteenth century, and ultimately ordered to be dismantled by James II 200 years later, after an eventful history. The countryside around the loch is now featureless moorland and the road to the loch is unclassified. Ardclach bell tower is due north of here, 8½ miles (14 km) south-east of Nairn and is an unusual dual-purpose two-storey structure. It was built in 1665 as a look-out post, but also to summon the faithful to worship. The key to the tower is available at the cottage. Its position affords a fine view of the Findhorn River, winding its course between steep wooded banks. The monument beside the track is to Donald Mitchell, Scotland's first missionary to India, born in 1782.

This route becomes less moorland and more wooded as we approach **Nairn**, which overlooks the Moray Firth at the mouth of the River Nairn. Now a popular seaside holiday resort, it was regarded in the past as the boundary point between the Lowlands and the Highlands. (James VI said that the people at one end of the town couldn't understand the language of the others. Be that as it may, Gaelic has long since ceased to be spoken here.) The Fishertown Museum at Laing Hall, Union Street, has items and photographs relating to the fishing industry of the Moray Firth, and domestic detail of fisherfolk's lives, while the other museum, the Literary Institute, displays archaeological and historical exhibits in the attics of the early sixteenth century Viewfield House. A pleasant place to eat is the Taste Bud restaurant in a well-restored cottage at 44 Harbour Street, where you can try Pâté Drambuie, Smoked North Sea Prawns, and Tweed Kettle among other local dishes. In the small town garden belonging to Elizabeth, Countess Cawdor, Constabulary Gardens makes a feature of unusual shrubs, worth visiting.

Unless you are in a hurry, avoid the A96 from Nairn to Inverness and take either the northerly B road, to include Fort George, or the southerly B road, not only much prettier but with three important places to visit on route. **Fort George**, eight miles (13 km) west of Nairn, overlooking the 'neck' of the Moray Firth, is Britain's best example of Hanoverian military architecture. Begun in 1748, it was built to accommodate 2,500 men, after the Jacobite rebellion, and now houses the Regimental Museum of the Queen's Own Highlanders, a chronological display of Highland regiment relics since 1778. After the museum, standing on the walls of the Fort, we felt very conscious of Scotland's military past, expressed fittingly in this setting.

The southerly road leads first to Cawdor Castle, magnificent in its park with fine old trees and lovely gardens. Most of the present building is seventeenth century, around an older central tower (1372) which was fortified in 1454. Parts of the interior are open to visitors, with a number of interesting exhibits, and there is a very pleasant coffee shop off the courtyard. A spiral stairway connects the tower room to the guard room, in the middle of which is an ancient hawthorn tree trunk, said to be the spot originally chosen for the building of the castle. An earlier Cawdor Castle (possibly where Macbeth murdered Duncan) was promised to Macbeth by the witches in Shakespeare's play, but the existing building is considerably later. Clava is an important stone/bronze-age site (2000–1500 BC) further along the B9006. Booklets describing it are sold at the Culloden Visitor Centre. From here the road proceeds to Culloden Moor, site of the last land battle in Britain, where the Young Pretender fought the Duke of Cumberland in 1746, finally ending the Stuart hopes of regaining the throne, also marking the beginning of the distintegration of the age-old Highland way of life. There is a Visitor Centre with audiovisual presentations to illustrate this momentous milestone in Scottish history, where in 40 minutes the Young Pretender lost 1,200 men. Old Leanach farmhouse is now restored as a battle museum, and Culloden House stands on the site of the house used as headquarters by the Young Pretender before the battle, built between 1772 and 1783.

II: Inverness – The Glens – Black Isle

Inverness, divided by the River Ness, is a busy Highland centre with Dalcross airport eight miles (13 km) north-east. There is an excellent Tourist Information Centre in Church Street, combining as a shop, not far from Abertarff House, now the home of the Highland Association with exhibitions on the Scottish Gaels. Church Street also has the High Church (1770) with fourteenth century tower. Near here, Dunbar's Hospital is an attractive example of restored seventeenth century domestic architecture, originally built in 1688 as an alms house. At the heart of the town, a restored Cross stands in front of the Town Hall on a base enclosing the 'Stone of the Tubs', where women used to rest their tubs returning with water from the river), whose origins are uncertain (local folklore has it that the prosperity of the city depends upon it never being moved from this position). The Museum and Art Gallery, just behind the Town Hall, has a pleasing layout, helpful staff and varied exhibits of local and Highland items, silver ware, wildlife, photographs and paintings. Across the river, St Andrew's Cathedral is an imposing building in pink stone built in 1868, with intricate interior. Note the octagonal chapter house. Next door is the modern Eden Court Theatre which incorporates a nineteenth century house built by Bishop Eden, and doubles as a gallery and conference centre. Half a mile (1 km) away is Tomnahurich (Hill of the Fairies), a 220 feet (67 m) high wooded mound, and very good vantage point.

Strategically well placed, Inverness has been the scene of much strife, and old buildings like the castle (finally blown up by the Young Pretender) and the Sconce (a fort built by Cromwell in the 1650s) have not survived, but Inverness is a lively and interesting town, with tempting little shops, especially for plaids, Fair Isle knitwear, kilts, kilt-socks and other Scots dress. There is a kiltmakers at 4–9 Huntly Street where individuals, or parties up to 20, can see kilts being made (*see* Directory p. 235). (Inverness is one of the few towns where it is still quite normal to see men dressed in the kilt for day wear.) There is also an extensive covered market (1886) and adjoining fish market (much older). (There used to be a Fish Wives' Rest Room here for the women who had to walk the seven miles (11 km) from Ardesier and back in a day.) Note the door in the market wall, which was used by the circus in days past. Animals and their paraphernalia were stored in the market hall when not performing in the adjoining circus. The market is still the focus of the town for food shopping, and take advantage of the hot smoked mackerel, ready to eat, smoked salmon, fresh herring, good range of savoury 'puddings' (Stornoway, Aultbea, white and black puddings recommended), freshly made haggis, meat pies and wide selection of fruit and vegetables (the latter is unusual in Scotland). The butcher's meat compares with French rather than English for skilled cutting and presentation.

Inverness station, near the market, always seems busy and welcoming, wide and airy. Crammed with bicycles, back-packs and hikers, there are hanging baskets suspended from the skylight roof, and planted tubs at floor level. The Station Hotel adjoins the station, and offers a warm atmosphere, very good food and helpful service. There are direct trains from London (Euston) day and night, and from Edinburgh, Glasgow and Aberdeen, and Inverness is a direct Motorail terminal from London, Birmingham, Crewe, York and Stirling. It is 40 minutes' flight from Glasgow to Inverness, 90 minutes from London, and airport coaches meet every incoming flight. In summer direct coach services operate to and from Edinburgh and Glasgow, so despite its northerly situation Inverness could never be described as inaccessible.

The A9 heads west from Inverness to **Beauly**, 'beautiful place' from the French 'beau lieu' which described the Priory founded in 1230 for French monks. Now a ruin, note the south wall with its surviving original triangular windows, and the west doorway of the south transept. Also in the main square is the old Cross, and a monument to the 16th Lord Lovat for his service to the South African War, when he 'desired to show that the martial spirit of their forefathers still animates the Highlands of today'. The River Beauly has cut a gorge through the scenic wooded valley which has two dams, Kilmorack and Aigas, opened daily to let the fish swim upstream. The Beauly valley extends into Strath Glass, into which run three glens, Strathfarrar, Glen Cannich and Glen Affric, all known for their beauty and splendour but especially Glen Affric which has been called the loveliest glen in Scotland. Dams and power stations for hydro-electricity have been built on the lochs, but cleverly designed not to mar the impression of nature untouched. The road up Glen Strathfarrar is private, precluding vehicles but not walkers, and leads through some of the best-preserved pine forest in the land (Strathfarrar National Nature Reserve, 5,409 acres (2,191 ha)), coming to a halt at the eastern end of Loch Monar, which is encircled by rugged Highland mountains reaching over 3,000 feet (914 m).

Cannich is the village at the meeting point of Glen Cannich, Glen Affric, Glen Urquhart and Strath Glass. The road along Glen Cannich passes a waterfall and rapids flowing through a ravine about two miles (3 km) up. (You might hear the water before you see it as the ravine is obscured by undergrowth.) The road ends at Loch Mullardoch nine miles (14 km) from Cannich, at the base of 3,500 feet (1,067 m) mountains, densely wooded on the lower slopes but barren above.

Glen Affric has the best road along it with most parking places, and at the end of the road a delightful walk is indicated, through woodland with splendid river vistas. More ambitious walkers can take the footpath beside Loch Affric as far as Alltbeithe Youth Hostel, then (next day!) skirt Beinn Fhada ('long montain') north or south to finish up at Morvich on Loch Duich.

Back at Cannich, Corrimony Cairn is a prehistoric burial cairn with roofed entrance passage, about three miles (5 km) along Glen Urquhart south of the road. A solitary crouched burial was discovered in this cairn, which is encircled by stones. From here follow the A831 along Glen Urquhart eastwards to join the A82 after Drumnadrochit (*see* p. 225), on Loch Ness.

The opposite bank of the firth from Inverness is a promontory about 20 miles long by 7 miles (32 × 11 km) wide, Black Isle, quickly reached across the Kessock Bridge (with wide views of Beauly and Inverness firths). On the eastern shores, **Fortrose** is Black Isle's main town, with under 1,000 inhabitants. Coinneach Odhar, renowned seventeenth century Scottish seer known as Brahan Seer, was murdered near here at Chanonry Point by the Countess of Seaforth, who had him plunged head first into a barrel of boiling tar as a revenge for hearing from him of her husband's infidelity. His 'prophetic' gift came as a result of placing a magical pebble to his eye, blinding that eye to all but the truth and the future. The predictions have since been recounted from generation to generation of Highlanders, and even the most sceptical have had to admit to powerful coincidence, when he foresaw, a century before the event, that the Highlanders would 'flee from their native country before an army of sheep' and 'emigrate to islands now unknown but which shall yet be discovered in the boundless oceans' (such as New Zealand?) leaving the Highlands 'utterly desolated and depopulated'! The charm of the small ruined Cathedral is slightly marred by the modern steeple surmounting the mellow octagonal clock tower of the original red sandstone church, founded by David I. Note the lovely thirteenth century chapter house beside it. On the golf course a stone indicates where Scotland's last witch was burned alive, or perhaps second to last as Dornoch makes the same claim. Take a walk up the Hill of Fortrose for extensive views, and look out from the signpost to Earth Pillars.

North of Fortrose, Rosemarkie is an unspoilt village with distinctive red sands and sheltered coves. The cliffs to the north-east are a breeding ground for fulmars, and pinkfeet in spring. There is a footpath to Fairy Glen and you can visit the lower part of Earth Pillars. Between here and Cromarty at the northern tip of Black Isle is a very good area for walks and birdwatching. Geologists will be familiar with the terrain through the writings of the well-known geologist, Hugh Miller (1802–56), whose thatched cottage birthplace is now a museum of his varied work. A statue of him (1859, by Ritchie) adjoins the chapel, and tombstones carved by Miller when he was a stonemason can be seen in the churchyard.

In **Cromarty** the Court House, the East Church (with three lofts) and the Cross are all of interest, and above the town is a ruined Gaelic chapel. In the early nineteenth century, before the railways, Cromarty thrived with coastal traffic, and the town prospered, note the three-storey merchants' houses. Now its main attraction is its seclusion. The road west and south follows the Cromarty Bay, Udale Bay and Cromarty Firth, overlooking the industrialised landscape around Invergordon (large aluminium smelter and distilleries) and the mountains westward. Invergordon can be reached by ferry across the narrow firth from Balblair. (At Castlecraig is a small fifteenth century ruined castle.) Udale and Nigg Bays form an important national nature reserve of 5,000 acres (2,025 ha) of flats for migratory wildfowl and waders. From St Michael's Chapel a delightful walk for birdwatchers is via Newhall Point and Balblair, and back, taking about one and a half hours.

III: Dingwall – Bonar Bridge – Helmsdale

Leaving the Black Isle on the A9, **Dingwall** is at the head of Cromarty Firth. Macbeth's birthplace, it was colonised by the Norsemen who named it 'Thing Vollr' (or council place) and made a royal burgh in 1226 by Alexander II. The Town House has a local history museum, with exhibit of General Sir Hector MacDonald (monument on Mitchell Hill).

The A834 heads west from Dingwall to form a triangle with the A9 and A832, through the quiet spa town of **Strathpeffer**, a good place to stop and look around. The sulphur springs used to bring people from afar, even in the eighteenth century, to take the 'therapeutic waters' which put Strathpeffer on the map. (These waters can still be taken here.) During the First and Second World Wars, the spa closed and hotels were commandeered, and in 1945 it was not reopened. As a Highland holiday resort it still prospers and has lost little of its old-fashioned charm, with its wide street and many pleasant houses and hotels. At the height of the spa's popularity, the railway was brought here on a branch line which was closed in the 1940s, but now the little Victorian station has been renovated (wood panelling painted maroon, with white wrought-iron work) and functions as a useful complex, with craft studios (unusual marquetry landscapes, framed, are on sale), an information centre and a little cinema where an excellent natural history film is shown (about Handa Island), as well as film of Strathpeffer Station as it used to be, with sound effects.

A signed path opposite the Ben Wyvis Hotel leads up to the Eagle Stone, commemorating a Clan Munro victory over the MacDonalds in 1411 (the eagle being the Munro crest). The Brahan Seer proclaimed that should the stone fall three times, ships would anchor to it. (It has already fallen twice since then. . . .) A worse defeat for the Clan MacDonald was at Kinellan (a mile (1½ km) to the south-west) in 1492. A young MacDonald woman was accepted by a Mackenzie as his bride but he was outraged on meeting her to find she was one-eyed. He sent her home on a one-eyed horse led by a one-eyed groom, accompanied by a one-eyed dog, and the affronted MacDonalds challenged them at Kinellan. The Mackenzie victory led to the MacDonalds also surrendering their title of Lords of the Isles, the penalty decreed by James IV.

With Ben Wyvis (3,429 feet/1,045 m) looming to the north, Strathpeffer is an excellent base for hill walking and exploring. The Rogie Falls, beside the A832, are worth visiting (good views, sometimes of salmon leaping, from the foot suspension bridge), and a booklet of local walks is available from the 'station' information centre. The Strathpeffer Highland Games are held on the first Saturday of August each year in the grounds of Castle Leod (1616), which is not open to the public. (The name is misleading: probably from Cul da Leothad, or 'behind the two slopes', not from any MacLeod connection.)

The A832 travels up through Garve past Loch Luichart, the first electricity generating loch in the Highlands, and on to Achnasheen (*see* p. 224) through lonely country. At the western tip of the loch at 4½ miles (7 km) a track can be found that climbs up to the wild and rugged Loch Fannich. (The equally remote 22-mile (35 km) dead-end road along Strath Conon leads from the A832 at Marybank, south-east of Contin). The rail route from Inverness to Kyle of Loch Alsh is the Great Scenic Railway, takes about three hours and is a restful way to travel through unspoilt Highland scenery. The route is losing money, and is threatened with closure, so go while the going's good!

Glen Glass joins the Cromarty Firth at Evanton, and is known as Black Rock Ravine, two miles (3 km) long, less than 12 feet (4 m) wide and in places over 200 feet (61 m) deep. The River Glass tumbles and thrusts its way along the cleft to the sea. It is worth following the road along its course, then the track up to the footbridge for fantastic views of the ravine. The 'Indian temple' on Knock Fyrish, 1,483 feet (452 m) above Evanton, was commissioned by General Sir Hector Munro, 1726–1805, to alleviate local unemployment. The A9 proceeds to Tain, on the southern banks of the Dornoch Firth, but the A836 provides a scenic shortcut northwards.

Tarbat Ness lighthouse (B9165) is one of the tallest in Britain, and a great spot for birdwatching. Seals can often be seen near the dangerous sandbanks across the Dornoch Firth. The village of Portmahomack is quite a popular resort, with harbour and interesting Reformation church. Near here Ballone Castle was built in the fifteenth to sixteenth century and abandoned in the early nineteenth century.

Back on the A9, **Tain** is a little town of long standing, its name a corruption of the Norse 'thing' meaning council. During 'the clearances' it was an administrative centre and the Tolbooth was known as the 'sharp-pointed house' by the Highlanders, because of its striking conical structure. St Duthus was born here and is Tain's patron saint. According to tradition, St Duthus' Chapel is on the site of his birthplace, and houses his bones, brought back in 1253 from Armagh in Ireland, where he died in 1065. The eleventh to twelfth century ivy-covered ruin, remarkable for not having an eastward altar, was originally a prayer cell, with residence for a hermit who protected it. St Duthus' Church stands on the site of a former church, of which traces can still be seen in the chapter house. Built in 1360, it became a place of pilgrimage in medieval times (James IV came yearly for 20 years as penance for the part he played in his father's death). Note the lovely stained-glass windows. From Tain quarry, two miles (3 km) south-west, Morangie Forest offers rewarding walks with the possibility of spotting blue hare, deer and wildcat.

Following the Dornoch Firth the A9 passes Struie Hill, with view indicator drawing attention to the impressive northward views. Before crossing the narrowing firth, Strathcarron runs from the moors about 10 miles (16 km) down to Ardgay on the firth. This valley witnessed some harsh confrontations during 'the clearances', and the church at Croick bears the names and messages, scratched on the windows, of the unfortunate people of Glencalvie who were evicted after sustained resistance together with their neighbours.

Bonar Bridge is reached by a bridge spanning the head of Dornoch Firth, with Kyle of Sutherland flowing to meet it. The forest area upstream is beautiful walking country (Kyle of Sutherland forest walks, all about two miles (3 km), lead through lovely scenery). Heading east from Bonar Bridge the A9 goes out towards Dornoch on the northern neck of the firth along the strip of land between mountains and sea.

Dornoch, dominated by its squat cathedral, is a quiet resort with fine sandy beaches and two golf courses. The cathedral was built in 1224 by the Bishop of Caithness, Gilbert de Moravia, and became the seat of the bishops. Castle of the Bishops was then built alongside, only the tower remaining (now part of a hotel). Some of the original stonework of the cathedral is still intact although it was badly damaged by fire in 1570, and underwent restoration both in the seventeenth and nineteenth centuries. Dornoch's town jail is now a craft centre where tartan is woven. The Witch's Stone marks the spot where Scotland's last witch, Janet Horne, was burnt in 1722, though this is arguable since Fortrose claims the same 'distinction'. She was condemned for turning her daughter into a pony, which she then rode to the witches' meeting place to have her shod by the Devil. . .

Rather than back-tracking to the A9, the road along the shore through Embo and Skelbo is more interesting. There are remains of stone-age burial chambers at the caravan site, about 2000 BC, which is also the site of a village where evicted crofters were settled during 'the clearances', and told to farm (the land is so sandy it was like attempting to farm a beach!) The ruin on the grass mound overlooking Loch Fleet is of fourteenth century Skelbo Castle. Loch Fleet is crossed at the head by a causeway first built in 1815. A ferry across the mouth of the loch was used previously.

At **Golspie**, a neat village backed by pinewoods, note the superb carved Sutherland Loft (1739) in the church. The enormous statue on top of Ben Vraggie is of the 1st Duke of Sutherland, who was as glorified for the improvements he instigated, as he was blamed for his part in 'the clearances' evictions (he died in 1833). On the left leaving Golspie is the Orcadian Stone Co. Ltd where you can see stones being sanded, drilled, ground, polished etc. See Directory p. 235.

Just outside Golspie, Dunrobin Castle stands impressively in a park beside the sea. It dates back to 1275, with numerous extensions over the years, notably in the nineteenth century by Sir Charles Barry, architect of the Houses of Parliament. Fire damage during the First World War, when used as a naval hospital, led to the most recent rebuilding, by Sir Robert Lorimer. The Castle collection includes two paintings by Canaletto, and note also in the drawing room the Mortlake tapestries. The summer house (1723) is also a museum.

At **Brora** note the remains of two brochs, the first just east of the road as it crosses the railway line, the other about three miles (5 km) north, again east of the road, and the better of the two with 31 feet (9 m) (internal) diameter, and domed wall chambers. (Two headless skeletons were discovered here in 1880.) There are a number of such remains in the district, another good example being inland, overlooking the Black Water, about nine miles (14 km) from Brora (take the little road that runs along the east shore of Loch Brora to Balnacoil). At the Sutherland Wool Mills you can see wool being manufactured, from raw material to travelling rug, tweed blanket, etc.

Helmsdale, a fishing town with colourful boats, has no remarkable features, but the road climbs and twists up to the rugged plateau of Ord of Caithness as it continues northwards along the coast. At Berriedale the meague remains of a castle/fortress stand beside the sea.

There is a castle at **Dunbeath**, to be viewed only from the outside, with a keep built in the fifteenth century and extended in 1870. Dunbeath also has the Laidhay Croft Museum, an eighteenth century croft with period interior. Due west of Dunbeath is Braemore where, at Eagle Rock, a monument marks the spot where the Duke of Kent (1902–42) was killed in an air accident. (The unclassified road through Braemore comes to a dead end beyond so you have to back-track to Dunbeath.)

Just north of Dunbeath, Latheronwheel (or Janetstown) is a village with a pretty harbour, and Latheron, on the junction with the A895 and A9, has a museum in the old parish church, the Clan Gunn Museum. There are interesting prehistoric sites in the area between here and Wick. The Achavanich Standing Stones, just east of the small road connecting the A895 to the A9 from Loch Rangag, (five miles (8 km) inland) are what remains of a ritual site originally of about 60 stones, forming a truncated oval open to the south-east. East and slightly north of this site are stone/bronze-age burial cairns, the Grey Cairns of Camster, on the road leading from Lybster (meaning 'farmstead' in the Norse) towards Watten, well worth diverting for. The Round Cairn and the Long Cairn (200 × 65 feet/61 × 20 m) both with complete entrance passages, are well restored and 'skylighted' for the benefit of visitors. Wide-ranging artefacts have been discovered here.

Returning to the A9, the Hill o' Many Stanes is marked from the road, and consists of 22 rows of smaller stones, at least eight per row, arranged on a hill, dating back to about 1800 BC. Though there are other similar combinations in the area, the point of them is unknown; some suggest a ritual mathematical alignment with the stars.

IV: Wick – Thurso – Drumrunie

Approaching **Wick** (or 'Vik' meaning Bay in the Norse), the ruined Castle of Old Wick stands on top of the cliffs by the foreshore about 1½ miles (2 km) south of the town. Built between the twelfth and fourteenth centuries as a square tower without windows, its main fault was lack of good water which led to its surrender in the sixteenth century, and total dereliction a century after that. The Brig o' Tram and the Brough are names of two stacks nearby, the former with a natural arch to the mainland, and the latter, flat-topped stack, with a tunnel running through it. Wick used to be a fishing port and lies on the estuary of the River Wick at the centre of a bay. A model village was commissioned on the southern edge of the bay in 1808, with inner and outer harbours, called Pulteneytown (R.L. Stevenson's grandfather carried out engineering improvements here in 1868). In 1960 the Caithness Glassworks were established here, to achieve an international name for hand-blown modern glassware. The High Street, north of the river, is still the shopping centre of the town, with Bridge Street. The burial place of the Earls of Caithness is Sinclair Aisle adjoining the newer parish church (1830) at the west end of High Street, and in Bridge Street is the Town House, with a curious cupola. The museum is in the Carnegie library, with exhibits covering local history, and a glimpse of the herring fishing days can be enjoyed at the Wick Heritage Centre, on Bank Row.

Caithness, the north easterly peninsula of the Scottish mainland, is not typical of Highland scenery. The mountains have been replaced by undulating country, culminating in dramatic cliffs at the coast where seabirds love to nest. The area is scattered not only with archaeological sites but with ruin after ruin. At Noss Head, north of Wick, with flat grass-topped cliffs dropping sheer into the sea, the ruins of the fifteenth century Castle Girnigoe, and seventeenth century Castle Sinclair, stand side by side on a rocky promontory, both once belonging to the Earls of Caithness, and both abandoned in 1679. Ackergill Tower, near the A9, a fourteenth century structure with square turrets, once belonged to the Earls Marischal. The stretch of coast from here to John o'Groats is probably the first part of Scotland to have been inhabited, during the middle stone age era. The remains of two ruined brochs can be seen north of Keiss harbour on the A9, and near the nineteenth century castle are the ruins of a former Keiss Castle which was the home of Sir William Sinclair, founder of the first Baptist church in Scotland. Inland to the west of Keiss (take one of the small roads off the A9 between Wick and Keiss) is an Arts Centre, at Lyth, where exhibitions of painting, photography, tapestry etc. by contemporary artists can be seen, in unusually remote setting.

John o' Groats is known as the most northerly place on mainland Britain, although Dunnet Head properly deserves that distinction. Bleakly situated facing the treacherous Pentland Firth, renowned for dangerous currents and whirlpools (the Well of Swona off the Isle of Swona, and the Swelkie off Stroma), it was probably named after a Dutchman, John de Groot, who operated a ferry service to South Ronaldsay and built an octagonal house here (see the mound near the hotel). A small road runs out to Duncansby Head lighthouse (210 feet/64 m) and to the south the three stacks of Duncansby stand resilient in the churning sea.

Taking the A9 west, the sixteenth century, restored, Castle of Mey, called Barragill Castle until 1952 when it was bought by the Queen Mother, overlooks Mey Bay with Dunnet Head to the west, a 400 feet (122 m) high promontory of sandstone supporting a lighthouse. The views all around are unforgettable from this point, which, it is believed, is the first place in Scotland to have been mentioned in writing (by the Roman geographer Diodorus Ciculus).

Thurso is a grey little town on the river of the same name with an attractive promenade overlooking Thurso Bay. In medieval days an important trading port with Scandinavia (to the extent that its weights and measures were adopted nationally), it is now a quiet spot dependent on tourism and fishing for its livelihood, though the installation of the experimental industrial nuclear research power station, at Dounreay, (with visitors' exhibition) about six miles (10 km) west, has brought some revenue to the town. Robert Dick (1811–66) was a Thurso baker, who became known as a botanist/geologist. The library's collection of fossils and stones includes his bequest, and in the new cemetary there is a monument to him. Note the Meadow Well, used for drawing water until the last century, and the twelfth to thirteenth century St Peter's Church, probably built by Bishop Gilbert de Moravia, which was rebuilt in the seventeenth century, and last used in 1862. The five-light window in the south gable is rather unusual. The Thurso Folk Museum in the High Street has exhibitions of Caithness folklore.

Scrabster, further round Thurso Bay, is the ferry point for Orkney (Stromness) and just beyond, at the entrance to the bay, is Holborn Head where extraordinary formations of rock appear to balance against each other. The Clett, further out to sea, stands alone, 150 feet (46 m) high, like a column designed for the use of seabirds. In summer there are boat trips around it.

Passing the sprawl of industrial development at Dounreay, reminiscent of a science fiction film set, the next place worth noting is Bettyhill, some 20 miles (32 km) further on. Named after Elizabeth, 1st Duchess of Sutherland, Bettyhill has an eighteenth century church, converted into the Strath Naver Museum which tells the chilling story of the Strathnaver Clearances (1812–19). East of Strath Naver there are 120 acres (49 ha) of natural blanket bog, Strathy Bog, a National Nature Reserve, in a visually uninspiring landscape. The Invernaver National Nature Reserve is 1,363 acres (552 ha) of mixed coastal and mountain plant communities, and breeding birds that include ring ouzel, twite and greenshank, around the River Naver mouth.

In 1972 a causeway was built over the shallow inlet, the Kyle of Tongue, beneath the looming Ben Loyal and Ben Hope. At low tide you can walk out to Rabbit Island in Tongue Bay – but don't get cut off by the incoming tide! Tongue village at the eastern end of the causeway is dominated by the scant ruin of Castle Varrich about which nothing much is known but probably once a stronghold of the Norsemen. On the opposite bank of the Kyle the road leads through a perfectly unspoilt landscape of islands, cliffs and sandy bays for over five miles (8 km), though you have to back track to return to the main road. Climbers wishing to tackle Ben Loyal should approach from Ribigill Farm (a couple of miles (3 km) south of Tongue) or from Loch Loyal. The west face is very steep, and Chaonasaid is the highest peak at 2,405 feet (733 m).

The Brahan Seer foretold that one day a war would end at Eriball, on a 10 mile (16 km) inlet as deep as the Kyle of Tongue is shallow, and in 1945 surrendering German submarines turned up in Loch Eriball. On the west bank of this beautiful 'loch' is an earth house in remarkably complete condition, with a curved stairway, and a corridor leading to a chamber. There is no artificial light, so take your own, and because of possible flooding it is best to wear waterproof boots.

Approaching **Durness**, the three large caves at the end of a deep cleft in the cliffs, known as Smoo Cave, can be visited at all times though it is impossible to get into the third cavern, and the second, with a waterfall, is not easy. Note the 'Gothic' arched opening to the first cavern as you go beneath it. Durness, the most northerly village on mainland Britain, is a good overnight stop with various accommodation. The Information Centre provides details, and of local sites of interest, notably prehistoric. Durness Old Church, early seventeenth century, is where an older church once stood which contributed, according to Vatican records, to the Third Crusade (twelfth century). Now roofless, it overlooks the beautiful white sand crescent of west-facing Balnakeil Bay. At Balnakeil the old RAF camp has been converted to a Craft Village with boat-builders, metalworkers, weavers, potters etc. at work. Opposite the church, the eighteenth century farmhouse is on the site of one of the summer residences of the bishops of Caithness. Cape Wrath can only be reached by passenger ferry across the Kyle of Durness, at Keoldale, connecting with an organised minibus service, from 1 May to 31 September. The rest of the year the ferry only operates by arrangement. The road crosses the Parph, a desolate moor once feared for its wolf populations, before reaching Britain's northernmost mainland extremity, precipitous gneiss cliffs, with pink streaked veins running through them, of 523 feet (159 m). The views, predictably, are incomparable for range and distance in clear weather. 'Wrath' is not connected with the English meaning, but with the Norse 'hvarf' ('turning point').

The A838 from Durness leads south-west towards the mass of Foinaven, reaching 2,980 feet (908 m), and the Gualin National Nature Reserve between the mountain and Strath Dionard, before veering past to Rhiconnich where a very small road heads four miles (6 km) north-west to Kinlochbervie, a village, with hotel, that has developed its lobster and white fishing industries since the Second World War, and beyond which the road eventually peters out. If you want to visit the superb and unspoilt Sandwood Bay in its remoteness, it entails over four miles (6 km) by footpath, but it's worth it in good weather. Be careful bathing in the bay as tidal currents can be treacherous here. Resuming the main road, at Laxford Bridge take the A894 towards **Scourie**. The terrain here is formidable and rugged interspersed with dark lochs, but Scourie is a long-established village, very popular in the summer holidays, with hotels etc. and boat trips can be arranged either from here or from Tarbet (due north and overlooking the Sound of Handa Bird Sanctuary, a haven for seabirds. (A nature film is shown at Strathpeffer Station about Handa, *see* p. 213).

The only way across Loch Cairnbawn is by the Kylesku ferry, operating daily from lighting-up time till 2300 hrs. Though it only takes five minutes to cross, delays can be long when the roads are busy. Cars without trailers, or caravans, have priority. The scenery is forbidding here, but above Loch Glencoul an impressive waterfall, Eas Coul Aulin, thunders down from a height of 658 feet (201 m), and can be visited by boat in summer (for details ask at the hotel, on south side of loch). The ruined Ardvreck Castle, a three-storey MacLeod stronghold, late fifteenth century, stands towards the eastern end of Loch Assynt, and nearby are the Calda House remains, a seventeenth century Mackenzie mansion that was burnt down.

The A837 runs along the northern shore of Loch Assynt and on to Lochinver, a large village, popular in the summer as a small centre in a very scenic stretch of coast. South of Loch Assynt on the A837, the Inchnadamph National Nature Reserve of 3,200 acres (1,296 ha) lies to the east, mainly of geological interest. The Allt nan Uamh caves in the reserve have yielded bones of prehistoric animals and traces of occupation by early man.

Taking the A835 at Ledmore, Knockan Cliff Nature Trail is about five

Eilean Donan, Highlands.

miles (8 km) along the road and is of great geological interest, as can be learned at the Nature Conservancy Visitor Centre here. A small road leads west at Drumrunie four miles (6 km) further on, and forms the start of the Motor Trail, leading either round the northern shores of the three lochs and down to Achiltibuie, or northwards, twisting and winding, to Lochinver, through superb and lonely country. Either way, climbers can approach Stac Polly from the road a couple of miles (3 km) before the turn off. The area within the Motor Trail circuit, via Lochinver, contains the Inverpolly National Nature Reserve, a crowded mass of peaks and crags with lochs intertwining, and certainly worth the extra mileage.

V: Ullapool – Wester Ross – Kyle of Lochalsh

Ullapool is a fishing town (listen to the scream of gulls when the boats come in) combined with a growing tourist centre, and port for car ferries to Stornoway, Lewis. The Lochbroom Highland Museum has a small collection with local emphasis, and there are diverse shops, cafes and pubs, where spontaneous singing and music is not unusual in the summer evenings. Cruises are organised to the Summer Isles, a scattering of sparsely populated islands in the wide mouth of Loch Broom (also accessible from Achiltibuie) one of which, Horse Island, possesses a herd of wild goats. There are good highland walks around Ullapool with lovely views over Loch Broom and in summer a passenger ferry crosses the loch to Altnaharrie, where a track leads up about six miles (10 km) to join the road between Gairloch and Corrieshalloch.

The A835 follows the loch south and at the head is the Lael Forest, whose Forest Garden has about 150 different trees and shrubs from all over the world, a rare pleasure to see. Two miles (3 km) south, Corrieshalloch is a dramatic gorge 200 feet (61 m) deep and a mile long (1½ km) with resounding waterfalls to add to the spectacle. The Measach Falls can best be viewed from the suspension footbridge above them.

'Destitution Road' is the name given to the Corrieshalloch to Poolewe Road (A832), built in 1851 in the midst of the dreadful famine. There are delightful sea loch views from the road, and sheltered sandy beaches, but the scenery is less fabulous than on the southern side of Loch Maree. **Poolewe**, at the head of Loch Ewe, is most famous for the Inverewe Gardens, founded in 1862 by Osgood Mackenzie and continued after his death in 1922 by his daughter, Mairi Sawyer. Their achievement was in the successful transformation of a barren headland into a resplendent fertile wooded garden, where, thanks to the warmer influence of the Gulf Stream, plants, shrubs and trees from all over the world can flourish, screened from the harsher effects of gales and storms by a judiciously planted belt of hardy trees. Years of trial and error have shown which species do well here, so you can be sure of an impressive show any time of the year. The 'natural' landscaping of the gardens, and their magnificent setting make it well worth visiting, even for less-than-keen gardeners. It was bequeathed to the National Trust for Scotland, and has an information centre, shop and restaurant.

From Poolewe to Gairloch there are fine views up Loch Maree inland, and seawards across to Skye and the mountains of Harris beyond, (view indicator on road). **Gairloch**, at the head of Gair Loch, is a sprawling village popular as a holiday destination and base for exploring the area. Gairloch Heritage Museum (1980 joint-winner of the Scottish Museum of the Year Award) is at the junction in the village centre, and has a comprehensive exhibition of local history. The road now twists eastward to meet Loch Maree at its widest point. In high summer this road becomes extremely busy and progress is bound to be slow. Note the waterfalls named after Queen Victoria after her visit here in 1877. The Slattadale Forestry Commission estate bordering the loch initially, has two forest trails, Slattadale, and Tollie Path which is longer (five miles/ 8 km) and leads up to Lóch Ewe. Where the loch broadens, a confusion of small islands cluster in the middle, forming Loch Maree Island's Nature Reserve, significant for the native juniper and pinewood. The Isle of Maree is said to be where the hermit monk, St Maree or Maelrubha, after whom the loch was named, is burried. There is a ruined chapel, and a well, whose waters were supposed to cure insanity! The Beinn Eighe Nature Reserve borders the southern stretch of the loch and was the first national reserve in Britain, established principally for the preservation of its ancient Caledonian pine forest. It combines to make the scenery of this area some of the most outstanding in Scotland.

Just before reaching **Kinlochewe**, it is worth stopping at the Aultroy Visitor Centre on the A832 to look at the illuminated physical model of the district for an excellent 'bird's eye view'. Information can be obtained also on the two local nature trails, starting from the car park two miles (3 km) north. Across the loch, the mass of Slioch dominates the skyline. This is a deer sanctuary, so keep clear during the stalking season.

From Kinlochewe take the A896 out to Shieldaig, returning to the A832 via Loch Carron and the A890. Together with the Beinn Eighe Reserve, the Torridon Estate (also NTS since 1967) covers about 26,000 acres (10,530 ha) of towering mountain landscape, as interesting to naturalists and ornithologists as to climbers and geologists, as it shelters abundant wildlife. There are two main mountains, Liathach and Beinn Eighe, and two lesser, Beinn Alligin and Beinn Dearg, nevertheless steep and challenging, and many visitors to the area come for the exciting hill walking and climbing that these peaks offer. (Guided walks can be arranged.) The Visitor Centre at the head of Upper Loch Torridon provides local information, audiovisual presentation, and a Deer Museum. The Loch Torridon Hotel here has atmosphere and style, beautifully situated, if you are lucky you will hear the bagpipes played here in the traditional manner.

From Kinlochewe to Sheildaig is a scenic drive to Torridon and along the loch, through the fringes of the Ben-damph Forest to **Sheildaig**, an attractive little lochside village. The A896 then cuts across the neck of the peninsular known as Applecross Forest, but you can take the small road, via Cuaig, leading right to Applecross (the stretch of road from Cuaig only opened in 1976). Applecross is called 'A Cromraich' in Gaelic which means 'sanctuary', from the days when the monastery, founded by the Irish Maelrubha in 673, was still here, making it an important Christian centre. The Norsemen destroyed it, and probably killed Maelrubha. The church and old burial ground is on the north-east corner of Applecross Bay. The road continues down from Applecross to Toscaig (dead end), past a scattering of deserted dwellings and the natural harbour of Camasterach Bay. The way back to the A896 is through the tortuous, hazardous but spectacular Bealach-na-Ba pass, 2,054 feet (626 m) high. This route rejoins the road at the head of Loch Kishorn, then turns east in Kishorn village to join Loch Carron on its north shore, at the village of Lochcarron (also called Jeantown). A small road leads south to the neck of the loch only (no ferry service) and the ruins of Strome Castle, a Macdonald stronghold blown up in the early 1600s by the Mackenzies, who were, supposedly, able to capture it because the women of the castle had inadvertently been pouring the water into the gunpowder vat instead of the water vat, thereby rendering the castle defenceless.

The A832, following Glen Carron, runs beside the railway through Achnasheen (*see* p. 224) and Garve finally parting from it south of Loch Garve to continue to Muir of Ord. The station at Achnasheen is the railhead of Gairloch, Loch Maree and Inverewe Gardens in Wester Ross.

Doubling back at the head of Loch Carron, take the A890 along the south shore to Stromeferry (no ferry service), then south to join the A87, which leads west to Kyle of Lochalsh. The railway approaches by the northern shore of the peninsula from Stromeferry, with lovely seaward views from the train, and it is worth checking at local stations for details of the train service from Inverness to Kyle of Lochalsh, as an observation coach (supplement payable) is attached to certain trains during the summer, with wide panoramic windows, ideal for enjoying such glorious scenery and for photography.

At Balmacara, north of the A87 to Kyle of Lochalsh, is the picturesque Lochalsh Woodland Garden with exotic plants, shrubs and trees, and an ecology exhibition. **Kyle of Lochalsh** is the principal road approach to Skye with frequent car ferries to Kyleakin on Skye. Less frequent services operate to Mallaig, in summer, and there are cruises to Crowlin Islands, Toscaig, Glenelg and Sandaig. Taking the A87 east, an islet at the neck of Loch Duich, connected to land by causeway, is a superb setting for Eilean Donan Castle, now used as a war memorial to Clan MacRae, overlooking the loch with mountains sloping to the water. Go up onto the old road for a better sight of the castle and the view beyond.

At the head of Loch Duich, **Morvich** has a NTS Visitor Centre, camp site, and audiovisual presentation of the walks and climbs to the Kintail estate. The Five Sisters of Kintail are the peaks to the east of the road south (four of them over 3,000 feet (914 m)) and beyond them, a strenuous walk from the end of the Morvich road, are the Falls of Glomach, whose water falls in two stages, 370 feet (113 m), making them amongst Britain's highest. From Sheil Bridge a small road leads to interesting broch sites over the scenic Pass of Mam Ratagan (1,116 feet/340 m), the road coming to an end at Arnisdale on Loch Hourn. The A87 meanders along Glen Shiel and to the spectacular Pass of Stachel, in which there is a car park and NTS Information Point. The road follows the north bank of Loch Gluanie which has a dam at the eastern end.

About a mile (1½ km) to the east of Ceannacroc on the A887, to the south side of the road, somewhat obscured by bushes, is a memorial to Roderick Mackenzie who, during the hunt for the Young Pretender after Culloden in 1746, allowed enemy soldiers to think he was the Young Pretender, with the result that he was beheaded and his head presented to Cumberland at Fort Augustus. Up the River Doe nearby is a cave called Corriedoe in which the Young Pretender took refuge from 24–28 August 1746. It is about 2½ miles (4 km) from the A887, which goes down Glen Moriston through woods beside the cascading river, to link with the A82 at Invermoriston on Loch Ness (*see* p. **225**).

After Loch Cluanie the A87 passes through grand mountainous scenery with superb views over Loch Loyne and Loch Garry to the west. The north bank of Loch Garry is skirted by a minor dead end road that only peters out at the head of Loch Hourn (Loch of Hell) in a desolate, barren landscape (walkers can continue by footpath across the Knoydart peninsula to Inverie, and around to Arnisdale nearing the mouth of Loch Hourn). The A87 comes down to join the A82 on Loch Oich.

VI: Loch Ness – Fort William – Glencoe

No visit to Inverness would be complete without a look at the Great Glen (Glenmore) consisting of Loch Ness, Loch Oich and Loch Lochy, forming a deep geological split across northern Scotland. The lochs are connected by the Caledonian Canal, 38 miles (61 km) of loch and 22 (35 km) of canal. The canal was constructed during the early nineteenth century. Telford, the original engineer, solved the problem of varying water levels with a total of 29 locks. Opened in 1822, it was found to be too shallow for many craft, and was not fully completed until 1847. It became an invaluable short cut across Scotland for seagoing traffic and as an inland waterway. Latterly, pleasure craft have tended to monopolise the canal as the lock capacity inhibits commercial efficiency. One of the best ways to enjoy the wonderfully contrasting scenery is by water, and pleasure cruises are arranged from Inverness as far as Urquhart Castle on Loch Ness. Boats can also be hired (details from the Tourist Information Office in Inverness). Buses run regularly from Inverness down to Fort William.

The Loch Ness monster, which has taken substance over the years from numerous reported 'sightings', is probably more famous than Loch Ness itself, though even with modern scientific techniques of investigation, no absolute proof of its (or their) existence has yet been found. The loch is 24 miles (39 km) long, about a mile wide (1½ km) most of its length, and in parts 900 feet (274 m) deep. Never been known to freeze due to its depth, it is fed by eight rivers and countless streams, the only outlet being the river Ness, to Moray Firth. Because of the peat content from the rivers and burns, underwater visibility is very poor, no doubt enhancing the mystery of the monster. There is a permanent Loch Ness Monster Exhibition at **Drumnadrochit**, behind the hotel.

The A82 runs along the north shore and becomes very busy in summer, while the B862 (with B852 on the shore) follows the south bank, and General Wade's military route. Wade was an English major-general (1673–1748) sent to Scotland in 1724 to build metalled roads and stone bridges, intended to bring the Highlanders under control. (One of his roads, now just a track, was followed by the Young Pretender and his army, across Corrieyarrick to the Spey.) Wade built 40 bridges while in

Glencoe, Highlands.

Scotland. 'Had you seen these roads before they were made, You would lift up your hands and bless General Wade' is the couplet by which he was remembered locally.

The south road is preferable during the tourist season, and is even more scenic in places, with Whitebridge View Point at 1,162 feet (354 m), and the Falls of Foyers. Now greatly reduced in volume, these falls once inspired Burns.

The A82 leads down towards Drumnadrochit (alternative route to The Glens) and the thrilling view of Castle Urquhart, once one of the largest castles in Scotland, given to John Grant of Freuchie by James IV in 1509. Now a sinister, but striking ruin, it is poised on a bluff at the loch's edge and is well viewed from the A82. Its destruction, in 1692, was to prevent the Jacobites taking it, but it stayed in the family of Grant for a further two centuries. At Invermoriston there is a Smithy Studio, with original cobbled floor, where crafts are sold.

Fort Augustus merits taking a little time to look around, with the Great Glen Exhibition explaining the local geography and history (housed in buildings beside a series of six locks on the canal). There is also an exhibition on 'Nessie', the Loch Ness monster here. The Abbey was originally a fort built by Wade whose headquarters were at this village (four of his metalled roads were started from this point). He named it Fort Augustus, replacing the name of Kilcumein, after William Augustus, Duke of Cumberland, then only a child, who grew up ultimately to defeat the Young Pretender at the battle of Culloden in 1746. It was he who was presented with the head of young Roderick Mackenzie, an Edinburgh lawyer who let the enemies of the Young Pretender believe he was the Prince, and whose memorial stands at Caennacroc on the A887 west of here. Lord Lovat bought the fort in 1867 and gave it to the Benedictine Order in 1876. Since 1878 there has been a boys' school here, Fort Augustus Abbey School, education being an integral part of Benedictine tradition. Cherry Island in the loch to the north of the town is one of the best examples of a pre-Christian crannog (man-made island), though since the construction of the Caledonian Canal the raised water level has somewhat reduced its size. (Crannogs were usually made by sinking a round wooden platform in shallow waters and piling stones onto it, access to land by sunken causeway, or boat.)

In **Invergarry** the remains can be seen of Invergarry Castle in the grounds of Glengarry Castle Hotel beside Loch Oich. There were two earlier castles on this site, long the seat of the MacDonells of Glengarry. A salmon hatchery has been established here by the North of Scotland Hydro-Electric Board, to compensate for the spawning grounds spoiled by dam building. The Young Pretender began his optimistic march south from the north end of Loch Oich. The isthmus between Loch Oich and Loch Lochy was the site of two clashes. In 1544 a skirmish took place between the Frasers and Macdonalds, which is known as the 'battle of the shirts', because they all abandoned their plaids in the summer heat to fight in shirtsleeves, and then the critical confrontation between government troops (two companies) and Highlanders 200 years later (August 1745) which could be said to mark the start of the '45 Rebellion. The government troops surrendered here, having retreated from a fight with about 12 Highlanders only, at Spean Bridge, utterly intimidated by the great noise they made with their pipes and drums. Within two days, these government prisoners were present at Glenfinnan to witness the Young Pretender raising his standard. The Well of Seven Heads is a gruesome monument on the west shore of Loch Oich. The heads surmounting the monument represent the seven brothers of the head of a branch of the MacDonells (Keppoch), in the seventeenth century. On Keppoch's death, his two sons being educated in France at the time, the control of his affairs went to his seven brothers, who were later responsible for murdering the two sons on their return. The family bard sought vengeance, and had all seven men decapitated. The spring at the foot of the monument is where the heads were washed before being presented to the Chief of the Clan of Glengarry.

Loch Arkaig lies to the west of Loch Lochy, with Achnacarry House on the isthmus between the lochs, built 1802–37, beside the remnants of a castle that Cumberland burnt down in 1746. A dead end road leads along the north shore to the west end of the loch, about 12 miles (19 km). Where the B8004 links up with the A82 just short of Spean Bridge is the Commando Memorial, by Scott Sutherland in 1952, surveying the scene of the commando training ground during the Second World War. There is a fine view south of Ben Nevis here (view indicator), and west towards the mountains of Lochaber. At Spean Bridge the A86 heads eastwards along Glen Spean to Newtonmore, and the A82 continues to follow the direction of the Caledonian Canal down to Fort William, where the canal finally joins Loch Linnhe. At the head of Loch Linnhe the A830 branches off the A82 along the north shore of Loch Eil, continuing west to Arisaig on the coast, where it twists north to Mallaig and ends. This route runs through grand Highland scenery, and also past the Glenfinnan Monument where the Young Pretender raised his standard, on 19 August, 1745. The monument supports a statue of a Highlander, and was erected in 1815 by a descendant of the devoted MacDonald with whom the Prince spent the night of 18 August, at Glenaladale, to be rowed up Loch Sheil next morning for the gathering at Glenfinnan. The monument has stairs inside the tower so you can climb up and stand beside the Highlander if you like. The Visitor Centre describes the Young Pretender's campaign from this point to his defeat the following April. At Fassfern House half way along the loch the Prince spent the night four days after raising the standard.

The road winds around the head of Loch nan Uamh (Loch of the Caves), where the Young Pretender initially landed. A cairn beside the road marks the spot. (He also left from here the following year, a dejected soul.) From Arisaig boat services operate to Eigg and Rhum. **Mallaig**, a small fishing port, is important for its ferry service to Skye and other Inner Hebridean islands. The railway virtually follows the road from Fort William to Mallaig.

Fort William is a busy, crowded town, with important road, rail and ferry links. Britain's highest mountain, Ben Nevis, to the south-east is a further attraction to visitors but the town itself is more practical than picturesque compared to most Scottish resorts. The West Highland Museum, though rather shabby, has interesting folk exhibits, tartan collection and Jacobite relics. Note the surveying level used by Telford.

Though Ben Nevis is 4,406 feet (1,343 m) at its highest, lacking dramatic peaks it appears less impressive than some smaller mountains. It is, however, easily climbed and very popular with walkers and climbers. Glen Nevis, a rugged and untamed valley, is a main feature, and 10 miles (16 km) of it can be driven, passing a youth hostel on the site of a medieval fort. Beside Achriabhach farm, about eight miles (13 km) up, the road crosses over the river, which is tumbling rapids at this point, and leads to a car park in a magnificent setting at the end of the road. There is a superb waterslide here.

The A82 follows the east bank of upper Loch Linnhe down to the narrow neck that separates it from the lower loch, across which a frequent car ferry service operates (five-minute crossing), giving useful access to the Ardgour district, (and thence south to Mull and Iona, via the ferry from Lochaline). The A82 then crosses the mouth of Loch Leven between North and South Ballachulish. Until 1975 there was a ferry here too, or a scenic, but slow, drive round the loch. **Kinlochleven** at the head of the loch is a small industrial town with aluminium works.

Glen Coe ('Glen of Weeping') was the scene of a bloody massacre in 1692, and is an area of grand and formidable scenery lying between Glencoe village on Loch Leven, and Kingshouse Hotel on the north side of the A82. Of the 200 inhabitants of the glen, 40 were killed in the massacre which was ordered by Sir John Dalrymple, Under Secretary of State, in Edinburgh. (The order is said to have been received written on a playing card, the 9 of Diamonds, known thereafter as 'the curse of Scotland'.) Although Scottish parliament decreed three years later that the action had been murder, Dalrymple was merely dismissed by William II (the reluctance of the Macdonalds of Glencoe to accept him as king had been behind the hostility). Some Macdonald gravestones can be seen on St Munda island in Loch Leven, where there are also some ancient burial places. The scene of the massacre was the lower glen and Glencoe village. The North Lorn and Glencoe Folk Museum, within two old cottages in the village, has an impressively varied display including toys, dolls, dolls' houses, games, lace, spinning wheels, copper, weaponry and old writing accessories. There is a monument to the battle of Glencoe a quarter of a mile (½ km) along the road off to the right before the bridge, through the village. It is up some steps through a hedge.

Driving up through the glen, look out first for the Pap of Glencoe to the north, a 2,430 feet peak (741 m), with steep corries, then for Signal Rock which used to be a Macdonald lookout point. At Clachaig there is a NTS Visitor Centre. (Some 14,000 acres (5,670 ha) of this area belong to the NTS.) The Study (from 'studdie' meaning 'anvil') is a high terrace north of the road 3½ miles (6 km) further on, commanding the best view of Glen Coe. Again on the north side, some three miles (5 km) further, the Devil's Staircase is part of an old military road, which crossed the hills for about four miles (6 km) to Kinlochleven. (The road is in disrepair.) Glen Etive, running south-west of the A82 a couple of miles (3 km) on, is a bleak and imposing glen with a small dead end road for 11 miles (18 km) to Lochetivehead, through Dalness where the river forms foaming rapids. Meall a Bhuiridh, near the head of the glen, offers good skiing, with chairlift and T-bars. The winding road from Kingshouse Hotel (a hotel off the road in open scenery) down to Bridge of Orchy was first built in 1751 by General Caulfield, crossing high, bare country, and incidentally the new Highland/Strathclyde regional boundary. At Loch Tulla, with beautiful views, there is a footpath up the glen, east of the road, to the ruins of Achallader Castle, where the Glen Coe Massacre is supposed to have been planned. (The path continues another 4½ miles (7 km).) Tyndrum is six miles (10 km) south of Bridge of Orchy, on the Strathclyde/Central regional boundary, and is a small Highland village with two stations, one for the Oban line and one for the Fort William line.

VII: Skye

Known also as the 'Misty Isle' because of its damp climate, Skye is nevertheless a beautiful island with very rugged scenery in parts, popular in summer but not to the point of overcrowding. Its Cuillin mountains, with peaks well over 3,000 feet (914 m), are Britain's most challenging for climbers (especially as the frequent mist shrouding them upsets magnetic compasses) and not many of the peaks can be reached without serious rock climbing, so take heed and only attempt what is within your range of experience! You can enjoy the lower reaches in safety, with impressive views of the barren crags and irregular boulders higher up. Of all the Hebridean islands, Skye is second only to Lewis in size, occupying about 600 sq. miles (155,400 ha), and is of course easily accessible from the mainland, taking only five minutes by car ferry from Kyle of Lochalsh to Kyleakin (continuous service), and from Glenelg to Kylerhea (frequent service in summer only), and half an hour from Mallaig to Armadale (five services daily in summer, less in winter). Loganair operate flights between Skye's airport near Broadford and Glasgow, daily except Sunday. Trains to Kyle of Lochalsh and Mallaig connect with ferries, and buses on the island.

Whichever car ferry you choose to take, the road from the port on the island will lead you to Broadford. **Armadale**, on the south-eastern coast of the Sleat peninsula, is only a landing place for the ferry, the village of Ardvasar being immediately to the south, but the road leaving Armadale quay leads straight to Armadale Castle within half a mile (1 km), which has a museum, the Clan Donald Centre (and a seventeenth century arboretum in attractive wooded grounds). The castle itself is early nineteenth century, build for Lord Macdonald, and the Centre portrays a history of the Macdonalds, and the Lords of the Isles – a useful introduction to the island. Just above the castle, off the A851, a narrow, awkward road snakes its way westwards, crossing the Sleat peninsula, travelling up its west coast for about three miles (5 km) then crossing back to rejoin the A851, making a detour of about 12 miles (19 km). The scenery is wild and lonely, with long views from the road across the Cuillin Sound. On the western stretch of coast Dunsgiath Castle, blending into its rocky habitat, is a ruin on the arm of a bay, but was once another robust Macdonald stronghold. The detour rejoins the main road just north of Knock Castle, another ruined castle, also on a bay and also once belonging to the Macdonalds (with a proviso that it should be kept ready to receive the king or his agents at all times). Continuing north towards Broadford, the fishing and the sea bathing is good at Isleornsay. Should you decide to land at Kylerhea, the little road from the ferry landing leads between mountains over 2,000 feet (610 m) high, following Glen Arroch to join the A850, from **Kyleakin**. Kyleakin is the most usual crossing point, and the road into Broadford passes the airport. At Kyleakin, a sprawling village with hotels for the ferry-users and plenty of parking space, the ruined Castle Moil overlooks the straits of Kyle Akin between the mainland and Skye, a good vantage point when it was used as a fortified look-out against Norse raiders long ago.

Broadford is an elongated village to the west of which a very picturesque road (dead end) winds around the head of Loch Slapin and down to Elgol, passing below Beinn na Cailleach (2,403 feet/732 m). The ruined church about two miles (3 km) from Broadford is said to stand where St Maelrubha, the seventh century hermit monk, had a cell. Note Skye's marble quarries on each side of the road. Near the little village of Kilmarie a footpath leads off westwards to Camasunary on the edge of Loch Scavaig (about three miles/5 km), and then continues along the coast to the wild and grand Loch Coruisk, beneath the looming mass of the Cuillins (but beware of the 'Bad Step' on this walk, a dangerous section recommended for experienced walkers only). Alternatively, it heads directly north from Camasunary some eight miles (13 km), to Sligachan, which is on the A850.

It was at the village of **Elgol** that the Young Pretender, after a 24-mile (37 km) walk, was feasted by the Mackinnons in a cave (now 'Prince Charlie's Cave') before being provided with a boat to Mallaig, back on the mainland. Beyong Elgol the road runs on for over a mile to Glasnakellie, just above a cave with stalagmites, Spar Cave, accessible at low tide only.

Taking the A850 out of Broadford, before reaching Sligachan, note the ferry jetty at **Sconser**, for crossing to **Raasay** (about four ferries daily, except Sunday) which is an island about 15 miles (24 km) long. Brochel Castle, over half way up on the east shore, is the ruined home of the Macleods of Raasay, Jacobites who sheltered the fugitive Young Pretender for two nights before his walk to Elgol. Soon after his departure, the Macleod estate was laid waste by Government troops.

Loch Sligachan, with the Duirinish peninsula, were the main centres for the crofter riots in 1881–85 following a series of bad fishing seasons and poor harvests. **Sligachan** village is a good walking centre, leaflets from hotel. From here the A863 travels north-west of Dunvegan (worth visiting for its castle) to be met by the A850 through Portree. The A863 leads first to Drynoch, at the head of a deep six-mile (10 km) sea loch. A smaller road leads round to the west of the loch to Carbost, and the Talisker distillery. Talisker village is some four miles (6 km) west, beside the River Talisker. The distillery can be visited by appointment. The A863 continues from Drynoch to **Dunvegan**, passing a broch ruin (the best-preserved on Skye) on the right, near Struan, and an earth house south of the road from the broch. A couple of miles (3 km) south of Dunvegan you can see the remains of two chambered cairns on the left of the road.

The massive Dunvegan Castle, seat of the Clan MacLeod chiefs since 1200 (at least) and formerly only accessible by sea, demonstrates every style of building from the fifteenth to the nineteenth century, and its many historic treasures include an early charter granted by James IV in 1498, the Dunvegan Cup (probably tenth century, with fifteenth centry silverwork), the magical Fairy Flag, a portrait of Dr Johnson, who was here in 1773, and a splendid carved sideboard (in the dining room) of 1603. The walls of the drawing room, which was originally the great hall of the keep, are 9 feet (3 m) thick, and note the view over Loch Dunvegan from the 'north' room. You can see letters from Dr Johnson, and from Sir Walter Scott in the exhibition. (Boat trips are arranged from the Castle jetty out to the seal rocks.)

Duirinish is the name of the bleak peninsula west of Dunvegan, scene of some of the worst crofter riots in the 1880s (memorial on the B884, west of the turn off to Boreraig). Taking the B884, south of Dunvegan, about four miles (6 km) in is an unusual museum, the Black House Museum. It is an authentic crofter's cottage with antique furniture, implements, and even a replica whisky still. Taking the road towards Dunvegan Head, the northernmost point of the peninsula, stop at Boreraig at the Piping Centre to learn the history of the bagpipes, and of the MacCrimmonds of Duirinish, who were the hereditary MacLeod pipers, and taught piping here for three centuries. (Don't confuse the Uig on this road with the Uig of Uig Bay on the Trotternish peninsula.) At Glendale on the B884 is a restored water mill. To return to the main road at the neck of the peninsula you have to back-track from here.

The Vaternish peninsula is penetrated by road (dead end) from Fairy Bridge as far as Trumpan, some three miles (5 km) from the northerly tip of Vaternish Point. A particularly gruesome conflict took place at Trumpan in 1579 between the Macdonalds and the MacLeods. When the MacLeods were attending a service in the church, the Macdonalds arrived by sea and set the building alight, killing all the MacLeod worshippers, only to find more MacLeods waiting for them at their boats, bearing the Fairy Flag that you can see in Dunvegan Castle. In their turn, the Macdonalds were all slain.

Continuing on the A850, **Portree** is Skye's only town, and therefore regarded as its capital, though not very large. A busy fishing port, it is popular with tourists, and boat trips operate here in summer, as well as coaches around Skye.

Trotternish is the most scenic of the island's northern peninsulas with impressive mountains and long seaward views. On the A856 towards Uig note the ruin of Caisteal Nisdein, in the seventeenth century the stronghold of pirate Hugh Gillespie, who was to die a nasty death near here. When his chieftain, a Macdonald, uncovered a treacherous plot against himself, he had Gillespie imprisoned in the dungeons of Duntulm Castle, with only a piece of salt-beef and an empty water jug.

Uig is important for its ferry services to the Outer Hebrides (North Uist and Harris), and is a pleasant, compact village. A couple of miles (3 km) north of Uig, Prince Charles' Point is where Flora Macdonald landed from Benbecula with the fugitive Young Pretender disguised as her maid, 'Betty Burke', in 1746 (about which a great deal of romantic poems and ballads have been written since). Flora Macdonald then led him to Sir Alexander Macdonald's house, Monkstadt, not a mile (1 km) up the coast (you can see the ruin) to find that Government officers were installed there, so the two of them proceeded south to Kingsburgh and Portree.

The Isle of Skye Cottage Museum, a mile or two (3 km) north of the ruins of Monkstadt House, is a croft museum with a box-type wall bed and a collection of bygones, and in Kilmuir graveyard you can see Flora Macdonald's grave and monument (beside a rather fine Crusader slab). The ruins of Duntulm Castle, a Macdonald stronghold from about 1616–1732, overlooks the sea from next to the road, which then heads east, and south through Flodigarry where Flora Macdonald lived after her marriage of Allan Macdonald of Kingsburgh in 1750, and where all her seven children were born. What was her home now forms part of the hotel here.

Just south of Flodigarry turn right for the Quiraing, a weird and spectacular natural confusion of towers and pinnacles, used in the past for driving cattle into during raids. Note especially 'the table' of flat green turf amidst all these rock formations, and 'the needle'.

Off the A855, Kilt Rock is a cliff whose strata resembles the pleats of a kilt with its horizontals and verticals, just north of Loch Mealt. If you walk about here, beware of the brittle and dangerous cliff edges. Note the little waterfall spilling over the cliff from Loch Mealt straight down to the sea.

The Storr is a strange mountain mass of crags and peaks, 2,360 feet (719 m) at its summit. The best approach to climing it is by a gully south of the highest point, but be careful not to slip on the loose ground where it is steep. At the top you are presented with a superb panorama of the mainland and the outer isles on a clear day. At the eastern end, the 'Old Man of Storr' is a 160-foot (49 m) black obelisk (first climbed in 1955).

About half way between Storr and Portree is a cave on the coast where the Young Pretender landed on his return from two days on Raasay, known as Prince Charles' Cave. He spent the night in a cowshed about two miles (3 km) to the south before embarking on the walk to Elgol.

VIII: Canna – Rhum – Eigg – Muck

These four islands are included in the Highland region together with Skye.

Canna is three miles (5 km) from Rhum, with its harbour at the eastern end, and a ruined tower at the harbour. The island is about 4½ miles (7 km) long, by less than a mile (1 km) wide.

Rhum is the largest of the group and was inhabited from the Stone Age until the Highland 'clearances' when all inhabitants (over 400) were forced to emigrate to America to make way for sheep. The sheep were later joined by red deer, for sport. Kinloch Castle was built in 1901 by the Bulloughs of Lancashire who had bought the island as a private estate in 1888. In 1957 the Nature Conservancy Council acquired it, and there is a deer park at Kinloch, as well as enjoyable nature trails. The island is about eight miles (13 km) square.

Eigg, five miles by 2½ (8× 4 km), is still privately owned and its distinguishing feature is the Sgurr of Eigg, 400 feet (122 m), a shiny black pitchstone mass surmounting a hill in the southern part of the island.

Muck is only a couple of miles (3 km) long, but has pleasant beaches.

All four islands can be visited easily in a day, and boat trips are organised by Caledonian MacBrayne usually four times a week. For details of all services, see Tourist Information Centres locally.

Access to Sites and Places of Interest

Aultroy
Visitor Centre
May–Sep. 1000–1700 Mon.–Sat.

Aviemore
Clan Tartan Centre; Highland Craft Village; Santa Claus Land
Jan.–Feb. 1000–1700 daily; Mar.–June, Sep.–Dec. 1000–1800 daily; July–Aug. 1000–2000 daily.
Fee for Santa Clause Land.
Reindeer: visitors may accompany the herdsman on his daily round. 1100, but depending on weather, 2–3 hours with some hill walking. Fee.

Cairngorm Chairlift
June, Sep.–Nov. 0900–1630 daily; July–Aug. 0900–1730 daily; Dec.–May 0900–dusk daily.
Fee.

Beauly
Priory
Standard.

Brora
Sutherland Wool Mills.
2 days notice, parties up to 30.
(Brora 366)

Caithness
Caithness Glass
0900–1200, 1230–1630 Mon.–Fri., 0900–1200 Sat.

Cawdor
Castle
Mid May–mid Sep. 1000–1730 daily.
Fee.

Cromarty
Hugh Miller's Cottage
May–Sep. 1000–1200, 1300–1700 Mon.–Sat.; June–Sep. 1400–1700 Sun.
Fee.

Culloden
Visitor Centre and Museum
Easter (or later) to mid Oct. 0930–1830 Mon.–Sat.; June–Aug. 0930–2130 Mon.–Sat., 1400–1830 Sun.
Fee.

The battlefield area, memorials, and Well of the Dead are accessible at all times.

Dounreay
Visitor Exhibition
May–Sep. 0900–1600 Mon.–Sat.
No dogs.

Dunrobin
Castle
May–Sep. 1030–1730 Mon.–Sat., 1300–1730 Sun.
Fee.

Fort Augustus
Abbey
Summer. Guided tours daily for parties between about 1100–1800.

Great Glen Exhibition
Apr.–Sep. 1000–1800 Mon.–Sat. Open till later in July & Aug.
Fee.

Fort George
Queen's Own Highlanders Museum
Apr.–Sep. 1000–1830 Mon.–Sat., 1400–1830 Sun.; Oct.–Mar. 1000–1600 Mon.–Fri.
Fee.

Fort William
West Highland Museum
0930–1300, 1400–1700 Mon.–Sat.; mid June–mid Sep. 0930–2100 Mon.–Sat.
Fee.

Glencoe
NTS Visitor Centre
Easter–mid Oct. 1000–1700 daily; mid May–mid Sep. 1000–1900 daily.
Fee.

North Lorn and Glencoe Folk Museum
June–Sep. 1000–1730 Mon.–Sat.
Fee.

Glenfinnan
Visitor Centre
Easter–Oct. 0930–1800 daily; June–Oct. 0930–2000 daily.
Fee.

Golspie
Orcadian Stone Co. Ltd.
24 hrs notice, parties up to 20.
(Golspie 483)

Gualin
National Nature Reserve
Permit required (NCC, NW Region).

Glen Farclas Distillery
0900–1630 Mon.–Fri.

Glen Fiddich and Balvenie Distilleries
1000–1230, 1400–1630 Mon.–Fri.

Glen Grant and Caperdonich Distilleries
1000–1200, 1400–1600 Mon.–Fri.; closed mid July–end Aug.

Inchnadamph
National Nature Reserve
Permit required in late summer and autumn (NCC, NW Region)

Inverness
Abertarff House
0900–1700 Mon.–Fri. In summer 0900–1300 Sat.

Museum
0900–1700 Mon.–Sat.

Caledonian Canal pleasure cruises.
Caledonian Canal office
(Inverness 33140)
Jacobite office
(Inverness 33999)

Kilt making at 4–9 Huntly Street
24 hrs notice.
(Inverness 222781)

Kincraig
Highland Wildlife Park
Mar.–early Nov. 1000–1800, or 1½ hours before dusk if earlier, daily.
No dogs (kennels).
Fee.

Kingussie
Highland Folk Museum
Apr.–Oct. 1000–1800 Mon.–Sat., 1400–1800 Sun.; Nov.–Mar. 1000–1500 Mon.–Fri.
Fee.

Laidhay
Croft Museum
Easter–Sep. 0900–1800 daily.
Fee.

Loch Garten
Nature Reserve
Mid Apr.–mid Aug. daily.
Donation.

Mey Castle
Gardens only, open three times yearly in aid of charity.

Morvich
Eilean Donan Castle
Easter–Sep. 1000–1230, 1400–1800 daily.
Fee.

Visitor Centre
Easter–Sep.

Nairn
Fishertown Museum
May–Sep. 1430–1630 Tue., Thur., Sat., 1830–2030 Mon., Wed., Fri.
Fee.

Literary Institute Museum
June–Sep. 1400–1600 Sat. Also Wed. in July.

Newtonmore
Clan Macpherson Museum
Easter–Sep. 1000–1200, 1400–1800 daily.

Poolewe
Inverewe Gardens
0900–2100 or dusk if earlier.

Visitor Centre
Apr.–mid Oct. 1000–1830 Mon.–Sat., 1300–1830 Sun., Centre closes at dusk if earlier than 1830.
Fee.

Strathnaver
Museum
Summer 1400–1700 Mon.–Wed., Sat.
Donation.

Strathspey Railway
Easter. Weekends May–Sep., but daily in July & Aug. 1030–1230, 1430–1700.

Tamdhu Distillery
May–Sep. 1030–1230, 1330–1630 Mon.–Fri.

Thurso
Folk Museum
June–Sep. 1000–1300, 1400–1700, 1900–2100 Mon.–Fri.
Fee.

Torridon
Visitor Centre
June–Sep. 1000–1800 Mon.–Sat., 1300–1800 Sun.
Fee.

Urquhart Castle
Standard.

Wick
Museum
July–Sep. 1000–1700 daily, but closed Wed. & Sat. afternoons.
Donation.

Hotels and Guest Houses

Achnasheen
Achnasheen Hotel IV22 2EF.
(Achnasheen 243)

Aviemore
Alt-na-Craig Hotel PH22 1RL.
(Aviemore 810217)

Corrour Hotel,
Inverdruie PH22 1QH.
(Aviemore 810220)

The Post House PH22 1PJ.
(Aviemore 810771)

Ravenscraig Guest Huose PH22 1RP.
(Aviemore 810278)

Beauly
Priory Hotel.
The Square.
(Beauly 2309/2572)

Cannich
Glen Affric Hotel.
(Cannich 214)

Carrbridge
Carrbridge Hotel.
(Carrbridge 202)

Caberfeidh Guest House,
Station Road PH23 3AN.
(Carrbridge 638)

Culloden Moor
Clava Lodge Hotel IV1 2EJ.
(Culloden Moor 461)

Dingwall
National Hotel,
High Street,
(Dingwall 62166)

Dornoch
Burghfield House Hotel IV25 3HN.
(Dornoch 212)

Trentham Hotel,
The Poles IV25 3HZ.
(Dornoch 391/551)

Dunbeath
Dunbeath Hotel.
(Dunbeath 208)

Durness
Cape Wrath Hotel IV27 4SW.
(Durnes 274)

Fort Augustus
The Brae Hotel.
(Fort Augustus 6289)

Fort William
Alexander Hotel.
(Fort William 2241)

Highland Hotel,
Union Road.
(Fort William 2291)

Milton Hotel,
North Road.
(Fort William 2331)

West End Hotel.
(Fort William 2614)
(Fort William 3288)

Glen Shiel Guest House,
Achintore Road.
(Fort William 2271)

Kismet Villa Guest House,
Heathercroft,
off Argyll Terrace.
(Fort William 4476)

Gairloch
Creag Mor Hotel IV21 2AH.
(Gairloch 2068)

Millcroft Hotel.
(Gairloch 2376)

Birchwood Guesthouse.
(Gairloch 2011)

Glencoe
　Ballachulish
　Ballachulish Hotel.
　(Ballachulish 239)

Glencoe
　Clachaig Inn.
　(Ballachulish 252)

Glenfinnan
Glenfinnan House Hotel.
(Kinlocheil 235)

Grantown-on-Spey
Ben Mhor Hotel PH26 3EG.
(Grantown-on-Spey 2056)

Dunvegan Hotel PH26 3HX.
(Grantown-on-Spey 2301)

Pines Hotel,
Woodside Avenue PH26 3JR.
(Grantown-on-Spey 2092)

Dunachton Guest House,
Grant Road PH26 31D.
(Grantown-on-Spey 2098)

Ravenscourt Guest House,
Seafield Avenue.
(Grantown-on-Spey 2286)

Helmsdale
Belgrave Arms Hotel KW8 6JX.
(Helmsdale 242)

Invergarry
Glengarry Castle Hotel PH35 4HW.
(Invergarry 254)

Inverness
Ardross Hotel,
2–4 Ardross Street.
(Inverness 30051/38864)

Cummings Hotel,
Church Street.
(Inverness 32531)

Haughdale Hotel,
Ness Bank.
(Inverness 33065)

Leinster Lodge,
27 Southside Road IV2 4XA.
(Inverness 33311)

Palace Hotel,
Ness Walk.
(Inverness 223243)

Royal Hotel,
Academy Street IV1 1JR.
(Inverness 30665)

Abermar Guest House,
24 Fairfield Road.
(Inverness 39019)

Ardnacoille Guest House,
1a Annfield Road.
(Inverness 33451)

Arran Guest House,
42 Union Street.
(Inverness 32115)

Ashland Guest House,
30 Telford Street.
(Inverness 30453)

Craignay Guest House,
16 Ardross Street.
(Inverness 33029)

Glencairn Guest House,
19 Ardross Street.
(Inverness 32965)

Redwood Guest House,
19 Culduthel Road.
(Inverness 32427)

Taymount Guest House,
(Inverness 32741)

John o'Groats
John o'Groats House Hotel KW1 4YR.
(John o'Groats 203)

Kingussie
Columba House Hotel,
Manse Road PH21 1JF.
(Kingussie 402)

Silverfijord Hotel PH21 1ES.
(Kingussie 292)

Kyle of Lochalsh
Lochalsh Hotel IV40 8AB.
(Kyle 4202)

Mallaig
Heatherlea Hotel,
Glasnacardoch.
(Mallaig 2184)

Primrose Cottage Guest House.
(Mallaig 2243)

Nairn
Alton Burn Hotel.
(Nairn 53325)

Golf View Hotel.
(Nairn 52301)

Newton Hotel.
(Nairn 53144)

Waverley Hotel,
High Street.
(Nairn 53001)

Orcadia Guest House,
2 Castle Lane.
(Nairn 52350)

Newtonmore
Alder Lodge,
Glen Banchor Road PH20 1EA.
(Newtonmore 376)

Mains Hotel.
(Newtonmore 206)

Coig na Shee Guest House PH20 1DG.
(Newtonmore 216)

Portmahomack
Caledonian Hotel.
(Portmahomack 345)

Shieldaig
Tigh-an-Eilean Hotel IV54 8XN.
(Shieldaig 251)

Strathpeffer
Ben Wyvis Hotel.
(Strathpeffer 323)

Hollylodge Hotel.
(Strathpeffer 254)

Tain
Mansfield Hotel,
Scotsburn Road.
(Tain 2052)

Thurso
Park Hotel KW14 8RE.
(Thurso 3251)

Ullapool
Altnaharrie Inn IV26 2SS.
(Dundonnell 230)

The Clubhouse,
West Lane IV26 2TY.
(Ullapool 2103)

Morefield Motel.
(Ullapool 2161)

Brae Guest House,
Shore Street IV26 2UJ.
(Ullapool 2421)

Wick
Ladbroke Mercury Motor Inn,
Riverside.
(Wick 3344)

Rosebank Hotel KW1 5LF.
(Wick 3244)

Accommodation for the Young

Beauly
Cannich Youth Hostel,
Cannich IV4 7LT.

Glen Affric Youth Hostel,
Allt Beathe,
Glen Affric,
Cannich.

Carrbridge
Dalrachney Beag PH23 3AX.
(Carrbridge 250)

Dalrachney Lodge Leisure and Study
Centre,
Dalrachney Lodge.
(Carrbridge 252)

Corrour
Loch Ossian Youth Hostel.

Durness
Durness Youth Hostel,
Smoo,
Durness IV2Y 4QA.

Fort William
Alltshellach,
Onich PH33 6SA.
(Onich 232)

The Holiday Fellowship,
142–144 Great North Way,
London NW4 1EG.

Gairloch
Carn Dearg Youth Hostel IV21 2DJ.

Glencoe
Carnoch Outdoor Centre,
Carnoch House.
(Ballachulish 350)

Glencoe Farm Bunkhouse,
Leacantuim.
(Ballachulish 256)

Glenmoriston
Loch Ness Youth Hostel,
Glenmoriston IV3 6YD.

Inverness
Inverness Youth Hostel,
1 Old Edinburgh Road IV2 3HF.

Kincraig
Insh Hall Hostel,
Insh Hall PH21 1NU.
(Kincraig 272)

Kingussie
Badenoch Christian Centre,
Kincraig PH21 1NA.
(Kincraig 373)

Kingussie Youth Hostel,
Viewmount PH21 1JS.

Kyle of Lochalsh
Kyle Youth Hostel IV40 8DA.

Lairg
Achmelvich Youth Hostel,
Recharn.

Lybster
Rumster Outdoor Centre,
Rumster Forest.
(Latheron 274)
Contact: Divisional Education Officer,
Education Office, Rhind House, West
Banks Avenue, Wick.
(Wick 2362/3)

Newtonmore
Mains Hotel,
Main Street,
(Newtonmore 206)

Onich
Creag Mhor PH33 6RY.
(Onich 205)
Contact: Booking Department,
Countrywide Holidays Association,
Birch Heys, Cromwell Range, Manchester
M14 6HU.
(Manchester 2887)

Thurso
Thurso Youth Club,
Old Mill,
Millbank KW14 8PS.
(Thurso 2964)
Dates: Apr.–Sep.

Torridon
Torridon Youth Hostel.

Ullapool
Ullapool Youth Hostel,
Shore Street.

Wick
John o'Groats Youth Hostel.

Camping and Caravanning

Applecross
Applecross Camp Site.
(Applecross 268)

Arisaig
Gorten Sands Caravan Site,
Gorten Farm.
(Arisaig 283)

Kinloid Caravan Site.
(Arisaig 666)

Portnadorran Caravan Site.
(Arisaig 267)

Tigh Loin Caravan Site,
Tigh An Loan.
(Arisaig 284)

Tigh Na Mara Caravan Site,
Back of Keppoch.
(Arisaig 257)

Aviemore
Aviemore Centre Caravan Park.
(Aviemore 810751)

Dalraddy Caravan Park.
(Aviemore 810330)

Glenmore Forest Park,
Forestry Commission.
(Cairngorm 271)

Speyside Caravan Park,
Craigellachie House.
(Aviemore 810236)

Badachro
Squer Glas Island,
Gairloch.
(Badachro 263)

Balmacara
Forestry Commission,
South Strome Forest,
Achmore.
(Strome Ferry 246)

Beauly
Cruivend Caravan & Camping Ground.
(Beauly 2367)

Lovat Bridge Caravan Site.
(Beauly 2374)

Bettyhill
Crigdhu Caravan & Camping Site.
(Bettyhill 273)

Boat of Garten
Boat of Garten Caravan & Camping Park.
(Boat of Garten 652)

Brora
Dalchalm Caravan Club Site,
Dalchalm.
(Brora 479)

Contin
Riverside Caravan Park.
(Strathpeffer 351)

Cromarty
Shore Mill Caravan Site.
(Poyntzfield 216)

Culloden
Broombank Caravan Club Site,
Newlands.
(Culloden Moor 625)

Daviot
Auchnahillin Caravan & Camping Park.
(Daviot 223)

Dingwall
Camping Club Site,
Jubilee Park.
(Dingwall 62236)
Booking enquiries: Sites Dept., Camping
Club of GB & Ireland, 11 Lower Grosvenor
Place, London. (out of season only)

Dornoch
Dornoch Links Caravan & Camping Site.
(Dornoch 423)
Booking enquiries: District Offices,
Golspie.
(Golspie 392)

Grannies Heilan Hame.
(Dornoch 260)

Pitgrudy Farm Caravan Park.
(Dornoch 291)

Seaview Farm Caravan Site.
(Dornoch 294)

Drumnadrochit
Highland Riding Centre,
Borlum Farm.
(Drumnadrochit 220)

Dunnet
Dunnet Bay Caravan Club Site.
(Castletown 319)

Durness
Sango Sands Caravan & Camping Site.
(Durness 262)

Fort Augustus
Mrs MacKnocker,
Markethill Caravan Site,
Fort William Road.
(Fort Augustus 6227)

Fort William
Glen Nevis Caravan & Camping Park.
(Fort William 2191)

Linnhe Caravan Park Ltd,
Corpach.
(Corpach 376)

Lochy Caravan Park,
Camaghael.
(Fort William 3446)

Gairloch
Sands Holiday Centre.

Garve
Garve Caravan Park,
Garve Hotel.
(Garve 205)

Glencoe
Invercoe Caravans.
(Ballachulish 210)

Red Squirrel Camp Site.
(Ballachulish 256)

Golspie
Golspie Caravan Site,
Ferry Road.
Booking enquiries: District Offices, Golspie.
(Golspie 392)

Grantown-on-Spey
Municipal Caravan Site,
Seafield Avenue,
(Grantown-on-Spey 2474)

Halkirk
Mr Thomson,
Banniskirk House Guest House Camping
& Caravan Site.
(Halkirk 609)

Helmsdale
Mrs Dudgeon,
Crakaig Caravan Site,
Loth.
(Brora 260)

Invergarry
Faichem Park,
Ardgarry Farm,
Faichem.
(Invergarry 226)

Faichemard Farm,
A. & D. Grant.
(Invergarry 276/334)

Inverinate
Caravan Club Site.
(Glenshiel 354)

Invermoriston
Loch Ness Caravan & Camping Park,
Easter Port Clair.
(Glenmoriston 51207)

Invernahavon
Invernahavon Caravan Park,
The Warden.
(Newtonmore 534/221)

Inverness
Bunchrew Caravan Park.
(Inverness 37802)

Torvean Caravan Park.
(Inverness 220582)

Invershin
Invershin Farm Caravan Site.
(Invershin 206)

John o'Groats
John o'Groats Caravan Site,
Last House.
(John o'Groats 250)

Stroma View Caravan Site.
(John o'Groats 313)

Kinlochbervie
Oldshoremore Caravan Site,
152 Oldshoremore.
(Kinlochbervie 281)

Kinlochewe
Kinlochewe Caravan Club Site.
(Kinlochewe 239)

Kinlochleven
Narrach Bridge Caravan Site.
(Kinlochleven 266)

Lairg
Fraser's Caravan Site,
Main Street.
(Lairg 2130)

Woodend Caravan & Camping Site,
Achnairn.
(Lairg 2248)

Lochinver
C. MacLeod,
102 Achmelvich.
(Lochinver 250)

Muir of Ord
Druimorrin Caravan Park,
Orrin Bridge.
(Urray 252)

Onich
Corran Caravans,
Moss Cottage.
(Onich 208)

Poolewe
National Trust for Scotland,
Inverewe Stage House Caravan Site.
(Poolewe 249).

Reay
Dunvegan Euro Caravan & Camp Site.
(Reay 405)

Roy Bridge
Bunroy Caravan Park,
Roy Bridge.
(Spean Bridge 332)

Scourie
Scourie Caravan & Camping Site,
Harbour Road.
(Scourie 2217)

Spean Bridge
Gairlochy Caravan Park,
Gairlochy.
(Gairlochy 229)

Stronaba Farm Caravan Site.
(Spean Bridge 259)

Tain
Meikle Ferry Caravan & Camping Park.
(Tain 2292)

Thurso
Thurso Caravan Site,
Scrabster Road.
Booking enquiries: Mr McPherson,
Caithness District Council,
Council Offices, Wick.

Ullapool
Ardmair Point Caravan Site.
(Ullapool 2054)

Watten
Oldhall Camping Site.
(Watten 215)

Wick
Riverside Caravan Club Site,
Janetstown.
(Wick 5420)

Self Catering

Applecross
A.D. Edwards, Manager,
Applecross Estates.

Arisaig
Gorten Sands Caravan Site,
Gorten Farm,
Arisaig.
(Arisaig 283)

Mr Henderson,
Traigh Farm,
Arisaig PH39 4NT.

Aultbea
Mrs S.W. Davidson,
Struan,
28 Mellon Charles,
Aultbea IV22 2JN.
(Aultbea 259)

Alexander MacKenzie,
30 Mellon Charles,
Aultbea.
(Aultbea 333)

Aviemore
Cairngorm Holiday Homes,
Thana,
Queens Drive,
Oxshott,
Leatherhead,
Surrey KT22 0PH
(Oxshott 3473)

Mrs Grant,
19 Craig na Gower Avenue,
Aviemore PH22 1RW.
(Aviemore 810318)

Mr & Mrs H.M.D. McWilliam,
Craigellachie House,
Aviemore PH22 1PX.
(Aviemore 810236)

Mrs S. Sanders,
Kincraig House,
Kincraig by Kingussie.

Beauly
Mrs C.M. Guthrie,
41 Barrow Point Avenue,
Pinner,
Middlesex HA5 3HD.
(01-866 5026)

Mrs MacDonald,
Lower Aultvaich,
By Beauly.
(Muir of Ord 870560)

Mrs J. Masheter,
Mains of Algas,
Beauly IV4 7AD.
(Beauly 2423)

Mrs M. Munro,
Tomich House,
By Beauly.
(Beauly 2225)

D.J. Turner,
Dunsmore Lodges,
Farley,
Beauly IV4 7EY.
(Beauly 2424)

Bettyhill
Mrs J. Atkinson,
8 Sinclair Street,
Thurso KW14 7AG.
(Thurso 3291 office hrs)

Mr and Mrs Donald M. MacKenzie,
Craidghu Caravan & Camping Site,
Bettyhill KW14 7SP.
(Bettyhill 273)

Mrs A. Todd,
Hoy Farm,
Halkirk KW12 6UU.
(Halkirk 544)

Boat of Garten
Mrs I. Anderson,
Corrour,
Drumullie Road,
Boat of Garten PH24 3BD.
(Boat of Garten 248)

Mr and Mrs W.B. Grant,
Mains of Garten Farm,
Boat of Garten PH42 3BY.
(Boat of Garten 228)

Mrs A.H. Harris,
25 Lime Tree Road,
Norwich NR2 2NQ.
(Norwich 53058)

Mrs Maureen H. Smyth,
Conifers Cottages,
Chapelton,
Boat of Garten PH24 3BU.
(Boat of Garten 327)

Cannich
Col J.A. Fraser,
Tomuaine,
Tomich by Beauly IV4 7LY.
(Cannich 220)

Carrbridge
Maj. and Mrs W. Dunlop,
Fairwinds,
Carrbridge PH23 3AA.
(Carrbridge 240)

Lochanhully Lodges,
Carrbridge PH23 3NA.
(Carrbridge 234)

Contin
A.S. Finnie,
Riverside Caravan Site IV14 9ES.
(Strathpeffer 351)

Culkein
Mrs V. MacLeod,
7 Mount Stuart Road,
Largs KA30 9ES.
(Largs 672931)

Culloden Moor
Mrs E.M.C. Alexander,
Culdoich Farm,
Culloden Moor
(Culloden Moor 268)

Miss Skinner,
Clave Lodge Hotel,
Culloden Moor.
(Culloden Moor 228)

Dalwhinnie
A.C. Gillies Jnr,
Gillies Leasing,
Dalwhinnie.
(Dalwhinnie 267)

Delny
Hoseasons Holidays,
Sunway House,
Lowestoft,
Suffolk NR32 3LT.
(Lowestoft 62292)

Dingwall
Eurecosse Holidays,
7 Greenhill Street,
Dingwall IV15 9JQ.
(Dingwall 62462)

Mrs Yvonne Mayer,
10 Cloudesley Place,
London N1 0JA.

Revd and Mrs Ross,
Free Presbyterian Manse,
Kingsway Avenue,
Tain.

Dores
Mr and Mrs A.I. Cameron,
Drummond Farm,
Dores.
(Dores 251)

Dornie
D.F. MacRae,
Rock House,
Dornie IV40 8DX.
(Dornie 268)

Dornoch
Mrs Sheila Board,
Park Restaurant,
Main StreetGolspie.
(Golspie 667/Dornoch 727)

Mrs A. Burnett,
Pulrossie Farm,
Dornoch IV25 3LR.
(Whiteface 206)

Mr MacDonald,
27 Stratherrick Road,
Inverness IV2 4LF.
(Inverness 34433)

Drumbeg
Elizabeth Johnson,
Low Alwinton,
Harbottle,
Morpeth,
Northumberland NE65 7BE.
(Rothbury 50224)

Drumbuie
Mrs F. MacLellan,
Northside,
Drumbuie by Kyle IV40 8BD.
(Plockton 337)

Drumnadrochit
Mrs S. Fraser,
Torbreck,
Lewiston,
Drumnadrochit IV3 6UW.
(Drumnadrochit 346)

Evanton
A.H. Munro,
Balconie,
Evanton IV16 9XG.
(Evanton 830218)

Fort Augustus
Hoseasons Holidays,
Sunway House,
Lowestoft,
Suffolk NR32 3LT.
(Lowestoft 62292)

Fortrose
John Bevan-Baker,
46 Ravenswood Drive,
Shawlands,
Glasgow G41 3UH.
(041 632 3698)

Mrs G.L. MacLeod,
The Pines,
13 Eveley Close,
Whitehill,
Bordon,
Hants.
(Bordon 2469)

Glenfinnan
Mr McKellaig,
Glenfinnan Information Centre,
Glenfinnan.
(Kinlocheil 250)
Glenmoriston.
(Glenmoriston 51200)

Glen Nevis
Mrs J. Cameron,
Springwell Cottage,
Glen Nevis Bridge,
Glen Nevis by Fort William.
(Fort William 2917)

Glenurquhart
Mrs MacDonald,
Lochletter Farm,
Balnain,
Glenurquhart.
(Glenurquhart 288/208)

Golspie
Mrs N. Grant,
Deo Greine,
Backies,
Golspie KW10 6SE.
(Golspie 306)

Grantown-on-Spey
Mrs J.R. Allan,
35 Heriot Row,
Edinburgh EH3 6JE.
(031 225 3581)

Mrs Joan Hay,
Larach Mor,
Kirk Road,
Gromdale,
Grantown-on-Spey PH26 3LP.
(Grantown-on-Spey 2556)

Mrs D. Laing,
Firhill,
Strathspey Drive,
Grantown-on-Spey.
(Grantown-on-Spey 2439)

Miss J.I.G. MacKenzie,
Milton of Delliefure,
Grantown-on-Spey.
(Grantown-on-Spey 2840)

A.E. Smith,
Auchernack,
Grantown-on-Spey.
(Grantown-on-Spey 2093)

Helmsdale
Mrs Cruickshank,
7 Hillpark Terrace,
Wormit-on-Tay.
(Newport 541794)

Mrs P. Weir,
Tigh mo Chridle,
Helmsdale KW8 6HH.
(Helmsdale 270)

Inverasdale
Mrs A.E. Kirk,
2 Coast,
Inverasdale IV22 2LR.
(Poolewe 267)

Mrs G. Meikle,
Abbeymount,
Ancrum Road,
Eskbank,
Edinburgh.
(031 663 3201)

Invergarry
Glengarry Castle Hotel (Reception)
Invergarry PH35 4HW.
(Invergarry 254)

A. and D. Grant,
Faichemard Farm,
Invergarry PH35 4HG.
(Invergarry 276)

Mrs Jennifer Gray,
Aldernaig,
Invergarry.
(Invergarry 201)

Invergordon
Mrs S.A. Fraser,
Greenlands,
Arabella,
Nigg.
(Nigg Station 209)

Invermoriston
Mrs W. Billings,
Point Clair House,
Invermoriston IV3 6YE.
(Invermoriston 51205)

Inverness
Mrs H. Allan,
5 Leyes Park,
Inverness.
(Inverness 30403)

R.M. Campbell,
85 Kenneth Street,
Inverness.
(Inverness 34711)

Mrs L. Colvin,
44 Thornbush Road,
Inverness.
(Inverness 32558)

Kingussie
P.J. Cook,
Scotts Hotel,
Kingussie.
(Kingussie 351)

Mrs L.B.H. Sandison,
Killiehuntly,
Kingussie PH21 1NZ.
(Kingussie 270)

Kinlochbervie
H. Elrich,
Achriesgill,
Rhiconich,
Sutherland.
(Kinlochbervie 228)

Mrs Georgina MacKay,
10 Manse Road,
Kinlochbervie IV27 4RG.
(Kinlochbervie 365)

Laggan
Mrs Shirley A. Grant,
Gaskbeg,
Laggan,
Newtonmore PH20 1BS.
(Laggan 255)

Mrs Cameron Ormiston,
Strathmashie Lodge,
Laggan by Newtonmore.
(Laggan 271)

Lochcarron

*Mrs K.A. MacKenzie,
Wilrijk,
Lochcarron IV54 8YG.
(Lochcarron 240)*

Lochinver
Mrs M. MacAskill,
Hamnavoe,
2 Inverkirkaig,
Lochinver IV27 4LR.
(Lochinver 239/267)

Mrs M. McCall,
Hillside,

Nethybridge
Abernethy Outdoor Centre,
The Resident Director,
Nethybridge PH25 3ED.
(Nethybridge 279)

Mrs A. Black,
Laintachan,
Nethybridge PH25 3EE.
(Nethybridge 641)

S. Davies,
Farthings,
The Causar,
Nethybridge PH25 3DR.
(Nethybridge 648)

Professor M. Dunn,
Culreach,
Grantown-on-Spey PH26 3NH.
(Nethybridge 269)

Mr and Mrs J. Fleming,
Dell of Abernethy,
Nethybridge PH25 3DL.
(Nethybridge 643)

Newtonmore
Blakes Holidays,
Wroxham,
Norwich NR12 8DH.
(Wroxham 2917)

Neil Campbell,
Station House,
Station Road,
Newtonmore.
(Newtonmore 469)

Mrs J. Fraser,
Creagbheag Cottage,
West Terrace,
Kingussie.
(Kingussie 547)

North Kessock
S. Fisher,
Tigh-na-Greine,
Drumsmittal,
North Kessock IV1 1XF.
(Kessock 227)

Plockton
Mackinnon Hathway,
Estate Agents,
Seawinds,
Church Road,
Kyle of Lochalsh.
(Kyle 4567)

Poolewe
Messrs MacAndrew & Jenkin,
Royal Bank Buildings,
5 Drummond Street,
Inverness.
(Inverness 33001)

Mrs A. Newton,
15 Londubh,
Poolewe,
Achnasheen.
(Poolewe 256)

Roy Bridge
Mrs L.P. Hawke,
Meadowcroft,
Roy Bridge PH31 4AQ.
(Spean Bridge 292)

Kinchellie Croft Motel,
Roy Bridge PH31 4RN.
(Spean Bridge 265)

Strathcarron
Mr and Mrs A. Petrie,
18 Drynie Terrace,
Inverness.
(Inverness 40338/Achnashellach 276)

Strathconon
Mrs A. Kellie,
The Croft House,
Curin,
Strathconon by Muir of Ord IV6 7QG.
(Scatwell 227)

Strathpeffer
Mrs I.M. Campbell,
Glenorchy,
Strathpeffer IV14 9DS.
(Strathpeffer 230)

Stromeferry
Eurecosse Holidays (R209),
7 Greenhill Street,
Dingwall.
(Dingwall 62462)

Tomatin
Mrs J.A. Glynne-Percy,
Tomatin House,
Tomatin IV13 7XX.
(Tomatin 210)

Tongue
Gordon R. Burr of
Messrs Peter Burr, Merchants,
Tongue IV27 4XF.
(Tongue 202)

Mrs Elliot,
Eriboll,
By Altnaharra,
Lairg.
(Durness 275)

Ullapool
Blakes Holidays,
Wroxham,
Norwich NR12 8DH.
(Wroxham 2917)

Mrs A. Campbell,
Clisham,
Rhue,
Ullapool.

G.B.N. Creswick,
Egford House,
Frome,
Somerset BA11 3JP.
(Frome 2794)

Highland Coastal Trading Company,
Coulmore,
Kessock by Inverness.
(Kessock 212)

G. MacDonald,
Rosedale,
Muir of Ord.
(Muir of Ord 281)

Watten
G. Calder,
Oldhall,
Watten by Wick KW1 5XL.
(Watten 215)

Wick
Mrs A. Innes,
Basquary,
Stirkoke.
(Wick 3695)

Golf

Boat of Garten
Boat of Garten Golf Club.
(Boat of Garten 282)
Secretary: R. Browne, Aldclune, Aviemore.
(Aviemore 810536)

Dornoch
Royal Dornoch Golf Course,
Golf Road.
(Dornoch 219)

Fort Augustus
Fort Augustus Golf Club.
(Fort Augustus 6333)

Fortrose
Fortrose & Rosemarkie Golf Club,
The Ness.
(Fortrose 20529)

Fort William
Fort William Golf Club,
Torlundy.
(Fort William 4464)

Gairloch
Gairloch Golf Club.
(Gairloch 2015)

Golspie
Golspie Golf Club,
Ferry Road.
(Golspie 266)

Grantown-on-Spey
Grantown-on-Spey Golf Club.
(Grantown-on-Spey 2079)

Helmsdale
Helmsdale Golf Course,
Strath Road.
(Helmsdale 224)

Invergordon
Invergordon Golf Club,
Cromlet Drive.
(Invergordon 852116)

Inverness
Inverness Golf Course,
Culcabock.
(Inverness 33422)

Torvean Golf Course,
Glenurquhart Road.
(Inverness 37543)

Kingussie
Kingussie Golf Club,
Gynack Road.
(Kingussie 374)

Mallaig
Traigh Golf Club,
Braeholm.
(Arisaig 2126)

Muir of Ord
Muir of Ord Golf Club,
Great North Road.

Newtonmore
Newtonmore Golf Course.
(Newtonmore 328)

Strathpeffer
Strathpeffer Spa Golf Club,
(Strathpeffer 219)

Tain
Tain Golf Club.
(Tain 2314)

Thurso
Thurso Golf Club,
Newland of Geise.
(Thurso 3807)

Wick
Wick Golf Club,
Reiss KW1 4RW.
(Wick 2726)

Riding Schools

Dores
Dores Riding Centre,
Drummond Farm.
(Dores 251)
Accommodation can be arranged near centre. Camping & caravanning facilities nearby.

Drumnadrochit
A.D. MacDonald-Haig,
Highland Riding Centre,
Borlum Farm.
(Drumnadrochit 220/434)
Accommodation can be arranged near centre. Camping & caravanning facilities nearby.

Forres
Kinloss Riding Stables,
Old Schoolhouse.
(Findhorn 2218)
Accommodation is available at the centre or can be arranged near centre. Camping & caravanning facilities.

Fort William
Great Glen Riding Centre,
Torlundy.
(Fort William 3015)
Accommodation is available at the centre

or can be arranged near centre. Camping & caravanning facilities nearby.

Invergarry
Garry Gualach.
(Tomdoun 230)
Accommodation can be arranged near centre. Camping & caravanning facilities nearby.

Melvich
Melvich Trekking Centre.
(Melvich 262)
Accommodation available at the centre or can be arranged near centre.

Nethybridge
Nethybridge Riding Centre,
(Nethybridge 693)
Accommodation can be arranged near centre. Camping & caravanning facilities available within 5 miles (8 km).

Game Fishing

Achall Loch
Salmon, sea trout, brown trout.
Permits: Highland Coastal Estates
(Rhidorroch) Office,
Shore Street,
Ullapool,
Ross & Cromarty.

Achiltibuie
Local lochs.
Salmon, sea trout, brown trout.
Permits: Badentarbat Lodge,
Achiltibuie,
Ullapool,
Ross & Cromarty.
(Achiltibuie 225)

Affric Hill Lochs
(Forestry Commission)
Rainbow trout.
Apply: Forest Office,
Cannich,
Beauly.

Alness River
Salmon, brown trout.
Permits: Coul House Hotel,
Contin by Strathpeffer.
(Strathpeffer 487)

Salmon, trout.
Permits: Dunraven Lodge Hotel,
Strathpeffer.
(Strathpeffer 210)

Alvie Loch; Spey River
Trout, salmon.
Permits: Lynwilg Hotel,
Loch Alvie,
Aviemore.
(Aviemore 810602)

Arkaig Loch
Lochiel Estate Fishings
Brown trout, sea trout, occasional salmon.
Permits: The West Highland Estates Office,
33 High Street,
Fort William.
(Fort William 2433 *or* Gairlochy 217)

Assynt
(34 lochs)
Brown trout.
Permits: Assynt Angling Club,
Baddidarroch,
Lochinver.
(Lochinver 253) *or*
Tourist Information Office,
Lochinver.
(Lochinver 330) *or*
Culag Hotel,
Lochinver.

Assynt Loch
Salmon, brown trout.
Permits: Inchnadamph Hotel,
Inchnadamph,
Sutherland.
(Assynt 202)

Avielochan
Brown trout, rainbow trout.
Permits: Mrs M. McCook,
Avielochan,
Aviemore.
(Aviemore 810450) *or*
G.G. Mortimer & Son (Fishing Tackle),
61 High Street,
Grantown-on-Spey.
(Grantown-on-Spey 2684)

Awe Loch
Salmon, brown trout.
Permits: Inchnadamph Hotel,
Inchnadamph.
(Assynt 202)

Badachro Loch and River
(plus 7 other hill lochs)
Trout, salmon.
Permits: Shieldaig Lodge Hotel,
Gairloch,
Ross & Cromarty IV21 2AW.
(Badachro 250)

Badanloch, Clar, Cor Na Mang, Fearnan, Rimsdale Lochs
Brown trout.
Permits: Navidale House Hotel,
Helmsdale.
(Helmsdale 258)

Balmacara Estate Lochs
Brown trout.
Permits: Balmacara Hotel by Kyle of
Lochalsh,
Ross & Cromarty.
(Kyle 283)

Beannach Loch
Brown trout.
Permits: Sutherland Arms Hotel,
Lairg.
(Lairg 2291)

Benevean Loch
(North of Scotland Hydro-Electric Board)
Trout.
Permits: J. Graham & Co Ltd,
27 Union Street,
Inverness.
(Inverness 33178)

Barriedale River
Salmon, sea trout.

Blackwater River
Upper beat (North of Scotland Hydro-Electric Board)
Salmon, brown trout.

Blackwater River, Conon River
Salmon, sea trout, trout.
Permits: Craigdarroch Lodge Hotel,
Craigdarroch Drive,
Contin by Strathpeffer.
(Strathpeffer 265)

Brora Loch
Salmon, sea trout, brown trout.
Permits: Estate Office,
Gordonbush,
Brora.
(Brora 323)

Brora River
About ¾ mile (1 km) of tidal water.
Sea trout, finnock, a few brown trout.
Permits: None required. Fly only.

Carron River
Salmon, sea trout.
Permits: Renton Finlayson,
Estates Office,
Bonar Bridge.

Catrine Loch
Brown trout.
Permits: Inveroykel Lodge Hotel,
Strathoykel by Ardgay.
(Rosehall 200)

Cluanie Loch
Brown trout.
Permits: Dochfour Estate Office,
Dochgarroch by Inverness.
(Dochgarroch 218/9)

Craggie Loch
Brown trout.
Permits: Ben Loyal Hotel,
Tongue.
(Tongue 216)

Craggie, Ailsh Lochs
Rainbow, brown & sea trout.
Permits: Oykel Bridge Hotel,
By Lairg.

Cuaich Loch
Brown trout.
Permits: Badenoch Angling Association,
29 Burnside Avenue,
Aviemore.

Drumbeg Lochs
(20 lochs near hotel)
Brown trout.
Permits: Drumbeg Hotel,
Assynt by Lairg.
(Assynt 236)

Findhorn
Salmon, brown trout.
Permits: Freeburn Inn,
Tomatin.
(Tomatin 205)

Fionn Loch
Salmon, brown trout.
Permits: Harold Davis,
Creag Mor Hotel,
Gairloch.
(Gairloch 2068)

Fuarloch
Brown trout.
Permits: Sutherland Arms Hotel,
Lairg.
(Lairg 2291)

Garvie and Polly Rivers
Salmon, sea trout, brown trout.
Permits: Royal Hotel,
Ullapool.
(Ullapool 2181)

Ghriama Loch
Brown trout.
Permits: Overscaig Hotel,
Overscaig by Lairg.
(Merkland 203)

Glenmoriston
(22 hill lochs)
Brown trout.
Permits: Glenmoriston Estate Office,
Glenmoriston.
(Glenmoriston 51202)

Helmsdale River
Sea trout, salmon.
Permits: Helmsdale River Board,
Fishery Office,
Strathnaver,
Kinbrace.
(Strathnaver 201)

Kyle of Sutherland Migdale Loch
Brown trout, sea trout.
Permits: Invershin Hotel,
Invershin,
Lairg.
(Invershin 202)

Kyle of Tongue
Sea trout.
Permits: Ben Loyal Hotel,
Tongue.
(Tongue 216)

Maree Loch
Salmon, sea trout, trout.
Permits: Shieldaig Lodge Hotel,
Gairloch,
Ross & Cromarty IV1 2AN.
(Badachro 250)

Sea trout, brown trout, salmon.
Permits: Kinlochewe Hotel,
Kinlochewe by Achnasheen,
Ross & Cromarty.
(Kinlochewe 253)

Maovally
Brown trout.
Permits: Ben Loyal Hotel,
Tongue.
(Tongue 216)

Meig Loch, Beannacharain Loch, Meig River
Brown trout.
Permits: East Lodge Hotel,
Strathconon.
(Strathconon 222)

Ness Loch
Salmon, trout.
Permits: Glenmoriston Estates Office,
Glenmoriston,
(Glenmoriston 51202)

Ness River
Salmon, sea trout.
Permits: Inverness Angling Club,
J. Fraser,
33 Hawthorn Drive,
Inverness.

Polly Lochs
Top, middle and lower.
Salmon, sea trout.
Permits: J. MacDonald,
Inverpolly,
Ullapool,
Ross & Cromarty.
(Lochinver 252)

Quoich Loch
Trout.
Permits: J. Sabin,
Lovat Arms Hotel,
Fort Augustus.
(Fort Augustus 6206)

Scaddle River
Salmon, sea trout.
Permits: Ardgour Hotel,
By Fort William.
(Ardgour 225)

Scourie Lochs
(and lochans over an area of 15,000 acres
(6,705 ha))
Brown trout, sea trout, salmon.
Permits: Scourie Hotel,
Scourie by Lairg.
(Scourie 2396)

Shin Loch
Brown trout.
Permits: Lairg Angling Club,

J.M. Ross, Secretary,
Post Office House,
Lairg.
(Lairg 2010) *or*
Lairg Pharmacy and local hardware fishing
tackle shop. *or*
Club Warden – club hut at lochside beyond
Lairg Dam.

Permits: Overscaig Hotel,
Overscaig by Lairg.
(Merkland 203)

Sionascaig, Lurgain, Badagyle Lochs
Salmon, sea trout, brown trout, ferrox.
Permits: Royal Hotel,
Ullapool,
Ross & Cromarty.
(Ullapool 2181)

Spean River
Permits: Spean Bridge Hotel,
Spean Bridge.
(Spean Bridge 250)

Spey Dam
Trout.
Permits: Badenoch Angling Association,
39 Burnside Avenue,
Aviemore. *or*
A. MacDonald,
6 Gergask Avenue,
Laggan.

Spey River
Salmon, sea trout, brown trout.
Permits: Osprey Fishing School,
Aviemore Centre,
Aviemore.
(Aviemore 810767/810911)

(6 miles/9 km, both banks)
Salmon, sea trout, brown trout.
Permit: The Boat Hotel,
Boat of Garten,
(Boat of Garten 258)

Spey, Feshie Rivers, Insh Loch
Salmon, brown trout, sea trout.
Permits: Invershie House Hotel,
Kincraig by Kingussie.
(Kincraig 332)

Spey, Feshie Lochs
Salmon, brown trout, sea trout.
Permits: The Osprey Fishing School,
The Fishing Centre,

Aviemore Centre,
Aviemore.

Strath Kanaird Loch
Brown trout.
Permits: Highland Coastal Estates
(Rhidorroch) Offices,
Shore Street,
Ullapool,
Ross & Cromarty.

Vaa Loch, Dallas Loch
Brown trout, rainbow trout.
Permits: Mrs M. McCook,
Avielochan,
Aviemore.
(Aviemore 810450) *or*
G.G. Mortimer & Son (Fishing Tackle
61 High Street,
Grantown-on-Spey.
(Grantown-on-Spey 2684)

Watten Loch
Brown trout.
Permits: Loch Watten Hotel,
Watten.
(Watten 232)

Watten Loch, Calder Loch, St John's Loch
Brown trout.
Permits: St Clair Hotel,
15 Sinclair Street,
Thurso.
(Thurso 3730)

Hotels with Fishing

Gairloch
Creag Mor Hotel
Fishing on River Kerry (½ mile/1 km),
Lochs Garbaig (6 miles/9 km) and Black
Lady Loch (1 mile/2 km).
Salmon, sea trout, brown trout.
(Gairloch 2068)

Shieldaig Lodge Hotel
Fishing in Loch and River Badachro (1–8
miles/13 km from hotel).
Trout and salmon.
(Badachro 250)

Glencoe
King's House Hotel
Fishing in Ba Loch.
Brown trout.
(Kingshouse 259)

Glenfinnan
Stage House Inn
Fishing in Loch Shiel, 1 mile/2 km from
hotel.
Salmon, sea trout, brown trout.

Glenurquhart
Kilmartin Hall
Fishing in River Enrick and Loch Meiklie
200 yards (183 m) from the hotel.
Trout, salmon.
(Glenurquhart 269)

Kingussie
Silverfjord Hotel
Fishing in Rivers Spey and Truim, and
seven Highland lochs.
Salmon, sea trout, brown trout.
(Kingussie 292)

Kinlochewe
Kinlochewe Hotel
Fishing in Loch Maree (1 mile/2 km from
hotel).
Sea trout, brown trout, salmon.
(Kinlochewe 253)

Lairg
Oykel Bridge Hotel
Fishing in Craggie and Ailsh Lochs.
Rainbow, brown and sea trout.
(Rosehall 218)

Sutherland Arms Hotel
Fishing in Loch Shin (adjacent to hotel)
and in Lochs Beannach and Fuaralach.
Brown trout, ferrox, sea trout.
Fishing may also be arranged on River Shin
and many other lochs.
Salmon, brown trout, sea trout, etc.
(Lairg 2291)

Lochinver
Culag Hotel
Fishing in River Kirkaig and Lochs Culag,
Fionn, Assynt, Cul Fraoich, Claise,
Crocach and Beannach all within 7 miles
(11 km) from the hotel.
Brown trout, rainbow trout, sea trout,
salmon.
(Lochinver 209/255)

Mallaig
Morar Hotel
Fishing in Loch Morar, 1 mile (2 km) from
hotel.
Salmon, sea trout, brown trout.

Newtonmore
Badenoch Hotel
Fishing on Badenoch Association Water in
Loch Shirra, Loch Laggan, Loch Cuaich,
Loch an Ericht and 14 miles (23 km) of .
River Spey, Feshie and Truim.
Salmon, sea trout, brown trout in river
water, and brown trout in other waters.
(Newtonmore 246)

Strathpeffer
Dunraven Lodge Hotel
Fishing in River Alness.
Salmon, trout.
(Strathpeffer 210)

Thurso
St Clair Hotel
15 Sinclair Street.
Fishing in Lochs Watten, Calder, St John's.
Brown trout.
(Thurso 3730)

Torridon
Loch Torridon Hotel
Fishing in Rivers Torridon and Baigy,
Lochs an Isacaigh and Damph all within 4
miles (6 km) of the hotel.
Brown trout, sea trout, salmon.
(Torridon 242)

Ullapool
Royal Hotel
Fishing on Lochs Sionascaig, Lurgan and
Badagyle, also Rivers Garvie and Polly
(spate).
Salmon, sea trout, brown trout, ferrox.
(Ullapool 2181)

Hotels with Shooting and Stalking

Gairloch
Shieldaig Lodge Hotel.
(Badachro 250)
Rough shooting and stalking.

Glenmoriston
Glenmoriston Arms Hotel.
(Glenmoriston 206)
Game, wildfowl, rough shooting.

John o'Groats
John o'Groats House Hotel.
(John o'Groats 203)
Rough shooting.

Kincraig
Invereshie House.
(Kincraig 332)
Game, wildfowl, rough shooting, stalking.

Lochailort
Lochailort Inn,
Road to the Isles.
(Lochailort 208)
Stalking.

Lybster
Portland Arms Hotel.
(Lybster 208)
Game, rough shooting.

Muir of Ord
Ord House Hotel.
(Muir of Ord 492)
Game, shooting, stalking.

Portmahomack
Caledonian Hotel.
(Portmahomack 345)
Game, wildfowl, rough shooting.

Scourie
Eddrachilles Hotel,
Badcall Bay.
(Scourie 2080)
Stalking.

Spean Bridge
Spean Bridge Hotel.
(Spean Bridge 250)
Stalking.

Struy
Cnoc Hotel,
Erchless Estate.
(Struy 264)
Game, rough shooting, stalking.

Whitebridge
Knockie Lodge Hotel.
(Gorthleck 276)
Game, shooting, stalking.

Special Interest Holidays

Osprey Fishing School
The Fishing Centre,
Aviemore Centre,
Aviemore.
(Aviemore 810767/810911)

School of Casting
Salmon & Trout Fishing (established 1964)
P.O. Box 10,
Inverness IV1 1TP.
(Cannich 214)

Abernethy Outdoor Centre
Nethy Bridge.
(Nethy Bridge 279)

Ardenbeg
Grant Road,
Grantown-on-Spey,
(Grantown-on-Spey 2824)
Skiing, ski-mountaineering, hillwalking,
mountaineering, snow/ice climbing and
mountain leader training.

Aviemore Sailing School
Cairdsport,
Aviemore Centre,
Aviemore.
(Aviemore 810310)
Windsurfing.

Garry Gualach Adventure Centre
Invergarry.
(Tomdoun 230)
Work camps, adventure holidays, wildlife
holidays.

*Glenmore Lodge National Outdoor Training
Centre*
Nr. Aviemore.
Contact: The Scottish Sports Council,
1 St Colme Street,
Edinburgh EH3 6AA.
(031-225 8411)
Mountaineering, canoeing, skiing, sailing.
Specialist courses arranged for colleges and
a variety of groups.
Accommodation is available at the centre.

Highland Guides
Inverdruie
Aviemore.
(Aviemore 810729)
Kayaks and Canadian canoes, Mirrors and
Wayfarers available.

Loch Insh Sailing School
Insh Hall,
Kincraig.
(Kincraig 272)
Sailing and canoeing.
Windsurfers, bicycles, canoes and sailing
boats for hire from the school.

John Ridgway Adventure School
Ardmore,
Rhiconich by Lairg.
(Kinlochlervie 229)

Outward Bound Loch Eil
Achdalieu,
Fort William.
(Corpach 320)

Aigas Field Centre
Beauly.
(Beauly 2443)

Cairngorm Gliding Club
Blackmill Farm,
Kincraig.
(Kincraig 339)

Cycling

Aviemore
Cairdsport Ski Schools Ltd,
Aviemore Centre.
(Aviemore 810310)

D'Ecosse Ski & Sports Ltd,
Main Road.
(Aviemore 810285)

Highland Guides,
Inverdruie
(Aviemore 810729)

Speyside Caravan Park & Chalets,
Craigellachie Hotel.
(Aviemore 810236)

Carrbridge
W. Dunlop,
Fair Winds.
(Carrbridge 240)

Fort William
Easyride Cycle Hire,
Farr Cottage,
Corpach.
(Corpach 315)

Inverness
Bishopleasure Bicycles Ltd,
11 Waterloo Place.
(Inverness 40352)

Thornton Cycles,
23 Castle Street.
(Inverness 222810)

Muir of Ord
John A. Urquhart,
The Cycle Shop,
Main Street.
(Muir of Ord 462)

Thurso
Autoparts,
52 Princes Street.

Where to Eat

Arisaig
Arisaig Hotel.
(Arisaig 210)

Aviemore
The Winking Owl,
Main Road.
(Aviemore 810646)

Lynwilg Hotel,
Loch Alvie,
nr Aviemore.
(Aviemore 810207)

Balmachara
(By Kyle of Lochalsh)
Balmacara Hotel.
(Balmacara 283)

Contin
Coul House Hotel.
(Strathpeffer 487)

Fort William
The Moorings Hotel,
Banavie,
nr Fort William.
(Corpach 550)

Inverness
Blen Mhor Hotel,
Ness Bank.
(Inverness 34308)

Station Hotel,
Academy Street.
(Inverness 31926)

Kingussie
Wood'n Spoon Restaurant & Creel Bar,
3 High Street.
(Kingussie 488)

Nairn
The Taste Bud,
44 Harbour Street.
(Nairn 52743)

Newtonmore
Alvey House,
Golf Course Road.
(Newtonmore 260)

Strathpeffer
Dunraven Lodge Hotel,
Golf Road.
(Strathpeffer 210)

Struy
Mauld Bridge Hotel,
By Beauly.
(Struy 222)

Car Hire

Achnasheen
Roderick A. MacLeod,
18 Midtown,
Inverasdale,
Poolewe.
(Poolewe 228)

Aviemore
Godfrey Davis Ltd,
Information Desk,
Aviemore Centre.
(Aviemore 810696)

Grants Service Station,
62 Grampian Road.
(Aviemore 810205)

Dingwall
MacRae & Dick Ltd,
Station Road.
(Dingwall 3223)

Fred Newton Ltd,
West End Garage.
(Dingwall 2323)

Dornoch
J.G. Gordon,
Broomfield,
Birichen.
(Dornoch 503 day, Dornoch 563/842 night)

Mackay's Garage,
The Square.
(Dornoch 232)

Fort William
Barclay House, Motors Ltd,
Barclay House,
Camaghael.
(Fort William 4141)

Ben Car Sales Ltd,
Argour Road,
Caol.
(Fort William 2408/9)

Wm Gilbert, (Ness Motors) Ltd,
North Road.
(Fort William 4913/4)

MacRae & Dick,
Gordon Square.
(Fort William 2345)

Gairloch
Gairloch Taxi Service,
5 Faolin,
Strath.
(Gairloch 2125)

Invergordon
Wm Munro, (Invergordon) Ltd,
Royal Garage.
(Invergordon 852351)

Inverness
Auto Sales,
Harbour Road.
(Inverness 30885)

Budget Rent-a-Car,
(Land Rovers),
c/o Macrae & Dick Ltd,
Academy Street.
(Inverness 39877/8)

Foss Self Drive/Europcar,
Millburn Road.
(Inverness 35486)

Godfrey Davis Ltd,
The Highlander Service Station,
Millburn Road.
(Inverness 34886/35337)

H.W. Jack (Car Hire) Ltd,
17 Ardconnel Terrace.
(Inverness 36571/2)

Ness Motors,
16 Telford Street.
(Inverness 222848)

SMT Self Drive Hire,
112 Academy Street.
(Inverness 34311/2)

Inverness Airport
Godfrey Davis (Car Hire) Ltd,
(Inverness 34886/35337)

Kyle of Lochalsh
Clan Garage (Kyle) Ltd,
(Kyle 4328)

Muir of Ord
D. Noble & Sons,
Glebe Garage.
(Muir of Ord 29617)

Tain
MacRae & Dick.
(Tain 2375)

Thurso
Northern Motors,
Couper Square.
(Thurso 2778/3553)

Ullapool
Mr McLeod,
Moss Road.
(Ullapool 2029)

Wick
Dunnet Motors Ltd,
Francis Street.
(Wick 2103)

MacRae & Dick,
Bridge Street.
(Wick 2195)

Mowatt's Garage,
George Street.
(Wick 2321/2)

Richard's Garage & Agric. Co.,
Francis Street,
(Wick 2240)

ISLE OF SKYE

Hotels & Guest Houses

Ardvasar
Ardvasar Hotel.
(Ardvasar 223)

Breakish
Langdale Guest House,
Waterloo IV42 8QE.
(Broadford 376)

Broadford
Beul-na-Mara Guest House,
Lower Harrapool.
(Broadford 487)

Flodigarry
Flodigarry Hotel.
(Duntulm 203)

Isle Ornsay
Duisdale Hotel.
(Isle Ornsay 202)

Kyleakin
Dunringell Hotel IV41 8PR.
(Kyle 4180)

White Heather Hotel IV27 4HW.
(Kyle 4577)

Portree
Bosville Hotel,
Bosville Terrace.
(Portree 2486)

Portree Hotel.
(Portree 2511)

Craiglockhart Guest House,
Beaumount Crescent.
(Portree 2233)

Struan
Ullinish Lodge Hotel.
(Struan 214)

Uig
Uig Hotel.
(Uig 205)

Accommodation for the Young

Broadford
Broadford Youth Hostel.

Glenbrittle
Glenbrittle Youth Hostel.

Uig
Uig Youth Hostel.

Camping and Caravanning

Loch Greshornish
Loch Greshornish Caravan & Camping
Site,
Edinbane,
Arnisport by Portree.
(Edinbane 230)
Apr.–Oct.

Portree
Torvaig Caravan & Camping Site.
(Portree 2209)
Apr.–Oct.

Staffin
Staffin Caravan & Camping Site.
(Staffin 213)

Self Catering

Ardvasar
Mrs E. Kendall,
The Cottage,
Tur Langton,
Leics.
(East Langton 281)

Borve
Borve Holiday Homes,
Borve.
(Skeabost Bridge 247/240)

Drumvuie
Mrs E. Morrison,
Ashlea, Viewfield Road,
Portree.
(Portree 2996)

Roskhill
Mrs Beevers,
Roskhill Guest House,
Roskhill.
(Dunvegan 317)

Sleat
Mrs M. MacLinnes,
10 Sasaig,
Teangue.
(Isle Ornsay 291)

Struan
Miss MacLeod,
4 Ullinish,
Struan.

Uig
Mrs MacLeod,
68 Queens Road,
Aberdeen.
(Aberdeen 38253)

Golf

Sconser Golf Club.
(Portree 2030)

Sea Angling

Glendale by Dunvegan
Shore fish at Poolteil Pier.
Glendale and Neist for information.
(Dunvegan 380)

Portree
Cod, haddock, whiting, coalfish, pollack,
mackerel.
Boats. Tourist Information Centre.
(Portree 2137)

Skeabost Bridge
Many types of sea fish can be caught by
boat. No shore fishing.
Boat available: Skeabost House Hotel.
(Skeabost Bridge 202)

Uig
Shore: coalfish, mackerel, pollack, whiting,
haddock, dogfish, flat fish, skate, cod.
Boats: J. Rankin. (Uig 213)
A. Mackinnon, Waternish. (Waternish
213)

Coarse and Game Fishing

Struan
Salmon, sea trout, brown trout.
Ullinish Lodge Hotel.
(Struan 214)

Hotels with Shooting and Stalking

Ardvasar
Ardvasar Hotel.
(Ardvasar 223)
Stalking.

Dunvegan
Harlosh Hotel,
Harlosh.
(Dunvegan 367)
Rough shooting and stalking.

Isle Ornsay
Kinloch Lodge Hotel,
Kinloch.
(Isle Ornsay 214)
Stalking.

Sleat
Tigh Osda Eilean Iarmain Camus Chros.
(Isle Ornsay 266)

Struan
Ullinish Lodge Hotel.
(Struan 214)
Game, rough shooting.

Uig
Uig Lodge Hotel.
(Timsgarry 286)
Wildfowl, rough shooting.

Cycling

Kyleakin
Skye Cycles.
(Kyle 4532)

Portree
A.D. MacDonald.
(Portree 2521)

Car Hire

Portree
N. Beeton,
Dunvegan Road.
(Portree 2002)

Hugh MacDonald,
3 Bayfield Road.
(Portree 2603)

E. MacRae,
West End Garage Ltd,
Dunvegan Road.

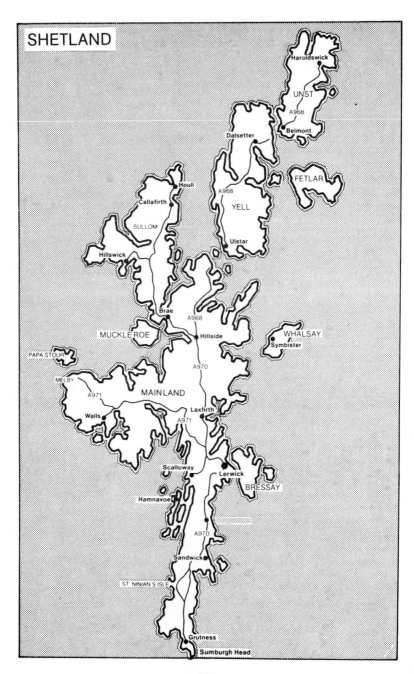

SHETLAND

Haroldswick

UNST

A968

Belmont

Dalsetter

Houll

FETLAR

Callafirth

A968

SULLOM

YELL

Hillswick

Ulstar

Brae

A968

MUCKLE ROE

Hillside

WHALSAY

Symbister

PAPA STOUR

A970

MELBY

MAINLAND

A971

Laxfirth

Walls

A971

Scalloway

Lerwick

BRESSAY

Hamnavoe

A970

Sandwick

ST NINIAN'S ISLE

Grutness

Sumburgh Head

Shetland

The Shetland group of islands numbers over 100, only 17 of which are inhabited, and they lie more than 60 miles (97 km) north of Orkney. Car ferries operate from Aberdeen to Shetland, and there are airstrips at Sumburgh and Tingwall. The largest, principal island is called Mainland and is about 50 miles (80 km) from north to south, the distance varying dramatically from west to east. This is the only one we have space to describe here, and is, in any case, easily the most interesting. Its 'capital' is **Lerwick** with about 7,000 inhabitants, on the east coast, facing the island of Bressay across the narrow Bressay Sound, and is the most northerly town in the British Isles. It is also one of increasing prosperity with the development of North Sea oil installations (and Sullom Voe as a tanker terminal) and Lerwick's waterfront and harbour are always busy, active areas.

The name of Shetland is derived from a Norse word meaning 'high land', and indeed the scenery is mostly rolling upland country. (Most of the place names here are of Norse derivation, including Lerwick, from 'leir vik' meaning clay creek.) Lerwick's town centre is concentrated around a narrow paved main street crowded with shops and offices, including many Shetland knitwear shops, where prices are still comparatively reasonable. The 'Lodberries' are attractive harbour buildings and warehouses over the water, with secret smugglers' passages leading to them. There is a fascinating museum in Lower Hillhead, with purely local exhibits explaining the story of the islands, and there is a Craft Workshop/Gallery worth visiting in Burns Lane. Fort Charlotte is the only surviving Cromwellian fort in Scotland. Based on a pentagon shape it was built in 1653, burned by the Dutch 20 years later, and rebuilt in the eighteenth century, garrisoned during the Napoleonic wars. Just outside Lerwick to the south-west is Clickhimin Broch which is 65 feet (20 m) in diameter with walls 18 feet (5 m) thick and 15 feet (4.5 m) high, on a great platform of rock, thought to have been in use in the Bronze Age.

Off the east shores of Bressay is the small bird sanctuary island of **Noss** where sea birds breed on the cliffs. In summer visits can be arranged (see Lerwick Tourist Information Centre).

Lerwick's annual Pagan 'Fire' festival, 'Up Helly Aa', welcoming the return of the sun, is on the last Tuesday in January and is renowned for its Viking torchlit procession with a replica of a Norse galley.

To the west of Lerwick, about seven miles (11 km) across, is the old village 'capital' of **Scalloway**, with its bleak ruin of Earl Patrick's Castle, built in 1600 but derelict since 1615 when the infamous Patrick was executed (*see* Kirkwall, Orkney, p. 265). Taking the A970 south the spectacular broch of Mousa is on the shores of a little island off the east

Walls, Shetland.

coast. One of the best examples of an iron-age broch in Scotland, it stands 45 feet (14 m) high, and has stairs and galleries within its thick walls, which taper from 12 feet (4 m) to 7 feet (2 m) at the top.

Just south of here the B9122 forks south-west across to the opposite coast, and **St Ninian's Isle**, attached to the mainland by a sand bank on a scenic stretch of coast. If you walk over the sand to the 'island' and climb the path up the shore-facing side, you will see the foundations of a twelfth century chapel in which a hoard of hidden eighth century Celtic silver was discovered in 1958. A bronze-age burial ground was discovered, and the remains of a pre-Norse church. (The silver is now in Edinburgh, in the National Museum of Antiquities.) With small sandy coves and beaches facing the shore, and towering cliffs seawards, it is a lovely spot to pass a few hours exploring and walking, to the accompaniment of the cry of gulls. You can follow the road southwards to rejoin the A970 near the Shetland Croft Museum, a complex of authentic nineteenth century croft buildings traditionally furnished with a little watermill nearby.

Jarlshof is the name given to the outstanding prehistoric settlement at the end of the road, dramatically situated beside the sea. The complex of extensive ruins demonstrates five separate periods of community habitation from the Bronze Age onwards, and is perhaps the most important archaeological site in Britain. There is a small museum where you can see some of the finds. The ruins are well-tended and very intriguing to investigate. You should allow plenty of time to do justice to this unique 'village'. Sumburgh airport, busy with helicopters from the oil rigs, is nearby to the east, where there is also an iron-age brooch.

Six miles (10 km) north-east of Lerwick is Tingwall, and the airport of Lerwick. There is an Agricultural Museum here, housed in eighteenth century buildings. The A970 heads on up north, while the A971 forks off to the west along the widest part of Mainland, to the head of the peninsula at Melby, facing the island of **Papa Stour** (boats three times a week). Several little roads lead off to right and left but the most interesting is the last which takes you to Staneydale Temple, in a lonely, deserted setting. Dating from the Stone Age, these remains were probably a dwelling house rather than a temple, showing thick walls and an oval-shaped internal chamber.

The A970 bears north then divides to branch along the various peninsulas. Sullom Voe Oil Terminal to the north of the fork in the main road, is Britain's biggest oil centre and sprawls across the Calback Ness peninsula.

Hotels and Guest Houses

Lerwick
Grand Hotel,
Commercial Street.
(Lerwick 2018)

Carradale Guest House,
36 King Harald Street.
(Lerwick 2890)

Scalloway
Scalloway Hotel,
Main Street.
(Scalloway 444)

West Mainland
Westings Hotel,
Wormadale,
Whiteness.
(Gott 242)

South Mainland
Barclay Arms Hotel,
Sandwick.
(Sandwick 226)

North Mainland
Brae Hotel,
Brae.
(Brae 456)

Island of Bressay
Shalder Brae Guest House.
(Bressay 263)

Fair Isle
Fair Isle Bird Observatory.
(Fair Isle 258)

Island of Yell
North Isles Motel,
Sellafirth,
Yell ZE2 9DG.
(Gutcher 293)

Accommodation for the Young

Lerwick
Isleburgh Youth Hostel,
King Harald Street.
(Lerwick 2114)

Isle of Unst
A. Fraser,
Crosbister,
Uyeasound.
(Uyeasound 237/259)

Camping and Caravanning

No official sites. It is possible to camp wild, but permission from landowner required.

Self Catering

Scalloway
Mrs R. Williamson,
Leagarth,
East Voe.
(Scalloway 376)

West Mainland
Capt. M. Fraser,
Bungalow,
Walls.
(Walls 219)

Westings Hotel & Chalets,
Wormadale,
Whiteness.
(Gott 242)

South Mainland
H.C. & M. Burgess,
Spiggie Hotel,
Scousburgh.
(Sumburgh 60409)

North Mainland
Mrs B. Leask,
15 Bruce Crescent,
Lerwick.
(Lerwick 3968)

Island of Burra
Mrs J.M. Christie,
Blimister,
Bridge End.
(Hamnavoe 274)

Island of Unst
Mrs M.P. Peterson,
Lower Toft,
Muness,
Uyeasound.
(Uyeasound 215)

Golf

Lerwick
The Shetland Golf Club,
Dale Golf Course,
PO Box 18.
(Gott 369)

Sailing

Shetland Isles Charter,
107 Commercial Street,
Lerwick.
(Lerwick 4387)

Sea Angling

Shore: coalfish, pollack, dogfish, mackerel,
dabs, conger and cod.
Boat: skate, halibut, ling, cod, torsk,
haddock, whiting, coalfish, pollack,
dogfish, porbeagle shark, Norway
haddock, gurnard, mackerel, cuckoo and
ballan wrasse.
Boats: *'Sula'*, E. Manson,
80 Commercial Street,
Lerwick.
(Lerwick 3488)
'Anderton', Mr R.H. Anderton,
Vaila Hall, Vaila,
Walls. (Walls 363)
'Quest', D. Black,
Tolob, Virkie.
(Sumburgh 243)
J. Cluness, Sandraquoy,
Uyeasound, Unst.
J. Harper, Meadowvale Hotel,
Virkie, (Sumburgh 352)
'Tystie', R. Hunter,
Tromso, Bressay.
(Bressay 270)
G. Laurenson, 3 Water Lane,
Lerwick. (Lerwick 2309)
'Whiniver', D. Robertson,
Guddon, East Yell.
(Burravoe 242)
A.W. Simpson,
115 North Road, Lerwick.
(Lerwick 3781)
S. Thomson, Quoy,
Fair Isle. (Fair Isle 241)
Boats can also be arranged through the
Shetland Tourist Organisations.

Game Fishing

Brown and sea trout.
Shetland Anglers Association,
3 Gladstone Terrace,
Lerwick.
Over 1,000 Lochs & Voes.
Controlled by the Shetland Anglers
Association.

Where to Eat

Brae
Busta House.
(Brae 209)

Orkney

The Orkney group of islands lies eight miles (13 km) to the north of the most northerly part of mainland Scotland, across the Pentland Firth, and consists of about 70 islands in all, the largest of which (known as Mainland) has the 'capital', Kirkwall, on the isthmus which joins East and West Mainland. Apart from the appeal of its remoteness most visitors are drawn to the Orkneys either for the abundance of prehistoric sites (by far the highest concentration in Britain) or for its natural history and the richness of the marine, plant and bird life. With Shetland, these islands were long under Norse control and evidence of this early influence is everywhere, from local names, to physical characteristics noticeable in the islanders.

Boats sail from Scrabster, near Thurso, on mainland Scotland, to Stromness on the west peninsula, and Kirkwall, both on Mainland, Orkney, the only two towns in the archipelago. **Stromness** has declined from being a principal port on sailing routes round the north of Scotland, to just the car ferry point from Scrabster, but look out for the natural history museum at the southern end of the long main street.

Kirkwall retains much of its ancient character and dignity. The dominant building is the Cathedral of St Magnus, a massive structure founded in 1137 by the nephew of St Magnus (the bones of both the saint and his nephew are concealed in chests within pillars of the choir, making the church unique in Britain, for housing the remains of both founder and patron saint, and also for technically belonging to the people of Kirkwall, rather than the Church). Building continued over several centuries so it is a combination of periods but with a style distinctly Norman. Beside it are the ruins of Bishop's Palace and Earl's Palace. Bishop's Palace is where King Hakon died after his defeat at the Battle of Largs in 1263. The tower, though apparently round, is square inside. Earl's Palace is a better ruin, for interest and appearance, with its attractive angle turrets, vast kitchens and great hall, once belonging to Earl Patrick, Steward of Orkney and Shetland, whose infamous ways were his downfall, and ended in his execution. The museum in Kirkwall is at Tankerness House, a sixteenth to eighteenth century merchant/laird's mansion, with a notable presentation of Orkney life from prehistoric times. The Scapa Malt Whisky Distillery is about two miles (3 km) south of Kirkwall.

To see the best of the Mainland sites, go to Finstown and take the A965 from Finstown to Stromness, then north to Skara Brae and on to Birsay, returning by Gurness Broch and Click Mill. First you can visit two bronze-age burial cairns by taking the small inland road to Finstown, Wideford Hill Cairn, and Cuween Cairn, or you can take the

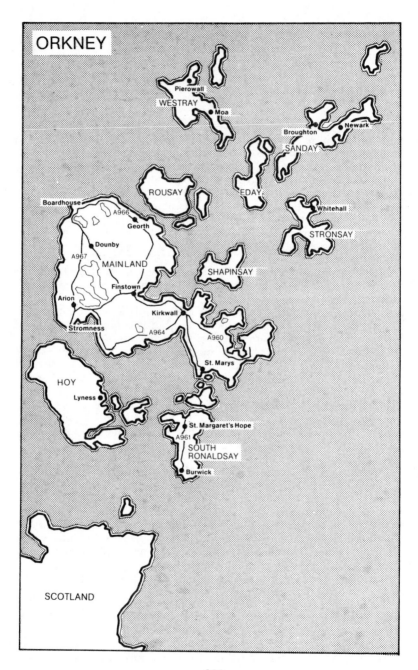

coast road, the A965 and see Grain Earth House just outside Kirkwall, then Rennibister Earth House.

After Finstown, Maes Howe is an exceptional megalithic tomb, 115 feet (35 m) in diameter and 24 feet (7 m) high with a 45-foot (14 m) ditch, showing outstanding masonry skill. The roof has been reconstructed and artificial lighting incorporated. The Standing Stones of Stenness are part of a 100-foot (30 m) diameter circle, about 2300 BC. The ring of Brodgar is a magnificent upright stone circle (27 of about 60 still in situ) encircled by a ditch cut into solid rock. Unstan Cairn is a circular mound, with three concentric walls, and one of the few with a cell and stalls. A collection of stone-age pottery was found here in 1844 (now in Edinburgh, at the National Museum of Antiquities). Skara Brae is at the southern end of Bay of Skaill, some seven miles (11 km) north of Stromness, and is an outstanding stone-age settlement, buried in sand from the time of its occupation until a freak storm revealed it in 1850. It demonstrates a different aspect of stone-age life, with primitive stone furniture, and dwellings. (The smaller finds are now in Edinburgh, at the National Museum of Antiquities.) At Marwick Head there is a prominent Kitchener Memorial. Lord Kitchener died at sea not far from here in 1916 when his ship was mined.

Within easy walking distance of Marwick Head is the Orkney Field Centre, where courses are run during the summer on subjects ranging from Orcadian Botany, to Archaeology and the Birds of Orkney. It offers simple accommodation and a very pleasant atmosphere. In Birsay village there is a post office, a general store, and the Earl's Palace, a dilapidated sixteenth century ruin built on the site of an earlier palace of the Earls of Orkney. At low tide walk across to Brough of Birsay where there are remains of a Norse settlement, an ancient church and a cloistered bishop's palace, with other ruins and foundations by the shore, and up the hill beyond. The cliffs around here are nesting sites for fulmar, kittiwakes and auks.

Rounding the north Mainland coast to the east, the road leads down to exposed Aiker Ness and the Broch of Gurness, the best preserved in Orkney, but so confused by other remains that you need to get a copy of the leaflet describing it in detail if you hope to understand it. There is a 10-foot (3 m) tower still standing. Continue down this road for Finstown, passing the Dale of Cottasgarth Nature Reserve, a heather valley with willows and a stream which forms a breeding area for kestrel, hen harrier, merlin and others. For Click Mill take the B9057 from Georth. The turf-roofed building is the only Orcadian horizontal watermill still in working order.

Of all the other islands forming the Orkney group, we can only include Hoy and South Ronaldsay. The North Islands are numerous, and many have ancient sites, but visitors tend to be deterred by the logistical problems of sailings, transport on the islands, food, accommodation and access to the sites. If you are determined to make the complete round of the major island sites, check first with the Orkney Tourist Office in

Kirkwall for full details of facilities.

Hoy is reached from Stromness or Scapa, and has an airstrip serviced by Loganair. It is different from all the other islands in that it is both hilly, and has indigenous trees growing. On the Atlantic side are some of the tallest sheer cliffs in Britain, and the individual stack of 450 feet (137 m) known as the Old Man of Hoy. Longhope is the island's main village, on the South Walls peninsula. There are Martello towers at Hackness and Crockness, and just off the road that crosses from Linksness to Rackwick you can see the stone-age rock tomb, unique in Britain, called Dwarfie Stone.

About six miles (10 km) south-west of Kirkwall beside the A964 you can see the ruined Orphir Church, a twelfth century circular structure which was the only one in Scotland. The fragment nearby is of a great hall of the Earls of Orkney.

To reach **South Ronaldsay** you can now drive across the Churchill Barrier, built to connect the chain of small islands to Mainland, and to act as a barrier to the east. The first island you cross is Lamb Holm where you can visit the Italian Chapel in two wartime Nissen huts, ingeniously fabricated from scrap metal by Italian prisoners of war working on the causeways, and quite beautiful. The village of St Margaret's Hope on South Ronaldsay is where, in 1290, the ship carrying the child Margaret, Maid of Norway, (grand-daughter of Alexander III) dropped anchor, after she had died at sea. She had been on her way to Scotland from Norway, and was to have been married to Edward I's son, whereas the outcome was soon to be bitter hostility between Scotland and Edward of England (who set about earning the nickname 'Hammer of the Scots'). The sea area contained within the Churchill Barrier, Kirkwall and Hoy is Scapa Flow, famous as an important naval base in the First and Second World Wars.

Hotels and Guest Houses

Kirkwall
Fovern Hotel,
St Ola.
(Kirkwall 2389)

Bellavista Guest House,
Carness Road.
(Kirkwall 2306)

Stromness
Braes Hotel.
(Stromness 850298)

Eday
Eday Hotel.
(Eday 263)

Self-Catering

Birsay
Mrs O. Flett,
Baord House,
Birsay KW17 2LY.
(Birsay 368)

Deerness
Mrs M. Foubister,
Esnaphy,
Deerness.
(Deerness 322)

Evie
Mrs Craigie,
Ingermas,
Evie KW17 2PH.
(Evie 268)

Stenness
Mrs Laidlaw,
Outbrecks,
Stenness.

Stromness
Mrs J. Chalmers,
Braehead Farm,
Cairston Road,
Stromness.
(Stromness 850410)

D. & I. Sinclair,
Milldam,
Stromness.
(Stromness 850432)

Sea Angling

Sea trout, plaice, pollack and coalfish,
mackerel, skate, halibut, ling, cod,
haddock.
Boats: Ron Spiers,
St Ola Hotel,
Kirkwall.

Further information:
J. Adam,
44 Quoybanks Crescent,
Kirkwall.

Game Fishing

Boardhouse, Harray, Hundland Lochs
Brown and sea trout.
No permits required.

Stenness Loch
Sea and brown trout.
No permits required.

Swannay Loch
Sea and brown trout.
No permits required.

Sailing

Orkney Yacht Charter.
(Kirkwall 2072)

Cycling

Kirkwall
Patersons Cycle Centre,
Tankerness Lane.
(Kirkwall 3097)

Where to Eat

Evie
(Nr Kirkwall)
Woodwick Restaurant.
(Evie 221)

Foveran
(Nr Kirkwall)
St Ola.
(Kirkwall 2389)

Quoyburray Inn,
Tankerness.
(Tankerness 255)

Stenness
Tormiston Mill,
Nr Stromness.
(Finstown 372)

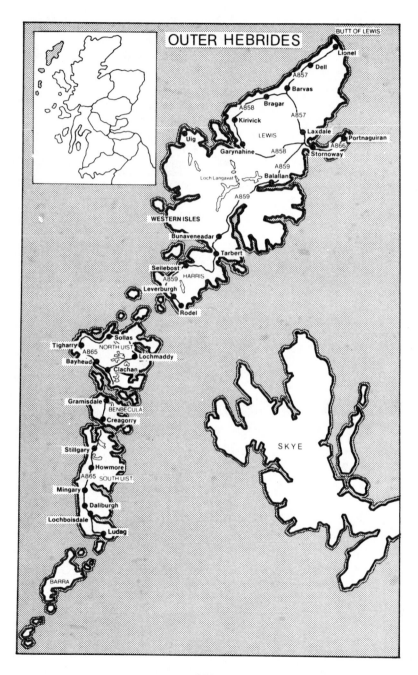

OUTER HEBRIDES

BUTT OF LEWIS

Lionel

Dell

A857

Barvas

Bragar

A858

A857

Kirivick

LEWIS

Laxdale

Portnaguiran

Uig

A866

Garynahine

A858

Stornoway

A859

Loch Langavat

Balallan

A859

WESTERN ISLES

Bunaveneadar

Tarbert

Seilebost

A859

HARRIS

Leverburgh

Rodel

Sollas

Tigharry

NORTH UIST

A865

Lochmaddy

Bayhead

Clachan

Gramisdale

BENBECULA

Creagorry

SKYE

Stillgary

Howmore

A865

SOUTH UIST

Mingary

Daliburgh

Lochboisdale

Ludag

BARRA

270

Outer Hebrides

The Islands of the Outer Hebrides are best described from one end to the other. If you land at Stornoway, you could leave from Tarbert, Lochmaddy, Lochboisdale or Barra, but be sure to check sailing times and book ahead when possible.

The islands form a string with scatterings of islands to each side. **Lewis**, with Harris in the south, is by far the largest, with **Stornoway** as its main town, (over 5,000 inhabitants), founded by James VI. It has a commercial and fishing harbour, and is a busy administrative and market town. In St Peter's Church in Francis Street, you can see the Prayer Book that used to belong to Livingstone, and perhaps the oldest font in Scotland. The town's main building is the Nicolson Institute, and the nineteenth century Lews Castle, beside the harbour, is now a technical college. Two miles (3 km) east you can visit the neglected ruin of fourteenth century Chapel of St Columba, or Ui Chapel (pronounced eye) founded by a MacLeod chief, and containing MacLeod tombs.

The A857 leaves Stornoway to cross the island north-westwards over bleak moorland. At Barvas it cuts north-east along the coast to the Butt of Lewis, through increasingly green and attractive scenery. The twelfth to thirteenth century Chapel of St Moluag in the village of Eoropie has been restored and sometimes holds Episcopal services. The road also passes a conspicuous 20-foot (6 m) monolith, the Trushel Stone, and a ruined burial cairn, east of the road, Steinacleit Cairn with stone circle and unusual outer surround.

Taking the A858 from Barvas you soon reach the Black House Museum, a preserved traditional crofter's cottage, at Arnol, then at Bragar you will see an arch made from whalebone, with the harpoon that killed the whale suspended from it. At Shawbost it is worth stopping for the Folk Museum which is the product of the Highland Village Competition in 1970. It vividly illustrates how Lewis islanders used to live, and there is a restored Norse watermill nearby. Dun Carloway broch is impressively situated overlooking the sea, and the 30-foot (9 m) wall is still intact on one side. Following the road round you come to Callanish. The Standing Stones of Callanish rank as one of the most complete, and ambitious prehistoric sites in Britain. In the form of a cross, there are nearly 50 stones, and the site is 400 feet (122 m) long. In the immediate vicinity there are several other megalithic sites. For the best scenery on Lewis, drive round the head of East Loch Roag. Bernera island can be reached by bridge.

From Stornoway the A859 weaves southwards round the many inland lochs to **Tarbert**, capital village of **Harris** on the narrow isthmus separating North Harris, mountainous and rugged, from South Harris,

271

A 'black house' on Lewis, the Outer Hebrides.

rocky wastes and small lochs in the east, and fine sandy beaches in the west. In North Harris the road following the north side of West Loch Tarbert has some lovely scenery with waterfalls splashing down the cliffs to the sea, an abandoned whaling station built by Norwegians, and a nineteenth century castle (not open to the public). From Tarbert you can take a car ferry to Uig on Skye, or Lochmaddy on North Uist.

There are two roads round South Harris, west coast with standing stones at Nisabost and Borvemoor, and east coast with craggy, more interesting terrain. Rodel is an isolated village at the southerly tip of Harris. St Clement's Church was originally built in 1500 but restored twice since. Note the unusual carved tower, and the splendid tomb recess with an armoured effigy of a MacLeod chief (1528). The Rodel Hotel bar is warmly recommended, especially if you have time to kill waiting to catch a ferry from **Leverburgh**.

The Leverburgh ferry goes to Newton Ferry at the north point of **North Uist**. Almost half of the total area of North Uist is taken up by lochs which are concentrated in the east on the moors. The west has superb and lonely beaches and is much more fertile. **Lochmaddy** is the main village, on the east side. In the south, at Carinish you can see the strange ruin of Trinity Temple, twin buildings founded by Beatrix, a daughter of Somerled, in the early thirteenth century, rebuilt by the wife of John Macdonald, 1st Lord of the Isles. There was a clan battle fought here in 1601 between the local Macdonalds and the MacLeods of Harris.

The North Ford causeway that links this island with **Benbecula**, via several little islands, was opened in 1960. Benbecula also has fine beaches to the west with a coast road running beside the dunes. Just past the airport is Dun Buidhe, possibly a place of strength at one time, judging from the stone remains. Balivanich is the main village, with the Ministry of Defence South Uist range. A mile (2 km) south is the ruin of a fourteenth century chapel once belonging to a nunnery, and a couple of miles (3 km) further is the remnant of Borve Castle, a Clan Ranald stronghold burnt by its own clansmen in the eighteenth century when they turned against their chief to follow George II.

The bridge over South Ford joins Benbecula and **South Uist**. There are beautiful stretches of unspoilt, and usually deserted beach along the west coast, flanked by the 'machar' inland, grassland which is bright with wild flowers in summer. The east coast is precipitous and dramatic in parts, with abandoned jetties, where you can sit and watch for the bobbing head of seals, or dangle a rod for mackerel. It was on this coast, at Glen Corrodale, that the Young Pretender landed in 1746, and hid himself in a hut. Through the well-disposed Neil MacEachain Macdonald he met Flora Macdonald, visiting from Skye, who agreed to return there, with the Prince disguised as her servant girl. The main road runs down the length of the island to its main centre, **Lochboisdale**, where there is a busy hotel overlooking the ferry landing quay. (At weekends the public bar of the hotel is the hub of the island's social life, therefore noisy and often rumbustuous!)

The island is 20 miles (32 km) long and roughly 7 miles (11 km) wide. Just across the South Ford bridge there is a small museum, the South Uist Folk Museum in a croft house. Our Lady of the Isles is a tall, distinctive Madonna and Child statue in granite by Hew Lorimer (1957) to the east of the road, erected by the Catholic community. Soon after, still on the east, you reach the Loch Druidibeg NNR, Britain's most important breeding ground for greylag geese. On the other side of the road is Howmore Church, notable as being one of the only two churches in Scotland with a central communion pew, (the other being at Achnaba on Loch Etive, on mainland Scotland). On a farm, 1½ miles (2½ km) off the road to the north-west, you can see the ruined Ormaclete Castle, another Clan Ranald stronghold, built between 1701–08, but built in vain because during the merry-making which followed the battle of Sheriffmuir in 1715, the place was accidentally burnt down. About 2½ miles (4 km) after the turn off and half a mile (1 km) north of Milton, you can see a memorial cairn from the road which indicates where Flora Macdonald was born in 1722.

At the Daliburgh crossroads turn left for Lochboisdale, the ferry point, or continue south to Ludag, an attractive little port overlooking Barra and Eriskay. **Eriskay** is known as the place where the Young Pretender first set foot on Scottish soil, on his arrival in July 1745. In 1941 there was another significant event – a ship carrying 20,000 cases of whisky was wrecked here (great delight all round) and this gave rise to Compton Mackenzie's book *Whisky Galore*. Eriskay is a nice little island to visit.

The road down to this point passes a sign to Kilpheder, just after Daliburgh. The little road leads through the village to the remains of an iron-age wheelhouse in the dunes. The modern church on the road at Garrynamonie is Our Lady of Sorrows, opened in 1964, and contains decorative Stations of the Cross designed by Calum McNeil, a priest on Barra.

Barra is the last of the islands included in this route, and is reached by car ferry from Lochboisdale, and from Oban (passenger ferry also from Ludag to Eoligarry), to Castlebay, the island harbour and main centre. Only eight miles by four miles (13 × 6 km), it has the unusual distinction of having an airport whose airstrip is the beach, so flights can only operate at low tide. The castle from which the bay takes its name is the ancient MacNeil stronghold here, Kisimul Castle, started in the eleventh century. After bad fire damage in the eighteenth century it was sold together with the island, but in 1937 repurchased by the 45th clan chief MacNeil, an American architect who set about restoring it, finally completing it in 1970.

A 14-mile (23 km) road runs round the island with several points of interest. After the Island of Barra Hotel (a very hospitable place, opened in 1974, much improving the island's facilities), you can see two small standing stones, supposed to mark the place where a local champion slew a Norse warrior in single combat, and where the Norseman was buried. Dun Barpha, on the road to Craigston, is a chambered cairn with some monoliths around it, and beyond the turn off to Craigston you will see Dun Cuier behind a small cemetery, with wall and side passages still surviving. The airport is in the north and Cille-Bharra, a group of three ruined chapels (possibly twelfth century), is just beyond at Eoligarry. Sir Compton Mackenzie is buried here. Over the road is St Barr's Well, where the saint is supposed to have struck water on arrival. There is a statue of St Barr, with stave raised ready to strike, on a loch island at North Bay (by local artist, Margaret Somerville, 1975). A 1954 marble Madonna, Lady Star of the Sea, stands high on the hill of Heavel.

Hotels and Guest Houses

Lewis – Stornoway
The Acres Hotel,
James Street.
(Stornoway 2740)

Lewis Hotel,
North Beach Street.
(Stornoway 4567)

Isles Guest House,
Lewis Street.
(Stornoway 2475)

Lewis - Borve
Borve House Hotel.
(Borve 223)

Lewis – Garrabost
Ceol Na Mara Guest House.
(Garrabost 372)

Lewis – Uig
Uig Hotel.
(Timsgarry 286)

North Uist – Lochmaddy
Lochmaddy Hotel.
(Lochmaddy 331)

Benbecula
Creagorry Hotel.
(Benbecula 2024)

South Uist – Lochboisdale
Lochboisdale Hotel.
(Lochboisdale 332)

South Uist – Grogarry
Ben More Guest House.
(Grogarry 283)

Barra
Castlebay Hotel.
(Castlebay 265)

Camping and Caravanning

South Uist
Loch Druidibeg Caravan Site.
(Grogarry 210)

Self-Catering

Lewis – Stornoway
Murdo MacLeod,
31 Urquhart Gardens,
Stornoway.
(Stornoway 2458)

Lewis – Dalbeg
Mrs MacKay,
1 Dalbeg.
(Shawbost 265)

Harris – Drinnishadder
Angus MacDonald,
10 Drinnishadder.
(Drinnishadder 207)

Kyles of Haris
Mrs Fiona Morrison,
School House,
Scalpay.
(Scalpay 245)

Golf

Lewis – Stornoway
Stornoway Golf Course.
(Stornoway 2240)

South Uist
Links-Land Golf Course,
Askernish Golf Club.
(Lochboisdale 277)

Sea Angling

Lewis – Stornoway
Conger, cod, skate, rays, ling, pollack,
whiting, dab, flounder, dogfish and
haddock.

Harris – Tarbert
Shore: mackerel, ling, coalfish, cod, pollack
and conger.
Boats: plaice, haddock and flounder.
Boats: J. MacLeod; J.M. Montgomery
(Piermaster).
W.D. Cameron, Hon. Sec.,
Harris Sea Angling Club,
Harris Hotel.

Game Fishing

Lewis
Loch Raonasgail (over 50 lochs)
Salmon, sea and brown trout.
Permits: Uig Lodge Hotel, by Stornoway.
(Timsgarry 286)

River Creed
Sea trout.
Permits: Stornoway Trust Estate Office,
Stornoway.
(Stornoway 2002)

Harris
Borve Carron and Sluice (lochs)
Sea trout.
Permits: Borve Lodge Estate,
Borve Lodge,
Scarista.
(Scarista 202)

Grisebat Collam (lochs)
Sea trout.
Permits: The Manager,
Neil MacDonald,
7 Diraclete,
Tarbet.
(Harris 2464)

Horsacleit House Grassy and Sheep Lochs
Salmon and sea trout.
Permits: The Manager,
Neil MacDonald, (*see* above).

South Uist
All hill lochs
Salmon, sea and brown trout.
Permits: Lochboisdale Hotel.
(Lochboisdale 332)

Hotels for Shooting and Stalking

Lewis
Borve House Hotel.
(Borve 223)
Game, wildfowl, rough shooting.

Cycling

Lewis – Stornoway
K. MacLennan, Cycle Shop,
Cromwell Street.
(Stornoway 2202)

Harris – Tarbert
D.M. Mackenzie,
Pier Road.
(Harris 2271)

Barra
Isle of Barra Hotel.
(Castlebay 383)

Post Office.
(Castlebay 286)

Where to Eat

South Uist
Lochboisdale Hotel.
(Lochboisdale 332)

Barra
Isle of Barra Hotel.
(Castlebay 383)

General Directory

Transport to Scotland

By Air

You can fly to Scotland direct from USA, Canada & Europe. The main airports are: Aberdeen, Edinburgh, Glasgow, Prestwick. For information write to:
British Airways,
85 Buchanan Street,
Glasgow G1 3HQ.
(041 332 9666)

British Caledonian,
127 Buchanan Street,
Glasgow G1 2JA.
(041 332 1681 reservations)

By Sea

From Ireland, for information write to:
Larne–Stranraer: British Rail (Sealink),
24 Donegal Place,
Belfast BT1 5BH.
(Belfast 27525)

Larne–Cairnryan: Townsend Thoresen,
The Harbour, Cairnryan, or
The Harbour, Larne.
(Cairnryan 276 or Larne 4321)

From Denmark, Norway, Iceland, Faroes, write:
c/o P & O Feries,
PO Box 5, Jamieson's Quay,
Aberdeen AB9 8DL.
(Aberdeen 572615)

By Rail

Main rail routes to Scotland are: London (Kings Cross) – Edinburgh, and London (Euston) – Glasgow. British Rail offer many different types of ticket. Sleeper carriages and car transportation (Motorail) available.
For information write to: British Rail,
Buchanan House,
58 Port Dundas Road,
Glasgow G4 0HG.
(041 332 9811)

By Coach

London (Victoria) – Edinburgh and Glasgow. Thee are many Express Coaches which operate from London.
For information write to:
Scottish Omnibuses Ltd,
Bus Station, St Andrew Square,
Edinburgh.
(031 556 8231)

W. Alexander & Sons, (Fife) Ltd,
Esplanade,
Kirkcaldy.
(Kirkcaldy 61461)

W. Alexander & Sons, (Northern) Ltd,
Bus Station, Guild Street,
Aberdeen AB9 2DR.
(Aberdeen 51381)

Cotters Coachline,
12 Crimea Street,
Glasgow G2 8PW.
(041 221 8042)

National Travel (London) Ltd,
Victoria Coach Station,
Buckingham Palace Road,
London SW1W 0TP.
(01 730 3455)

Parks of Hamilton,
Warren Road,
Hamilton,
Lanarkshire ML3 9QT.
(Hamilton 33481)

Stagecoach,
Friarton Road,
Perth.
(Perth 33481)

White Horse Tours,
Western Chambers,
Station Road,
Hayes,
Middlesex UB3 4BL.

Transport within Scotland
Air Routes
For information write to:
Air Ecosse,
Edinburgh Airport.
(031 333 3277)

Air Ecosse,
Aberdeen Airport.
(Aberdeen 724782)

British Airways,
85 Buchanan Street,
Glasgow G1 3HQ.
(041 332 9666)

Loganair Ltd,
St Andrew's Drive,
Glasgow Airport.
(041 889 3181)

Sea Ferries
For ferries to Orkney and Shetland contact:
P & O Ferries,
Orkney & Shetland Services,
Jamieson's Quay,
Aberdeen AB9 8DL.
(Aberdeen 572615)

For ferries to the Hebrides contact:
Caledonian McBrayne Ltd,
The Ferry Terminal,
Gourock PA19 1QP.
(Gourock 33755)

For ferries to Dunoon contact:
Western Ferries (Argyll) Ltd,
16 Woodside Crescent,
Glasgow G3 7UT.
(041 332 9766)
Dunoon Terminal (Dunoon 4452)

Coach Information
Scottish Omnibuses Ltd,
Bus Station,
St Andrew Square,
Edinburgh.
(031 556 8231)

Useful Addresses

British Tourist Authority
Queen's House,
64 St James Street,
London SW1.
(01 629 9191)

The Countryside Commission for Scotland
Battleby House,
Redgorton,
Perth PH1 3EW.
(Perth 27921)

Department of the Environment
Argyle House,
3 Lady Lawson Street,
Edinburgh EH3 9SD.
(031 229 9191)

Forestry Commission
Information Office,
231 Corstorphine Road,
Edinburgh EH12 7AT.
(031 334 0303)

(East Scotland Region)
6 Queen's Gate,
Aberdeen AB9 2NQ.
(Aberdeen 33361)

(North Scotland Region)
21 Church Street,
Inverness IV1 1EL.
(Inverness 32811)

(South Scotland Region)
Greystone Park,
55/57 Moffat Road,
Dumfries DG1 1NP.
(Dumfries 2425)

(West Scotland Region)
Portcullis House,
21 India Street,
Glasgow G2 3PL.
(041 248 3931)

Highlands and Islands Development Board
Bridge House,
Bank Street,
Inverness.
(Inverness 34171)

Mountaineering Council of Scotland
Hon. Secretary, 11 Kirklee Quadrant,
Glasgow G12 0TS.
(041 339 7713 home;
041 959 1207 business)

National Trust for Scotland
5 Charlotte Square,
Edinburgh EH2 4DU.
(031 447 4784)

Nature Conservancy Council
12 Hope Terrace,
Edinburgh EH9 2AS.
(031 226 5922)

Ramblers Association (Scottish Area)
43 Polmaise Road,
Stirling.
(Stirling 2323)

Royal Society for the Protection of Birds
17 Regent Terrace,
Edinburgh EH7 5BN.
(031 556 5624)

Scottish Mountaineering Club
Hon. Secretary: Donald J. Bennet,
4 Morven Road,
Bearsden,
Glasgow G61 3BU.
(041 942 1387)

Scottish Sports Council
1–3 St Colme Street,
Edinburgh EH3 6AA.
(031 225 8411)

Scottish Tourist Board
23 Ravelston Terrace,
Edinburgh EH4 3EU.
(031 332 2433)

5–6 Pall Mall East,
London SW1.
(01 930 8661/2/3)

Scottish Wildlife Trust
8 Dublin Street,
Edinburgh EH1 3PP.
(031 557 1525)

Scottish Youth Hostels Association
7 Glebe Crescent,
Stirling FK8 2JA.
(Stirling 2821)

Scottish Tourist Information Centres in England

London
Scottish Tourist Board,
5–6 Pall Mall East,
London SW1.
(01 930 8661/2/3)
May–Oct. 0900–1800 Mon.–Fri.;
Nov.–Apr. 0900–1700 Mon.–Fri.

Scottish Representative,
Tourist Information Centre,
British Tourist Authority,
63–65 St James Street,
London SW1A 1NF.
(01 629 2121)

Southwaite (M6)
Tourist Information Centre,
M6 Service Area,
Southwaite,
Carlisle CA4 0NS.
(Southwaite 445)
July & Aug. 0900–2000 Mon.–Sun.; Apr.,
May, June & Oct. 0900–1800 Mon.–Sun.;
Nov.–Mar. 0900–1700 Mon.–Sat., 1200–
1400 Sun.

Scottish Tourist Information Centres Overseas

Argentina
British Tourist Authority,
Avenida Córdoba 645 (Piso 28)
1054 Buenos Aires.
(392 9955)

Australia
British Tourist Authority,
171 Clarence Street,
Sydney NSW 2000.
(29 8627)

Belgium
British Tourist Authority,
52 rue de la Montague Bte 2,
Berystraat 52 Bus 2,
1000 Brussels.
(5114390)

Brazil
British Tourist Authority,
Avenida Ipiranga 318-A,
128 Andar, Conjunto 1201,
01046 S«ao Paulo-SP.
(257 1834)

Canada
British Tourist Authority,
151 Bloor Street West, Suite 460,
Toronto, Ontario M5S 1T3.
(925 6325)

Denmark
British Tourist Authority,
Montergade 3,
DK - 1116 Copenhagen K.
(12 10 93)

France
British Tourist Authority,
6 Place Vendôme,
75001-Paris.
(296 47 60)

Germany
British Tourist Authority,
Neue Mainzer Strasse 22,
6000 Frankfurt-am-Main.
(23 64 28)

Italy
British Tourist Authority,
Via S Eufemia 5,
Rome 00187.
(678 55 48/678 49 98)

Japan
British Tourist Authority,
Tokyo Club Building,
3-2-6, Kasumigaseki,
Chiyoda-ku, Tokyo 100.
(581 3603/581 3604)

Mexico
British Tourist Authority,
Rio Tiber 103 - 6 piso,
Mexico 5DF.
(511 39 27/514 93 56)

Netherlands
British Tourist Authority,
(written enquiries only)
Leidseplein 5,
1017 PR Amsterdam.
(23 46 67)

British Travel Centre,
(personal callers only)
Leidseplein 23,
Amsterdam.

New Zealand
British Tourist Authority,
PO Box 3655,
Wellington.

Norway
British Tourist Authority,
Mariboes gt. 11,
Oslo 1.
(41 18 49)

South Africa
British Tourist Authority,
7th Floor,
PO Box 6256, JBS Building,
107 Commissioner Street,
Johannesburg 2001 RSA.
(29 6770)

Spain
British Tourist Authority,
Torre de Madrid 6/4,
Plaza de Espana,
Madrid 13.
(241 13 96)

Sweden
British Tourist Authority,
Visitors: Malmskillnadsg 42 (1st floor),
Correspondence: Box 7293,
s-103 90 Stockholm.
(08 21 24 44)

Switzerland
British Tourist Authority,
Limmatquai 78,
8001 Zurich.
(01/47 42 77 *or* 47 42 97)

USA
British Tourist Authority,
680 Fifth Avenue,
New York NY 10019.
(212 581 4700)

British Tourist Authority,
612 South Flower Street,
Los Angeles,
California 90017.
(213 623 8196)

British Tourist Authority,
John Hancock Centre (Suite 3320),
875 North Michigan Avenue,
Chicago,
Illinois 60611.

Access to Sites and Places of Interest
Standard times apply to most Ancient
Monuments (Scottish Development Dept)
and are Mon.–Sat. 0930–1900, Sun. 1400–

1900. From Oct.–Mar. incl., sites close at 1600.

In most cases there is an entrance fee. Unless otherwise stated months are inclusive i.e. May–Oct. = 1 May–31 Oct.

Whisky
Many whisky distilleries welcome visitors. Local Tourist Information Offices will supply visiting times. Prior notice should be given in some cases. Large groups should check what the maximum number is.

Hotels and Guest Houses
The lists in the Directory sections are compiled from Tourist Offices around Scotland. Prices have not been included as they are always changing. When asking for prices check whether or not VAT is included. July and August are normally busy so book well in advance.

The disabled can obtain information on suitable Hotels and Guest Houses from: Information for the Disabled, 18–19 Claremont Crescent, Edinburgh. (031 556 3882) and Scottish Tourist Board publication *Holidays with Care.*

Accommodation for the Young
Applicable either to groups of youngsters, or individuals, the accommodation is either self-catering, or meals and other services can be obtained. Book well in advance.

Self Catering
Types of accommodation listed in the Directory sections are caravans, chalets, cottages, houses and flats. Your travel gent should be able to help you book. If you write direct, send a stamped addressed envelope.

Camping and Caravanning
We have only listed the larger sites. Prices can be obtained by writing.

Pets: If you take your pet(s) on holiday with you please check if they are allowed on site.
Touring Passing places should only be used for passing, not as lay-bys.

Lay-Bys are not to be used for over night stops.
Camping outside sites please obtain permission from landowner before stopping for the night.

Golf
Scotland is known the world over for its golf courses. Some clubs require a letter of introduction from your own golf club, though many require only a fee. A list of competitions can be obtained from Scottish Tourist Board or from clubs.

Adventure and Special Interest Holidays
This type of holiday has become more widely applicable as the various centres have increased their scope. Many pursuits can now be followed. Accommodation has also improved.

Sea Angling
Scotland is a paradise for the sea angler. The Scottish Tourist Board can provide detailed information on sea angling events.

Rules to abide by
Wear or carry a life jacket.
Wear warm clothing and lightweight waterproof anorak and trousers.
Don't wear heavy thigh boots – use half-wellingtons which can easily be kicked off in the water.
Never crowd a small boat, and remember an outboard weighs the same as one extra person.
Don't stand upright or mess around in a small open boat.
If you need to move, keep your centre of gravity as low as possible.
Take with you a spare oar, fire extinguisher, basic first aid, flares and other simple emergency equipment.
Tell people where you are going and when you expect to return.
If your boat does capsize, stay with it.

Weather and safety information
Available through VHF radio or by telephone.
MRCC Clyde (Greenock 29988/29014)
MRSC Oban (Oban 4256)

MRSC Stornoway (Stornoway 2013/2014)
MRSC Shetland (Lerwick 2976/4600)
MRSC Orkney (Kirkwall 3268)
MRSC Wick (Wick 2332/2333)
MRSC Moray (Peterhead 4270/4278)
MRSC Aberdeen (Aberdeen 873347)
MRSC Forth (Crail 666/667)

Fishing (Game and Course)
Permits
Can be obtained from angling clubs, tackle shops, hotels and other sources. (*See* Directory sections.)

Cost
It is worth trying some of the lesser known lochs, streams and rivers, as they tend to be cheaper than better known waters.

Best times for fishing
Spring, early summer and autumn. (Also good for motoring, so you can change location frequently.)

Choosing your loch
We have given a limited selection in each area. For more detail contact the local Tourist Information Office.

Fishing for the Disabled
A list of suitable locations can be obtained from:
Denis Gow,
20 West Court,
The Thistle Foundation,
Edinburgh EH16 4EA.
(031 661 2494)

Shooting and Stalking
Scotland's main attractions for the shooting and stalking enthusiast are:

Deer
Red, Sika, Roe, Fallow.

Small Game
Black game, pheasant, capercailzie, ptarmigan, grouse, snipe, partridge, woodcock.

Wildfowl – Ducks and Geese
Common pochard, common scoter, gadwell, garganey, teal, goldeneye, long-tailed duck, mallard, pintail, scaup, shoveller, tufted duck, widgeon, bean, canada, greylag, pinkfoot, whitefront.

Also
Hare, rabbit, woodpigeon and in certain areas wild goats.

Gun Licences
Under the provision of the *Firearms Act* 1968, a certificate is required by all persons owning or using either a rifle or a shotgun.

Overseas Visitors
Visitors to Britain from overseas may obtain a Firearms Certificate in advance from the Area Police Headquarters where they are going to shoot. This should be done through your travel agent.

Useful Addresses
WAGBI For Shooting and Conservation,
Boquhan,
Kippen,
Stirlingshire.
(Kippen 5343)

British Field Sports Society,
Glenmore Lodge,
Old Edinburgh Road,
Moffat,
Dumfriesshire.
(Moffat 20571)

British Deer Society,
Hazelwood,
Methven,
Perth.
(Methven 303)

Cycling
Most holiday centres hire cycles. If you use your own cycle, there are many repair facilities. Hire costs are low but try to book in advance.

Food
Buying fresh meat in Scotland is a nicer experience than in some other parts of Britain because of the care taken in preparing the raw meat cuts, and the range of prepared sausage-shaped meat and savoury products, such as black puddings, red puddings and haggis. Mutton, beef, venison and poultry are generally of a very high standard, and bacon bought from the butcher (as opposed to supermarket).

Salmon is always associated with Scotland, but the abundance of inland and coastal fish makes it possible to sample many other species, including trout (fresh and sea-water), halibut, whiting, skate, mackerel, and shellfish (crab, lobster, scollops, prawns etc.) There is a strong Scandinavian influence in the smoking of fish. Fish and chip shops are to be recommended in Scotland.

A number of cheeses are indigenous to Scotland, among the best being various kinds from Orkney, caboc and cream cheese from Arran (by the end of 1983 there will be a Scottish version of the Greek fetta!) but all in all, Scottish cuisine is best-known for its baking, with a wide variety of traditional breads, cakes, scones (including potato scones), biscuits, oatmeal products and pies.

The restaurants we have mentioned are, in the main, ones in which we have personally eaten, or which friends and acquaintances have recommended to us.

Comments on menus: If soup is offered, always check if it is home-made because if it is, it's usually excellent. Meat, fish and poultry are normally well cooked, sometimes superb, but beware of over-cooked vegetables and uninspired salads. The standard of ice cream is above the British average, with the strong Italian influence in Scotland. A pot of tea is still a better bet than a pot of coffee, though the quality of coffee-making is starting to improve, specially in towns. (If you order a ham sandwich you might be given a bacon sandwich, so specify boiled ham, unless of course you want bacon!)

Hired Transport Available

Self-drive or chauffeur-driven cars; motor caravans; self-drive and chauffeur-driven mini-buses; self-drive vans; 'Hire here and leave there'.

Motoring

Road and Weather Reports
For the whole of Scotland can be obtained from:
AA (031 246 8021)
AA (041 246 8021)
Can also be obtained from the Radio (local radio stations have information of 'What's On', from jumble sales to Highland games).

Radio Stations

Radio Forth	194 M	96.8 VHF
Radio Clyde	261 M	95.1 VHF
Moray Firth	1100 M	95.9 VHF
Northsound	290 M	96.9 VHF

Meteorological Offices
Aberdeen Airport: (Aberdeen 722331)
Glasgow: (041 248 3451)
Kirkwall Airport: (Kirkwall 2478/2233)
Leuchars: (Leuchars 224)
Pitreavie (Fire): (Inverkeithing 2566)
Prestwick: (Prestwick 78475)

Driving on Single-Track Roads
Use passing places only for passing or overtaking. No picnics. Beware of sheep and deer.

Petrol Stations
In towns and major areas petrol can be easily obtained. In remote areas always fill your tank for the weekend.

INDEX